Sources of Holocaust Insight

Sources of Holocaust Insight

Learning and Teaching about the Genocide

JOHN K. ROTH

CASCADE Books · Eugene, Oregon

SOURCES OF HOLOCAUST INSIGHT
Learning and Teaching about the Genocide

Copyright © 2020 John K. Roth. All rights reserved. Except for brief quotations in critical publications or reviews, no part of this book may be reproduced in any manner without prior written permission from the publisher. Write: Permissions, Wipf and Stock Publishers, 199 W. 8th Ave., Suite 3, Eugene, OR 97401.

Cascade Books
An Imprint of Wipf and Stock Publishers
199 W. 8th Ave., Suite 3
Eugene, OR 97401

www.wipfandstock.com

PAPERBACK ISBN: 978-1-5326-7418-1
HARDCOVER ISBN: 978-1-5326-7419-8
EBOOK ISBN: 978-1-5326-7420-4

Cataloguing-in-Publication data:

Names: Roth, John K., author.

Title: Sources of Holocaust insight: learning and teaching about the genocide / John K. Roth.

Description: Eugene, OR: Cascade Books, 2020. | Includes bibliographical references and index.

Identifiers: ISBN: 978-1-5326-7418-1 (paperback). | ISBN: 978-1-5326-7419-8 (hardcover). | ISBN: 978-1-5326-7420-4 (ebook).

Subjects: LCSH: Holocaust, Jewish (1939–1945). | Holocaust, Jewish (1939–1945)—Moral and ethical aspects. | Rubenstein, Richard L. | Wiesel, Elie, 1928–2016—Criticism and interpretation. | Littell, Franklin H. (Franklin Hamlin), 1917–2009. | Hilberg, Raul, 1926–2007. | Kofman, Sarah. | Delbo, Charlotte—Criticism and interpretation. | Camus, Albert, 1913–1960—Criticism and interpretation. | Levi, Primo. | Améry, Jean.

Classification: BJ1031 .R75 2020 (print). | BJ1031 (ebook).

Manufactured in the U.S.A. 02/21/20

Unless otherwise noted, Scripture quotations are taken from the New Revised Standard Version Bible, copyright © 1989 National Council of the Churches of Christ in the United States of America. Used by permission. All rights reserved worldwide.

Scripture quotations marked (JB) are taken from The Jerusalem Bible © 1966 by Darton Longman & Todd Ltd and Doubleday and Company Ltd.

In Memoriam

My Parents, Doris and Josiah

and to

My Students

Whatever else you get, get insight.
—Proverbs 4:7, NRSV

Contents

Acknowledgments | ix

PROLOGUE: **Acts of Recognition** | 1

1. **Richard L. Rubenstein** | 10
2. **Elie Wiesel** | 27
3. **Friends and Teachers I** | 47
4. **Franklin H. Littell** | 69
5. **Raul Hilberg** | 88
6. **Friends and Teachers II** | 114
7. **Sarah Kofman and Charlotte Delbo** | 140
8. **Philip Hallie and Albert Camus** | 165
9. **Friends and Teachers III** | 184
10. **Primo Levi** | 207
11. **Jean Améry** | 232

EPILOGUE: **Take Nothing Good for Granted** | 257

Bibliography | 261
Index | 277

Acknowledgments

This book recognizes people who have profoundly influenced the learning and teaching about the Holocaust that I have been doing for more than fifty years. My parents, Doris and Josiah, top that list. Dedicated to them, *Sources of Holocaust Insight* is also for my students, who have taught me in irreplaceable ways.

Support, inspiration, love—these gifts, sources of deep insight, have been abundantly bestowed upon me, day in and day out, by my wife, Lyn, my children, Andy and Sarah, and their spouses, Liz and Erik, and by a most special person, my granddaughter, Keeley Brooks. In addition, valued guidance and needed encouragement have been generously supplied by my editor, K. C. Hanson, his colleagues Jeremy Funk, Ian Creeger, Daniel Lanning, and Matthew Wimer—and the entire, highly capable team at Cascade Books.

As the book developed, I increasingly appreciated that my sources of Holocaust insight include many more women and men than those discussed in the pages that follow. I could not write about them all in the ways they deserve, but I mention some of them—an inadequate gesture, but it must suffice—especially in three chapters about friends and teachers. Even then, I know my acknowledgments lack completeness. Unnamed though my writing leaves the many other persons who have given me Holocaust insight, their presence decidedly informs this book. I can only hope that, in some way, my reflections convey how much I gratefully owe them.

PROLOGUE

Acts of Recognition

Call me odd—an American Christian philosopher who has studied, written, and taught about the Holocaust for more than fifty years. That experience makes me melancholy. It also makes me determined to keep doing what I can to resist genocidal attitudes and actions.

What backstories, including the styles of inquiry as well as the findings and moods in my investigations, contribute most to that identity? How have events and experiences, family and friends, scholars and students, texts and testimonies—especially the questions they raise—affected my Holocaust studies and guided my efforts to heed the biblical proverb: "Whatever else you get, get insight" (Prov 4:7)?

My friend Debórah Dwork, a superb historian, calls the Holocaust her compass. It works that way for me as well, orienting my attention, guiding my priorities, directing my discernment about what's right and wrong. The compass keeps me aware that absent the facts of history, the insight this book seeks could not exist. Thus, the quest gets underway by noting that World War II claimed the lives of at least fifty million people, more than half of them civilians. Operating largely under the cover of war, Nazi Germany's system of concentration camps, murder squadrons, and killing centers took millions of defenseless lives. The toll included most of Europe's Jews, who were targets of the mass-atrocity crimes that came to be called the Holocaust.[1]

1. For an overview of World War II death statistics, see Winter, "Demography," 224–27. Regarding Holocaust statistics, reliable scholars have differed, but the numbers are always large. Raul Hilberg calculated that 5.1 million Jews perished in the Holocaust. Israel Gutman and Robert Rozett put Jewish losses between 5.5 and 5.8 million. More recently, the German historian Wolfgang Benz contended that the number of Jewish deaths exceeded 6.2 million. The figures remain imprecise for several reasons, including the years and demographical boundaries used to determine prewar census data;

2 Sources of Holocaust Insight

My understanding of the term *Holocaust* agrees with the definition provided by the United States Holocaust Memorial Museum, which states that "the Holocaust was the systematic, bureaucratic, state-sponsored persecution and murder of six million Jews by the Nazi regime and its collaborators."[2] The genocide committed by the Nazis aimed to rid Europe of Jews. Hitler intended that result to be permanent so that Jews could never return to or enter Europe again. That goal could be fully achieved only if every Jew on planet Earth was destroyed. The Third Reich was crushed militarily before Hitler could implement what his genocidal logic entailed, but he went far in achieving what the Nazis called the "Final Solution of the Jewish Question." Two-thirds of Europe's Jews were dead by the end of World War II.

For racial, cultural, or political reasons, the Third Reich's murderous policies also destroyed millions of other people, including Roma and Sinti (Gypsies) and Polish citizens as well as homosexuals, disabled people, Jehovah's Witnesses, and other political and religious dissidents within Germany itself. Additionally, in their German captivity, which ruthlessly disregarded international conventions pertaining to civilized treatment of war prisoners, an estimated 3.3 million Soviet POWs lost their lives to starvation, inadequate medical treatment, forced marches, or outright murder. These atrocities were related to but not synonymous with the Holocaust, which names the Jews' fate under Hitler.

My decision to call this book *Sources of Holocaust Insight* is inspired by titles and themes from two other books. First, *Sources of Holocaust Research*, published in 2001, is a significant but not widely studied book by Raul Hilberg, who is best known for his magisterial three-volume work called *The Destruction of the European Jews*. Having focused on the Holocaust for five decades, Hilberg said that he had thought of his sources—primarily the German documents he scrutinized in detail—as "raw material that would enable me to fashion a description of the destruction process . . . But then I stopped to ask myself: what is the nature of my sources? They are Not identical to the subject matter. They have their own history and qualities,

---

the margins of error in death reports from German and Jewish sources; the difficulties of comparing prewar and postwar populations; and the fact that the Germans and their collaborators did not record the death of every victim. See Hilberg, *Destruction*, 1320–21; Gutman and Rozett, "Estimated Jewish Losses," 1797–802; Benz, *Holocaust*, 152–53.

2. See the United States Holocaust Memorial Museum, *Holocaust Encyclopedia*, "Introduction to the Holocaust." For a helpful discussion of how the term *Holocaust* has been interpreted, see Lipstadt, *Holocaust*.

which are different from the actions they depict and which require a separate approach."[3]

Hilberg's *Sources of Holocaust Research* deeply moved me. It led me to ask about my sources and to see that "the attribution of significance to sources, or a differentiation between them, or the fitting of pieces into a larger structure, is an act of recognition."[4] Having focused on the Holocaust for a long time, I recognize that more sources than I can acknowledge have informed my encounters with that catastrophe. But looking back on my efforts to fathom the Holocaust, particular persons and writings loom especially large. Some of them affected me early on, others more recently. In the chapters that follow, I revisit my sources of Holocaust insight. I do so not only to pay tribute to them but also to refocus the insight, which includes and encompasses the expanding plural insights that decades of Holocaust studies continue to give me. In addition to showing what such inquiry can and ought to teach, I hope that this book, which concentrates on the ethical, philosophical, and religious implications of the Holocaust, will encourage renewed recognition of key challenges and responsibilities that the Holocaust and its reverberations confer upon anyone who cares about human well-being in the twenty-first century.

Second, in 1912, about a century before *Sources of Holocaust Research* appeared, an American philosopher named Josiah Royce published a book called *The Sources of Religious Insight*. A leading thinker in his day, and one still relevant in ours, Royce lived in a pre-Holocaust world, but early on he and his Harvard colleague William James significantly affected my thinking.[5] Royce's astute understanding of *insight* helps to explain my use of that term.

Beyond affirming that insight connotes clear, accurate, and deep-down understanding, Royce held that insight is knowledge defined by what he called "breadth of range, coherence and unity of view, and closeness of personal touch."[6] Absent an accurate grasp of diverse facts, plans, and events, insight does not exist. Nor is it present if sound judgment is lacking about how those realities fit together—to the extent that they do—and what their meanings and implications may be. Insight includes encounters with people but depends on discerning their character, their moral fiber, including their trustworthiness and commitment to truth. Hearsay and rote learning do not produce insight, which requires personal experience. But without coherence

---

3. Hilberg, *Sources*, 7–8.
4. Hilberg, *Sources*, 194.
5. See, for example, Roth, *Freedom*; and Roth, ed., *Josiah Royce*.
6. Royce, *Religious Insight*, 6.

and breadth of range, Royce argued, individual experience is not by itself sufficient to produce insight. That is true because insight is not something one possesses finally and completely, let alone in isolation from others who are pursuing insight too. Seeking and finding insight are ongoing actions. They require interpersonal exchanges that challenge and correct, augment and amplify even the most reliable insights that are ours here and now. To have insight is to recognize that learning is never finished, that my grasp of things is fallible and incomplete, and that "an insight that is superior in grasp, in unity, in coherence, in reasonableness to [my] momentary insight" is not only possible but imperative to seek and discover.[7]

In addition to depending on memory, which is essential for clear perspective, sound comparative judgment, and penetrating acts of recognition, insight takes time to be born, to grow and mature. Insofar as insight exists, lucidity intensifies, comprehension increases, and understanding expands. Royce saw insight illustrated in a skilled artist's vision of a landscape or an observant biographer's portrayal of a person's life. Encountering a landscape, the skilled artist sees it distinctively and with discernment that finds insightful expression through a painting's shadings of light and color, its mood and emotion, uses of foreground and background, degrees of abstraction or realism, and angles of interpretation. Considering a person, the perceptive biographer also sees distinctively and with discernment that turns the facts of a life into a narrative that reveals the subject's complexities and contradictions, successes and shortcomings, through shadings of personality and disposition, decisions about which plans and choices should be in the foreground, degrees of detail or generalization, and the angles of interpretation that are most needed to shed light on a person's path toward death.

Outlooks and qualities of that kind affect what I mean by Holocaust insight, which is not something simply stated because it must be shown as much as said. So, my effort to get insight *about* and *from* the Holocaust probes the human contours and configurations that produced the catastrophe, gauging especially the moral failure that led to vast and still rumbling destruction. As I explore the Holocaust and its aftershocks, my quest for lucidity, comprehension, and understanding cannot rely on firsthand experience of that genocide. I have none of that. Nor can I claim extensive archival research of the kind that Hilberg pursued with such grit and diligence. Nevertheless, in varied ways I have encountered Holocaust-related landscapes and people who have inhabited them. I have sources of Holocaust insight. They include persons I have known—some of them Holocaust survivors, many of them scholars and students of the Holocaust. Among my

---

7. Royce, *Religious Insight*, 108.

most valuable sources are Holocaust-related writings, which for me are akin to archival documents. Crucially, my sources also consist of questions—indispensable for insight—that drive my inquiries.

Asking questions (who, what, where, when, how, and above all, *why*?) is one of the most significant features of human life. If we do not ask questions and follow where they lead, life will be impoverished and endangered. Curiosity and inquiry will be stunted, maybe absent altogether. Learning will be hampered, if it takes place at all. Critical thinking will be unthinkable; creativity will diminish. Error, lying, dogmatism, tyranny, injustice, and violence will gain traction they do not deserve.

Questions seek answers, but in key ways asking questions is more important than getting "answers," because so often the "answers" we get are incomplete, short-sighted, limited and limiting, mistaken, partisan, stupid and false, life-threatening and life-destroying. On the other hand, asking questions keeps inquiry going, encourages us to look further and better, urges us to think twice rather than to plunge ahead recklessly, murderously. Asking questions well requires seeking evidence to support or correct judgments, makes us wonder if we might be mistaken, and tests what we think and believe. Asking questions can help us to make good choices, or at least to steer clear of bad ones, and prevent taking good things for granted.

Rich and extensive, challenging and encouraging, my resources of Holocaust insight develop and enlarge, their imperatives always insisting "never stop asking *why*." Engagement with my resources often arouses feelings and emotions that embody the "closeness of personal touch" that Royce regarded as a necessary condition for insight. Thus, my acts of recognition about the significance, differentiation, and connection of the sources that enliven my quest for Holocaust insight include a moment at the beginning of *Night*, Elie Wiesel's classic memoir, which details his experiences as a young man in Auschwitz. That episode introduces one of Wiesel's early teachers. His name was Moishe, the year 1941. Although underway, the Holocaust had not yet wrecked Sighet, Wiesel's hometown in eastern Europe. One day, the twelve-year-old Elie asked Moishe, his teacher, "Why do you pray?" The reply: "I pray to the God within me that He will give me the strength to ask Him the right questions." Wiesel adds, "We talked like this nearly every evening."[8]

When Elie Wiesel died at the age of eighty-seven on July 2, 2016, his passing was emblematic of the fact that few Holocaust survivors remain, and that the Holocaust itself recedes into the past even as other disasters,

---

8. Wiesel, *Night*, trans. Rodway, 3. A more recent translation refers to "the real questions." See Wiesel, *Night*, trans. Marion Wiesel, 5.

real and probable, vie for attention and resources. When I began to study the Holocaust, dates like 9/11 and acronyms like ISIS meant nothing. Ethnic cleansing in the former Yugoslavia, genocide in Rwanda and Darfur, an ongoing twenty-first-century refugee crisis of immense proportions—to say nothing of devastating terrorism, resurgent antisemitism and racism, upsurges of xenophobic nationalism, obstinate political and religious tribalism, and burgeoning threats of climate change and thermonuclear war—were not on computer screens because the technology and communication revolution that now dominates and complicates the world—including "tweets" and "hacking," "fake news" and "cyberwarfare"—had barely begun. Nevertheless, no event exceeds the Holocaust's power to raise what Wiesel called the right and real questions and to beckon us to reckon with them. To a large degree, moreover, the Holocaust—and the mass-atrocity crimes that deepen the scars of a post-Holocaust world—happened because too many people, especially but not only the perpetrators of those disasters, failed to ask the right and real questions long or well enough.

Such questions are fundamental: Who are we? What is right and what is not? What is good and what is most important? Are we doing the best we can? What about God, or is that question absurd? How can we forestall despair and resist injustice? Where are we or should we be going? What are we or should we be doing? What must change to curb and heal the wasting of the world? Are our judgments true? Can our responses to such questions withstand scrutiny, or do they require further inquiry and evidence to support them? Wrestling with those questions will not be sufficient to resist further disasters, but that struggle may be a necessary condition for doing so.

I am a philosopher, and I believe that philosophy thrives, first and foremost, on questions. Immanuel Kant was on the mark when he defined philosophy as the discipline that pursues three fundamental questions: *What can I know? What should I do? For what may I hope?* Those are some of the right questions for human beings to wonder about. Early in my philosophical training and career, I worked on them with little reference to the Holocaust. Then—in 1972—I took a friend's suggestion and began to study Wiesel's writings. His brief description of the conversation with Moishe in 1941 continues to stand out for me. As well as any, Moishe's few words—"I pray to the God within me that He will give me the strength to ask Him the right questions"—sum up one reason why my philosophical work took a decisive Holocaust studies turn.

Philosophy always deals with questions, but Holocaust studies gave me insight that some ways of approaching them are more important and powerful than others. Specifically, I began to discover, questions do not give us the best possible insight when they are posed abstractly, without reference to real human experiences and histories. Wiesel's words showed me that. So did Hilberg's.

When the late filmmaker Claude Lanzmann produced *Shoah* in 1985, he created a cinematic counterpart to Hilberg's *The Destruction of the European Jews*. Hilberg played an important part in Lanzmann's epic film about the Holocaust. In a segment on the Warsaw ghetto, for example, Hilberg discusses the dilemmas faced by Adam Czerniakow, the man who headed the Judenrat, the Jewish administrative council that the Germans required to aid and abet their destruction of the Jews in that place. For almost three years, Czerniakow wrote a diary to document what he did. It survived the war, but Czerniakow did not. He took his own life on July 23, 1943, the day after the Germans began to liquidate the Warsaw ghetto by deporting its Jews to Treblinka. The last entry in Czerniakow's diary says, "It is three o'clock. So far four thousand are ready to go. The orders are that there must be nine thousand by four o'clock." Hilberg adds: "This is the last entry of a man on the afternoon of the day that he commits suicide."[9] Hilberg knew the details of Czerniakow's life because he helped to edit and translate the diary.

In another segment of Lanzmann's *Shoah*, Hilberg studies a different kind of document: Fahrplananordnung 587, a railroad timetable that scheduled death traffic. Conservative estimates indicate that Fahrplananordnung 587, which outlines a few days in late September 1942, engineered the transport of some ten thousand Jews to Treblinka's gas chambers. Hilberg spent his life detailing how such things happened. In his first appearance in Lanzmann's film, he observes, "In all of my work I have never begun by asking the big questions, because I was always afraid that I would come up with small answers; and I have preferred to address these things which are minutiae or details in order that I might then be able to put together in a gestalt a picture which, if not an explanation, is at least a description, a more full description, of what transpired."[10]

As a philosopher confronting the Holocaust, I keep in mind Hilberg's warning about "big questions." He did not deny that the Holocaust raises them—first and foremost the question *why*? However, that a question can be asked does not mean that it can be answered well, if at all, particularly when it is one of the "big," fundamental, and sweeping questions that typically characterize philosophical and religious inquiries. So, Hilberg concentrated on details instead. His minutiae, however, were much more than minutiae. Their particularity speaks volumes and forms a terribly vast description.

9. The quotations are from Lanzmann, *Shoah*, 188.
10. See Lanzmann, *Shoah*, 70.

So full of life distorted and wasted, that accumulated detail makes the "big questions" less simple to raise but even more important too.

Put into perspective by insight such as Hilberg's, the "big questions" become what Wiesel's teacher, Moishe, called the "right questions," the real ones, and thus they deservingly command respect. That respect enjoins suspicion about "answers" that are small, inadequate for the facts they must encompass. That same respect also conveys the insight that the big questions raised by the Holocaust nonetheless need to be kept alive. For the political scientist's details and the historian's minutiae, far from silencing the big questions, ought to intensify wonder about them. Otherwise we repress feeling too much and deny ourselves the insight that can be deepened only by asking the "right questions."

As a philosopher confronting the Holocaust, I find that my guiding compass is provided by one more statement about asking questions that are properly big and right: "The Holocaust demands interrogation and calls everything into question. Traditional ideas and acquired values, philosophical systems and social theories—all must be revised in the shadow of Birkenau."[11] Birkenau was the killing center at Auschwitz, and those words are more of Wiesel's. One of the insightful points they make is this: whatever the traditional ideas and acquired values that existed, whatever the philosophical systems and social theories that human minds devised, either they were inadequate to prevent Auschwitz or, worse, they helped to pave the way to that place.

A few of us philosophers work on these problems. Philosophy and perhaps the world would be better if there were more. But at the same time, when Holocaust scholars from the fields of history or literature, political science or sociology, ask the right questions, they move into the area that too many philosophers have ignored. Fortunately, when these scholars who do not identify themselves primarily as philosophers get to the big questions, they often do so with immense philosophical sensitivity and insight.

But what about philosophers and the discipline of philosophy in relation to Holocaust studies? I think philosophers and philosophy have avoided the Holocaust primarily because so much history is involved. To encounter the Holocaust philosophically, at least to do so insightfully, one must study what happened, to whom, where, when, and how. Reckoning with detail and particularity of that kind is not what philosophers are naturally inclined or usually trained to do. So, it is likely that only a relatively few of us philosophers—maybe those who have grown impatient with the abstraction and distance from history that much contemporary philosophy

---

11. This statement is from Elie Wiesel's foreword to Cargas, *Shadows*, ix.

reflects—will immerse ourselves in this field of study. Once there, however, we are unlikely to want to be anywhere else, for the work is so intense and important.

Think again of the big questions that will always need to be explored and must be carefully handled if they are to be the right questions: How did the Holocaust happen? Who is responsible for it? How can we best remember that history? What about God and religion after Auschwitz? What about human rights and ethics in a post-Holocaust world? What can I know, what should I do, for what may I hope in the shadow of Birkenau?

"Whatever else you get," advises the biblical proverb, "get insight." Philosophers should ask the right questions. At least some of us should let our questioning be informed by the Holocaust in ways that heed Raul Hilberg's warnings about "big questions." We should join scholars in other fields, using the insights that philosophy can bring, to revise traditional ideas and acquired values, philosophical systems and social theories. Such acts of recognition might lead to the insight we need, to a better picture, which, if not an explanation, would at least be a description, a fuller description, of what transpired in the Holocaust and how the persistence of mass atrocities can be curbed if not eliminated.

1

Richard L. Rubenstein

In an essay called "To a Young Jew of Today," Elie Wiesel said that "you will sooner or later be confronted with the enigma of God's action in history."¹ No one has confronted that enigma more decisively and with greater insight than Richard L. Rubenstein. I did not become well acquainted with him until 1976, but he had influenced me well before our initial meeting and eventual collaboration on writing projects.²

In 1976–77, I was a fellow at the National Humanities Institute at Yale University, an initiative underwritten by the National Endowment for the Humanities. During that year, I wrote a book called *A Consuming Fire: Encounters with Elie Wiesel and the Holocaust*. Focusing on my Christian tradition, it too probed the enigma of God's action—or lack of it—in history. My thinking was enriched, my writing complicated, by a growing friendship with Rubenstein, who was also one of the twenty fellows at the Institute. A year earlier, he had published *The Cunning of History: The Holocaust and the American Future*. Its visibility rose when the American novelist William Styron discussed the book in the *New York Review of Books* in 1978 and then referenced it at some length in his award-winning novel *Sophie's Choice* a year later. *The Cunning of History* concluded that we live in a "*functionally godless*" world.³

Almost every day during lunch at the Institute, Rubenstein and I talked about such matters, which he had put on my mind ten years before

---

1. Wiesel, *One Generation After*, 176.

2. My first publishing about the Holocaust focused on Rubenstein. See Roth, "Death of God in American Theology," 224–30. For an example of my writing with Rubenstein, see Rubenstein and Roth, *Approaches to Auschwitz*. To the best of my knowledge, this book is the first about the Holocaust coauthored by a Jew and a Christian.

3. Rubenstein, *Cunning of History*, 91 (italics original).

with the 1966 publication of his *After Auschwitz: Radical Theology and Contemporary Judaism*. Appearing as I completed my doctoral dissertation at Yale, Rubenstein's book anticipated themes in *The Cunning of History* by arguing that the Holocaust had "permanently impaired" long-held beliefs and assumptions about God, humanity, and ethics.[4] A chief casualty was the idea that God acts providentially in history.

Usually friends do not agree completely. It has been that way with Rubenstein and me, but his influence on my thinking has been immense. I am not convinced that we live in a functionally godless world, but if we do not, then quarreling with God's failures—something that Wiesel helped me to discern as an ethical act in its own right—looms large as a factor in protesting against injustice and the moral shortcomings that aid and abet it. Such insights are among those that guide me through the aftershocks and reverberations of the Holocaust.

Religion was not a sufficient condition for the Holocaust, but it was a necessary one. What happened in the Nazi killing fields and at Treblinka and Auschwitz is inconceivable without beliefs about God first held by Jews and then by Christians. Holocaust and genocide scholars have explored the similarities and differences between the Holocaust and other genocides. Although the field of comparative genocide does not often make the point, one aspect of the Holocaust that is qualitatively different from other systems of extermination and mass destruction in the modern period can be stated as follows: No example of mass murder exceeds the Holocaust in raising so directly or so insistently the question of how or even whether such a catastrophe can be reconciled with God's providential involvement in history. More than any other disaster in modern times, the Holocaust resonates and collides with the theological and ethical traditions of biblical religion. It does so to such an extent that the nineteenth-century French writer Stendhal (Marie-Henri Beyle) likely hit the mark when he said, "The only excuse for God is that he does not exist."[5]

After Auschwitz

In 1970, the first Annual Scholars' Conference on the Holocaust and the Churches took place at Wayne State University. Organized by Franklin Littell and Hubert Locke, this ongoing annual conference, the oldest continuing initiative of its kind, still produces groundbreaking scholarship about the Holocaust. None of the work from those meetings, however, has sustained

---

4. Rubenstein, *After Auschwitz*, xx.
5. Quoted in Camus, *Rebel*, 67.

more attention than an exchange between Rubenstein and Wiesel during the first meeting.[6] "Some Perspectives on Religious Faith after Auschwitz," Rubenstein's main contribution to the exchange, included his refusal "to say *Gott mit uns* under any circumstances."[7] The idea that "God is with us" has a lineage that is ancient and biblical; it has given encouragement, solace, and hope, and the causes it has been invoked to serve have often been laudable. But Rubenstein remembered that "Gott mit uns" was inscribed on the belt buckles of the German Wehrmacht during World War II. In that carnage, "Gott mit uns" helped to encourage and legitimate the destruction of the European Jews. "God is with us"—Rubenstein found the meanings of that phrase too problematic. The costs of blood and suffering to be paid for invoking God in that way were too high.

Reasons for that outlook were rooted in Rubenstein's experiences during the summer of 1961. On Sunday, August 13 of that year, Rubenstein planned to begin a research trip to West Germany. That same day, the East Germans created a major Cold War crisis by building a wall between East and West Berlin. Postponing his trip for two days, Rubenstein arrived in Bonn, the West German capital, and accepted an invitation from his hosts, the Bundespressamt (Press and Information Office) of the Federal Republic to fly to Berlin to see the unfolding crisis. In an atmosphere charged with fear that nuclear war might erupt, Rubenstein took the opportunity to interview Heinrich Grüber, a prominent German Christian leader who had resisted the Nazis, rescued Jews, and suffered imprisonment in Sachsenhausen.[8] Earlier in 1961, Grüber had been the only German to testify for the prosecution at the Jerusalem trial of Adolf Eichmann, a leading perpetrator of the Holocaust.

With American tanks rumbling through the streets of Dahlem, the West Berlin suburb where Grüber lived, Rubenstein interviewed him in the late afternoon of August 17. When their conversation turned to the Holocaust, this meeting became a turning point in Rubenstein's personal and intellectual life. Grüber affirmed a biblical faith in the God-who-acts-in-history. More than that, he held that the Jews were God's chosen people;

---

6. The Rubenstein–Wiesel exchange can be found in Roth and Berenbaum, eds., *Holocaust*, 346–70. It appeared first in Littell and Locke, eds., *German Church Struggle*, 256–77.

7. Rubenstein, "Perspectives on Religious Faith," 356.

8. Rubenstein's essay, "The Dean and the Chosen People," recounts these events. See Rubenstein, *After Auschwitz*, 3–13. See also Rubenstein, *Power Struggle*. In the 1992 version of *After Auschwitz*, nine of the original edition's fifteen chapters were replaced. Those that remain were substantially rewritten. Although earlier versions of them first appeared elsewhere, ten chapters in the 1992 edition were new. In this chapter, the quotations from *After Auschwitz* are from the second edition.

therefore, he believed, nothing could happen to them apart from God's will. When Rubenstein asked Grüber whether God had intended for Hitler to attempt the destruction of the European Jews, Grüber's response was yes. However difficult it might be to understand the reason, he told Rubenstein, the Holocaust was part of God's plan.

Rubenstein was impressed that Grüber took so seriously the belief that God acts providentially in history, a central tenet of Judaism and Christianity. To Grüber, that belief meant specifically that God was ultimately responsible for the Holocaust. Although Grüber's testimony struck him as abhorrent, Rubenstein appreciated the consistency of Grüber's theology, and the American Jewish thinker came away convinced that he must persistently confront the issue of God and the Holocaust. The eventual result was *After Auschwitz*. A second edition of the 1966 original, so extensively enlarged and revised as to be virtually a new book, was published in 1992 with a different subtitle: *History, Theology, and Contemporary Judaism*.

When *After Auschwitz* first appeared, it was among the first books to systematically probe the significance of Auschwitz for post-Holocaust religious life. Rubenstein's analysis sparked controversy and ongoing debate because it challenged beliefs that many people have long held dear. After Auschwitz, Rubenstein contended, belief in a redeeming God—one who is active in history and who will bring a fulfilling end to the upheavals in the human condition—is no longer credible.

In the late 1960s, the stir caused by *After Auschwitz* linked Rubenstein to a group of young American Protestant thinkers—Thomas Altizer, William Hamilton, and Paul M. van Buren among them—who were dubbed "death of God" theologians. The popular media amped up the buzz—*Time* magazine's cover story on April 8, 1966, featured the topic—and the movement ignited public discussion for some time.[9] Although the spotlight eventually moved on, these thinkers' contributions—especially Rubenstein's—did not fade. Their outlooks posed questions and their testimonies raised issues too fundamental to disappear. Yet neither the labeling nor the clustering of these thinkers was entirely apt. None was atheistic in any simple sense. Nor were their perspectives, methods, and moods identical. What they loosely shared was the feeling that talk about God did not—indeed could not—mean what it apparently had meant in the past. In that respect, the term "radical theology" described their work better than the more sensationalistic phrase "death of God." Creating breaks with the past and intensifying discontinuities within traditions, the radical theologians talked about experiences that were widely shared even though most people lacked the words

---

9. See Haynes and Roth, eds., *Death of God Movement*.

or the encouragement to say so in public. Unlike his Protestant brothers, however, Rubenstein put the Holocaust at the center of his contributions to radical theology in the 1960s. The insights of *After Auschwitz* provoked Holocaust-related searches that continue to this day.

At the time, the three American Protestants hailed "the death of God" with considerable enthusiasm. They concurred that secularization—manifested especially in an expanding consciousness of human freedom, technological power, and responsibility—called into question the need for or even the possibility of a traditional, transcendent God who exercised providential care by episodic interventions in human history. Later, van Buren would concentrate on the Holocaust as he rejected his earlier position and developed a Christian theology that was deeply sensitive to Jewish tradition, but the Holocaust did not center the early discourse of these "radical" Christian theologians. Rubenstein's outlook differed. If he was not alone among those thinkers in denying that he literally believed "God is dead," Rubenstein made clearer than most his view that "the ultimate relevance of theology is anthropological," a perspective reflected in his long-standing use of psychoanalytic insights when he spoke about religion.[10] Rubenstein meant that whenever we speak of God, we are talking about what we believe about God, which is not the same as talking about God directly. Thus, it can make sense to say that "we live in the time of the death of God," but, he explained further, we cannot say whether "the death of God" is more than an event within human culture.[11]

Nor should it be expected, Rubenstein added, that living in the time of the death of God means the end of religion. On the contrary, in such a time important upsurges of religion, new and old, will appear. Far from being paradoxical, such expressions of religion are understandable because people seek meaning for their lives, and they may do so most intently when meaning is uncertain. Religion is not going away anytime soon. Revitalized in surprising ways, it may manifest itself in new forms or in the reaffirmation of old ones, even in the time of the death of God.

Rubenstein's emphasis on what he called the anthropological dimensions of theological discourse did not mean that he was indifferent to the nature of ultimate reality. One place, for example, where he parted company with the Christian radical theologians involved his impression that with very little regret, they "'willed' the death of the theistic God."[12] By contrast, as he found himself unwillingly forced to conclude that the idea of a God

---

10. Rubenstein, *After Auschwitz*, 250.
11. Rubenstein, *After Auschwitz*, 250.
12. Rubenstein, *After Auschwitz*, 248.

of history lacked credibility after Auschwitz, Rubenstein reports being saddened. He recognized that history had shattered—at least for him—a system of religious meaning that had sustained people, especially Jews and Christians, for millennia. For him, the destruction of such a pattern of meaning was no cause for celebration. On one occasion, Rubenstein summed up his melancholy as follows:

> If the God of history does not exist, then the Cosmos is ultimately absurd in origin and meaningless in purpose. We have been thrust into the world in which life proliferates, has its hour, only to disappear amidst further proliferation of life. As human beings we are divided by historical and geographical accident into the tribes of mankind, to no ultimate reason or purpose. We simply are there for but a moment only to disappear into the midnight silence of Eternal Chaos.[13]

The concerns that drove Rubenstein to reject the traditional God of history were never governed by unsatisfactory attempts to answer the abstract question, "If the world contains radical evil, how can God be omnipotent, all-knowing, and completely good?" His issue was far more concrete and historical than that. With Auschwitz at the epicenter of his insight, what sense could be made of a Jewish tradition of covenant and election, a perspective in which Jews interpreted themselves to be specially chosen by God, bound to God in a covenant that entailed God's blessing for faithfulness and God's judgment against infidelity? Common to that tradition's self-understanding was the belief that "radical communal misfortune," as Rubenstein called it, was a sign either that God found the chosen people wanting and dispensed punishment accordingly, or that God called upon the innocent to suffer sacrificially for the guilty, or than an indispensable prelude for the messianic climax of Jewish history was underway, or some combination of such outlooks. In any case, the Holocaust, an event in which Nazi Germany was hell-bent on destroying Jewish life root and branch, made Rubenstein collide head-on with the biblical tradition of covenant and election, which seemed to lead consistently to a positive answer to the question, "Did God use Adolf Hitler and the Nazis as his agents to inflict terrible sufferings and death upon six million Jews, including more than one million children?"[14] Rubenstein survived the collision, but in his view the God of history could not.[15]

13. Rubenstein, "Some Perspectives," 355.
14. Rubenstein, *After Auschwitz*, 162.
15. Rubenstein's analysis of relations between the Holocaust and the God of history focused primarily on Jewish understanding and by extension on Christian

Human Rights

Rubenstein's early conviction that "the ultimate relevance of theology is anthropological" foreshadowed how his work would concentrate increasingly on history, politics, economics, and sociology, usually with reference to religious thought and practice but with the emphasis on the conditions that produce human conflict and the safeguards that must be shored up to limit human destructiveness. One result of that focus was *The Cunning of History*, which argued that "the Holocaust bears witness to *the advance of civilization*."[16] Rubenstein took the "Final Solution"—the Nazis' euphemism for the destruction of the European Jews—to be symptomatic of the modern state's perennial temptation to destroy people who are regarded as undesirable, superfluous, or unwanted because of their religion, race, politics, ethnicity, or economic redundancy. The Nazis identified what they took to be a practical problem: the need to eliminate the Jews and other so-called racial inferiors from their midst. Then they moved to solve it. Consequently, the Holocaust did not result from spontaneous, irrational outbursts of random violence or even from antisemitism alone. Nor was the Holocaust a bizarre historical anomaly. It was instead a state-sponsored program of population riddance made possible by modern technology and planned by contemporary political actors and organizations.

Significantly, the Holocaust did not occur until the mid-twentieth century, but conditions necessary, though not sufficient, to produce it were forming centuries before. Decisive in that process was Christian anti-Judaism and its demonization of the Jew. For example, Rubenstein appraised the Christian New Testament correctly when he wrote that "no other religion is as horribly defamed in the classic literature of a rival tradition as is Judaism."[17] The reason for that defamation was the Christian belief that the Jews were, as Rubenstein put it, "the God-bearing and God-murdering

---

understanding as well. In this regard, see Anderson, *Ethics and Suffering*, 137–67. But as the philosopher Norman Kenneth Swazo points out, Rubenstein's insight also has significant implications for Islamic understanding. Swazo's perceptive article, "Questioning Islamic Belief," 272–90, explores a crucial question: "how an omnibenevolent and omnipotent Allah permitted Muslims to slaughter and rape hundreds of thousands of other Muslims along with tens of thousands of others." His essay ends on a note that echoes Rubenstein: The Bangladesh genocide suggests that "it is difficult—if not impossible—to justify belief in Allah, and that therefore that belief is to be accounted a questionable, even dishonest, rational post-genocide commitment" (272, 286). Debate on such issues deserves ongoing attention in Muslim circles.

16. Rubenstein, *Cunning of History*, 91 (italics original).
17. Rubenstein, *After Auschwitz*, 131.

people *par excellence*."[18] Jesus, the incarnation of God according to Christian tradition, was one of the Jewish people, but the Christian telling of this story depicted the Jews as collectively responsible for his crucifixion and thus for rejecting God through deicide, the most heinous crime of all. Christian contempt for Jews was advanced further by the belief that the dispersion of the Jews from their traditional homeland after the Judeo-Roman War and the fall of Jerusalem in 70 CE—and perhaps all of their subsequent misfortune—was God's punishment for their failure to see the light. The effect of this centuries-old tradition was, as Rubenstein said, "to cast them [the Jews] out of any common universe of moral obligation with the Christians among whom they were domiciled. In times of acute social stress, it had the practical effect of decriminalizing any assault visited upon them."[19] Building on a long history that went beyond religious to racist antisemitism, the assaults reached their zenith when Nazi Germany became a genocidal state.

The Nazis' antisemitic racism eventually entailed a destruction process that required and received cooperation from every sector of German society. What's more, the killers and those who aided and abetted them directly—or indirectly as bystanders—were civilized people from a society that was scientifically advanced, technologically competent, culturally sophisticated, efficiently organized, and even religiously devout. These people were, as the Holocaust scholar Michael Berenbaum cogently observed, "both ordinary and extraordinary, a cross section of the men and women of Germany, its allies, and their collaborators, as well as the best and the brightest."[20] There were, for example, pastors and priests who led their churches in welcoming Nazification and the segregation of Jews it entailed. Teachers and writers helped to till the soil where Hitler's racist antisemitism took root. Their students and readers reaped the wasteful harvest. Lawyers drafted and judges enforced laws that isolated Jews and set them up for the kill. Government and church personnel provided birth records to document who was Jewish and who was not. Other workers entered such information in state-of-the-art data processing machines. German philosophers, Martin Heidegger prominent among them, welcomed the rise of National Socialism.[21] University administrators curtailed admissions for Jewish students and dismissed Jewish faculty members. Bureaucrats in the Finance Ministry handled confiscations of Jewish property and wealth. Postal officials delivered mail about definition and expropriation, denaturalization and deportation.

18. Rubenstein, *After Auschwitz*, 131 (italics original).
19. Rubenstein, *After Auschwitz*, 132.
20. Berenbaum, *World Must Know*, 223.
21. See Knowles, *Heidegger's Fascist Affinities*.

Driven by their biomedical visions, physicians were among the first to experiment with the gassing of *lebensunwertes Leben* (lives unworthy of life). Scientists performed research and tested their racial theories on those branded sub- or nonhuman by German science. Business executives found that Nazi concentration camps could provide cheap labor; they worked people to death, turning the Nazi motto *Arbeit macht frei* (Work makes one free) into a mocking truth. Stockholders made profits from firms that supplied Zyklon B to gas Jews and from companies that built crematoriums to burn the corpses. Radio performers were joined by artists such as the gifted film director Leni Reifenstahl to broadcast and screen the polished propaganda that made Hitler's policies persuasive to so many. Engineers drove the trains that transported Jews to death, while other officials took charge of the billing arrangements for this service. Factory workers modified trucks so that they became deadly gas vans; city policemen became members of the squadrons that made mass murder of Jews their specialty. As partners who supported these efforts, women as well as men were deeply implicated in the social structures and cultural life that made the Third Reich genocidal.

Short of Germany's military defeat by the Allies, no other constraints—social or political, moral or religious—were sufficient to stop the "Final Solution." That fact led Rubenstein to write *The Cunning of History* and to wonder about truths whose status is far more fragile and precarious than Thomas Jefferson assumed when he contended that they should be held as "self-evident." None of those truths is more crucial than the claim made by Jefferson in the American Declaration of Independence, namely, that persons are "endowed by their Creator with certain unalienable Rights." Those rights, Jefferson believed, are not merely legal privileges that people grant to each other as they please. Rather, his philosophy held, reason—rightly used—shows that such rights are "natural." Part and parcel of what is meant by *human* existence, they belong equally to all humanity and presumably cannot be violated with impunity. But the sense in which rights are unalienable—inviolable, absolute, inherent—is an elusive part of Jefferson's Declaration, for it also states that "to secure these rights, Governments are instituted among Men." Apparently unalienable rights are not invulnerable; but if they are not invulnerable, then in what way are the unalienable?

One answer could be that what *is* and what *ought to be* are usually not the same, and reason can make the distinction. To speak of unalienable rights, therefore, is to speak of conditions of existence so basic and integral to human identity that they ought never to be abrogated. Persuasive though it may be, such reasoning gives too little comfort in actual historical circumstances. No matter how fundamental we take them to be, rights to life, liberty, and the pursuit of happiness are qualified repeatedly and very often trampled, even by governments that seek to secure them. Rubenstein questioned the *functional* status of unalienable rights. The Holocaust, genocide, and related instances of state-sponsored population elimination indicated to him that "there are absolutely no limits to the degradation and assault the managers and technicians of violence can inflict upon men and women who lack the power of effective resistance."[22]

True, nearly everyone says that certain rights must not be usurped. Still, if those rights are violated completely and all too often with impunity—and they are—how can they convincingly be called natural or unalienable? Is that not an idealistic illusion that deserves to be unmasked by Rubenstein's realism? It holds that "the dreadful history of Europe's Jews has demonstrated that *rights do not belong to men by nature*. To the extent that men have rights, they have them only as members of the polis, the political community . . . Outside of the polis there are no inborn restraints on the human exercise of destructive power."[23]

Rubenstein's insight questions dearly held assumptions. They include beliefs that the most basic human rights are a gift of God, and that nature and reason testify to a universal moral structure that underwrites them. But what if we live in the time of the death of God? What if Rubenstein's "omnipotent Nothingness is the Lord of all Creation"?[24] What if there is no God, not even omnipotent Nothingness? What if nature is amoral? Granting that reason can make critical distinctions between what *is* and what *ought to be*, what if reason also insists that the most telling truth of all is that history is what Hegel, the nineteenth-century German philosopher, called it: a slaughter bench,[25] a realm where unalienable rights are hardly worth the paper they are written on—unless political might ensures them?

In our carnage-filled, post-Holocaust twenty-first century, it is no longer clear that anything except human power can secure a person's rights, and if rights depend on human power alone, then they may well be natural and unalienable in name only. In such circumstances, to call rights unalienable may still be a legitimate rhetorical device, perhaps buttressed by religious discourse, to muster consensus that certain privileges and prerogatives must not be taken away. But ideas do not necessarily correspond to facts any more than dreams do to waking life. It appears increasingly that rights are functionally unalienable only within a state that will successfully defend and honor them as such. Harsh though it is, Rubenstein's realism informs mine.

22. Rubenstein, *Cunning of History*, 90.
23. Rubenstein, *Cunning of History*, 89 (italics original).
24. Rubenstein, *After Auschwitz*, 305.
25. Hegel, *Philosophy of History*, 24.

Surplus People

The world's population is likely to reach 8 billion by 2025, 9 billion by 2040, and 11 billion by 2100.[26] In addition, according to 2018 reports from the office of the United Nations High Commissioner for Refugees (UNHRC), recent conflict forcibly displaced 68.5 million people from their homes, including 25.4 million refugees and 3.1 million asylum seekers.[27] Rubenstein could not have had these figures in mind when he wrote *The Cunning of History*, but he understood that demography and destiny are intertwined. While concentrating on the rights that most need to be honored and how state power could defend them, Rubenstein saw increasingly that those issues were complicated by a fundamental fact: more people exist than anyone needs.

A version of that insight found expression in an arguable but perceptive thesis in *The Cunning of History*: "The Nazi elite clearly understood that the Jews were truly a *surplus people* whom nobody wanted and whom they could dispose of as they pleased ... In terms of German ideology, the Jews were a *surplus population* because of the kind of society the Germans wanted to create."[28] Rubenstein expanded those claims in his 1983 book *The Age of Triage: Fear and Hope in an Overcrowded World*, but already his point was that established interests had for centuries engaged in the riddance of redundant populations through eviction, compulsory resettlement, expulsion, war, or outright extermination. As he saw it, the Nazis' handling of the Jews implemented an extremely calculated procedure for dealing with an old problem. It also involved a host of particular features, which included the blending of ancient strands of Christian anti-Judaism with modern ideologies of nationalism and racism. But in addition to arguing that the Holocaust—though exceptional—was still one of many instances of state-sponsored population elimination, Rubenstein claimed that the category of "surplus people" was crucial because it could help us to understand not only how the Holocaust was distinctive but also how it remains symptomatic of endemically destructive features in current ways of life.

"The concept of a surplus population is not absolute," Rubenstein noted in *The Cunning of History*. "An underpopulated nation can have a redundant population if it is so organized that a segment of its able-bodied human resources cannot be utilized in any meaningful economic or social

---

26. See the data supplied by The World Counts, on its World Population Clock Live.

27. See the United Nations High Commissioner for Refugees (UNHCR), "Figures at a Glance."

28. Rubenstein, *Cunning of History*, 18, 83 (italics original).

role."[29] Thus, as he succinctly put the point in *The Age of Triage*, "a surplus or redundant population is one that for any reason can find no viable role in the society in which it is domiciled."[30] Underscoring that *triage* is a socioeconomic sorting that saves some ways of life by dispatching others, Rubenstein recognized that redundancy exists partly because of sheer numbers but even more because the dominant intentions that energize modern society tend to be governed by the belief that money is the measure of all that is real. More than any other, he claimed, that belief drives the modernization process, which has been underway and intensifying over the past five centuries. One effect of that process is that the intrinsic worth of people diminishes. Human worth is evaluated functionally instead. Hence, if persons are targeted as not useful—they can be so regarded in any number of ways, depending on how those in power define their terms—a community may find it sensible to eliminate the surplus. In modern times, that action has been facilitated, indeed instigated and promoted, by governmental power. As Rubenstein understood it, triage entails state-sponsored programs of population elimination. The winnowing process, more or less extreme in its violence, enables a society to drive out what it does not want and to keep what it desires for itself.

Rubenstein's contention—the Holocaust, exceptional though it was, is still one of many instances of state-sponsored population elimination—provoked criticism. Critics argued that his outlook ignored (1) the Nazis' use of Jewish labor; (2) the Nazi outlook that Jews were not "superfluous" but evil, owing to the racial threat they posed; and (3) the centrality of antisemitism rather than economics as a key condition for the genocide against European Jews. Critics also argued that Rubenstein's understanding of "surplus people" was too broad and relative to be helpful in explaining why genocide happens in its specific circumstances, times, and ways. Responses asserted that such criticisms ignored (1) that Jewish workers were often dispatched to the gas chambers or worked to death; (2) that people are not likely to be demonized unless they already are unwanted in the extreme; (3) that economic factors inseparable from antisemitism made the Third Reich genocidal; and (4) that if one focuses only on the many and varied particulars that lead to genocide, continuities among those events would be overlooked.

Elaborating on the last point, Rubenstein's insight was that the specific reasons for genocide also involve a shared pattern, one to which his intentionally elastic concept of surplus populations directs attention. The explanatory power of the concept may not be its primary hallmark—for

---

29. Rubenstein, *Cunning of History*, 10.
30. Rubenstein, *Age of Triage*, 1.

explanation one must go to the details in particular cases. The concept's strength is instead its synthesizing capacity, which in turn enables insight before it is too late regarding the diverse ways and places in which people might find themselves functionally redundant and destined to be targets for riddance. Importantly, Rubenstein emphasized that people do not have to be overtly labeled as surplus to be redundant; nor must the controlling powers explicitly identify a problem of population superfluity for their actions to show that they do, in fact, think one exists. The ultimate documentation is population riddance itself. In Rubenstein's view, genocidal action reveals population redundancy even if the perpetrators of genocide use other terms to explain and justify their acts of population riddance.

Meanwhile, as Rubenstein advanced his analysis of surplus people and population riddance, he boldly asserted that the Holocaust "can be fully comprehended in terms of the normal categories of history, social science, demography, political theory, and economics."[31] At this point, Rubenstein's reach exceeded his grasp. For if "the Cosmos is ultimately absurd in origin and meaningless in purpose," if human lives disappear into "the midnight silence of Eternal Chaos," if human experience cannot ultimately account for itself—and it cannot—then it is hard to see how "the normal categories of historical and socio-political analysis" can fully comprehend the Holocaust or, for that matter, anything else.[32] Yet, even if Rubenstein's assertion on this matter was not well-founded, a major point in its favor remains. He defended the Holocaust's comprehensibility to contest perspectives that mystify the Holocaust by stressing that the event eludes rational understanding. Probably the truth is closer to Rubenstein's side than not. Admitting that we lack the requisite metaphysical certainty to comprehend any historical occurrence fully, the disciplines of history, social science, demography, political theory and economics nevertheless do tell much about how and why the Holocaust happened.

Despite the bleak portents of his *Age of Triage*, Rubenstein still found room to say, "We are by no means helpless in meeting the challenge confronting us."[33] Economically, he argued, the basic remedy for triage would be to create a social order that provides a decent job for any person who is willing to work. His optimism was muted, however, because he saw that implementation of his economic remedy is not an economic matter alone. In fact, the forms of practical rationality that govern modern economic

---

31. For Rubenstein's articulation of this perspective, see his "Naming the Unnamable," 43–55.

32. Rubenstein, "Some Perspectives," 355; and Rubenstein, "Naming the Unnamable."

33. Rubenstein, *Age of Triage*, 224.

initiatives—they now include job-killing realities portended by robotics and artificial intelligence—tend to mitigate against full employment of the kind that Rubenstein envisioned. The challenge that confronts us, then, is largely a spiritual one. Unless people are resensitized religiously and morally, the resources to avert triage are likely to be hopelessly inadequate.

Rubenstein contended that we need nothing less than "an inclusive vision appropriate to a global civilization in which Moses and Mohammed, Christ, Buddha, and Confucius all play a role."[34] To call Rubenstein's vision demanding understates the case. Their universalizing tendencies notwithstanding, the major religious traditions have themselves been instrumental in "triaging" people "into the working and the workless, the saved and the damned, the Occident and the Orient."[35] Rubenstein hoped that a new religious consciousness could build on the inclusive aspects of the major religious traditions, excluding the exclusive features in the process. It would take "authentic religious inspiration" to produce that transformation.[36] Unfortunately, such inspiration cannot be called into existence at will, least of all by intellectuals, and religion's presently dominant forms are characterized more by tribalism than by the inclusiveness that Rubenstein advocated. This dilemma intersects with a story that Rubenstein has liked to tell.

The Swami's Insight

The story features Swami Muktananda of Ganeshpuri.[37] Meeting Muktananda on two occasions in the mid-1970s, Rubenstein was deeply moved by the first words that Muktananda spoke to him, for it seemed, says Rubenstein, that the guru knew instinctively what he needed to hear: "You mustn't believe in your own religion," the swami advised him; "I don't believe in mine. Religions are like the fences that hold young saplings erect. Without the fence the sapling could fall over. When it takes firm root and becomes a

34. Rubenstein, *Age of Triage*, 240.
35. Rubenstein, *Age of Triage*, 240.
36. Rubenstein, *Age of Triage*, 239.
37. A controversial figure owing to allegations about sexual and financial misconduct, the Hindu Muktananda nevertheless remains significant as the founder of the spiritual and meditative path called Siddha Yoga. Emphasizing enlightenment and self-realization, Muktananda taught that "God dwells within you as you," and that people can and should "see God in each other." See the website for Siddha Yoga, and especially the webpage on its essential teachings, whose URL is given at the end of the bibliography. At various times, Muktananda left his native India to travel the world. In the 1970s, he lived and taught in the United States, where he established meditation centers, ashrams, and the SYDA (Siddha Yoga Dham Associates) Foundation, which advances and supports his legacy.

tree, the fence is no longer needed. However, most people never lose their need for the fence."[38]

Rubenstein found Swami Muktananda to be a deeply religious man. What, then, did Muktananda mean when he said that he did not believe in his own religion, and that Rubenstein ought not to believe in his? Rubenstein found the Swami's insight particularly helpful because, Rubenstein says, he received it at a time when he was feeling "bitterly pessimistic about almost every aspect of the human condition," a mood that included what he acknowledged as an intolerance toward people in his own Jewish tradition who apparently declined to face what Rubenstein called "the difficulties involved in affirming the traditional God of covenant and election after Auschwitz."[39] As Rubenstein interpreted Muktananda, the Swami was urging Rubenstein not to give up his fundamental insights but to use them to look deeper and to see beyond their limited meanings. The point was not that the place where one stands is unimportant. Nor was it to contend that particular religious traditions are insignificant and undeserving of loyalty, finite and fallible if not ultimately false though they may turn out to be. On the contrary, the issue is to draw on what is best in a tradition and to filter out what is not. Building on the Swami's insight, Rubenstein discerned and helped me to grasp a fundamental truth: When it comes to the multiple shortfalls and shortcomings of thought, character, decision, and action that tempt us human beings to betray what is good, right, virtuous, and just, and incite us to inflict incalculable harm, the responsibility to curb those inclinations and resist their power falls to us human beings. That recognition invites little optimism. If we do not rise to that occasion, nobody or nothing else will.

Influenced by the Swami's insight, Rubenstein's outlook and mine took further post-Holocaust turns as the twenty-first century arrived. His 2010 book, *Jihad and Genocide*, revealed one of them. Introducing the book by explaining why he wrote it, Rubenstein recalled the early morning of September 11, 2001. As he put his finishing touches on the revised edition of *Approaches to Auschwitz*, which he coauthored with me, Rubenstein pondered how he had "devoted the better part of a career of half a century to research, writing, and lecturing on the Holocaust and the terrible phenomenon of genocide."[40] When he turned on the television for the morning news on that fateful day, his reflection was profoundly interrupted as he learned about al-Qaeda's deadly terrorist attacks against the World Trade

---

38. Rubenstein, *After Auschwitz*, 293.
39. Rubenstein, *After Auschwitz*, 293.
40. Rubenstein, *Jihad and Genocide*, 1.

Center in New York City and the Pentagon in Washington, DC. Rubenstein's introduction to *Jihad and Genocide* continued as follows:

> Apart from sheer horror, my immediate reaction was to ask myself whether our book on the Holocaust had instantly become an exercise in futility. Without delay, I sent John Roth an e-mail message saying that, as important as was the Holocaust, it happened sixty years ago and we were facing a very real present danger. I told him that henceforth my efforts were less likely to be focused on the Holocaust than on the threat of radical Islam. John was supportive in his reply, but insisted that both were equally important. He was, of course, correct. As is evident from much of the material in this book, there is more than a little affinity between National Socialism and Islamic extremism. As partners in World War II, both sought the utter destruction of the Jewish people, a project Islamists have never abandoned. As is evident from a multitude of hateful sermons, media propaganda, and street demonstrations (all too many of which are available on the Internet), today's Islamists have recycled some of National Socialism's most vicious anti-Semitic propaganda while peddling the obscene canard that the Israelis are latter-day Nazis.[41]

Once again, my experience did not replicate Rubenstein's, but his insight influenced mine. The evening before the 9/11 attacks, I addressed the first-year students at Claremont McKenna College. More prescient than I could imagine, my theme was "take nothing good for granted." My reflection drew on *Holocaust Politics*, a book of mine published just a few days earlier.[42] Its eclipse by 9/11 left me wondering whether my work on the Holocaust might be, in Rubenstein's words, "an exercise in futility." Both of us, however, rejected that conclusion, albeit in different ways.

Rubenstein's analysis of radical Islam proved distinctive because it showed affinities between National Socialism and Islamic extremism. The Holocaust was the backdrop, and sometimes center stage, in each of *Jihad and Genocide*'s six chapters. Post-9/11, my work on the Holocaust turned to ethics even more than before.[43] What had happened to ethics during and after the Holocaust? Is it a forlorn cause to think that the failures of ethics can be curbed, if not corrected and overcome? Among other things, that

---

41. Rubenstein, *Jihad and Genocide*, 2.
42. See Roth, *Holocaust Politics*.
43. See, for example, Roth, *Ethics*; Roth, *Failures of Ethics*; Roth, ed., *Genocide*; Grob and Roth, eds., *Losing Trust*; Rittner and Roth, eds., *Rape*; and Rittner and Roth, eds., *Teaching about Rape*.

inquiry led me to participate in Jewish–Christian–Muslim trialogue, which, I have hoped, might lend support to Muslims who defend Islam against its extremists.[44]

Dubious about that approach, Rubenstein contended that Islamist terrorism has deep and arguably irreversible roots in centuries of Islamic tradition. With the threats posed by Hamas and a potentially nuclear-armed Iran in the foreground, Rubenstein senses that the genocidal destruction of the State of Israel is an objective required by Islamic extremism's understanding of jihad. My approach is more sanguine about Islam than Rubenstein's, but I do not discount key insights that *Jihad and Genocide* underscores: (1) "Believe those who promise to kill you, especially when they seek the weapons with which to do it." (2) "Unless a strategic national interest is at stake, no nation will risk its blood and treasure to rescue citizens of another country."[45]

Such insights, Rubenstein maintains, are the result of knowledge he gained over decades. For many reasons, he remains a source of Holocaust insight for me, but particularly because my long knowledge of him drives home this summary recognition: (1) Nothing is likely to matter more than who holds power and how power is used. (2) The twentieth century revealed the immense, untamed human capacity to unleash mass atrocities and the untold suffering they inflict. Thus far, little if anything in the twenty-first century has significantly interrupted, let alone reversed, that trend. (3) Understanding religion is crucial for understanding the Holocaust, genocide, and other mass-atrocity crimes; understanding the Holocaust, genocide, and other mass-atrocity crimes is crucial for rethinking politics, economics, ethics, and religion. (4) Never lose sight of or underestimate religion's importance in human affairs. (5) Even when I disagree with Rubenstein—perhaps especially then—I recognize anew that his words are ignored at humanity's peril.

---

44. See, for example, Grob and Roth, eds., *Encountering the Stranger*.
45. Rubenstein, *Jihad and Genocide*, 124–25.

2

Elie Wiesel

In his classic Holocaust memoir called *Night*, Elie Wiesel describes the deportation of Jews from Sighet, his hometown in what was then Nazi-occupied Hungary, during the spring of 1944. That railroad journey reduced his world to "a hermetically sealed cattle car."[1] Wiesel recalls "the heat, the thirst, the stench, the lack of air," but "all that was nothing compared to her screams, which tore us apart."[2]

---

1. Wiesel, *Night*, trans. Marion Wiesel, 24. Quotations are from this translation. Arguably, no Holocaust-related book has had more widespread influence than *Night*, but controversy has swirled around the differences between the Yiddish, French, and English versions of that memoir. At the controversy's epicenter is Seidman, "Elie Wiesel," 1–19. Seidman argues that the early Yiddish (*Un di Velt Hot Geshvign*, 1956) and the abridged French (*La Nuit*, 1958) versions are substantially different accounts, and that Wiesel toned down the anger in the former to make the latter more palatable to non-Jewish readers. (Translated from the French version, the English version of *Night* was published in 1960.) In addition, see Seidman, *Faithful Renderings*, esp. 199–242. In his preface to the 2006 English edition of *Night*, translated by Marion Wiesel from the French, Wiesel discusses some of the differences among the versions of *Night*. See Wiesel, *Night*, trans. Marion Wiesel, vii–xv. On these topics, see also Bloom, ed., *Elie Wiesel's "Night"*; Katz and Rosen, eds., *Elie Wiesel*; Manseau, "Revising *Night*," 387–99; Rosen, ed., *Approaches to Teaching*; Wyatt, "Translation."

The saga of *Night* has gone further. In 2009, Wiesel asked his friend Joel Rappel to archive his papers and manuscripts—about a million documents in all—a task that took Rappel seven years. That work unearthed an overlooked Hebrew version of *Night*. Probably written in the late 1950s, Wiesel's Hebrew *Night* is harsher than the later Hebrew translation of the softer French version. What becomes clear is that *Night*'s multiple versions tell and retell what Wiesel remembered, felt, interrogated, and strived to communicate. On those themes, see Greenspan, "Humanities of Contingency," which focuses on what the author calls "retelling." For further information about Rappel and his discovery of the Hebrew version of *Night*, see Aderet, "Newly Unearthed Version." See also, Aderet, "Why the Opening."

2. Wiesel, *Night*, 26.

The screams were those of a middle-aged woman whom Wiesel identifies only as Mrs. Schächter, although he adds that he knew her well. Her husband and two older boys had been deported earlier. Now she was imprisoned in the cattle car with her ten-year-old son. "The separation," says Wiesel, "had totally shattered her . . . Mrs. Schächter had lost her mind."[3] Her disorientation was revealed not only by moans and increasingly hysterical screams but also by the visions that provoked them.

Mrs. Schächter could not see outside the rail wagon, but on the third night of the seemingly endless journey, she saw flames in the darkness. "I see a fire!" she kept exclaiming. "I see flames, huge flames."[4] At first, the screams led some of the men to look through the small windows that allowed a little air into their cattle-car prison, but they saw no flames. "There was nothing," reports Wiesel, "only the darkness of night."[5]

Some took pity and tried to calm Mrs. Schächter. Others were less kind. Wanting her quiet, they bound, gagged, and even struck her—with "blows," Wiesel acknowledges, "that could have been lethal." Meanwhile, he observes, "her son was clinging desperately to her, not uttering a word. He was no longer crying."[6]

Dawn's arrival stilled the bewildered woman. She remained quiet throughout the next day, but the fourth night again brought her screaming visions of fire. On the following day, the train stopped at a station. None of Mrs. Schächter's flames were to be seen, but signs indicated that the train had reached Auschwitz. "Nobody," says Wiesel, "had ever heard that name."[7]

For an afternoon and on into the evening, the train waited, but with nightfall, Mrs. Schächter's mad cries renewed. "As she went on howling," says Wiesel, "she was struck again. Only with great difficulty did we succeed in quieting her down." At last the train began to move, taking the rail spur that had recently been constructed to facilitate the arrival of transports at Birkenau, the killing center at Auschwitz. Mrs. Schächter had almost been forgotten, but "suddenly there was a terrible scream: 'Jews, look! Look at the fire! Look at the flames!'" This scream was right. "This time," says Wiesel, "we saw flames rising from a tall chimney into a black sky."[8] Lighting up the darkness as they reached skyward from crematorium furnaces, those flames turned Jewish lives into smoke and ash.

3. Wiesel, *Night*, 24.
4. Wiesel, *Night*, 25.
5. Wiesel, *Night*, 25.
6. Wiesel, *Night*, 26.
7. Wiesel, *Night*, 27.
8. Wiesel, *Night*, 27–28.

With the transport's arrival at Birkenau, the cattle cars opened, and the prisoners were rousted toward the selection process that determined their fate: a gas-chamber murder or the slave labor that eventually resulted in death for most of those who were chosen. The selection process began. It spared Wiesel and his father Shlomo but condemned his mother Sarah and his little sister Tzipora. *Night* also indicates that Wiesel caught one last glimpse of Mrs. Schächter and the boy who held her hand. Mrs. Schächter and her son were of no use to the Germans. Birkenau's furnaces soon consumed them. As for Wiesel and his father, their Auschwitz path took them toward a fiery pit in which little children were being burned. Wiesel recalls his father's words: "Do you remember Mrs. Schächter, in the train?"[9] The immediate response in *Night* does not contain an explicit answer to his father's question, but the words that follow are among Wiesel's most powerful:

> Never shall I forget that night, the first night in camp, that turned my life into one long night seven times sealed.
>
> Never shall I forget that smoke.
>
> Never shall I forget the small faces of the children whose bodies I saw transformed into smoke under a silent sky.
>
> Never shall I forget those flames that consumed my faith forever.
>
> Never shall I forget the nocturnal silence that deprived me for all eternity of the desire to live.
>
> Never shall I forget those moments that murdered my God and my soul and turned my dreams to ashes.
>
> Never shall I forget those things, even were I condemned to live as long as God Himself.
>
> Never.[10]

Initially studying Wiesel's *Night* almost fifty years ago, I became a philosopher tripped up by Holocaust history. In my early thirties at the time, my American life was progressing well, and despite the fact that my philosophical interests focused on questions about injustice, suffering, and evil, the Holocaust was not at the center of my attention. The experiences that Wiesel reported in *Night*, even his use of words and silences, were distant from my experience. Nevertheless, what had happened to Madame Schächter and her son, to Elie Wiesel and his family, had taken place during my lifetime. My life, their lives, indeed all our lives, unfold in one world, and the resulting collisions of consciousness and concern would drive me to find out as much as I could about how and why the Holocaust happened.

9. Wiesel, *Night*, 34.
10. Wiesel, *Night*, 34.

Wiesel's memory of Madame Schächter did not fade away. Decades after writing *Night*, Wiesel recalled her in his 1995 memoir, *All Rivers Run to the Sea*. "Certain images of the days and nights spent on that train invade my dreams even now," he wrote. "Anticipation of danger, fear of the dark, the screams of poor Mrs. Schechter, who, in her delirium, saw flames in the distance; the efforts to make her stop; the terror in her little boy's eyes."[11] Such recollections made Wiesel wonder: "And what of human ideals, or of the beauty of innocence or the weight of justice? ... Why all these deaths?"[12] Questions shape the Holocaust's legacy. Wiesel explored them in ways that remain challenging sources of Holocaust insight.

It Started with Tears

Wiesel taught at Boston University for nearly four decades. As Ariel Burger, one of his assistants, has aptly observed, Wiesel saw teaching as "the core of his life's mission, . . . his writing as an extension of this role, and his activism as its public face."[13] Although I never had the privilege of being in Wiesel's Boston classroom, he remains my teacher. So, as I reflect on my learning and teaching about the Holocaust, I often recall that Wiesel's mood turned somber during one of my visits with him in his New York home. He wondered whether his work had changed the world very much, whether it had made a substantive difference. "Well," I replied, "you definitely changed me."

Prior to my earliest encounters with Wiesel, the Holocaust had affected me through the writings of Richard Rubenstein, especially his *After Auschwitz*, which I read shortly after its publication in 1966. Indeed, my first Holocaust-related publication focused on him.[14] Not until I read Wiesel, however, did my life take the Holocaust turn that changed me personally and professionally forever.

The change began in earnest during the summer of 1972 when I followed the suggestion of the late Frederick Sontag, my Pomona College philosophy teacher and for many years my special friend and colleague. Sontag thought that I would find it worthwhile to read Wiesel's writings. Without knowing what awaited me, I bought some of Wiesel's books, and started to

11. Wiesel, *All Rivers*, 76. The change in the spelling of Mrs. Schächter's name is Wiesel's.

12. Wiesel, *All Rivers*, 79.

13. Burger, *Witness*, xi. For further testimony about the impact of Wiesel-as-teacher, see Berger, ed., *Elie Wiesel*.

14. See Sontag and Roth, "Death of God in American Theology," 224–30. In this chapter I have discussed Rubenstein's thought. For further discussion on that theme, see Haynes and Roth, eds., *Death of God Movement*; and Roth, "Is God Dead?" 43–57.

read them a few days after my second child, Sarah, was born on July 4 of that year, just a few weeks, as it turned out, after Wiesel became a father when his son, Elisha, was born on June 6.

Circumstances, emotions, and words conspired to make that reading experience the most intense of my life. In two weeks, I read all of Wiesel's books that had thus far been published in English. The collision I experienced then between my good fortune—fatherhood, a promising academic career at Claremont McKenna College—and the destruction of family and hope explored in Wiesel's Holocaust-related reflections left lasting marks upon me.

Many years have passed since I wrote about Wiesel for the first time. "Tears and Elie Wiesel" that piece was called. "Lately something has been puzzling me," it began. "I do not regard myself as an emotional person, so why do I sometimes find myself about to weep?"[15] In writing that initial article, I began to understand that my tears were partly a response to the Holocaust and especially to Wiesel. Not long after my early essay appeared, Wiesel read it. He sent me an encouraging note, and I wrote back. Three years elapsed before we met face-to-face in 1975, but friendship grew as dawning insight made me see what I continue to discern: No catastrophe challenges treasured beliefs and cherished hopes more than the Holocaust. Fueled by virulent, racist antisemitism, that disaster, which targeted Judaism as well as every Jewish life within the Third's Reich's lethal grasp, still underlines the fragile status of human rights and ethics, still undercuts optimism about human progress, and still undermines confidence about God's moral authority, providential engagement with human history, and even God's existence itself.

Do such negations have the last word? Life persists, history continues, and they embody so much that is good and precious, so much that must not be abandoned lest failure be compounded to the point of no return. What is good and precious includes the people who—sometimes for religious reasons but often without such motivations—have resisted genocide and other mass atrocities and have rescued, often at the risk of their own lives, and helped to heal at least some of those targeted by human destructiveness. Not to stand in solidarity with the resisters and rescuers, not to emulate them as best one can, only contributes to history's human-inflicted wrack and ruin. Although confrontations with the Holocaust, genocide, and other mass atrocities produce aftershocks of melancholy and despair, the face of the other is still present, conferring responsibility upon us.

15. Roth, "Tears," 42.

Wiesel sometimes said that he did not like answers but loved stories. He was a masterful storyteller, and one of his favorites, as demanding as it is brief, comes from the Hasidic tradition in Judaism:

> A disciple made the following remark in front of Rebbe Menahem-Mendl of Kotzk: God, who is perfect, took six days to create a world that is not, how is that possible? The rebbe scolded him:
>
> —Could you have done better?
>
> —Yes, I think so, stammered the disciple, who no longer knew what he was saying.
>
> —You could have done better? the Master cried out. Then what are you waiting for? You don't have a minute to waste, go ahead, start working![16]

According to Wiesel, Rebbe Mendl, who lived a century before the Holocaust raged, was obsessed with truth, which often made him feel "trapped in a universe doomed to falsehood and decay."[17] And yet that same obsession made him resist and protest against such failure and loss. "Having learned of the new pogroms that were laying waste the Jewish communities of Poland and Russia," writes Wiesel, "the Rebbe reportedly flew into a rage and pounded the table with his fist, roaring: 'I demand that justice be done, I demand that the Supreme Legislator obey his own Laws!'"[18] Apparently Mendl of Kotzk did not succeed in forcing God's hand. Truth may even have produced lucidity that it was ultimately futile to try. At the same time, despite finding life without release from suffering short of death, Rebbe Mendl affirmed humanity as precious by living defiantly to the end. It is said that he affirmed "*Avinu malkainu*, our Father, our King, I shall continue to call You Father until You become our Father."[19] It is also said that his last words were, "At last I shall see Him face to face." Wiesel adds that "we don't know—nor will we ever know—whether these words expressed an ancient fear or a renewed defiance."[20] But what can be firmly grasped are lifelines that, in Wiesel's words about Rebbe Mendl, "prepare us, demanding that we be strong, intransigent, capable of resisting evil no matter what form it takes, . . . capable of resisting even God and the hope in God."[21]

16. Wiesel, *Messengers*, 35–36.
17. Wiesel, *Souls on Fire*, 233.
18. Wiesel, *Souls on Fire*, 230.
19. See Wiesel, *All Rivers*, 85.
20. Wiesel, *Souls on Fire*, 254.
21. Wiesel, *Souls on Fire*, 254.

One day I heard Wiesel say that despair is not the end but the beginning. His depiction of Rebbe Mendl echoes that theme. The Rebbe's stories or those about him, said Wiesel, "rarely make one smile. They do not amuse, they do not appease."[22] Instead, Wiesel took those tales to emerge from "a world where man, despairing of his condition, deliberately, lucidly, chooses to probe deeply into his despair to seek, to hunt down a possibility of victory, however imprecise, however obscured by night."[23]

Where Are We Going?

Well known for defending human rights as well as for bearing witness to the Holocaust, Elie Wiesel received the Nobel Peace Prize in 1986 and led work that resulted in the opening of the United States Holocaust Memorial Museum in 1993. There is even the Elie Wiesel Genocide and Atrocities Prevention Act, which was signed into US law on January 14, 2019.[24] But my admiration for him is based less on his public accolades than on his being a dedicated teacher and a profound writer. His books have been vital for me. The best of Wiesel's versatile writing—novels, essays, plays—includes the brief Holocaust-related dialogues that appear in his books from time to time. Spare and lean, they often consist of a few hundred words or less. These dialogues are distinctive not only for their minimalist quality but also because their apparent simplicity, unidentified settings, unnamed characters, abrupt beginnings, and open endings raise fundamental questions in moving ways. In Wiesel's *A Jew Today*, one of these dialogues comes from "A Mother and Her Daughter." "Where are we going?" it begins. "Tell me. Do you know?" The mother tells her daughter, "I don't know," but when the child asks again, "Where are we going?" her mother says, "To the end of the world, little girl. We are going to the end of the world."[25]

Personal and poignant, this dialogue is ominous and dark, reflecting as it likely does, Wiesel's attempt to retrieve a conversation that he could not have heard, if it took place, as his mother and little sister approached the gas chambers of Birkenau after he was separated from them. Where are we going? In that dialogue between a mother and a daughter, the little girl tells

---

22. Wiesel, *Souls on Fire*, 233.
23. Wiesel, *Souls on Fire*, 233–34.
24. Passed with overwhelming bipartisan support in the US Congress, the act in Wiesel's honor aims to prevent genocide and other atrocities "which threaten national and international security, by enhancing United States government capacities to prevent, mitigate, and respond to such crises."
25. Wiesel, *Jew Today*, 144.

her mother that she is "really tired. Is it wrong, tell me, is it wrong to be so tired?" Her mother answers: "Everybody is tired, my little girl." A question in response: "Even God?" And, echoing Rebbe Mendl, this reply: "I don't know. You will ask Him yourself."[26]

Wiesel claimed that he "never intended to be a philosopher."[27] Nevertheless, his probing of the depths of questioning, which drove Wiesel's hard-won insistence that the essence of being Jewish is "never to give up—never to yield to despair," showed me that he was a philosopher of immense importance.[28] I credit him in that way because Wiesel emphasized that "the only role I sought was that of witness. I believed that, having survived by chance, I was duty-bound to give meaning to my survival, to justify each moment of my life."[29] Despite finding that "all words seemed inadequate, worn, foolish, lifeless," Wiesel wrote searing words that were faithful to the Holocaust's victims, loyal to his Jewish tradition, and true to the purpose of his writing: "To wrench those victims from oblivion. To help the dead vanquish death."[30]

My Holocaust insight is inseparable from Wiesel's work. Eight of his major teachings—two sets of four that focus on *understanding* and *doing*—are among those that continue to influence me most. Simple and yet complex, none is an abstract principle; all are forged in the Holocaust's fire, and each has integrity, credibility, and durability.

Understanding

Wiesel sought understanding—but not too much. While wanting people to study the Holocaust, he alerted them to the dangers of thinking that they do or can or even should know everything about it. While wanting people to meet as friends, he cautioned that such meetings will be less than honest if differences are glossed over, minimized, or forgotten. While wanting humankind and God to confront each other, he contended that easy acceptance is at once too much and too little to accept. Wiesel's understanding was neither facile nor obvious and automatic. Nevertheless, I found, its rhythm could be learned. Four of its movements follow.

1. "*The Holocaust demands interrogation and calls everything into question. Traditional ideas and acquired values, philosophical systems and social*

26. Wiesel, *Jew Today*, 144–45.
27. Wiesel, "Why I Write," 200.
28. Wiesel, *Jew Today*, 164.
29. Wiesel, "Why I Write," 200–201.
30. Wiesel, "Why I Write," 201, 206.

theories—all must be revised in the shadow of Birkenau."[31] A key insight I took from Wiesel is that nothing exceeds the Holocaust's power to evoke and intensify the question *why*? That authority puts everything else to the test. Whatever the traditional ideas and acquired values that have existed, whatever the philosophical systems and social theories that human minds have produced, they were either inadequate to prevent Auschwitz or, worse, they helped pave the way to that place. The Holocaust insists, therefore, that how one thinks and acts needs revision in the face of those facts, unless one wishes to continue the same blindness and corruption that produced the darkness of *Night*. The needed revisions, of course, do not guarantee a better outcome. And yet failure to use the Holocaust to call each other, and especially ourselves, into question diminishes chances to mend the world.

Wiesel did not place his greatest confidence in answers. Answers—especially when they take the form of philosophical and theological systems—made him suspicious. No matter how hard people try to resolve the most important issues, Wiesel insisted that "the questions remain questions."[32] To encounter the Holocaust, to reckon with its disturbing whys?—without which our humanity itself is called into question—that is enough to make Wiesel's case. Typically, however, we want not only answers but also certainty and closure about them. Wiesel aimed for sound responses to questions, but he resisted the temptation to settle questions that ought to remain unsettled and unsettling. For if answers aim to settle things, their ironic, even tragic, outcome is often that they produce disagreement, division, and death. Hence Wiesel wanted questions to be forever fundamental.

People are less likely to savage and annihilate each another when their minds are not made up but opened up through questioning. The Holocaust shows as much: Hitler and his Nazi followers "knew" they were "right." Their "knowing" made them killers. Questioning might have redeemed them and spared their victims. Wiesel's point is not that responses to questions are simply wrong. They have their place and can be essential too. Nevertheless, questions deserve lasting priority because they invite continuing inquiry, further dialogue, shared wonder, and openness.

2. "*And yet—and yet. This is the key expression in my work.*"[33] Wiesel's writings keep me moving. Always suspicious of answers but never failing for questions, he confronted problems not simply for their own sake but to inquire, what is the next step? Reaching an apparent conclusion, he went further. Such forms of thought reject easy paths in favor of hard ones. Wiesel's

---

31. This statement is from Wiesel's foreword to Cargas, *Shadows*, ix.
32. Wiesel, "Telling the Tale," 234.
33. Wiesel, "Exile," 183.

"and yet—and yet" affirms that it is more important to seek than to find, more important to question than to answer, more important to travel than to arrive. It can be dangerous to believe what you want to believe, deceptive to find things too clear, just as it is also dishonest not to strive to bring them into focus. He cautioned against overlooking that there is always more to experience than our theories admit, even though we can never begin to seek comprehension without reasoning and argument. So, Wiesel told his stories, and even their endings resist leaving me—or him—with a fixed conclusion. He wanted his readers to join him in feeling his "and yet—and yet," which provides a hope that people may keep moving to choose life and not to end it.

3. *"There is a link between language and life."*[34] The Holocaust's origins were partly in "paper violence"; they grew from and depended on words. Laws, decrees, orders, memoranda, even schedules for trains and specifications for gas vans and crematoria—all of these underwrite Wiesel's insistence that care must be taken with words, for words can kill. Wiesel used words differently. He spoke and wrote to protest injustice, to relieve suffering, and to save life. His words, including the silences they contain, brought forgotten places and unremembered victims back to life just as they could jar the living from complacency and indifference.

Doing these things, he understood, requires turning language against itself. In the Third Reich, language hid too much: euphemisms masked reality to lull; rhetoric projected illusions to captivate; propaganda used lies to control. Those efforts were hideously successful. Language and life are linked in more ways than words can say. Nonetheless, priorities after Auschwitz enjoin that words must decode words, speech must say what speech hides, writing must rewrite and set right what has been written, language must express and defend truth against the lies and falsehoods that the corruption of language aids and abets. None of this can be done perfectly, once and for all. The task is ongoing, but only as it is going on will lives be linked so that "and yet—and yet" expresses hope more than despair.

4. *"Rationalism is a failure and betrayal."*[35] Wiesel was scarcely an enemy of reason and rationality, but he did stand with philosophers who believe that one of reason's most important functions is to assess its own limitations. And yet Wiesel's critique of reason was grounded differently from David Hume's or Immanuel Kant's. Theirs depended on theory. Wiesel's rested on history and on the Holocaust in particular. The Holocaust happened because human minds became convinced that they could figure

---

34. Wiesel, "Exile," 182.
35. Wiesel, "Use of Words," 79.

everything out. Those minds "understood" that one religion had superseded another. They "comprehended" that one race was superior to every other. They "realized" who deserved to live and who deserved to die.

One can argue, of course, that such views undermined rationality and perverted morality. They did. And yet to say that much is too little, for one must ask about the sources of those outcomes. When that asking occurs, part of its search leads to reason's tendency to presume that indeed it can, at least in principle, figure everything out. With greater authority than any theory can muster, Auschwitz shows where such rationalism can lead. Wiesel's antidote was not irrationalism; his rejection of destructive madness testified to that. What he sought was understanding that includes fallibility, comprehension that looks for error and revises judgment when error is found, and recognition that knowing is not a matter of fixed conviction but of continuing dialogue.

From time to time, Wiesel contended that the Holocaust "can be compared to no other event," or that the Holocaust goes beyond or transcends history.[36] Critics have attacked him for mystifying the Holocaust and removing it from history because in his judgment the event ultimately eludes final human comprehension. I do not share these critics' reading of Wiesel. He knew that although every event is singular, all of them have features in common. But Wiesel rightly saw that no event could be equated with the Holocaust, and he correctly resisted comparison that distorts, trivializes, and denies truth about the Holocaust by diminishing the differences between the Holocaust and other events, including other genocides and mass-atrocity crimes. In his view, any reasoning that did otherwise was a failure and betrayal.

Wiesel's belief that the Holocaust goes beyond or transcends history, which entails that this event ultimately eludes final human comprehension and thus reduces us to silence, has much to commend it. It need not be understood as denying either that the Holocaust is thoroughly a historical event or that we can comprehend a great deal about it. Nevertheless, Wiesel was on target in thinking that our comprehension of the Holocaust has serious limits, partly because of our finite and fallible human capacities, and partly because the event raises questions and possesses implications that are more than historical analysis can settle and even more than history can contain.

---

36. See, for example, Wiesel, "Trivializing the Holocaust," 158; Wiesel, "Gates of the Holocaust," 211; Wiesel, "What Is a Jew?," 272. These three essays appear in volume 1 of Abrahamson, ed., *Against Silence*.

Doing

Wiesel's insights about understanding urge one not to draw hasty or final conclusions. Instead, he emphasized exploration and inquiry. It might be objected that such an outlook tends to encourage indecision and even indifference. However, one of Wiesel's most significant philosophical contributions runs in just the opposite direction. His perspective on understanding and on morality is of one piece. Thus, dialogue leads not to indecision but to an informed decisiveness. Tentativeness becomes protest when unjustified conviction asserts itself. Openness results not in indifference but in the loyalty of which friendship is made and on which it depends. Wiesel's doing is demanding, but it, too, has a rhythm that can be learned. Here are four of its movements.

1. "*Indifference to evil is worse than evil . . . We must take sides. Neutrality helps the oppressor, never the victim. Silence encourages the tormenter, never the tormented.*"[37] Wiesel never understood the world's killers, at least not completely. To do so completely would be to legitimate them by showing that they were part of a perfectly rational scheme. Though for very different reasons, he never fully understood their victims, either; their silent screams call into question every account of their dying that presents itself as a final solution. Wiesel insisted that understanding should be no less elusive where indifference—including its accomplices, passivity and neutrality—prevails. Too often indifference exists among those who could make a difference, for it can characterize those who stand between killers and victims but aid the former against the latter by doing too little, too late. Shortly after learning that he had won the 1986 Nobel Peace Prize, Wiesel put these insights in some of his best remembered words.

> Indifference, to me, is the epitome of evil. The opposite of love is not hate, it's indifference. The opposite of art is not ugliness, it's indifference. The opposite of faith is not heresy, it's indifference. And the opposite of life is not death, it's indifference. Because of indifference, one dies before one actually dies. To be in the window and watch people being sent to concentration camps or being attacked in the street and to do nothing, that's being dead.[38]

---

37. Wiesel, "Why Should People Care?" This essay is the prologue to Roth, *Consuming Fire*, 15. See also Wiesel, "Acceptance Speech" (Oslo, Norway, December 10, 1986) delivered by Elie Wiesel in English and reprinted in *Night* (trans. Marion Wiesel), 118.

38. Wiesel, "One Must Not Forget," 68.

Wiesel amplified these themes in a talk he gave at the White House at the invitation of Bill and Hillary Clinton on the evening of April 12, 1999. At the time, American and NATO forces had intervened in Kosovo to impede Slobodan Milosevic's genocidal campaign against the ethnic Albanians who sought Kosovar independence from Serbia. In that context, Wiesel's topic was "The Perils of Indifference: Lessons Learned from a Violent Century."[39]

Emphasizing that indifference "is not only a sin, it is a punishment," Wiesel underscored how indifference to evil multiplies suffering and enlarges death's toll. In devastating ways, indifference is both sin and punishment because its temptation and seduction make it "easier to look away from victims . . . For the person who is indifferent, his or her neighbors are of no consequence . . . Indifference reduces the other to an abstraction." As it does so, indifference also robs the indifferent person of humanity. In its always corrupting ways—including the failure to resist it—indifference "makes the human being inhuman." By contrast, being human in the best senses of that term requires resistance against those who oppress and torment. That conviction defined Wiesel's moral insight.

2. *"It is given to man to transform divine injustice into human justice and compassion."*[40] Abraham and Isaac, Moses and Job—those "messengers of God," as Wiesel called them—saw how people abuse the freedom that makes life human. They also wrestled with the fact that human existence neither accounts for nor completely sustains itself. Their dearly earned reckoning with that reality led them to a profound restiveness. It revealed, in turn, the awesome injunction that God intends for humankind to have hard, even impossible, moral work until and through death.

One may not see life the way those biblical messengers saw it. Whatever one's choices in that regard, it is nevertheless as hard as it is inhuman to deny that injustice too often reigns divine and that moral work is given to us indeed. Wiesel presumed neither to identify that work in detail for everyone nor to insist, in particular, where or how one should do it. Those are the right questions, though, and he wanted people to take them seriously. That exploration, he urged, is not likely to be done better than through Holocaust lenses. Enhancing vision sensitively, they can help to focus every evil that should be transformed by human justice and compassion.

3. *"If I still shout today, if I still scream, it is to prevent man from ultimately changing me."*[41] While "and yet—and yet" may be the key expression in Wiesel's writings, a close contender could be phrased "because of—in

---

39. For the text of Wiesel's talk, see Wiesel et al., "Remarks."
40. Wiesel, *Messengers*, 235.
41. Wiesel, *One Generation After*, 77. See also, Wiesel, *Testament*, 9.

spite of." Here, too, the rhythm insists that, no matter where one dwells, there is and must be more to say and do. On this occasion, though, the context is more specific, for the place where "because of—in spite of" becomes crucial is the place where despair most threatens to win. So, because of the odds in favor of despair and against hope, in spite of them, the insistence and need to rebel in favor of life are all the greater.

How Wiesel's logic works is reflected in a story that he often told. A Just Man came to Sodom to save that ill-fated place from sin and destruction. A child, observing the Just Man's care, approached him compassionately:

> Poor stranger, you shout, you scream, don't you see that it is hopeless?
>
> Yes, I see.
>
> Then why do you go on?
>
> I'll tell you why. In the beginning, I thought I could change man. Today, I know I cannot. If I still shout today, if I still scream, it is to prevent man from ultimately changing me.

The Just Man's choice is one that others can make as well. Thus, a future still awaits our determination, especially if the rhythm "because of—in spite of" is understood and enacted.

4. "*As a Jew I abide by my tradition. And my tradition allows, and indeed commands, man to take the Almighty to task for what is being done to His people, to His children—and all men are His children—provided the questioner does so on behalf of His children, not against them, from within the community, from within the human condition, and not as an outsider.*"[42] Some of Wiesel's most forceful writing involved the Jewish tradition known as Hasidism.[43] Many features impressed him as he traced this movement from its flowering in eighteenth-century Europe to its presence in the death camps and to its continuing influence in a world that came close to annihilating Hasidic ways root and branch. One of the rhythms of understanding and doing stressed by Wiesel derives at least in part from a Hasidic awareness of the relationships between "being for" and "being against."

Hasidism combines a genuine awe of God with direct and emotional reactions toward God. It finds God eluding understanding but also as One to whom people can speak. The Hasidic masters argued with God, protested

---

42. Wiesel, "Trial of Man," 176.

43. In addition to Wiesel, *Souls on Fire*, see, for example, Wiesel, *Four Hasidic Masters*; Wiesel, *Somewhere a Master*; Wiesel, *Sages and Dreamers*; and Wiesel, *Wise Men and Their Tales*. Wiesel's many public lectures often focused on Hasidic teachers. He spoke frequently at the 92nd Street Y in New York, which has a significant digital archive of Wiesel's lectures: https://www.92y.org/archives/featured-series/elie-wiesel/.

against God, feared, trusted, and loved God. All of this was done personally and passionately, without compromising God's majesty and beyond fear of contradiction. Levi Yitzhak of Berditchev, for example, understood his role as that of attorney for the defense, reproaching God for harsh treatment the Jews received. Joining him was Rebbe Israel, Maggid of Kozhenitz, author of one of Wiesel's favorite Hasidic prayers: "Master of the Universe, know that the children of Israel are suffering too much; they deserve redemption, they need it. But if, for reasons unknown to me, You are not willing, not yet, then redeem all the other nations, but do it soon!"[44] Nahman of Bratzlav held another special place in Wiesel's heart. Laughter was Nahman's gift: "Laughter that springs from lucid and desperate awareness, a mirthless laughter, of protest against the absurdities of existence, a laughter of revolt against a universe where man, whatever he may do, is condemned in advance. A laughter of compassion for man who cannot escape the ambiguity of his condition and of his faith."[45] And a final example, Menahem Mendl of Kotzk embodied a spirit whose intense despair yielded righteous anger and revolt so strong that it was said, "a God whose intentions he would understand could not suit him."[46] This rebel embraced life's contradictions both to destroy and to sustain them. Short of death, he found life without release from suffering. At the same time, he affirmed humanity as precious by living defiantly to the end.

Anything can be said and done, indeed everything must be said and done, that is for men, women, and children. Wiesel understood this to mean that standing against God is sometimes required. But he hastened to add that such a stance needs to be from within a perspective that also affirms God. Otherwise we run the risk of being against humankind in other ways all over again. Those ways include succumbing to dehumanizing temptations which conclude that only human might makes right, that there is human history as we know it and nothing more, and that, as far as the Holocaust's victims are concerned, Hitler was victorious. For . . . against—that rhythm involves taking stands. It means to be against God when being for God would put one against humankind. It also means to be for God when being against God would put one against humankind by siding with forces that waste human life. Wiesel was fiercely humanistic. His humanism, however, remained tied to God. The lesson here is that without enlivening and testing those ties and their ways of being for and against humankind, a critical resource for saving life and mending the world will be lost.

44. Quoted in Wiesel, *Souls on Fire*, 133.
45. Wiesel, *Souls on Fire*, 198.
46. Wiesel, *Souls on Fire*, 245.

Wiesel's insights about understanding and doing never cancelled his conviction that "everything to do with Auschwitz must, in the end, lead into darkness."[47] Nevertheless, that end ought not to be the ending. Remembering and acting accordingly could lead beyond. Honesty permits no greater optimism in the twilight that forms the post-Holocaust world. And yet some light remains. Though not as much as we need, might it be enough to keep destruction's nighttime madness at bay so that day can dawn again?

Toward a Post-Holocaust Christian Humanism

Elie Wiesel died on July 2, 2016. The next day at the funeral, his son, Elisha, noted that while he questioned God's existence, his father "questioned God's decisions."[48] God was never absent, at least not completely, in Wiesel's universe, but God was never present unambiguously either. One of the reasons that Wiesel has moved me is that his writings and lifelines press a conversation, a debate—often one-way and ever disconcerting—with God after Auschwitz.

In mid-June 2011, Wiesel had emergency surgery that saved his life. Less than a year later, he published a brief but noteworthy book called *Open Heart*, which reflected not only on the operation and his recovery but also on his life and work. I first read *Open Heart* uneasily because I remembered "A Prayer for the Days of Awe," a *New York Times* essay by Wiesel that appeared on October 2, 1997, the eve of the Jewish High Holy Days that year. "Master of the Universe," it began, "let us make up. It is time. How long can we go on being angry?"[49]

Fifty years after the Holocaust, Wiesel was not letting God off easy. He admitted that anguish and perplexity filled his religious outlook more than fervor or piety. He owned what he called the harsh and burning words he had written about God's apparent silence, absence, indifference and abandonment while the Holocaust raged. He insisted that the survivors' wounds would never heal, and he implored God not to forgive the killers and their accomplices. Nevertheless, the tone of that 1997 essay was more conciliatory than contentious, its outlook more settled than unsettling: "Let us make up, Master of the Universe. In spite of everything that happened? Yes, in spite."

Early on, when I read, taught, and wrote about him, a younger and seemingly more religiously rebellious Wiesel spoke profoundly to me. I liked the earlier Wiesel's stormy protest more than his composed prayer. As

---

47. Wiesel, "Auschwitz—Another Planet," 293.
48. See Blau, "Family and Friends."
49. For Wiesel's essay-prayer, see Wiesel, "Prayer."

I started to read *Open Heart*, one of the last books he published before he died, I wondered whom I would encounter in his pages this time.

Open Heart did not disappoint. True, I found a mentor much frailer than he was when we met for the first time. But far from burning out, Wiesel's fire still blazed as his persistent questions called humankind and God to account. Wiesel recalled that a journalist friend had asked what he would say if he stood before God. One word, said Wiesel, *Why?*[50] And then he went on to wonder how God could justly reply to silence that protesting inquiry. Whatever the response might be, Wiesel hoped that he would have the audacity and strength not to accept it.

I especially respect and love that Elie Wiesel because his disputatious interrogations of God, his ways of being *for* humanity and even *for* God by being *against* God, emphasize ethics and especially justice. If protest against God does not lead us to resist injustice, then such protest is senseless. But absent protest against God—or against whatever ultimately grounds our tragic if not absurd existence—we are likely to accept too much, and our resistance against injustice may be needlessly muted, weak, and bereft. If God is silent, that silence must be broken. If God is indifferent, we should at least try not to be. If God refuses to be accountable, we ought to be responsible all the more. If God dishonors his own imperative—"You shall not murder"—by permitting if not enabling genocide, then human accountability requires affirming that we ought always to obey that commandment. If God is absent, we should be present wherever injustice wracks and ruins life. If God has abandoned the suffering and forsaken the hopeless, then we must try our best to diminish their pain, despair, and grief. Nothing guarantees that such aims will gain the success that is needed. Pursuing them may be a forlorn cause. But as Wiesel puts the point in *Open Heart*, "I belong, after all, to a generation that has learned that whatever the question, indifference and resignation are not the answer . . . If life—mine or that of my fellow man—is not an offering to the *other*, what are we doing on this earth?"[51]

The nineteenth-century Christian philosopher Søren Kierkegaard emphasized that life is understood backward but must be lived forward. As I look back on decades of Wiesel's influence within me, I see increasingly how he emboldened me to live forward by finding my own voice and intensifying the post-Holocaust Christian humanism that keeps daring me. Here are some of that outlook's key perspectives:

- Human life, God's creation and gift, is precious; it can be good beyond description.

50. Wiesel, *Open Heart*, 65.
51. Wiesel, *Open Heart*, 73, 75.

- Failure and especially ethical shortcomings—God's as well and humanity's—riddle existence. Short of falsifying the past by erasing apprehension of it, there is no way to move totally beyond the atrocity and waste that scorch and scar history; not even life beyond death can redeem them, at least not completely.
- We should live with gratitude, respect, and awe for all that is good, including the capacity to question and the responsibility to resist all that is not.
- No one can do everything that needs to be done, but the quality of human existence depends mightily on how well we respond to the question, Are we doing the best we can to salvage life from wrack and ruin?
- Meaning, purpose, and what I call an *in-spite-of* joy, which refuses to let indifference dominate and despair prevail, can and must be found in opposing injustice and heeding the call that we are in the world to do what is right and good.
- Jesus, a Jew from Nazareth, underscores that caring for the suffering and forlorn matters more than religion and theology; he can hearten those who strive to love their neighbors as themselves and to do unto others as we would have them do unto us.
- Not exclusively but decisively, Christianity's integrity depends on honoring the Jewish roots of Christianity, confessing Christian complicity in the Holocaust, learning from Judaism as a spirited and living tradition, and standing in solidarity and community with Jews and all people who seek to mend the world.

Now in my late seventies, I understand more profoundly than I did when Wiesel first moved me in 1972 that my ongoing quarrel with God, Jesus, and Christianity does not repudiate them but instead reveals what the New Testament, reflecting its Jewish roots, calls a hunger and thirst for righteousness. Christian Scripture reports that Jesus said, "Blessed are those who hunger and thirst for righteousness, for they will be filled" (Matt 5:6). I doubt that Jesus was completely right about that, but the verse's yearning, passion, hope, and anticipation of joy remain on target to me, even as I recognize that fulfillment of the tasks of righteousness can never be complete.

At its fullest and best, *righteousness* requires thinking wholeheartedly and acting not only justly but also compassionately. It compels being accountably offended—especially at oneself—when such opportunities are bypassed or squandered. Such qualities, I believe, are as well summarized as they are persuasively reinforced by a Methodist tradition in Christianity that interprets hunger and thirst for righteousness as follows:

> Do all the good you can,
> By all the means you can,
> In all the ways you can,
> In all the places you can,
> At all the times you can,
> To all the people you can,
> As long as ever you can.

Wiesel was born on September 30, 1928. Over the many years of our friendship, geographical distance kept us from meeting very often, and it became my custom to send him a birthday letter. In September 2015, *The Failures of Ethics*, a recent reflection of mine at the time, accompanied my greeting. What I told Wiesel about that book also bears witness for and to me as life goes on. "Your influence is present in every chapter," I told him, "so much so that the book owes its very existence to you. I hope that I have done justice to that impact. Your presence to me is vivid, immediate, and constant—always." Now his death and my memory of him reinforce the conviction that his insights must remain challenging and encouraging to me in ways that keep paying tribute to him.

When a person dies, a conventional wish is "rest in peace," but my hope for Elie Wiesel is different. May he keep doing all the good he can by protesting to God on behalf of humanity. May memory of him be a blessing that strengthens hunger and thirst for righteousness in ways that are oppression-resisting, death-defying, hope-sustaining, life-giving, and joy-creating.

Elie Wiesel called *The Oath*, his 1973 novel, "bleak . . . devoid of hope."[52] His evaluation is understandable, but that book remains fundamental for me, a reminder of Wiesel's brilliance as a teacher, an emblem of his life-changing and life-sustaining impact upon me. *The Oath* works that way because I found something immensely meaningful and encouraging in that story about a pre-Holocaust Jewish community engulfed and destroyed by violence except for one surviving witness, a man named Azriel, who had taken an oath to be silent about whatever would befall his people. Years later, torn between speech and silence but true to his oath, Azriel meets a despairing young man who wishes he were dead. Azriel decides to intervene, but how to make the young man choose life is the question. Azriel responds by breaking his oath. He tells his tale-that-cannot-be-told, hoping to instill rebellion against despair, passionate responsibility in the place of emptiness, concern to thwart indifference, life to counter death. Apparently

---

52. Wiesel, *Sea Is Never Full*, 52.

Azriel has some success. "By allowing me to enter his life," the young man testifies, "he gave meaning to mine."[53]

The dire straits from which Azriel's testimony rescues that young man in *The Oath* are far removed from me, but not the experience of finding that Wiesel has been a profound source of Holocaust insight for me. Entry into his life—through reading and writing, through friendship, through questions—gives meaning to mine. "Not to transmit an experience," said Wiesel, "is to betray it."[54] Far from betraying his Holocaust insights, Wiesel transmitted them in ways that have lasting impact. Small though it may be, one sign of his success is that his insights became mine.

---

53. Wiesel, *Oath*, 16.
54. Wiesel, "Why I Write," 201.

3

Friends and Teachers I

In *Souls on Fire* and other books, Elie Wiesel used thematic interludes to augment and link major chapters. Following that example, the first of three reflections supplements this book's primary discussions by identifying additional people who have deepened my learning and advanced my teaching about the Holocaust. Here, I sketch vignettes about historians who are especially important to me and representative of many others who are my friends and teachers.[1]

Historical research is the bedrock for learning and teaching about the Holocaust, for understanding how and why that disaster happened and for grasping the ethical issues and insights that flow from such study. Anyone who approaches the Holocaust as student or teacher is indebted to scholars who do the painstaking work of archival research, where documents are the coin of the realm. The Holocaust's documents, of course, come in many shapes and sizes. There are the railroad timetables that Raul Hilberg has shown to be invaluable for grasping how the perpetrators made the Holocaust happen, but there are also the memoirs of Charlotte Delbo and Primo Levi, and the USC Shoah Foundation has more than fifty thousand survivor testimonies in its holdings. But historians also grapple with the fact that much of the Holocaust's documentation has been lost forever. The murdered cannot speak. The Germans destroyed massive amounts of

---

1. More historians than I can name have been sources of Holocaust insight for me; but in addition to those discussed in this chapter, I acknowledge Götz Aly, Victoria Barnett, Omer Bartov, Doris Bergen, Donald Bloxham, David Cesarani, Alon Confino, Martin Dean, Patrick Desbois, Debórah Dwork, Robert Ericksen, Richard J. Evans, Peter Fritzsche, Wolf Gruner, Patricia Heberer, Marion Kaplan, Ian Kershaw, Claudia Koonz, Thomas Kühne, Deborah Lipstadt, Jürgen Matthäus, Steve Paulsson, Gitta Sereny, Timothy Snyder, Alan Steinweis, Robert Jan Van Pelt, Nikolaus Wachsmann, and Gerhard Weinberg.

evidence, or war's devastation turned it to rubble. Nevertheless, advances of knowledge take place as historians diligently do their work. Underscoring that those advances are not automatic, Hilberg stressed that "they become possible when someone steps out of a habitual framework of thought to recognize complications or connections not seen before, or when fortuitously a missing fact is found, or when patient sifting through large collections of records allows glances at life as it was lived."[2] Seven historians are special sources of Holocaust insight for me because they have advanced knowledge in ways that fit Hilberg's description.

Christopher R. Browning

I was with my father, Josiah, in Claremont, California, when he died at the age of ninety-six in the early morning of Tuesday, October 2, 2001. During the fall semester of that academic year, Tuesdays were teaching days for me at Claremont McKenna College. That morning, my class on the Holocaust was scheduled to meet at 9:40. I made the decision that I knew my father would want: go and teach. With respect and care, the students received the news about my loss, and then they agreed that the most meaningful thing to do was to keep studying together. That hour with them remains as vivid as my memory of my father's face.

The lesson for that October morning concentrated on writing by Christopher Browning. We first met at a symposium on "Western Society after the Holocaust," which was held at the University of Washington, Seattle, in November 1978. His friendship as well as his scholarship mean much to me. Few historians have authored books that become widely read classics used repeatedly in college and university courses on the Holocaust. Browning deservedly enjoys a place in that select company because of *Ordinary Men: Reserve Police Battalion 101 and the Final Solution in Poland*. The book's 1992 publication was followed by a 1998 edition and then by a twenty-fifth anniversary edition in 2017. The later versions were less revised editions of the original text than occasions for Browning to add an "Afterword" (1998) and an essay called "Twenty-five Years Later" (2017). In the former, Browning continued a tussle with Daniel Goldhagen, whose research findings on Police Battalion 101 competed with Browning's in controversial ways. In the latter, Browning commented on and sometimes quarreled with research by others that might update, expand, and contextualize Browning's primary analysis. Important though they are, Browning's postscripts are minor reasons for the book's ongoing impact. The major reason for that

---

2. Hilberg, "Incompleteness," 91.

result continues to be Browning's powerful narrative, which leads him and his readers to conclude that "within virtually every social collective, the peer group exerts tremendous pressures on behavior and sets moral norms. If the men of Reserve Police Battalion 101 could become killers under such circumstances, what group of men cannot?"[3]

On that October morning in 2001, my class focused on related issues using Browning's *Nazi Policy, Jewish Workers, German Killers*, a book lesser known than *Ordinary Men* but not less important. Specifically, we focused on Browning's findings about the dispositions and motivations that characterized the units of the German Order Police—Reserve Police Battalion 101 was one of many police battalions—who killed tens of thousands of Jews in eastern Europe during the Holocaust. Those units were not monolithic. They typically contained three cohorts. The largest group, says Browning, "followed orders and complied with standard procedures but did not evince any eagerness to kill Jews."[4] Smaller in number was "a significant core of eager and enthusiastic killers." Smaller still was "a minority of men who sought not to participate in the regime's racial killing." Browning concluded that they "had no measurable effect whatsoever," but the eager killers "formed a crucial nucleus for the killing process in the same way as eager and ambitious initiators at the middle echelons and Hitler, Himmler, and Heydrich at the top." The influence of such ambitious and determined people, added Browning, "was far out of proportion to their numbers in German society." Nevertheless, combined with a compliant majority, that zealous minority produced untold suffering and death. That day in October—and on many others too—Christopher Browning helped my students and me to wonder about the meaning of such results, what they imply about justice, and whether death is the last word.

Peter Hayes

A story began when my phone rang one morning in early September 2005. The call was from Lucy Qureshi, then the commissioning editor for religion and theology at Oxford University Press. She wondered if I would be interested in compiling and editing what eventually would become *The Oxford Handbook of Holocaust Studies*. Of course, I told Qureshi, I was very interested in the handbook project but a historian would need to be my partner in the editorial work.

3. Browning, *Ordinary Men*, 189.

4. Browning, *Nazi Policy*, 167. Subsequent quotations in this paragraph can be found on the following pages of Browning's book: 166, 169, and 175.

"Fine," she said, "do you have anyone in mind?"

"Yes," I replied without hesitation, "Peter Hayes."

Five years later—big scholarly projects take time—the book appeared, co-edited by Hayes and me.

Hayes and I had met some fifteen years earlier, primarily through his leadership in the Holocaust Educational Foundation's Lessons and Legacies conferences and renowned summer institutes at Northwestern University. Hayes's location at Northwestern in Illinois and mine at Claremont McKenna College in California meant that we did not see each other frequently, but I became a keen, appreciative, and admiring observer of him and his work. I saw that he knew almost everyone in the field of Holocaust studies and that he deservedly enjoyed their profound respect. As I read his scholarship and, from time to time, heard him lecture and teach, I was impressed by his exemplary clarity, depth, and insight.

Two Claremont-related moments are emblematic of what I am underscoring. In early February 2004, the forerunner of the Mgrublian Center for Human Rights at Claremont McKenna College sponsored a conference called "Gray Zones: Ambiguity and Compromise in the Holocaust and Its Aftermath." Hayes's paper, which became the lead chapter in the conference volume, concentrated on the German corporate world in the Third Reich and the role of slave labor in its enterprises. Drawing on his expertise as an economic historian, Hayes's study went into fascinating detail about the production of carbon black, an ingredient essential for the durability of rubber used in tires and other crucial war-related products. Absent carbon black, there might have been no Holocaust, but the Germans produced it, and the Third Reich's troops rode on the tires it made possible. Hayes's mastery regarding carbon black was as gripping as it was informative. Increasingly, I realized, he was becoming my teacher.

Two years later, in November 2006, the biennial Lessons and Legacies conference came to Claremont McKenna College for the first time. I organized the final plenary session, "Ethics during and after the Holocaust," which gave me the opportunity to invite Christopher Browning, Claudia Koonz, Rebecca Wittmann, Berel Lang, and Hayes to reflect on what their Holocaust study had led them to discern about ethics. "My response to this challenge," Hayes said, "will seem banal, I am afraid, but it goes as follows: I have been reminded that ethical behavior is hard."[5] Anything but banal and certainly not as simple as it sounds, that insight—clear, forthright, and as ethically accurate as it is challenging—was aptly amplified ten years later in Hayes's 2017 book, *Why? Explaining the Holocaust*. The Holocaust's

---

5. Hayes, "Ethics and Corporate History," 302.

"dreadful history," he wrote, "shows that doing the right thing can have costs that are multiplied by the unwillingness of most people to pay them, so bravery is not enough—wit, wiliness, shrewd judgment, persistence, and creativity in challenging evil are also indispensable."[6] Indispensable scarcely means sufficient, but nonetheless Hayes's insight stands.

Holocaust historians tend to be rationalists. Hayes is no exception. He holds that "the Holocaust was not mysterious and inscrutable." I, too, want lucidity and resist mystification, but my friend leaves me thinking that explanation for the Holocaust is bound to fall short if it depends too much on seeing that catastrophe, in Hayes's words, as "the work of humans acting on familiar human weaknesses and motives: wounded pride, fear, self-righteousness, prejudice, and personal ambition being among the most obvious."[7] The last word in Hayes's *Why?* is "Beware the beginnings," a proverbial German warning to look and think twice about the origins of human shortcomings and why the brakes against them are so frail. More than that, wariness about the beginnings and their aftermath entails not being too sure that we can identify and understand them without remainder. Hayes's footing is firmer in *How Was It Possible?*, his comprehensive 2015 anthology of Holocaust history. "In the study of history," he aptly says, "most answers are provisional, subject to alteration on the basis of new information and insights. But that prospect does not relieve us of the responsibility, here and now, to do the best we can with what we have."[8] Whether that outlook dismisses mystery and inscrutability altogether is dubious. Nevertheless, partly because of disagreements I may have about the degree to which Hayes or any historian has fully explained the Holocaust, he remains a source of insight for me because he so often fulfills the responsibility, here and now, to do the best we can with what we have.

Michael R. Marrus

Anyone who has met Michael Marrus, a distinguished colleague and valued friend for several decades, is likely impressed by his deep voice. I hear it resounding throughout his *Lessons of the Holocaust*, which, in ways both persuasive and paradoxical, plumbs the depths of the fraught but vital topic that its title identifies, increasing my Holocaust insight in the process.

The book recapitulates and extends Marrus's career as Holocaust historian, which he describes as "a never-ending quest to get to the bottom of

6. Hayes, *Why?*, 341.
7. Hayes, *Why?*, 342.
8. Hayes, ed., *How?*, xiv.

things."⁹ Two outlooks govern Marrus's version of that quest. First and foremost, with a premium placed on clear-eyed judgment and close attention to the best evidence available, Marrus wants to understand the Holocaust, whose status as an "epoch-making . . . watershed in the history of our times" derives from that event's most telling and boggling features: "unprecedented human wrongdoing . . . the gravest atrocities, murder, and other horrors, on a practically unimaginable scale."¹⁰ Second, Marrus distrusts attempts to promote lessons in response to such carnage. As he mines the problems that beset even the best-intentioned aims to advance lessons of the Holocaust, his skepticism reaches a bottom line akin to Hayes's: "beware of lessons."¹¹

Marrus gets his caution honestly. Taking lessons about the Holocaust to be admonitions, directions, and prescriptions for future behavior and courses of action—typically intended to prevent repetition of atrocities or to "make the world a better place"—Marrus shows in his analysis that such lessons are problematic: they are vague, contradictory, changeable, overgeneralized, lacking nuance, contested, or insufficiently grounded in history.

Beware of lessons—that, says Marrus, is his "principal lesson of the Holocaust."¹² Persuasive though that lesson needs to be, *Lessons of the Holocaust* also reveals it to be paradoxical, a quality that helpfully resists premature closure about lessons of the Holocaust. Furthermore, taking *paradox* to refer to statements or circumstances that are puzzling because they are conjoined in ways that are apparently at odds, consider that, contrary to Marrus's assertion, "beware of lessons" may not really be his principal lesson of the Holocaust. A rival for that distinction could be his imperative to "get the history right."¹³

As he makes clear through strong and frequent appeals to ongoing critical inquiry, careful research, sifting of evidence, objectivity, and commitment to truth—fundamental pursuits required to harness the passion to get to the bottom of things—Marrus teaches that "when speaking about the Holocaust we all have a fundamental duty to be as faithful as we can be to the epoch-making events from which we issue statements that are supposedly validated by the campaign against European Jewry."¹⁴ Which, then, is or ought to be the principal lesson of the Holocaust: beware of lessons *or* get the history right? Probing further within and beyond *Lessons of the*

9. Marrus, *Lessons*, 174.
10. Marrus, *Lessons*, 160, 162, 166, 168.
11. Marrus, *Lessons*, 160.
12. Marrus, *Lessons*, 160.
13. Marrus, *Lessons*, 159.
14. Marrus, *Lessons*, 160.

Holocaust, good responses to that question, paradoxically, might be, either and/or both, especially if the tension between the two lessons is dialectical—mutually critical, corrective, and illuminating.

If "beware of lessons" is primary, then it would need to apply to the duty or lesson to "get the history right." Marrus's own analysis shows that "get the history right" is an admonition as elusive as it is idealistic. Errors of historical judgment can be corrected, new evidence can be found and integrated, narrative accuracy can be improved, best historical practices can be followed, but, as Marrus accurately observes, probably nobody can "master all of the literature that appears."[15] The historian's work is never done—one has to "keep at it."[16] Strictly speaking, then, no one does or ever will get the history right, for the Holocaust shows itself to be an event so vast, complex, and far-flung in its origins and implications that all human inquiry about it will be forever incomplete and wanting in one way or another.

Historical analysis, moreover, always entails interpretation, which does not stay fixed, partly because scholars do not want to agree with their colleagues, at least not completely. Otherwise, they would have little, if anything, to say. Knowledge about "what really happened" is scarcely to be taken for granted, not least of all because truly getting the history right involves questions—philosophical, religious, psychological—that "fall outside the historian's province."[17] Such realities do not disparage understanding of the Holocaust, let alone render understanding impossible, but they do suggest that it is wise to "beware of lessons," including the lesson "get the history right."

On the other hand, if the Holocaust's primary lesson is "get the history right," where that injunction's meaning encompasses the fallibility, frailty, and failure of even our best efforts to do so, then the caution about lessons, still needed though it is, could be better nuanced and contextualized. Marrus's urging to get the history right would clarify what lessons of the Holocaust, at their best, can be and do. The point needs to be put that way because toward the end of his book, Marrus explains that his "quarrel is not necessarily with the probity of any of the purported lessons . . . The problem is not with intentions or goals; the problem is an insufficient acquaintance with Holocaust history."[18]

One would have to address what constitutes acquaintance with Holocaust history sufficient to support lessons of the Holocaust—another place

---

15. Marrus, *Lessons*, 67.
16. Marrus, *Lessons*, 170.
17. Marrus, *Lessons*, 166.
18. Marrus, *Lessons*, 158.

to be wary—but Marrus does soften his skepticism. Well he should, too, because sound lessons of the Holocaust remain badly needed. Primarily, as he underscores, such lessons will be grounded in and emerge from the paradoxical possibility that careful study of the Holocaust, its gravest atrocities and unprecedented human wrongdoing, can change people for good—by enhancing understanding of the world and the human condition, by helping us to have better judgment, and by making us, even in small ways, wiser than we otherwise would have been. The immensely important results of such learning and teaching could be that they instill what Marrus calls "a capacity to meet the unanticipated."[19]

With approval, Marrus quotes the late American historian Carl Becker: "The value of history is . . . not scientific but moral."[20] We rightly strive to get the Holocaust's history right for ethical reasons. To paraphrase Marrus's further quoting of Becker, getting that history right, as best we can, may liberalize the mind, deepen the sympathies, and fortify the will in ways that help people to live more humanely in the present and encourage them "to meet rather than to foretell the future."[21] No doubt it is wise to put that lesson to the test, but "get the history right," in moral as well as analytical ways, pairs well with "beware of lessons" to drive home in tandem a profoundly ethical lesson—beware of lessons *and* get the history right. That lesson is well worth practicing. For me, the deep voice of Marrus's *Lessons of the Holocaust*, paradoxes and all, makes that insight as clear-eyed as it is imperative.

Yehuda Bauer

I first met Yehuda Bauer in the summer of 1988 at an international conference on the Holocaust called "Remembering for the Future," which took place at Oxford University. Before and after that first meeting, my understanding of the Holocaust and its aftereffects has been informed by his research and writing and my interactions with him. No encounters with Bauer were more instructive than my wrestling with his *Rethinking the Holocaust*, which appeared in 2001, the same year in which Raul Hilberg published *Sources of Holocaust Research*. Over the years, Bauer thought I mystified the Holocaust, a judgment I reject but understand because I disagreed with rationalistic claims he made about the explicability of the genocide.

---

19. Marrus, *Lessons*, 39.
20. Marrus, *Lessons*, 39.
21. Marrus, *Lessons*, 39.

Rethinking the Holocaust, "an attempt to rethink categories and issues that arise out of the contemplation of that watershed event," required "historiosophy," Bauer's term denoting investigations where philosophy and Holocaust history intersect.[22] Seeking to correct shortcomings he found in other interpretations of the Holocaust, Bauer stressed that antisemitism provides "a central explanation for the Holocaust."[23] In addition, balancing the emphasis on German perpetrators characteristic of historians such as Browning and Hayes, Bauer stressed that the Holocaust is best understood from a Jewish perspective. Three other major claims of his grabbed my attention even more: (1) The Holocaust remains unprecedented. (2) The Holocaust, at least in principle, is explicable. (3) Study of the Holocaust involves political aims.

At the end of the twentieth century, debate about the Holocaust's uniqueness swirled through Holocaust studies.[24] Bauer defended a version of that contested thesis, although his rethinking led him to prefer the term *unprecedentedness*. Switching terminology, he tried to elude a criticism, namely, that the concept of *uniqueness* lacks meaning because all historical events are particular and therefore unique in one way or another. Bauer contended that this criticism is neither telling nor helpful, for it overlooks the point that sound analysis entails comparison of historical events. When comparison takes place, and one event exhibits an element—especially one of immense importance—that all others lack, then a claim for that event's uniqueness, far from being trivial, is appropriate and significant. Bauer hoped to avoid misunderstanding by using *unprecedented* instead of *unique*, but nonetheless the change reaffirmed the Holocaust's uniqueness.

To advance his claim about the Holocaust's unprecedentedness, Bauer acknowledged that the Holocaust was a genocide but that much more needs to be said to answer the question, What was the Holocaust? As the term *genocide* is commonly used, it refers primarily to the destruction of a national, ethnic, religious, or so-called racial group. Genocide does not necessarily mean that the murder of every single member of such a group is intended. But that goal was the one that Adolf Hitler and his Nazi followers intended for the Jews. In ways never seen before or since, said Bauer, Nazi ideology, a "pure fantasy" that combined racial antisemitism with belief in a global Jewish conspiracy to control the world, condemned Jews "anywhere

---

22. Bauer, *Rethinking*, ix, xiv.
23. Bauer, *Rethinking*, 74.
24. See, for example, Rosenbaum, ed., *Is the Holocaust Unique?*

in the world" to death "just for being born" and murdered them in killing centers that were brought "to a totally new stage of development."[25]

But if the Holocaust is unique, especially in the sense that no event before or since has been driven by such lethal intentions, couldn't it be argued that the Holocaust defies explanation? The brutality involved was so senseless, the vastness of the catastrophe so immense, the suffering of the victims so devastating that we would seem to be at a loss to understand how the Holocaust could happen. Bauer, however, rejected such reasoning. Far from making the Holocaust inexplicable, the Holocaust's unprecedentedness depends on the fact that its horror was unleashed by one group of human beings and inflicted on another. Unless we claim that human beings cannot be understood, which we do not, the Holocaust can be comprehended by historical analysis because it was a human event from start to finish.

Up to a point, Bauer realized that his position about the Holocaust's intelligibility involves problems. Thus, he underscored that he was not saying that anyone has fully comprehended how the Holocaust happened and why. He stressed that historians develop interpretations and theories to explain events. Not only do these efforts involve alternative and even competing views, but the historians' accounts do not—indeed cannot—encompass everything. They are incomplete, subject to correction as errors are discovered, and destined for revision as new evidence is found.

Bauer hedged his bets on the degree of explicability we can expect, but still his analysis did not probe deeply enough. Because historical analysis is a human endeavor, one that inevitably lacks omniscience, no good reason exists to assume that full historical comprehension of the Holocaust is possible. If full historical comprehension is impossible, then claims that the Holocaust is explicable—even "perfectly explicable," at least in part, as Bauer sometimes said—are in more trouble than he thought.[26] God might possess the comprehension needed to make the Holocaust fully explicable, but while Bauer finds Holocaust-related theology fascinating, he concludes it is "a dead end," and thus does not turn to God for the explicability he seeks. Still, Bauer-the-historian insisted, the Holocaust remains explicable *in principle*.[27]

Unfortunately, Bauer's rationalism betrayed him at this point, for his appeals to explicability in principle, let alone his claims about "perfectly explicable," are too problematic to be trusted completely. If no one, in fact, can finally explain the Holocaust through historical analysis—and that is where

---

25. Bauer, *Rethinking*, 265, 267.
26. Bauer, *Rethinking*, 22, 27.
27. Bauer, *Rethinking*, 15, 212.

the logic of Bauer's historiosophy leads—then how does it make sense to say that, in principle, the Holocaust is explicable historically? At best, we ultimately seem to be left with hypotheses that are "likely stories"—some far better documented and more accurate and reliable than others—but probably not more than that. The point is not that the Holocaust escapes human understanding altogether, but rather than clinging to the specious reed of explicability *in principle*, Bauer would be on firmer ground to settle for the fact that our historical comprehension of the Holocaust, real though it is, has serious, terminal limits, partly because of our finite and fallible human capacities, and partly because the event raises questions and possesses implications that are more than historical analysis alone can contain. Ultimately, the question, Why did the Holocaust happen? is the most important question of that kind.

If historical analysis always remains inadequate to respond to that question sufficiently, that shortcoming does not compromise Bauer's third key thesis: study of the Holocaust involves political aims. *Rethinking the Holocaust* ends with a speech that Bauer gave to the Bundestag, the German House of Representatives, on January 27, 1998. (On November 1, 2005, the United Nations General Assembly designated January 27 as International Holocaust Remembrance Day. On that date in 1945, Soviet forces liberated Auschwitz.) As Bauer concluded his speech, he alluded to the biblical Ten Commandments, suggesting that in confronting threats of mass murder, genocide, or "a Holocaust-like tragedy," the Decalogue should be supplemented by three additional imperatives: You shall not become a perpetrator. You shall not allow yourselves to become victims. You shall not become bystanders.[28]

Rethinking the Holocaust reinforces the insight that we study the Holocaust because it happened, but not only for that reason. "Too many humans have been murdered," says Bauer, "and the time has come to try and stop these waves that threaten to engulf us."[29] The Holocaust compels attention because, unprecedented though it may be, we continue to need the warning that it could become—and to some extent already has been—a precedent in our time. If Bauer's historiosophy has flaws, the moral intentions that inspired it are not among them.

---

28. Bauer, *Rethinking*, 273.
29. Bauer, *Rethinking*, xiv.

Saul Friedländer

Yehuda Bauer argued that the Holocaust is "a specifically Jewish tragedy," and thus it would never be enough to research it from the perspective of the Nazi perpetrators.[30] Saul Friedländer agreed but went further. His monumental effort attempted to produce what he calls an integrated history of the Holocaust. This project, he said, was necessary for three main reasons. First, a singular focus on German decisions and measures could not include initiatives and reactions in the occupied and satellite countries of German-controlled Europe. Second, "at each stage Jewish perceptions and reactions, collective or individual, cannot and should not be considered as a separate domain within any general historical rendition, as they affected, in various degrees, all other elements of this history." Third, only by reaching for "a simultaneous representation of the events—at all levels and in all different places"—could adequate analysis of the magnitude, complexity, and interrelatedness of the Holocaust's events be approached.[31]

Late in his academic career, Friedländer taught at UCLA, while I was sixty-some miles east at Claremont McKenna College. From time to time, I saw this distinguished, gracious scholar, a child survivor of the Holocaust, but I did not know him as well as the other historians discussed in this chapter.[32] I did know his work, however, and the project he set for himself is extraordinary in its scope and ambition. As a source of Holocaust insight, Friedländer and his attempt at an integrated history of the Holocaust are as awesome as they are instructive.

The first volume of Friedländer's two-part history of the Holocaust concentrated on what he called "the years of persecution," the period from 1933 to 1939.[33] Analyzing Hitler's consolidation of power and its increasingly disastrous but not yet fully murderous impact on German and Austrian Jews, Friedländer held that a "redemptive antisemitism" characterized Nazi ideology. He also showed how sound historical investigation of the Holocaust depends on integrating the experiences of the German perpetrators, their Jewish victims, and many other groups and individuals who were also involved in that catastrophe.

Friedländer's emphasis on "redemptive antisemitism" clashed with so-called functionalist interpretations of the Holocaust, which contended that

---

30. Bauer, *Rethinking*, xiii.

31. Friedländer addressed these points at the 2006 Lessons and Legacies conference at Claremont McKenna College. See Friedländer, "Prologue," 3–15, esp. 5.

32. Friedländer has written two memoirs: *When Memory Comes* and *Where Memory Leads*.

33. Friedländer, *Years of Persecution*.

Nazi Germany was not necessarily a genocidal regime from the beginning but evolved toward its "Final Solution" when other options for solving the Nazis' "Jewish question" proved unworkable. Friedländer disagreed, contending that Nazism early on harbored potentially genocidal intentions. Hitler and his followers saw "the Jew" as the worst threat to civilization. The world's redemption required the elimination of that menace.

This analysis did not mean, however, that Nazi leadership in the 1930s already had a blueprint for mass murder, let alone specific designs for killing centers such as Treblinka and Auschwitz. Friedländer maintained that the decisions to commit mass murder, the attention to detail needed to implement them, did evolve over time, eventually involving persons and places scattered far and wide in the Holocaust's vast continental scope. Nevertheless, as Friedländer showed in his second volume, *The Years of Extermination,* his chronologically organized account of the wartime period from 1939 to 1945, Nazi Germany's fervent, indeed fanatical, commitment to those decisions and details cannot be adequately understood absent the implicitly genocidal "redemptive antisemitism" that motivated them.

Throughout the two volumes, Friedländer defended and acted upon his long-held conviction that sound investigation of the Holocaust depends on integrating the histories of the German perpetrators, of their Jewish victims, and of many other groups and individuals as well. Neither the perpetrators nor their victims acted independently; they were always related and intertwined. As obvious as that point may be, the attempt to write the Holocaust's history with that convergence in the foreground is herculean because too much happened all at once. No Holocaust scholar knows that predicament better than Friedländer, who, arguably more than any historian thus far, has written a profoundly integrated history of the Holocaust.

No photographs are reproduced in *The Years of Extermination,* but to see what Friedländer's prodigious work required, consider that he begins the book by describing what happened in a picture that was taken at the University of Amsterdam in the Netherlands on September 18, 1942. A medical student named David Moffie is receiving his medical degree. Surrounded by his professors, family, and friends, the young doctor wears a tuxedo. On its left side is a star, the word *Jood* upon it. "Moffie," Friedländer explains, "was the last Jewish student at the University of Amsterdam under German occupation."[34]

34. Friedländer, *Years of Extermination,* xiii. For more detail on Moffie, including the photograph that Friedländler describes, see Zeidman and Cohen, "Walking a Fine Line," 252–75, esp. 262–63. (The photo is reproduced on page 262.) Moffie was the ninth of ten students who took medical doctorates under the supervision of Ariëns Kappers, a distinguished scientist who resisted the Nazis and helped to save Dutch

Unearthing such details was indispensable to Frielander's work. In the narrative he constructs, they show the interrelationships he finds so important for documenting and delineating the Holocaust's years of extermination. Importantly, much is not revealed in the Moffie photograph. It is silent, for example, about the words that were spoken at his graduation. Probably they are completely lost, and no history of the Holocaust will ever contain them. Further research indicates, however, that shortly after Moffie's graduation, he was deported to Auschwitz-Birkenau. His survival put him in the 20 percent of Dutch Jews who lived through the Holocaust. Most of the Jews in the Moffie photo, Friedländer observes, were among the other 80 percent of Dutch Jewry, those killed, one way or another, by the Germans and their collaborators.

Friedländer helps his readers to see that the window on the Holocaust provided by the Moffie photograph opens still wider if one pursues key questions implicit in that image. How, for instance, was it possible that a Jewish medical student could receive a degree at a Dutch university in September 1942? German forces had occupied Dutch soil since the spring of 1940. By 1942, the Nazis' continental "Final Solution" was underway. Deportations of Dutch Jews to Auschwitz and other places of death in the East had started on July 14 of that year. Later, on September 8, a German decree excluded Jews from Dutch universities. Nevertheless, Moffie's graduation took place in an official ceremony ten days later. It did so, Friedländer's meticulous research shows, because the calendar provided a loophole that allowed some Dutch and Jewish resistance against German power. In Dutch universities, the 1941–1942 academic year ended on Friday, September 18. The 1942–1943 academic year started on Monday, September 21. The exclusionary decree of September 8 was not effective until the beginning of the new academic year. In conferring Moffie's degree, the Dutch university took an action that was clearly contrary to the spirit if not the letter of German intentions. The photograph, says Friedländer, "documents an act of defiance, on the edge of the occupier's laws and decrees."[35]

As Moffie received his degree, he, his family, and their Jewish friends were going forward with their lives as best they could. For the Dutch Jews in the early autumn of 1942, as Friedländer's analysis shows, it was immensely precarious to do that. With deportations already in full cry, Jews were regularly rounded up by Germans and the Dutch police, who helped them to fill

---

Jews. After barely surviving Auschwitz, Moffie became a notable neurologist. In 2003, the year after his death, the Amsterdam Neurological Association created the David Moffie Prize, an annual award in his honor. The photograph is also accessible online; see the bibliography for the URL that links to the photograph.

35. Friedländer, *Years of Extermination*, xiv.

the weekly transport quotas. Amsterdam's Jewish Council, leaders required to comply with German orders, were also implicated in the deportations. Moffie and the Jews who attended his graduation ceremony would not have been there if they had not received certificates that exempted them, albeit only temporarily, from deportation.

According to Friedländer, there were seventeen thousand of these special certificates for Amsterdam's Jews—by no means enough to go around. Thus, deep probing of the Moffie photograph reveals the gray zone in which some Dutch Jews found themselves. German authority gave Jewish leaders the opportunity to reprieve, if only for a time, some but not all their fellow Jews from slave labor and death in the East. Saving a few meant condemning others. In the end, however, there were no exemption certificates, because while Moffie received the degree that certified him to be an individual trained to restore health and entrusted to save life, German authority had affixed a Jew-labeling star to his chest. That emblem stole Moffie's individuality and virtually sentenced him to death because "the Jew" had to be wiped off the face of the earth.

The Moffie photograph illustrates what an integrated history of the Holocaust entails. It must include much more than German decisions and measures alone. It must go beyond a singular focus on Jewish perceptions, initiatives, and reactions. In addition, such history writing requires attention to what was happening concurrently and simultaneously as well as concentration on intermediate and long-term relationships of cause and effect. Still further, Friedländer's project reaches overwhelming proportions when one realizes how many Holocaust-related artifacts await the same scrutiny that he gave to a single photograph.

Just as the words spoken at Moffie's commencement ceremony are unlikely to be retrieved, there are countless documents pertaining to the Holocaust that are lost forever. The number that remains is large, however, and more documents and artifacts are still being recovered. They include German records that chronicle the years of extermination and Jewish diaries that recall the onslaught day-by-day. The amount of Holocaust-related evidence is matched by its complexity because these sources cover vast geographical terrain and more places than any single map can identify. Interpreting these Holocaust data also involves understanding of the cultural and religious differences that contextualize them, as well as expertise in the diverse languages in which Holocaust-related experiences are recorded. No matter how extensive, Friedländer's attention could never encompass all the important moments, their interrelationships and juxtapositions.

To some extent, Friedländer's project was destined to be self-defeating. Odds in favor of that outcome even increased as he tackled other integrative problems—narration, contextualization, and comprehension—that are related to but beyond detail gathering. No history of the Holocaust, especially an integrated one, can be only a collection of episodes, even if they are interpreted as well as Friedländer handles the Moffie photograph. Friedländer had to put the episodes together so that a sustained narration resulted. This work required careful and difficult decisions about where to start and stop a thread, such as the one about Moffie. It entailed complicated judgments about how to connect Holocaust moments in ways that show accurately, not for literary effect, how one thing led to another in the destruction process.

Putting the episodes together was not enough. To get the compelling narrative he wanted, Friedländer had to keep context in mind as well, for just as one Holocaust moment relates to others, these events unfolded in social, economic, political, and religious settings that were larger than the individual episodes and arguably more than the sum of their parts. If all these tasks could be handled satisfactorily, there would still be the problem of what, if anything, to conclude about the Holocaust, how to end an integrative and integrated two-volume work that is well over a thousand pages in length. In this area, Friedländer had to decide what, if anything, to do about lingering questions that elude closure and that further historical analysis may not be able to answer.

Friedländer's project was self-defeating, but it brims with integrated detail—his best accomplishment—and his refusal to give up produced significant light that had never before been shed on the Holocaust. *The Years of Extermination* ends without a definitive summing up or conclusion. As though exhaustion intervened, Friedländer's account stops rather abruptly with events in May 1945. While he has little to say about the Holocaust's aftereffects, his final paragraph concentrates on the few hundreds of thousands of Jews who stayed in Nazi-occupied Europe and survived the Holocaust. Probably with his own experiences in mind, he notes that the years of destruction "remained the most significant period of their lives. They were entrapped in it: Recurrently, it pulled them back into overwhelming terror and, throughout, notwithstanding the passage of time, it carried along with it the indelible memory of the dead."[36] Friedländer's conclusion is no more—or less—than that. If it leaves his reader wanting more, perhaps the author's wisdom, and his appropriate modesty about the all-but-impossible task he set for himself, is simply to recognize that while we can know much about the Holocaust, how and why it happened, there is no closure for an event that leaves one staring into an abyss as unacceptable as it is unfathomable.

36. Friedländer, *Years of Extermination*, 663.

Friedländer's nonconcluding ending circles back to the beginning and to the book's governing epigraph, whose sense is more intense and ominous after one reads *The Years of Extermination*. Stefan Ernest, the epigraph's author, lived in Warsaw, Poland. Like Friedländer, he was a Jew in hiding in 1943. Ernest wrote his version of Holocaust history, hoping that the narrative would survive although he would not. Ernest imagined readers asking him whether his account was the truth. "I reply in advance," he says. "No, this is not the truth, this is only a small part, a tiny fraction of the truth . . . Even the mightiest pen could not depict the whole, real, essential *truth*."[37] With those words, Friedländer's remarkable research and mighty pen find a fitting place for study of the Holocaust to stop momentarily, but not end, and then to begin again.

Two Claremont Colleagues

A few years after my retirement, Claremont McKenna College endowed a professorship in my name. I was honored twice when Wendy Lower became the inaugural holder of that chair. Two decades earlier, during the summer of 1992, she traveled to Ukraine to do archival research. Some of the documents she studied contained "the names of young German women who were active in the region as Hitler's empire-builders."[38] That discovery put Lower on the twenty-year path that led to her deservedly praised *Hitler's Furies: German Women in the Nazi Killing Fields*, which appeared in 2013.

During that same summer of 1992, I tried to find a publisher for a book that I was completing with Carol Rittner. Failures seemed to prevail as rejections accumulated—not because of the book's quality, the various editors kept saying, but because they doubted there would be a market for its topic: women and the Holocaust. Rittner and I eventually found a publisher, and the book helped to break taboos about the subject.[39]

Meanwhile, Lower's perpetrator-oriented research shows that while genocide is committed primarily by men, "genocide is also women's business."[40] If the German women who became killers in the East numbered "only" a few thousand, the evidence, says Lower, shows that "at least half a million women witnessed and contributed to the operations and terror of a genocidal war in the eastern territories."[41] Driven by motivations that

37. Quoted in Friedländer, *Years of Extermination*, vii.
38. Lower, *Hitler's Furies*, 2.
39. See Rittner and Roth, eds., *Different Voices*.
40. Lower, *Hitler's Furies*, 166.
41. Lower, *Hitler's Furies*, 166.

included ambition and opportunism, patriotism and senses of duty, most of these women were not full-fledged perpetrators of mass murder, but their complicity and partnership raise crucial questions.

Decades later, it is hard to imagine the indifferent and at times hostile responses that once were commonplace about gender-focused research on the Holocaust. Lower and *Hitler's Furies* ensure that confrontations with the Holocaust, genocide, and other mass atrocities must have a focus of that kind. That focus, however, raises difficulties, as Lower acknowledges toward the end of her book when she wonders why the history of the Holocaust and in particular the history of German women in the Nazi killing fields "continue to haunt us," as they surely do.[42] My contention is that a key reason why those histories haunt us—indeed why they *must*—has much to do with the failures of ethics. No book has done more than Lower's to reinforce that Holocaust insight for me.

After publishing *Hitler's Furies*, Lower continued her groundbreaking work by assessing where historical research about the Holocaust ought to go in the future.[43] Underscoring that more scholars are pursuing Holocaust research than ever before, she stresses that the work is far from finished. What's more, the work that needs attention is so vast that individuals or groups may approach success but not achieve it. For example, Lower values Saul Friedländer's attempt to write Holocaust history that integrates the experiences of Jews and the German perpetrators of genocide. He succeeded up to a point, but Lower urges an even more ambitious and complicated project that focuses on the Europeanization of the Holocaust. She is right: the Holocaust was a European event and "a European history of the Holocaust has not been written."[44] But to say that writing such a history would be daunting is an understated understatement. Lower shows why.

Such research and writing require mind-boggling abilities, including, to identify a few of them—mastering "the enormity of source material in multiple languages"; meeting "the intellectual challenge of comprehension and comparison," which is all the more inescapable because digitized archives make access easier; pivoting "away from the fragmentation of microstudies and nationalist paradigms toward the search for unifying themes and syntheses" that transnational analysis demands; comprehending and prioritizing how countless concurrent events are related.[45] A truly European

---

42. Lower, *Hitler's Furies*, 200.

43. See Lower, "Holocaust Studies"; Lower, "History and Future"; and Lower, "Decentering."

44. Lower, "Holocaust Studies," 568.

45. Lower, "Decentering," 33–34.

history of the Holocaust, Lower suggests, "may not be achievable."[46] Time will tell, but Lower adds that even a European history of the Holocaust may not be enough. Indeed, "it may not be the right goal in the end, because when one reads the sources closely and listens to individual testimonies, one discovers new factors and phenomena that defy explanation and comparison."[47] These recognitions might require a global history of the Holocaust, whose dimensions and ramifications definitely have that scope. The reach of such an ambitious project, however, likely exceeds any realistically conceivable grasp.

In the meantime, Lower judges that "the overall growth in Holocaust Studies is impressive but fractured."[48] She describes the field as "fertile" and "expanding" but paradoxically finds that "few debates" are driving it.[49] One debate that could insightfully fill that gap is provoked by a question that historians may or may not welcome: What is the burgeoning historical research on the Holocaust *for*? Is it done for its own sake, or are larger goals involved? If so, what are they, and how does more and more research advance them? Lower suggests that future historical research "could open up new areas of understanding social, cultural, and political history."[50] That goal is admirable, but where do new areas of understanding lead, and where should they go? More historical research may not answer such questions as much as is needed, but focusing future directions for research may underscore their importance.

Taking up the challenge of writing the needed European history of the Holocaust—or even a history on a larger scale than that—is not a fool's errand, at least not completely. Much will be learned by attempting it, not least that any success will be partial at best. By implication, if not explicitly, Lower seems to sense this outcome when she concludes that "taken together, the voluminous library of case studies and grand narratives reveals how the Holocaust happened, but not why. No single explanation, be it antisemitism, Nazi colonialism, Nazi culture, Hitler, or working towards the Führer, suffices. There were many causes, which are still being identified, explained, and compared."[51] Attempting bigger projects may not be the wisest way to make up for the shortfalls and shortcomings of smaller ones, even if those outcomes help to show why something bigger and better is needed. Be that

46. Lower, "Holocaust Studies," 576.
47. Lower, "Holocaust Studies," 576.
48. Lower, "Holocaust Studies," 574.
49. Lower, "Holocaust Studies," 574, 576.
50. Lower, "Holocaust Studies," 574.
51. Lower, "Holocaust Studies," 566.

as it may, whether the focus of historical research about the Holocaust is large or small, it must continue. Only in that way will Holocaust insight be deepened and enhanced.

Prior to Lower's arrival, Jonathan Petropoulos became my colleague at Claremont McKenna College in 1999. We soon became friends, teaching together, teaming up on conference and book projects, and joining forces to launch the college's Center for the Study of the Holocaust, Genocide, and Human Rights (now the Mgrublian Center for Human Rights). Early on, I saw that Petropoulos frequently traveled to Washington, DC. He needed to be there because in 1998 the Presidential Advisory Commission on Holocaust Assets in the United States had been established to investigate what to do about the property of Holocaust victims that fell into US possession or control. Petropoulos led the Commission's research team tasked with probing matters pertaining to art and cultural property. His academic qualifications for this important role included a distinctive blending of expertise in art history, Nazi culture, and Holocaust studies.

One result of that expertise was *The Faustian Bargain: The Art World in Nazi Germany*, which appeared in 2000. Soon after that, the two of us began to teach a course called Researching the Holocaust. Working seminar-style with advanced undergraduates, we explored books in the field of Holocaust studies that were new at the time. *The Faustian Bargain* was on the list. While studying the book, the students wrote questions about it. One student asked Petropoulos, "What would you do if you walked into someone's house or gallery and recognized a piece of art that you knew had once belonged to a Jewish family whose art had been plundered?"

I do not recall exactly what Petropoulos said in response, but his book and life's work show why this friend and teacher is an important source of my Holocaust insight. First, as I studied *The Faustian Bargain*, I saw not only perceptive historical analysis but also a deep-seated moral passion. Petropoulos wrote about Ernst Buchner, Karl Haberstock, Kajetan Mühlmann, and other now nearly forgotten people in the Third Reich who, one way or another, trafficked looted art. His analysis of them is as fascinating as it is detailed and documented. But Petropoulos's scholarship, appropriately dispassionate, also had an unmistakable ethical edge. My friend wants to hold those "second rank" Nazis accountable. Petropoulos left no doubt that he found the art looting deplorable and that he saw his scholarship as doing at least something to right the wrong. His conclusions included these judgments: "This book has stressed the ethical implications of the art experts' behavior. Granted, this is but one possible approach, but morality lies at the center of history . . . It may be true that the figures who implemented the Nazi cultural program were not entirely without a conscience and that there were limits to resistance, but this does not mitigate their actions . . . The art experts of the Third Reich largely avoided punishment while they were alive; it is therefore imperative that they not be exonerated by history."[52]

Second, just as Christopher Browning has testified in courtrooms where Holocaust perpetrators and deniers have been brought to justice, Jonathan Petropoulos has worked year in and year out—sometimes in courts and museums, sometimes in confrontations with dealers of dubious repute—to help Jewish families recover valuable artworks that were lost to Nazi Germany, whose plunder and theft of Jewish property was so vast that no restitution or recompense can render adequate justice no matter how long efforts in that direction continue. But Petropoulos's practical application of scholarship—sometimes its personal cost has been high—teaches me that historical research no less than philosophical reflection can make a restorative difference in people's lives, and that my task, like his, is to put learning and teaching about the Holocaust in that service.

Postscript

For a long time, I have observed historians of the Holocaust. They know a great deal—more, in some ways, than even survivors of that catastrophe. Working with Holocaust historians, learning from them, admiring their tenacity and perseverance, I nevertheless find sometimes that they make me puzzled, impatient, and exasperated. Those relationships have enhanced my Holocaust insight in many ways, including my recognition of an instructive paradox: the pursuit of Holocaust history is self-defeating, but its self-defeat is related to its most important contributions.

To see how that paradox works, note that every Holocaust historian—at least those who have been most influential—has a project. That project involves two elements that are in tension as much as they are linked. On one hand, the Holocaust historian's project is shared with other historians of that kind. Its goal is to understand and explain an immense and reverberating catastrophe. On the other hand, this shared aim manifests itself concretely in particularity. The particularity shows that Holocaust historians are not copycats. Individually, their project is not to say, "Oh, I just agree with Hayes," or, "I think Bauer is great—he got everything right and there's nothing more to say." Like philosophers, Holocaust historians tend to think that no one—at least nobody before them—got enough right, to say nothing of everything, and thus there is much that needs to be said that no one else can show and say as well. It is no exaggeration to say that Holocaust historians,

---

52. Petropoulos, *Faustian Bargain*, 277, 280.

like philosophers, are stubborn, arrogant at times, even as they insist that the pursuit of Holocaust history must be open-ended and self-corrective because, like every form of human inquiry, its scope is finite, its reach fallible and prone to error.

The pursuit of Holocaust history involves so much differentiation and even disagreement that the unity within that pursuit is inseparable from diversity. That diversity—it grows from the finding that no version of Holocaust history deserves to have the last word—defeats the pursuit insofar as the aim is attainment of some comprehensive, unified, and knowable truth.

At their best, Holocaust historians know better than anyone that the event unavoidably has the effect of eluding the closure that narratives, theories, and explanations try to impose upon it. But even though the pursuit of Holocaust history defeats itself and is also defeated by the Holocaust itself, that pursuit nevertheless achieves a fundamental success. It consists of insight: finite and limited though every Holocaust historian's project surely is, sound historical inquiry of that kind keeps attention focused on key questions—how and why did the Holocaust happen? Failure to pursue them dooms humankind.

4

Franklin H. Littell

On February 25, 2004—it was Ash Wednesday, the beginning of the Christian season called Lent—*The Passion of the Christ*, a film directed and produced by Mel Gibson, a conservative Roman Catholic, opened in American theaters. Critics rightly charged that Gibson's portrayal of the trial and crucifixion of Jesus contained antisemitic tropes and stereotypes as well as excessive violence, but ticket sales soared, and the US screenings alone grossed some $370 million.

As the excruciatingly bloody, precrucifixion scourging of Jesus reaches it climax in *The Passion of the Christ*, one of Pontius Pilate's lieutenants intervenes and chastises the Roman soldiers for unwarranted brutality. "You weren't supposed to beat him to death!" he exclaims. That moment was only one of many that jarred me when I saw Gibson's film two days after it opened. Given the scourging that Gibson created, the judgment of Pilate's lieutenant seemed ludicrous and incredible. After such a beating, scarcely anyone could have remained alive, as Jesus had to be for his crucifixion to follow. Of course, a caveat in that judgment is needed, and this point is no doubt one that Gibson wanted to make: namely, Jesus was not "anyone"; he was the incarnation of God and thus able to take any punishment, any abuse, that human beings could devise and still triumph over it.

Four Insights

Problematic though it remains, *The Passion of the Christ* helped me to focus at least four insights. First, few if any events in human history have had more volatile consequences and potent implications than the Roman execution by crucifixion of a relatively obscure Jewish teacher from Galilee whose name was Jesus. To employ one of several shorthand equations that I use to put key issues in bold relief, *No crucifixion of Jesus = No Western civilization as we know it.*

Second, that equation holds because the crucifixion of Jesus has always played a decisive part in the Christian tradition's understanding of God, the world, and the meaning of our individual lives. These connections are so strong that they warrant another equation: *No crucifixion of Jesus = No Christianity.* Absent Christianity, Western civilization and indeed the world as we know it would be inconceivable.

Taking the New Testament Gospels as the historically accurate source, Gibson's film arrived amid claims that it truthfully portrayed what really happened during the last twelve hours of Jesus's earthly life. However, as many have pointed out, the film is not authentic as history or as a representation of the Gospels, at least as far as the details are concerned. To one watching the film, checking the New Testament texts, and tracking Gibson's use of sources, it is apparent that *The Passion of the Christ* is a highly idiosyncratic interpretation of events whose reality remains elusive. Thus, a third key point emerges: beyond the barest of outlines, no one today can be confident that they know precisely what happened during the last twelve hours of Jesus's life. That Jesus was crucified is not in question, but precisely how and why the crucifixion took place is profoundly contested. Hence, another equation holds: *No crucifixion of Jesus = No Christian–Jewish rivalry.*

Fourth, the Christian–Jewish rivalry had such catastrophic implications that particularly after the Holocaust, we Christians should be especially careful about how the crucifixion of Jesus is interpreted and portrayed. Nazi Germany's attempt to destroy the Jewish people would have been virtually inconceivable without Christianity's (my tradition's) negative depictions of Jews. To say the least, that conjunction creates a challenging legacy for Christians and Christianity. For anyone like me who has lived within the Christian tradition and often found it rich and meaningful, that challenge leads not only to repentance about the Christian tradition's long-standing and only recently reformed stance toward Jews but also to fundamental rethinking about what it should and should not mean to be a Christian after Auschwitz. Among the many shortcomings of Gibson's film, therefore, I found none more egregious than its insensitivity about the Holocaust, its failure to acknowledge another telling equation: *No crucifixion of Jesus = No Holocaust.*

In some circles, constructive Christian–Jewish dialogue preceded the Holocaust, and respectful postwar Christian–Jewish relationships have often been motivated by desires to improve communal cooperation and to extend interreligious understanding that are unrelated to, or at least not focused explicitly on, the Holocaust. In general, Christian–Jewish relations are better in the twenty-first century than they have been for centuries. Nevertheless, no event haunts Christian–Jewish relations more than Nazi Germany's genocide against the Jews, for that mass atrocity cannot be separated from the centuries of anti-Jewish hostility that have been deeply rooted in Christian thought and practice. Neither Christianity nor any single person, institution, or motivation—from the power of Adolf Hitler and the SS, for example, to the widespread racist antisemitism embraced by millions of ordinary Germans during the Nazi period—was *enough* by itself to make the Holocaust happen. But Christianity was a *necessary* condition for that catastrophe. That scar should remain unsettling.

The Harpoon

The Passion of the Christ was not the only source for the insights I have identified. The pioneering Christian scholar Franklin Littell did much more to help me see the devastating links between Christianity and the Holocaust. So, I recall that on July 23, 1998, Littell's friend, the distinguished historian Yehuda Bauer, interviewed him in Jerusalem at Yad Vashem, Israel's official Holocaust memorial, where they frequently led seminars. This interview, a good synopsis of Littell's primary concerns in Holocaust studies, concluded with remarks emblematic of the character, outlook, and aspiration of this remarkable man, who died on May 23, 2009, at the age of ninety-one. Underscoring that his conviction about the Holocaust was "above all . . . to avoid premature closure," Littell ended the 1998 interview by emphasizing his aim "to keep this thing [the memory of the Holocaust] irritating—you know, be the harpoon that the fish can't escape."[1]

Those who knew Littell can still hear his voice in those words—earthy and earnest, intense and impassioned, edged at times with laughter and humor, but always cutting to the chase. That voice came from one whose eyes glistened with insight, whose embrace and grip expressed warm friendship, and whose jaunty, feisty spirit inspired courage. His insight, friendship, and courage invited others to join him in work governed by the conviction that the unredeemable atrocities of the Holocaust and all genocides must provoke resistance against the injustice and indifference that produce them.

The presence of a necessary irritant such as Littell's harpoon is a cause for celebration in a world like ours, whose brutality cries out for aroused

---

1. See Littell, "Interview." This interview is available online. For the URL that links to the interview, see the bibliography. Parts of this chapter are adapted from Roth, "Connections and Exchanges."

conscience and energized political will against injustice. All who care about human rights, all who work in the field of Holocaust and genocide studies have abundant reasons to be grateful for and indebted to him. At the same time, glimpses of his life show that Littell's absence leaves a void and a challenge, for his absence reminds one of how exceptional he was and how much the world needs scholars, organizers, and committed people to support his causes, which have no closure

The catalog of the United States Library of Congress contains more than thirty Littell entries. The earliest books, from the 1950s, suggest that this ordained Methodist minister, his doctorate in theology and religious studies, might have had a conventional professorial career as a scholar concentrating on church history in the United States, with an emphasis on Protestant Christianity and church-state relationships. Early on, however, much more was gestating. A visit to Nazi Germany in 1939 made an indelible impression on him, which was deepened and intensified during and after work in postwar Germany, where he served as the chief Protestant advisor for the US occupation forces. These experiences honed the harpoon that Littell would thrust at multiple targets, including, first and foremost, his own Christian tradition.

Two books in Littell's Library of Congress list loom largest. In 1975, he published *The Crucifixion of the Jews*. I will focus on that book shortly but note first that Edward Flannery and James Parkes were Christian scholars who preceded Littell in documenting their tradition's culpability for antisemitism. Littell's book was groundbreaking nonetheless because it drove home Christian responsibility for and complicity in the Holocaust. Written in the aftermath of attacks on the State of Israel in 1967 and 1973, it also staunchly defended "the right of the Jewish people to self-identity and self-definition," which was one of his lifelong commitments.[2]

Littell often referred to the Holocaust as an "alpine event," his way of identifying its distinctive, watershed significance. In his view, the Holocaust constituted the most severe "credibility crisis," one of his favorite terms, to strike the Christian tradition. Its "teaching of contempt" about Judaism and Jews had contributed mightily to genocide against the Jewish people. Only profound contrition and reform, including fundamental theological revision that tackled the New Testament's anti-Judaic themes, could restore integrity to post-Holocaust Christianity. An essential irritant for his own religious tradition, Littell held that tradition accountable for its part in the Holocaust and sought the changes that might take Christianity through its credibility crisis.

2. Littell, *Crucifixion*, 3.

Littell's belief that Christianity faced a monumental credibility crisis was not based solely on the centuries-old history of Christian hostility toward Judaism and Jews. More immediately, his postwar experiences in Germany made him painfully aware of the welcoming embrace that most German churches had given to Adolf Hitler and Nazism, the complicity of German churches in the Holocaust, and the widespread indifference of the churches outside Germany when it came to the plight of Jews under the swastika. That awareness was nuanced by his understanding that some Christians and churches in Germany had resisted Nazism and, at least to some extent, assisted Jews. Thus, even before Littell published *The Crucifixion of the Jews*, his pioneering work included the other entry that looms largest in his Library of Congress list, *The German Church Struggle and the Holocaust*, a volume coedited with his friend Hubert Locke.

Important in its own right—among other things it contains a memorable exchange between Richard Rubenstein and Elie Wiesel—this book signaled the pivotal role that Littell played as an organizer and leader in Holocaust studies and Christian-Jewish relations. *The German Church Struggle and the Holocaust*, which appeared in 1974, emerged from a conference that Littell and Locke convened at Wayne State University in 1970. Focused on Germany's Christian support for and resistance against Nazism and on the implications of that struggle for the future of Christianity and its relationship to Jews and Judaism, the 1970 meeting was the first of what became the Annual Scholars' Conference on the Holocaust and the Churches, an interfaith, interdisciplinary, and international gathering of scholars, educators, clergy, and community leaders. A tribute to Littell's persistence, this conference remains the longest continuously running initiative of its kind. Its work, including many publications, has significantly influenced and advanced the field of Holocaust and genocide studies.

Littell determined that his harpoon's thrust needed to find more than the Christian tradition. He showed that the professions—for example, medicine, law, and engineering—had dirty hands that contributed to the Holocaust. He revealed that universities had shirked ethical responsibilities in their teaching and research, for the Holocaust was not perpetrated primarily by the uneducated. Littell kept holding professional and academic feet to the ethical fire. As his work on the Holocaust continued in decades that saw crimes against humanity and genocide in Rwanda, the former Yugoslavia, and Darfur, Littell held governments and political leaders accountable too, encouraging both the development of early warning networks to prevent genocide and the political will to intervene against genocide.

Littell's distinguished academic career took him to Emory University, Temple University, Hebrew University in Jerusalem, the Richard Stockton

College of New Jersey (now Stockton University), and other institutions. In those places he broke new ground in Holocaust education. A founding member of the United States Holocaust Memorial Council, which oversees the US Holocaust Memorial Museum in Washington, DC, he was also the first Christian named to Yad Vashem's International Governing Board. Everywhere he went, his harpoon was the right kind of irritant.

A Photograph

Littell appears in the photograph embedded in this chapter. It is immensely meaningful to me because the connections and exchanges, the stories and testimonies, embodied in it provide further insight that has transformed my thinking and sustained my living. Taken on September 29, 1988, at Webster University in St. Louis, Missouri, the photo captures a moment during a symposium called "Elie Wiesel: The Man and His Work." Conceived and convened by Harry James Cargas, a legendary member of Webster's faculty, the symposium celebrated both the thirtieth anniversary of *Night*, Wiesel's famous Holocaust memoir, and his sixtieth birthday, which took place the next day.

Photo (September 29, 1988) courtesy of Webster University Archives
Front row, left to right: Franklin H. Littell, Leo Eitinger, Elie Wiesel, Paul Braunstein, and Raul Hilberg
Second row, left to right: Harry James Cargas, Dorothee Soelle, John K. Roth, Irving "Yitz" Greenberg, and William Heyen

More than three decades later, most of the people in the photo are gone. Looking at the picture, one sees Elie Wiesel seated in the center of the first row. He died at the age of eighty-seven in 2016. Flanking him are two medical doctors. To Wiesel's right is Leo Eitinger, a brilliant Jewish physician-psychiatrist from Norway, who endured the Holocaust and went on to study and treat survivor trauma. In January 1945, Eitinger, an Auschwitz prisoner himself, operated to stop life-threatening infection in Wiesel's right foot and knee.[3] Eitinger was eighty-three when he passed away in 1996. Absent his care, Wiesel would have perished in Auschwitz. To Wiesel's left is Paul Braunstein, the Catholic orthopedic surgeon who brought Wiesel back to health after a New York taxi ran down the young journalist one autumn day in 1956. Inflicting multiple fractures, which required a ten-hour surgery to repair them, the accident rendered Wiesel semicomatose for several days and put him in a cast from neck to foot for some time. Braunstein, said Wiesel, "saved my life."[4] One of Wiesel's early novels is dedicated to this skilled physician, who died at the age of eighty-six in 2011.[5]

At the end of the first row, to Braunstein's left, is Raul Hilberg. Well known for his magisterial study called *The Destruction of the European Jews*, Hilberg was eighty-one when cancer took his life in 2007. Next to Eitinger, at the other end of the row, is Franklin Littell, who was significantly influenced by Wiesel. In ways that are part of what Littell called "the deepest mystery of life and death," all five of these men profoundly affected me—the doctors by saving Wiesel, whose testimony, authorship, and friendship, along with that of Hilberg and Littell, conferred responsibilities upon me.

Standing at the ends of the second row are William Heyen (on the far right as one views the photo), a prize-winning poet who has reflected about the Holocaust with great sensitivity and discernment, and (on the far left)

---

3. The account in *Night* does not identify Eitinger because Wiesel did not know his name at the time. But Wiesel's description of his medical plight does recollect the treatment given him by "a great Jewish doctor," adding that "every one of his words was healing and every glance of his carried a message of hope." See Wiesel, *Night*, 77–84. In later memoirs, Wiesel related how he was reunited with his Auschwitz doctor after Wiesel gave a speech at the University of Oslo. He pays high tribute and expresses deep gratitude to Eitinger. See Wiesel, *All Rivers*, 89–91; and Wiesel, *Sea Is Never Full*, 24–25.

4. See Wiesel, *All Rivers*, 294.

5. Dedicated to Braunstein, Wiesel's third book—it follows the memoir *Night* and his first novel, *Dawn*—was called *The Accident* when it was first published in English in 1962. Originally published in French as *Le Jour* in 1961, the English translation was appropriately retitled *Day* in 2006 and republished with a new preface by Wiesel. The novel's protagonist is struck by a taxi in New York City, but *Day* is a novel, not an autobiography. Taken together, however, *Night*, *Dawn*, and *Day* do form a trilogy. Their publication in a single volume, as well as in individual editions, helps to highlight that relationship. See Wiesel, *Night Trilogy*.

Harry James Cargas, a prolific author who called himself a "post-Auschwitz Catholic," produced seminal interviews with Wiesel, and died too young at the age of sixty-six in 1998. To Heyen's right is the distinguished Modern Orthodox rabbi Irving "Yitz" Greenberg, whose insight and leadership have done much to advance Holocaust education, Jewish–Christian relations, and the United States Holocaust Memorial Museum. To Cargas's left is Dorothee Soelle, the German Protestant theologian who taught at Union Theological Seminary in New York and wrote important books on ethics, suffering, and justice before she died at the age of seventy-three in 2003. Rounding out the ten, I stand between Soelle and Greenberg and directly behind Eitinger and Wiesel.

Telling the Tale

When I look at that photo, I sense the presence of all those participants from that symposium long ago. Especially I am moved by connections and exchanges that involve Wiesel and Littell and Richard Rubenstein too. Although Rubenstein was not at Webster University on September 29, 1988, his presence could nevertheless be felt because Littell's presentation that day referred to the well-known exchange between Wiesel and Rubenstein that had taken place in 1970 at the first Annual Scholars' Conference on the Holocaust and the Churches.[6]

On that inaugural occasion in 1970, Wiesel planned to speak on "The Literature of the Holocaust." Instead he responded to Rubenstein, who had explored why the Holocaust led him, an ordained rabbi, to spurn the Jewish tradition's covenantal God of history and, at the time, to embrace "what Camus has rightly called the courage of the absurd, the courage to live in a meaningless, purposeless Cosmos rather than believe in a God who inflicts Auschwitz on his people."[7] Significantly, the phrase "rather than" in Rubenstein's statement underscored the abhorrent implication that he took to follow from the "logic" of what he called "Covenant Theology." As Rubenstein saw it, "if one takes Covenant Theology seriously, . . . Auschwitz must be God's way of punishing the Jewish people in order that they might better see the light, the light of Christ if one is a Christian, the light of Torah if one is a traditional Jew." Refusing to accept that implication, which he regarded as obscene, Rubenstein turned away from the God of history and covenant

---

6. Reprinted in Roth and Berenbaum, eds., *Holocaust*, 346–70, the Rubenstein–Wiesel exchange appeared first in *German Church Struggle*, 256–77.

7. For the Rubenstein quotations in this paragraph, see Rubenstein, "Some Perspectives," 354–55.

theology. Meanwhile, indicating back in 1970 that he shared Rubenstein's "anger and his despair," Wiesel emphatically resisted such closure and passionately rejected Rubenstein's abandonment of God, insisting instead that "to be a Jew is to have all the reasons in the world not to have faith in language, in singing, in prayers, and in God, but *to go on telling the tale, to go on carrying on the dialogue*, and to have my own silent prayers and quarrels with God."[8]

At Webster University in 1988, Franklin Littell underscored that Wiesel's most important contributions to Jewish religious philosophy and Christian theology included liberating his listeners and readers to "debate with God."[9] Indeed, Littell told Harry James Cargas on another occasion, Wiesel's writings showed him a way beyond "radical denial of the God of whom the Bible speaks." In Littell's understanding, that path led to "the right, indeed the duty, of a believing person . . . to argue and debate with God when he [God] acts, or lets things happen, contrary to his own declared nature and promises."[10]

Earlier, Littell had explored variations on those themes in *The Crucifixion of the Jews*, whose culminating chapter is called "The Debate with God." Much of that chapter extended and amplified the book's preceding themes, quintessential to Littell's outlook: (1) abhorrence of Christian antisemitism; (2) alarm that far from being quelled after the Holocaust, antisemitism, in one form or another, stubbornly remained and was even resurgent; (3) lamentation about Christian apostasy during the Holocaust, especially among so-called German Christians; (4) sorrow about the Confessing Church's lack of success in the German church struggle during the Hitler era; (5) anger about the tepid, even insipid quality of American Christianity, whose "falsely optimistic view of human nature and social progress" has failed to take seriously the immensity of the Holocaust and the complicity of Christianity in the Nazi attempt to destroy the Jewish people; (6) loathing of "timeless truths and placeless abstractions that ring in the ear but never move the feet"; (7) denunciation of modern educational systems that produce the ever-dangerous "technically competent barbarian."[11]

At first glance, such distress seems unrelated to debate with God, for it results from human failure. A key theme, however, in Littell's experience that Wiesel liberated him to debate with God makes the connection. If history, particularly Holocaust history, includes the right and duty to argue

---

8. Wiesel, "Talking and Writing," 363, 369 (italics original).
9. Littell, "Proclaiming the Silence," 63.
10. See the quotations from Littell in Cargas, "Elie Wiesel," 283–84.
11. Littell, *Crucifixion*, 115, 124, 126.

with God when things go so terribly wrong as to be at odds with God's most pronounced commandments and promises, then that debate not only must challenge God but also must protest human actions and resist human institutions that fail to do the best they can. If we are free and even accountable to debate with the everlasting and transcending God, Littell insisted, how can we not be emboldened and on notice to confront and contend with human powers—always transient and finite, no matter how strong they appear to be—when they are hell-bent on destruction and waste? "The debate with God," Littell went on to say, "is best carried forward not in pursuit of direct encounters with an unmediated divinity, but through dealing—in all human vigor and with all human limitations—with the concrete issues and decisions affecting one's fellows and one's self. The insistent question is not whether God exists, nor whether his ways make sense in terms of known systems of thought. The insistent question is what must be done here and now by specific persons facing specific choices."[12]

The context for Littell's emphasis on "the insistent question" was more complicated than might be suggested by his warning against "pursuit of direct encounters with an unmediated divinity." What Littell called "the agony of doubt" could not be easily assuaged because it was intensified by Holocaust challenges to the credibility of traditional biblical claims regarding God's working in history.[13] Littell did not follow Rubenstein in thinking that those challenges were primarily about the punishment implications in covenant theology. A different, though related, dilemma gripped Littell: Was Christianity's crime of crucifying the Jews during the Holocaust compounded by God's forsaking and abandoning them in that catastrophe? More than that, "the deepest agony," said Littell, "arises from the thought that God himself is an ally of evil," a dire prospect reinforced by Littell's quoting from an early Wiesel novel in which the protagonist submits that "God is capable of the most flagrant injustice."[14]

Such unsettling reflections made Littell confront what he called "the appalling thought": namely, "that one must choose between a cruel God or none."[15] For Littell, that option was doubly challenging. Not only was its dichotomy abysmal, but also Littell found himself unwilling, indeed unable, to deny "the God of whom the Bible speaks."[16] His affirmation instead was that "a way needs to be found for a walk of faith that practices a vital dialogue

---

12. Littell, *Crucifixion*, 117.
13. Littell, *Crucifixion*, 113–18, esp. 117.
14. Littell, *Crucifixion*, 116. The Wiesel quotation is from *Day*, 34.
15. Littell, *Crucifixion*, 116.
16. Littell quoted in Cargas, "Elie Wiesel," 284.

with the past and looks for the Kingdom to come. A sign pointing to that way is the tale or story."[17] So, Littell's choice was to try his best, in Wiesel's words, *"to go on telling the tale, to go on carrying on the dialogue."* In *The Crucifixion of the Jews*, that decision required holding Christians and Christianity accountable for centuries of lethal anti-Jewish hostility and especially for *"the mass murder of Jews by Christians in the heart of Christendom."*[18] No less, Littell's decision also meant that, arguments to the contrary notwithstanding, biblical stories about the God who acts in history must still be told. What's more, he thought, their testimony about God's ongoing and everlasting fidelity to the Jewish people remains valid, complicated and challenging though it is to affirm and bear witness to that testimony.

Crucifixion and Resurrection

Coming as it did from a fellow Christian, Littell's wrestling with these issues instructed me. Arguably nothing anchored his post-Holocaust fidelity to biblical narratives more deeply than his discerning that "the crucifixion of the Jews" in the Holocaust, "an unavoidable reality" that "raises the most insistent question about the credibility of Christianity," had been followed by what he called the "resurrection of the Jewish people."[19] Arguably nothing embodied that resurrection more than what Littell called "the restitution of Israel," which surely included the establishment of the State of Israel in 1948 and its prevailing against existential threats such as in the 1973 Yom Kippur War, a key part of the geopolitical situation in which Littell wrote *The Crucifixion of the Jews*. As Littell told the tale in 1975, not only was it true that "so far as biblical teaching is concerned, Jewish peoplehood and nationhood and attachment to the land is the only kind of ethnic identity to which God has given explicit approval," but it was also true that "the crucifixion and resurrection of the Jewish people is a sign that God is not mocked, that pride brings the biggest battalions low in the end, that the Author and the Judge of history blesses the Suffering Servant and brings the human hero low."[20]

As his appeals to crucifixion and resurrection underscored, Littell did not shy away from a boldly religious interpretation of the Holocaust. The tale he told defended the biblical God of history—no ally of evil, at least in Littell's reckoning—whose covenantal bond with the Jewish people, far from being abrogated or destroyed in the killing fields and death camps

17. Littell, *Crucifixion*, 62.
18. Littell, *Crucifixion*, 60 (italics original).
19. Littell, *Crucifixion*, 2, 6.
20. Littell, *Crucifixion*, 95, 98–99.

of the Holocaust, resulted in "the renewal of Jewish life, the most striking theological development today."[21] For Littell, that outcome, as impressive as it was unlikely, as decisive as it was unexpected, included "*the right of the Jewish people to self-identity and self-definition.*"[22]

Littell detested "thoughtless utterance" and "premature closure" and despised even more what he called "the babbling of fools."[23] Such qualities never characterized Littell's reflection about the Holocaust and its reverberations, but it would also be a telling example of thoughtless utterance and premature closure to say that Littell's outlook in *The Crucifixion of the Jews*, highly significant though it remains, is without problems that may prove to be insurmountable. The following questions point to two of those problems: (1) What happened after *The Crucifixion of the Jews*? (2) What happened regarding the debate with God?

Sometimes insight depends on disagreement. My responses to these questions underscore my respect for Littell, his telling of the tale, and acknowledge his influence upon me while also indicating how my thinking differs from his.

History's Slaughter Bench

Littell lived a long life. More than thirty years passed between the publication of *The Crucifixion of the Jews* in 1975 and his death in 2009. During that time, as well as in the decade after Littell's passing and beyond, what the philosopher Georg W. F. Hegel called "the slaughter bench of history" has continued to have its grisly way. To name only a few illustrative catastrophes, ethnic cleansing and genocide engulfed the former Yugoslavia and Rwanda in the 1990s. With the arrival of the twenty-first century, al-Qaeda's 9/11/2001 attack on the World Trade Center and the Pentagon in the United States raised the levels of Muslim-related terrorism to new highs and portended the horror unleashed later by the jihadist Islamic State, Boko Haram, and a resurgent al-Qaeda as well.

Midway through the century's second decade, anti-Muslim hostility intensified in Europe and in the United States, where the American president Donald Trump pushed to limit, if not ban altogether, Muslim immigration to the country. Meanwhile, as Trump urged restrictions on refugee entry to the United States, the war-torn Syrian city of Aleppo became the site of a humanitarian disaster of immense proportions. In early 2017, the

---

21. Littell, *Crucifixion*, 96.
22. Littell, *Crucifixion*, 3 (italics original).
23. Littell, "Proclaiming the Silence," 64.

centennial year of Littell's birth, twenty million people—1.4 million children among them—faced famine in northern Nigeria, Somalia, South Sudan, and especially Yemen, even though the world's food excess was enough to feed them all.

Meanwhile, the Palestinian–Israeli conflict showed no sign of abating as prospects for a two-state solution dwindled in a tangle that includes not only the Boycott, Divest, Sanctions (BDS) movement aimed at Israel but also expansion of Jewish settlements in the West Bank, almost daily Palestinian attacks against Israelis, and the problematic relocation of the American embassy in Israel from Tel Aviv to Jerusalem. Furthermore, antisemitism has intensified: in the US and elsewhere, bomb threats target Jewish schools and community centers, shootings happen at synagogues, and Jewish cemeteries are desecrated.[24]

In addition, escalating cyberwarfare, spearheaded by Russia, endangers democracy in Europe and the United States, while global woes worsen, erratic North Korea and Iran pivotal in the dangerous mix. Threats of nuclear war are now greater than at any time since the 1960s during the Cold War.

Obviously, *The Crucifixion of the Jews* could not address circumstances and events at play since its publication in 1975. Nevertheless, given how human history has unfolded since that time, a reader can wonder how the book's voice sounds several decades later. In many cases, Littell's words are as timely now as they were then. When Littell wrote, for example, that "the question naturally arises whether the claim to be 'Christian' is anything but a sham, whether 'Christendom' itself is anything but a fraud," his question resounds.[25] When he contended that "the Holocaust is the unfinished business of the Christian churches, the running sore unattended by its leaders and weakening to its constituents," Littell remains on target, especially when that challenge includes his insight that the story of the churches' insufficient struggle against Hitler has a dangerous sequel in their embrace, especially in the United States, of "new and apocalyptic figures of prestige," who are actually "false prophets . . . and public servants who do not serve."[26]

When Littell said that "a 'Christian' civilization's attitude to Jewish history and treatment of the Jewish people afford the litmus test as to how it will act on all critical decisions involving the resistance of helpless or weaker peoples," it makes sense that Christian failure to do everything possible to

---

24. For an important contemporary analysis of antisemitism, see Lipstadt, *Antisemitism*.

25. Littell, *Crucifixion*, 86.

26. Littell, *Crucifixion*, 129, 124–25.

protect and save Jewish life under the swastika remains a warning for Christians not to forsake others who are in similarly dire straits.[27] That warning does not define, let alone prescribe, priorities and policies with regard to dilemmas such as those that riddle the Middle East, but the warning's injunction against indifference, a stance that Wiesel especially deplored, still stands. Yet, because so much devastation has happened after *The Crucifixion of the Jews*, the relevance, insistence, and urgency of Littell's admonitions create unintended consequences, including some of the possibly insurmountable problems in his outlook.

God with Us?

Central to that outlook, pivotal in Littell's telling of the tale, is his fidelity to the Author and the Judge of history, who, in Littell's narrative, resurrected the Jewish people after the Holocaust. Some of Littell's readers may find that story—and his sticking to it—foolish babbling, but it would be a mistake to draw such a conclusion, because that tale may be needed more than ever as a "sign point," a reminder that premature closure about the finality of despair, death, and meaninglessness, which deserve no more victories, ought not to be anyone's story. What the human story should be instead, however, remains immensely complex. Probably inadvertently and unintentionally, Littell illustrated that point when he made the seemingly uncontroversial and indeed even imperative claim that "the Jewish people has a right to self-definition."[28]

Denial of that right led to the Holocaust, but that truth does not cancel out another, namely, that the assertion and defense of a right to self-definition for any "people"—Jewish or any other—are rarely uncontestable and uncontested. That dilemma exists not only because so many human groups will claim a right to self-definition and act on it in a crowded and conflicted world but also because the boundaries and meanings of such a right are neither self-evident nor conflict-free. What's more, human groups are prone to use the right to self-definition as an occasion to exclude, demonize, and destroy the "other," those who do not fit with or who conflict with a group's or people's self-definition. All too often, religion is invoked and complicit, sometimes it is even a driving force, in such "othering." The destructive history of Christian antisemitism bears witness to that and so, typically, do any ideologies, especially nationalism—including its Islamic, American, and Israeli varieties—that proclaim God to be on "our" side.

27. Littell, *Crucifixion*, 40.
28. Littell, *Crucifixion*, 96.

In the exchange between Richard Rubenstein and Elie Wiesel to which Littell referred in *The Crucifixion of the Jews* and elsewhere, Rubenstein emphasized that "I refuse to say *Gott mit uns* under any circumstances."[29] Rubenstein's point—the meanings and implications of that phrase are too problematic, the price in blood and suffering to be paid for invoking God in that way are too high—was not lost on Littell, who knew well enough the costs of "Gott mit uns." Still, Littell would not, could not, draw Rubenstein's conclusion that it did not make moral sense to defend the view that there is a God of history who resurrected the Jewish people after the Holocaust. But if God did that redemptive work, then what of the accumulated wreckage of post-Holocaust disasters—to say nothing of even worse events that may be coming—after *The Crucifixion of the Jews*? Littell's book does not show a way out of that dilemma, at least not adequately. So, he left work for his readers to do, but whether anyone, even God, can accomplish what needs to be done remains unclear, an enigma that leads back to the debate with God.

Insightful and challenging though it is, *The Crucifixion of the Jews* is also disappointing because the book promises more debate with God than it delivers. Despite Littell's emphasis on the importance of arguing and quarreling with God, his dispute is muted in comparison to his insistence that "the crucifixion and resurrection of the Jewish people is a sign that God is not mocked, . . . that the Author and the Judge of history blesses the Suffering Servant."[30]

Unfortunately, and arguably contrary to Littell's theological claims about the resurrection of the Jewish people, history itself mocks God aplenty. Evil and suffering keep accumulating, escalating, apparently without end. If God exists, God seems to have been unable or unwilling to prevent the carnage that took place during the Holocaust and its aftermath, including all the waste that happened after *The Crucifixion of the Jews*. Perhaps God suffers too amid the wrack and ruin, but the comfort in that possibility seems scant because nothing—not even Littell's purported resurrection of the Jewish people—can set right the unjust maiming and dying.

Why is preventing or intervening against the wasting of life so hard—for God as well as for humanity? Life will go on, justice will be sought, and suffering may diminish with time's passage. But the brute facts of unjust death and suffering persist, including the unredeemable losses of Jewish life in the Holocaust. Evil and suffering rage to such an extent that the universe is cracked beyond complete repair and redemption. The debate with God must move a step beyond where Littell took it. In light of the

---

29. Rubenstein, "Some Perspectives," 356.
30. Littell, *Crucifixion*, 98–99.

world's countless innocent victims, God's goodness (if God exists) must be acknowledged to be flawed, at the very least.

Continuing the Debate with God

In 1975, the same year in which *The Crucifixion of the Jews* appeared, Editions de Seuil, one of Elie Wiesel's French publishers, released his *Célébration biblique: Portraits et legends*, which was translated and published the next year as *Messengers of God: Biblical Portraits and Legends*. When Wiesel emphasized his commitment "*to go on telling the tale, to go on carrying on the dialogue*," that decision entailed a lifelong engagement with biblical stories and their characters' contentious encounters with God.[31]

Adam and Eve, Cain and Abel, Abraham and Isaac, Jacob, Joseph, Moses, and Job—the Third Reich sought to burn stories about them and to eradicate the moral accountability emphasized in those narratives. The protesting and resisting task that Wiesel set for himself in *Messengers of God* was to tell and retell the stories of those biblical people, the contemporary implications those tales contain, and the responsibilities they confer.

According to *Messengers of God*, the tasks set for us are monumental: "It is given to man to transform divine injustice into human justice and compassion."[32] Moses did such work. "After him," says Wiesel, "nothing was the same again."[33] Life without Moses? Think of it. No Torah. Nothing to distinguish Jews from other human groups. No Christianity, no antisemitism, and no Holocaust. Not even God, at least as Jewish and Christian traditions have understood God. But there is Moses standing before his homeless people, setting before them life and death, urging them to choose well. Moses set so much of history's course.

Moses knew God as One who sets people free. He also knew God as a consuming fire, and even as One who "tried to kill him" (Exod 4:24). It was not Moses's first choice, but, "he filled two equally difficult roles: he was God's emissary to Israel and Israel's to God."[34] More than one writer contends that the God of history, not to mention God's covenants with human creatures, went up in smoke from Nazi ovens. That conclusion is hard to resist if we encounter God only in terms of traditional notions of full omnipotence and total goodness, but Wiesel's Moses never had such illusions.

---

31. Wiesel, "Talking and Writing," 369.

32. Wiesel, *Messengers*, 235. My discussion of *Messengers* is adapted from Roth, *Consuming Fire*, 158–69.

33. Wiesel, *Messengers*, 181.

34. Wiesel, *Messengers*, 200.

He recognized the sovereignty of God and knew that to confront God was to stand on ground that was holy but not simply good. Thus, he came to understand that to enter self-consciously into relation with God is to find oneself in a struggle for liberty that requires people to contend with God as well as with themselves and each other.

Moses discovered that the God of history encountering him was more likely problematic than providential. What Moses found is that the One sustaining and dealing with humanity is a God who cares, but who does so largely by leaving people to sort out a gift of freedom that is at once incredibly vast and wonderful and yet immensely destructive. Directives are given, and pacts are established as part of the bargain, but they increase the tension more than they release it because too often God seems not to keep his part of the bargain, let alone to follow his own commandments consistently. Amazing, then, that Moses did not find God a cosmic sadist, a hollow mask of indifference broken only by mocking laughter.

Reasons why? First, Moses saw that people are forgetful, foolish, cowardly—and, even worse, that they are deceitful, calculating, treacherous, and ready to sell and destroy souls for almost any price. And yet the counterpoint was that people could be different—not perfectible but surely less imperfect. Second, an irreplaceable source of courage to struggle for good against evil could come through a sense of covenant with God, so long as it was understood that human service for God required one to be against God too. Moses, so often pictured as the obedient leader who constantly had to deal with a people stubborn in their rebelliousness, that Moses was the most profoundly rebellious of all. Without God, Moses could be nothing. With God, Moses saw ways to bring people to places from which they could at least catch glimpses of a promised land. Perhaps how Moses acted made a difference to God, challenged God too. Without Moses, who would God be? With Moses, who might God become? Wiesel's Moses dares humanity—and perhaps God as well—to decide whether we can envision and enliven not a God of history who pulls the strings of events, nor even a God who uses people as instruments of God's own judgment, but rather One whose covenant with a world of freedom requires our moral rebellion if that world's goodness—and God's redemption—is to flourish.

Job also experienced and understood these relationships. Wiesel gives him a voice this way: "Job spoke his outrage, his grief; he told God what He should have known for a long time, perhaps since always, that something was amiss in His universe. The just were punished for no reason, the criminal rewarded for no reason. The just and the wicked were subjected to the same fate—God having turned His back on them, on everyone. God had lost interest in His creation; He was absent."[35]

If Wiesel's Job, a just man, were here today in a post-Holocaust world where atrocity rages on and on, what would he have to say? Maybe, "I would speak to the Almighty, / and I desire to argue my case with God . . . See, he will kill me; I have no hope; / but I will defend my ways to his face" (Job 13:3, 15). Would he say, "I know that my Redeemer lives, / and that at the last he will stand upon the earth; / and after my skin has been thus destroyed, / then in my flesh I shall see God, / whom I shall see on my side, / and my eyes shall behold, and not another" (Job 19:25–27)? After God "answers" him out of the whirlwind—"Where were you when I laid the foundation of the earth?" (Job 38:4)—would Job say, "Now, having seen you with my own eyes, / I retract all I have said, / and in dust and ashes I repent" (Job 42:5–6, JB)?[36]

The last passage is especially troubling because it suggests, at the end of the day, a simple resignation. Or is more going on than meets the eye at first glance? Wiesel suggested that, far from resignation, Job's answer is one of resistance and rebellion instead, masked and expressed in hasty abdication. Ultimately, God cannot be defeated. That fact may be both Job's and our hope and despair, Job's and our cause for lamentation and thanksgiving. But in confessing and repenting—when God, with greater reason to do so, did not—Job, said Wiesel, "continued to interrogate God."[37] The world's fate—maybe God's too—hangs in the balance of that interrogation's quality and persistence.

Wiesel's reflections in *Messengers of God* are among the most important places where he argued more boldly with God than Littell's embrace of the crucifixion/resurrection motif regarding the Holocaust allowed Littell himself to do. Wiesel's love for the Jewish people and for the State of Israel was steadfast and unwavering, but God's role in the emergence of the State of Israel remained for him, I believe, something that produced more questions than answers about God. At the end of the day, Wiesel rejected Rubenstein's denial of the God of history, but Wiesel, I think, was less sure than Littell about the extent to which God is a providential, resurrecting God of history. So am I.

---

35. Wiesel, *Messengers*, 229–30.
36. See also Wiesel, *Messengers*, 231–32.
37. Wiesel, *Messengers*, 235.

Tender Traces

As the 1988 Webster University symposium on Elie Wiesel: The Man and His Work came to an end, Wiesel responded to the presentations he had heard. His comments included a story about his exchange with Rubenstein in the conference that Franklin Littell and Hubert Locke organized at Wayne State University in 1970. After he had finished his response to Rubenstein that evening, Wiesel recalled, Rubenstein stood and stated that he wished to say something. His expectation at that time, said Wiesel at Webster University, was that Rubenstein would try to refute him. Instead, said Wiesel, Rubenstein's reply to him was simply, "I as a rabbi want to give you my blessing."[38]

Drawing this chapter to a close, I see that photograph from a long-gone symposium. I sense its tender traces of a blessing, which threads its way through connections and exchanges that affect me more deeply than words can say. In their different but always special ways, Richard Rubenstein, Elie Wiesel, and Franklin Littell continue to give me insight. They help me—and countless others—to face the mystery of life and death and to try to do so without thoughtless utterance and premature closure that produce foolish babble. As good friends do, they encourage me to tell the story in my own way and to carry on the dialogue as best I can in my prayers and quarrels with God

---

38. Wiesel, "Talking and Writing," 369.

5

Raul Hilberg

In 1966, I completed my doctoral dissertation in philosophy at Yale University. It focused on the American philosopher William James, whose lifelong conviction held that "philosophical study means the habit of always seeing an alternative, of not taking the usual for granted, of making conventionalities fluid again, of imagining foreign states of mind."[1] Those insights have informed my understanding of philosophy's responsibilities.

My dissertation explored James's moral philosophy. Ever since, my work has explored ethical questions: How should I understand ideas such as *right* and *wrong, justice* and *injustice, good* and *evil*? Why do we human beings—so often, so gravely—intend and unleash harm? What most needs to change, and how could such transformation take place, for individuals and institutions to waste life less and respect each other more? Not long after I finished my dissertation, the Holocaust decisively influenced my understanding of those questions, intensifying their urgency and complexity. My writing, including its reflections on religion and God, tries to advance that understanding, for striving to meet the highest ethical standards is as important as anything we do.

Defined by the intention to encourage human action that fits sound understanding about what is right and wrong, just and unjust, good and evil, virtuous and corrupt, ethics arguably is civilization's keystone. At its best, ethics emphasizes careful deliberation about the differences between those fundamental realities, promotes encouragement not to be indifferent toward those the differences, honors cultivation of virtuous character, and supports action that defends what is right and resists what is wrong. Absent the overriding of moral sensibilities, if not the collapse or collaboration of ethical

---

1. James, "Teaching," 178. I am indebted to Henry Greenspan for the quotation. Parts of this chapter are adapted from Roth, *Ethics*; and Roth, *Failures of Ethics*.

traditions, the Holocaust, genocide, and other mass atrocities could not take place. Although these catastrophes do not pronounce the death of ethics, they show that ethics is vulnerable, subject to misuse and perversion, and that no simple reaffirmation of ethics, as if nothing disastrous had happened, will do. Raul Hilberg, who called the failure of morality to stop the Nazi genocide "a phenomenon of the greatest magnitude," shaped and sharpened my ethical insight in pivotal ways.[2] His instruction keeps reminding me that reflection on the Holocaust yields its best results when one starts with details—an event, a person, a place—and then brings questions to bear so that inquiry spirals from the particular in something like concentric circles to the more general perspective and then drills back down to the details that test and ground any generalizations or philosophical observations. Only commitment to a process of this kind can keep one from small answers to big questions.

Detecting Hilberg's Ethics

In *The Politics of Memory*, an autobiographical account of his Holocaust studies journey, Hilberg recalled boyhood railroad trips with his parents in the 1930s. "The train," he said, "opened the world to me."[3] As events unfolded, trains provided not only Hilberg's "awakening to space" but also one of his most penetrating perspectives for analyzing "the so-called Final Solution, which entailed the transfer of Jews from all parts of Europe to death camps or shooting sites."[4]

In the mid-1970s, I heard Hilberg lecture for the first time. He spoke about the Deutsche Reichsbahn, as the German railroads were named before and during World War II. His research broke new ground as he showed the centrality of the Reichsbahn's bureaucracy and personnel to the destruction of the European Jews. As he noted in a key journal article that appeared in 1976, "more than five million Jews were killed during the destruction process in ghettos, on shooting grounds, and in gas chambers. In the three-year period between October 1941 and October 1944 the Reichsbahn transported more than half these people to their deaths. Throughout that time, despite difficulties and delays, no Jew was left alive for lack of transport."[5]

---

2. Hilberg, *Destruction*, 1085. In this book, citations from *The Destruction of the European Jews* refer to the third edition.

3. Hilberg, *Politics of Memory*, 39.

4. Hilberg, *Politics of Memory*, 39–40.

5. Hilberg, "German Railroads," 60–74, esp. 70. For further analysis of Hilberg's article and its findings, see Browning, *German Railroads*.

Organized in a bureaucracy as specialized and efficient as it was vast, the Reichsbahn's personnel numbered about 1.4 million. Those people were not "specialists in Jewish affairs," but their training and expertise were nonetheless brought to bear on facilitating Jewish deaths. "Many of the men who made the railways their career," wrote Hilberg, "worked ceaselessly to increase the capacity of the network for all the transports projected in the German Reich, and to the very end they found purpose in that endeavor. In their hands the railways became a live organism which acted in concert with Germany's military, industry, or SS to make German history." The Reichsbahn men, continued Hilberg, "were solid individuals, not mindless robots. As intelligent men they were capable of understanding the tenor of their time. They could not fail to obtain an 'overview' of their situation; they could not 'bypass' their reflections. The fact is that they were part of Nazi Germany, ruthless, relentless, and Draconian practitioners in every respect . . . No one resigned, no one protested, and hardly anyone asked for a transfer."[6] Most of them continued their careers with the renamed, postwar Bundesbahn.

Owing to Hilberg's extensive research, the French filmmaker Claude Lanzmann tracked Hilberg down at his Burlington, Vermont, home during a winter several years before *Shoah*, Lanzmann's epic film about the Holocaust, appeared in 1985. Lanzmann showed him a Holocaust-related railway document, which Hilberg seized "like an addict to explain the hieroglyphic contents to him."[7] Seizing, in turn, on Hilberg's gift of explanation, Lanzmann got him to repeat for the camera his decoding of the German timetable. The result was that a miniature version of Hilberg's masterful study, *The Destruction of the European Jews*, and other aspects of his scholarship, particularly Hilberg's work on *The Diary of Adam Czerniakow*, became a key informing thread in Lanzmann's film. One of Lanzmann's strategic decisions was how to introduce Hilberg in *Shoah*, a film that featured survivors, perpetrators, and bystanders but not scholars, let alone the "talking heads" of conventional documentaries. Lanzmann determined that Hilberg's first words would not deal with German railroads or even with the Holocaust directly. Instead they compactly identified Hilberg's methods and standards as a Holocaust scholar. "In all of my work," he stated in his opening line, "I have never begun by asking the big questions, because I was always afraid that I would come up with small answers; and I have preferred to address these things which are minutiae or details in order that I might then be able

---

6. Hilberg, "German Railroads," 60, 70–72.
7. Hilberg, *Politics of Memory*, 40.

to put together in a gestalt a picture, which, if not an explanation, is at least a description, a more full description, of what transpired."[8]

One sentence could not be enough to guarantee Hilberg's credibility to an audience that had never laid eyes on him. A few words of that kind did not ensure that Hilberg's analysis would be instantly embraced by people who had never studied his writings. In *Shoah*'s context, however, Hilberg's "entry" could scarcely have been more compelling. For me, and I expect for many others, the effectiveness of his opening statement emerged from the sense that it conveyed ethical insight—not explicitly but still profoundly—about his commitment and approach to Holocaust studies. Not only in the Lanzmann film but long before and after, Hilberg's appeal, his authority one could say, was never exclusively found in his immense knowledge about the Holocaust and its German destruction process. The appeal and authority of this serious man resided in a combination of extensive knowledge plus a style of inquiry, an expression of feeling (often muted or understated), and a determination to keep going despite frustration, melancholy, and despair. Observing Hilberg and learning from him for decades, I think that his contribution to analysis of the Holocaust, not only its history but also its consequences and implications, cannot be sufficiently grasped unless one consciously detects Raul Hilberg's ethics.

For several reasons, I refer to detecting Hilberg's ethics, a task that takes careful work. First, one needs to refine the scope and limitations of the concept *Hilberg's ethics*. The detective work I have in mind is not to offer a biographical account, let alone an appraisal, of Hilberg's personal or professional life, except insofar as his scholarship and analysis of the Holocaust involve reflection that has ethical content and insight. The two elements are intertwined and sometimes inseparable, but the emphasis here is less on Hilberg's conduct than on what can be called his moral philosophy. Arguably every person lives more or less consistently but imperfectly with respect to his or her ideals. No one lacks ethical shortcomings. Hilberg was no exception to that rule. What concerns me, however, is an exploration of the ethical insights embedded in his Holocaust studies. Hilberg practiced well what his insights reveal, but my analysis will fall on the latter, leaving the work of biography to others.

A second reason why it is appropriate to speak of detecting Hilberg's ethics and why the detection requires careful work is that he did not think of himself as a philosopher, and even less did he want to be considered a theologian. He was known as a historian of the Holocaust, but he frequently reminded his readers and audiences that he was a political scientist, which

---

8. See Lanzmann, *Shoah*, 70. This book contains the complete text of the film.

goes far toward explaining not only his interest in bureaucracy, decision-making, and the ways documents contain information and reflect and communicate decisions that have been made, but also his judgment that sheets of paper, "artifacts of the administrative machinery itself," can constitute "a form of action."[9] Repeatedly and in depth, Hilberg's scholarship dealt with human choices and decisions, with human responsibility for their implementation and their consequences, which are all key factors in ethics. His main interest was to find out how decisions were made, what led them to go one way or another, and how a web of decision-making and responsibility created a destruction process. He was always on the edge of overt ethical reflection, but he usually held it back, or at least in reserve, so that he could focus on the process more than on the ethical appraisal of it. The result was that Hilberg only occasionally spoke overtly and explicitly about ethics, and yet ethical concerns were always nearby, awaiting exploration, beckoning to his readers and listeners because Hilberg, the historian and political scientist, concentrated on a moral disaster.

Hilberg's writings and lectures do not offer more than fragments of an ethical theory. Nevertheless, it is difficult to study his work without sensing that ethical impulses and passions run deep in his scholarship. Sometimes they dwell between the lines or beneath the surface of his unembellished prose; sometimes they are implied in the tenacity that the clarity of his expression reveals as it seeks to leave a lasting record of how a catastrophe took place. Thus, Hilberg's written and oral expression points toward a third reason why it is appropriate to speak of detecting Hilberg's ethics and to recognize the complexity involved in such work.

Hilberg remarked that an editor once complained that he wrote short sentences.[10] The editor's observation was correct but not his complaint. One of Hilberg's virtues was that his prose was spare, lean, and therefore robust. Clarity and precision, characterized not only by attention to organizational structures but also by understatement that conveys a keen sense of irony as well as a melancholy mood, are among the hallmarks of his expression. His skill as a speaker and a writer was to master a vast amount of detail and then to communicate his findings in ways that showed how an exploration of twigs and bushes enables the landscape they compose to stand out in bold relief.[11] But if one looks for Hilberg's ethics in the projects that occupied

---

9. Hilberg, *Destruction*, xii. The quoted words are from Hilberg's preface to the second edition (1985) of *The Destruction of the European Jews*. The third edition (2003) contains Hilberg's prefaces to all three of the editions, the first of which appeared in 1961.

10. See Hilberg, *Politics of Memory*, 46.

11. I owe the metaphor to Christopher Browning. See Browning, *Collected*

his life, the task is a complex one of detection because there is a need to consider not only what he said overtly and explicitly but also what was not said but still conveyed, what was left in silence but nonetheless voiced, what was pointed at but not directly because to divert attention in that way would be to deflect attention from the details that have to be identified and related so as to obtain the "picture which, if not an explanation, is at least a description, a more full description, of what transpired."

Hilberg stressed that documents, especially written documents from the Holocaust itself, are the gold standard for understanding how and why the Holocaust took place. Although their content may be elusive when it comes to detecting Hilberg's ethics, the written documents—in this case his books, essays, lectures—are the documentary source. That source, however, creates problems even as it remains indispensable for identifying Hilberg's ethical perspectives. Thus, a fourth problem encountered by an interpreter of Hilberg's ethics can be stated as follows: The question that governs such an inquiry—What is Hilberg's ethics?—may be one of those "big questions" that would make him cautious, if not skeptical, about answering for fear that the answers, which would have to be made with the Holocaust to test them, might be small. When the Holocaust is the context and the testing ground for ethical thinking, careful thought hesitates because ethical statements may end up being abstract, superficial, inadequate, or unpersuasive.

Sources of Hilberg's Moral Insight

Giving these reservations and cautionary notes their due, it is nevertheless instructive to identify and reflect upon Hilberg's ethical insights. Few if any scholars thought longer and with greater care about the Holocaust. He witnessed the Anschluss in his native Austria, fled by train with his parents to France in the spring of 1939, and then by ship to Cuba before he reached Miami, Florida, on September 1, 1939, the day that Hitler invaded Poland and World War II began. Eventually the reunited family settled in New York. After graduating from college, Hilberg, still in his teens, returned to Europe with the US Army. By 1948, while a graduate student at Columbia University, he decided to focus on the destruction of the European Jews, convinced that "without an insight into the actions of the perpetrators, one could not grasp this history in its full dimensions. The perpetrator had the overview. He alone was the key. It was through his eyes that I had to view the happening, from its genesis to its culmination. That the perpetrator's

---

Memories, x. Browning quotes the late historian George Mosse, who once said, "Those of us who survey the broad landscape still love the twigs and bushes."

perspective was the primary path to be followed became a doctrine for me, which I never abandoned."[12]

When Hilberg proposed this project for his doctoral dissertation, Franz Neumann, a distinguished political scientist who had escaped from Nazi Germany in 1933, agreed to direct Hilberg's research, but not without a warning. Neumann, recalled Hilberg, "knew that at this moment I was separating myself from the mainstream of academic research to tread in territory that had been avoided by the academic world and the public alike. What he said to me in three words was, 'It's your funeral.'"[13] That remark is well known in Hilberg lore, but far from being his funeral, Hilberg's project led to the first edition of *The Destruction of the European Jews*, which appeared in 1961 and eventually had a significant impact on the academic world and the public alike.

Hilberg spent a lifetime studying, researching, writing, and rewriting about the Holocaust. How is such a commitment to be understood? What insights about ethics did that work focus for him? Such questions are important, for Hilberg's life and work gave him angles of vision that no one else could have. He saw that the Holocaust revealed an immense moral failure. The dimensions of that failure are made even more extensive because of Hilberg's scholarship, which showed again and again how the steps that led to Nazi Germany's genocide against the Jews were carried out by ordinary people who were not bloodthirsty killers but willing nonetheless to make choices and take decisions that were genocidal. Hilberg was a witness of a distinctive kind. Having immersed himself in this history for such a long time, Hilberg gleaned insights about the Holocaust that humankind can ill afford to lose.

What's more, the ways Hilberg did his Holocaust research may be an important source for thinking about ethics in a post-Holocaust context. Not only did he spend a lifetime trying to find out what happened during the Holocaust, how that catastrophe happened, and why, but also he reflected deeply and repeatedly on how that research is best carried out, what pitfalls need to be avoided, and how one should proceed in a field where evidence is both vast and incomplete and where the perpetual threat of error requires vigilance and a willingness to admit and correct mistakes. One could easily overlook the broader implications of Hilberg's methodological reflections, but his hard-won insights in this area turn out to be among the richest veins to mine in detecting not only Hilberg's ethics but also the ways his insights can and should inform ethics generally after Auschwitz.

12. Hilberg, *Politics of Memory*, 61–62.
13. Hilberg, *Politics of Memory*, 66.

An Ethical Perspective's Ingredients

To detect Hilberg's ethics, one must consider several questions that are fundamental for identifying an ethic's perspective, content, texture, type, and significance: (1) What moods are echoed in, constitutive of, and promoted by a thinker's reflection? (2) What principles, maxims, injunctions, or imperatives are central for the ethic's content? (3) What virtues or characteristics are most highly valued? (4) On what foundations do the ethical principles and virtues rest, or, if the ethical perspective neither articulates nor assumes a single grounding of some kind, then how are those ingredients derived, and on what basis is the outlook's credibility commended? Then, after one identifies sound responses to those questions, (5) what conclusion should be drawn about the ethical perspective, its strengths and weaknesses? Some further detail about these matters can contextualize the analysis of Hilberg's ethics that follows.

Ethics does not and cannot exist without distinctions between *right* and *wrong*, between what *ought* and *ought not* to be done. These distinctions both imply and advance a vision about what is good and what is not. Neither the distinctions nor the visions are unencumbered by history and a thinker's experience of and within it. That experience is thick with feelings, emotions, memories, and particularities that affect a person deeply. When thinking turns, implicitly or explicitly, to consider how well or poorly life is unfolding—not only one's own but also the lives of others with whom one shares the world—the place of what can be called *moods* becomes significant. These moods reveal much about what could be called one's sense of things overall. Hence, we can detect whether a thinker is basically optimistic or pessimistic, hopeful or gripped by senses of tragedy and despair. Ethical outlooks vary in style and substance depending on the moods embedded in and projected by them. In Hilberg's case, his moods are among the richest sources of his ethical insights.

Next, when one notes that ethics does not and cannot exist without distinctions between *right* and *wrong*, between what *ought* and *ought not* to be done, or without a vision of the good, it is important to underscore that these elements of ethics are typically expressed in the form of *imperatives*, principles, or judgments that imply a maxim or an injunction. "Do unto others as you would have them do unto you" would be an example of such an ethical principle or imperative. "It is important to study the Holocaust" could be a judgment that implies a maxim or an injunction to remember so that one does not live blindly in the present or take decisions about the future lightly. In detecting Hilberg's ethics, one needs to identify his imperatives and the judgments that lead to them.

Ethics is neither completed by nor reducible to moods, imperatives about right and wrong, or visions of the good. It also involves habits of mind, qualities of judgment, characteristics of will, dispositions to act, and senses of responsibility. When such elements of personality and behavior are positive and desirable, one thinks of them as *virtues* (thoughtfulness, for example, or wisdom, determination, courage, and caring). When negative and undesirable, they are often called *vices* (blindness, for instance, or imprudence, arrogance, rigidity, stupidity, and irresponsibility). In detecting Hilberg's ethics, one needs to identify the virtues that he took to be most important and the vices that he most deplored.

If there are ethical principles and imperatives that ought to be followed, what is their source? What *grounds* them? At the end of the day, why is virtue better than vice? Can the sources and grounds of ethics be located? What makes an account of virtue persuasive and a discussion of vice convincing? Philosophical approaches to ethics include questions such as these. It does not follow that the responses to them will agree, which raises the additional question of what to do about the variety and disagreement that seem to be unavoidable in ethical reflection. When the issue is about the sources or the groundings for ethics, a variety of positions, sometimes mutually supportive and sometimes at odds with one another, have traditionally been advanced, explored, and criticized. The sources and grounds might be found, for example, in appeals to divinity, reason, intuition, conscience, social evolution, neuroscience, or individual subjectivity and feeling, to name a few. When the issue is about priorities among virtues and vices, similar justifying mindscapes present themselves. As one identifies and reflects on Hilberg's ethics, it will be helpful to consider these traditional sources of moral authority, for Hilberg understood that some or even all these sources have been shattered or wounded by the Holocaust. His position about the grounding of ethics, usually implied but sometimes explicit, was formed with awareness of, indeed in spite of, the Holocaust's harm to ethics.

One of the complexities that ethical reflection includes is that the identification of a person's ethical outlook does not ensure that the ethic can withstand criticisms that may be brought against it. On the other hand, it does not follow that there is some neutral, purely objective, context-free Archimedean point from which such criticisms flow and appraisals derive. Recognition of that situation can produce skepticism about humanity's ability to discriminate rationally among different ethical outlooks, at least if the assumption is that one or more of them can rightly be called true while others are false. If that skepticism escalates, the result is moral relativism, which holds that it is difficult, to the point of impossibility, to discriminate rationally between competing ethical viewpoints. According to the relativist's outlook, discrimination can and does take place, but it hinges much more on matters of taste, culture, historical context, privilege, gender, or power than on objectivity, rationality, and truth. Persuasive though it may look at first glance, the relativist's outlook has its own problems. One of the most telling is that unless moral relativism lays claim to objectivity, rationality, and truth, it cannot reasonably occupy the privileged position it tries to maintain. On the other hand, that recognition does not banish the corrosive effects of skepticism, at least not entirely. It is unlikely, though not impossible, that any particular ethical perspective will be able to defend itself perfectly against every reasonable criticism that can be brought against it. Thus, ethical pluralism, which is not the same as ethical relativism, is likely to remain. No single view will outdo every other outlook. Universal agreement about ethical matters will be less, probably far less, than complete. In the process of detecting Hilberg's ethics, one will eventually face the question, How sound, ethically, is his perspective? What will be important to discern is whether Hilberg's ethics contains insights that can help one to cope with the dilemmas of objectivity, skepticism, and relativism that are embedded in a post-Holocaust question of that kind.

Moods

In Lanzmann's film *Shoah*, Hilberg interprets Fahrplananordnung 587, a German railroad timetable that routed Polish Jews to the gas chambers at Treblinka in the autumn of 1942. Summing up what the document reveals, he tells Lanzmann that the timetable refers to four different transports, each one doomed. "We may be talking about ten thousand dead Jews on this one Fahrplananordnung here," he states, but Lanzmann, following the calculations closely, insists "more than ten thousand." Hilberg counters: "Well," he says, "we will be conservative here." Letting Hilberg's judgment stand, Lanzmann moves to another question. Why, he asks, does Hilberg find the timetable so fascinating? "When I hold a document in my hand, particularly if it's an original document," Hilberg replies, "then I hold something which is actually something that the original bureaucrat held in his hand. It's an artifact. It's a leftover. It's the only leftover there is. The dead are not around."[14]

My description of this exchange cannot do it justice, but I believe that Hilberg's expression—the intense look on his face, the measured cadences and focused inflection of his voice, as well as the words caught by Lanzmann's soundtrack—reveal that *anger*, at times close to seething but controlled rage, is a dominant mood in Hilberg's ethics. How could it not be?

14. For the quoted passages, see Lanzmann, *Shoah*, 141–42.

Writing twenty years later in his preface to the third edition of *The Destruction of the European Jews,* Hilberg noted that his research on the Holocaust was destined to end because exhaustion, if not death, would overtake him. Nevertheless, as that edition appeared in 2003, he remarked that he had not yet "come to an end, and I knew that no topic was more important to me than this one."[15]

Perhaps the answer is obvious without asking the question, but why was study of the Holocaust and of the German destruction process in particular so important to him? No evidence suggests that a credible answer could be found in any fame or fortune that such work could produce. Nor would routine or even the history's vast and lethal scope be fully adequate to explain Hilberg's passionate commitment. Closer to the truth of the matter is recognition that in Hilberg's view the destruction of the European Jews was immensely devastating and utterly wrong. It could have been prevented; it might have been stopped before the worst took place, but "the dead are not around," and to a large extent the murderers got away with their crime. In my judgment, it is this moral anger that accounted for Hilberg's impassioned, dispassionate scholarly commitment to study of the Holocaust. His outraged sense of justice beats within the heart of his ethics.

Righteous anger, however, is not the only mood that governed Hilberg's moral outlook. It blended with melancholy and sadness. In *The Politics of Memory,* Hilberg recalls a September Sunday in Boston. The year was 1992. His book *Perpetrators Victims Bystanders* had just been published, but a *New York Times* review was less favorable than he had hoped, and when Hilberg visited a large Barnes & Noble store, his new book was not to be found. As he took his lunch that day in a hotel dining room above a street-level restaurant called The Last Hurrah, Hilberg reports feeling "an indescribable sadness."[16] Alone in that moment, he felt that he was saying goodbye to his life.

Many writers receive ungenerous reviews. Even more have been disappointed when their writings are absent from bookstore shelves. One could read Hilberg's lament as self-indulgence, but his sadness and melancholy are not simply or best explained by his feeling slighted. I think that the sadness and melancholy were most importantly prompted by his awareness that the history he cared about so much, the moral failure that angered him so deeply, the loss of the dead who are not around might be receding toward oblivion no matter how hard he tried to stem the tide of forgetfulness and ignorance. A related disposition affected Hilberg's 2001 study, *Sources of*

---

15. Hilberg, *Destruction,* ix.
16. Hilberg, *Politics of Memory,* 18.

Holocaust Research, which speaks about the researcher's ideal of accessing and preserving "the past in its pristine state" but ends by acknowledging that "the reality of the events is elusive, as it must be" and by suggesting that the researcher's work goes forward not so much to achieve mastery as to prevent the past, and awareness of the Holocaust's destruction process in particular, from being "relinquished and forgotten."[17]

About two months after that Sunday in Boston when Hilberg felt his indescribable sadness, he returned to Vienna, the city of his boyhood, which he had not visited since 1976. There a woman named Evelyn Adunka interviewed him, calling Hilberg's attention to a letter she had found in an archive. Its author was the distinguished scholar and novelist H. G. Adler, a survivor of Theresienstadt and Auschwitz. Dated March 6, 1962, the letter contained commentary about *The Destruction of the European Jews*, whose first edition had appeared in the previous year. Adler praised Hilberg's book. "It is not likely to be surpassed very soon," he observed, "even though it is by far not yet the final portrayal. No one until now has seen and formulated the total horrible process so clearly." What was especially moving about *The Destruction of the European Jews*, Adler went on to say, was "the hopelessness of the author . . . At the end nothing remains but despair and doubt about everything, because for Hilberg there is only recognition, perhaps also a grasp, but certainly no understanding."[18] Upon reading these comments, Hilberg observed that Adler "had peered directly into the core of my being."[19]

Impassioned anger, melancholy, sadness—these are part of Hilberg's mood but not the whole of it. At least two other feelings affected his ethical outlook. Paradoxically, the passion of Hilberg's anger was both masked and muted but also revealed and communicated through subdued prose and plain description. Such sentences—short, compact, restrained, understated, overtly dispassionate, matter-of-fact—such sentences characterized Hilberg's speech and writing.

Hilberg's style, I believe, was far from emotionless, but he controlled and condensed, at times repressed, emotion so that he could report as straightforwardly as possible what took place. The cool prose, moreover, was supported as thoroughly as possible by documentation that undermines

---

17. Hilberg, *Sources*, 71, 204.

18. Adler is quoted in Hilberg, *Politics of Memory*, 202–3. Using the initials H. G., Adler erased his given name, Hans Günther, when he discovered that a Nazi with that name headed the Central Office for Jewish Emigration in Bohemia and Moravia, making him accountable for deporting Adler and thousands of other Czech Jews to Theresienstadt. For more on Adler, see Filkins, *H. G. Adler*.

19. Hilberg, *Politics of Memory*, 202.

disconfirmation and short-circuits disbelief. The Holocaust precludes the possibility that justice can prevail, but Hilberg brought the case against the perpetrators, bystanders, and to some extent against the victims nonetheless. On the latter score, Hilberg assessed responsibility wherever he must, but with empathy for the constraints and pressures that faced a Jewish leader such as Czerniakow, who led the Jewish Council in the Warsaw ghetto.

Hilberg reports that, figuratively, he "spent about six years with Czerniakow" while working on the diary of a man who took his own life upon learning that there was no reprieve for the Jews of Warsaw when the Germans ordered deportations from the ghetto to begin on July 22, 1942. Czerniakow's diary was filled with short statements and factual descriptions. Hilberg paid a kind of tribute to him by writing about Czerniakow in a similar vein. "When the deportations began," Hilberg remarks as he considers Czerniakow's final hours, "he wanted to save the Jewish orphans, and when he could not secure even their safety, he killed himself."[20] In *Shoah*, Lanzmann's film, Hilberg's last words are about Czerniakow. They refer to reports that after Czerniakow had closed his diary for the last time, he wrote a note in which he said: "They want me to kill the children with my own hands."[21] After Lanzmann had heard Hilberg speak about Czerniakow, again capturing his commentary on film, he said of Hilberg, "You were Czerniakow."[22] Lanzmann could well have been referring to the mood of Hilberg's understated expression, which conveyed rage and despair with authority and power.

At times, especially when Hilberg wrote or spoke about the perpetrators, notes of irony and dark humor infused the mood that pervaded his ethics. As he analyzed the decisions that led to the "Final Solution," Hilberg underscored that bureaucrats had to become initiators and that other perpetrators had to become innovators and inventors. Such terms are often part of a vocabulary of "progress," where they signal "virtues" of one kind or another. The "Final Solution" was a kind of "progress," and it demanded and received creative thinking so bent on destruction that it produced what Hilberg called "a turning point in history."[23] Hilberg's irony contains ethical warnings to which I will return. Meanwhile, it sometimes involved the dark humor contained in anecdotes that he recounted in his typically understated way. In 1976, for example, Hilberg was doing archival research in Germany when a group of lawyers invited him to a party. They were investigating

---

20. Hilberg, *Politics of Memory*, 187.
21. See Lanzmann, *Shoah*, 190.
22. Hilberg, *Politics of Memory*, 188.
23. See Lanzmann, *Shoah*, 71.

and prosecuting "National Socialist Crimes."[24] Hilberg asked one of the attorneys what he thought about Hitler's role. He replied that prosecutors had "often fantasized about drawing up an indictment against Adolf Hitler" for the Holocaust. But then, the German lawyer added, it dawned upon them that "we didn't have the evidence." Hilberg's direct comment on this story consisted of three words about the lawyer: "And he laughed." Hilberg did not say that he did likewise, but one can sense a wry, ironic smile as the prelude to the task of holding Hitler and his followers accountable, which was Hilberg's passion.

Toward the end of *The Destruction of the European Jews*, Hilberg included a twenty-two-page list of Holocaust perpetrators, which identifies their role in the Nazi regime, the outcome of any legal proceedings that may have been brought against them, and, in some cases, their postwar careers and fate. "An all-encompassing roster of perpetrators," noted Hilberg, "would fill a multivolume directory . . . For the large majority there is no postwar report . . . By the law they had not lived. By the law they did not die."[25] One of the entries in Hilberg's catalog refers to Hermann Pook, an official in the SS Wirtschafts-Verwaltungshauptamt (WVHA, Economic-Administrative Main Office) who "had salvaged the gold from the mouths of the gassed." Without commentary, Hilberg simply states a fragment of absurdity from the defense that Pook's lawyer offered on behalf of his client: "The corpse has no more rights of any sort, but no one has any right to the corpse either. The body, so to speak, from a legal point of view, floats between heaven and earth."[26] This less-than-convincing defense brought the convicted Pook a five-year sentence from a US military tribunal. Hilberg notes, however, that the sentence was reduced to time served. With its darkly humorous twists and turns, the Holocaust's irony multiplies irony. Its nuances affected Hilberg's mood by making him do all that he could to ensure that men such as Pook are not rehabilitated by obscurity and oblivion.

Imperatives

In 1971, Hilberg published a book called *Documents of Destruction: Germany and Jewry 1933–1945*. This edited volume, which contained Hilberg's commentary, includes documents from German and Jewish sources that recorded and constituted actions in the destruction of the European Jews. The book's front matter features two epigraphs that highlight the most

24. Hilberg tells this story in "Holocaust," 99–100.
25. Hilberg, *Destruction*, 1173.
26. Hilberg, *Destruction*, 1157, 1187.

important imperative in Hilberg's ethics.[27] The first comes from Heinrich Himmler's speech to his SS and police leaders in October 1943. Himmler praises his men for remaining decent and for having been "hardened" under the stress and strain resulting from having "gone through this"—Himmler's nonspecific way of referring to mass killing. What has been accomplished, Himmler states, "is a page of glory in our history," but also one "never written and never to be written." In juxtaposition to Himmler's injunction that silence must cover the "page of glory," Hilberg sets the following words from a Jewish survivor named Jacob Celemenski: "Today I am one of the survivors. For twenty years I have constantly heard within my mind the very cry of the murdered: Tell it to the world!"

The contrast between these two passages is of fundamental importance in Hilberg's ethics. Himmler referred to a "page of glory" but ordered silence about it. Celemenski broke the silence. He unmasked the "glory" by indicating that it refers to mass murder. Himmler wanted the "page of glory" to be unwritten, but the absence of dead Jews resounded in the cries that reverberated in Celemenski's mind. Those cries, moreover, had a specificity, which insisted upon remembrance and testimony: Tell it to the world!

Ethical imperatives direct attention and guide action, but their meaning is not always self-evident. If, for example, a well-known imperative is to love your neighbor as yourself, then questions such as "who is my neighbor?" and "how should loving yourself be understood?" have their place. The same can be said of Celemenski's "Tell it to the world!" What is to be told, by and to whom, and how should the telling be done? One can even reflect on what "telling" does and does not involve. Hilberg's work sheds light on his most crucial imperative—Tell it to the world!—by illustrating what it means and what is entailed by it.

The *it* that must be told has at least three dimensions. First, nothing is more important than telling what happened and doing so as thoroughly, honestly, and persistently as possible. So, one must reckon with both Himmler and Celemenski, with who they were, what they did, and what they said. Himmler and Celemenski, of course, are not only particular persons, but also they are emblematic of countless others who played their parts in the destruction of the European Jews. That recognition took Hilberg on his quest for what he called the "minutiae" that constitute the Holocaust's immensity.

Second, recording and telling the history of the Holocaust is both an end in itself and the means to something more than that. "Telling it to the world" may be the best that one can do to remember the dead, to mourn the

---

27. See Hilberg, ed., *Documents*, vi.

loss, and to hold accountable those who perpetrated the Holocaust but have eluded justice. Such telling has value that is not reducible to instrumentality. Among other things, it is distinctive for its power to differentiate between *right* and *wrong*. It may not be universally impossible, but it would certainly be difficult to read the epigraphs in Hilberg's edition of documents, to study those items, and then to return to the difference between the statements of Himmler and Celemenski without feeling that what took place was wrong.

Third, when "telling it to the world" arouses and deepens feelings about the difference between right and wrong, the telling becomes more than an end in itself. If wrong has been done, then it ought to be set right as far as possible, and at the very least the wrong ought not to be repeated. "Telling it to the world" means persistent, ongoing, and ever-more-detailed and firmly documented reporting so that forgetfulness does not make it easier for others to create more never-to-be-written pages of "glory." Commenting on Himmler's speech of October 1943, Hilberg put the point as follows: "There are some things that can be done only so long as they are not discussed, for once they are discussed they can no longer be done."[28]

Hilberg knew that "telling it to the world" is an imperative that strives for more than it can achieve. Just as "an all-encompassing roster of perpetrators would fill a multivolume directory," no way exists to remember every victim or to appraise the conduct of every neighbor and bystander.[29] "All that has gone on in the world," said Hilberg, "can be preserved only in fragments, and these leftovers constitute our material . . . Empirical historiography is by definition salvage. It cannot be more."[30] Completeness, finality, closure—these are not qualities that fit "telling it to the world." Their absence and impossibility require the telling to continue in spite of the melancholy and sadness that such awareness evokes.

Such factors help to explain the high esteem in which Hilberg held a little-known book by the sociologist John K. Dickinson. First published in 1967, *German & Jew: The Life and Death of Sigmund Stein* focused on a single German Jew—his real name was Hermann Reis—a lawyer of "obscure prominence" in Marburg before the Nazis' rise to power ruined his career, destroyed his family, and left him dead, probably at a satellite camp of Auschwitz that Dickinson identified as Golleschau.[31]

In his introduction to the 2001 reissue of this book, Hilberg praised the work as unique and lamented that same fact about it. Although Hilberg

---

28. Hilberg, *Destruction*, 1090.
29. Hilberg, *Destruction*, 1173.
30. Hilberg, "Incompleteness," 81.
31. Dickinson, *German & Jew*, viii.

was often skeptical about the value of oral testimony, he credited Dickinson for interviewing 172 people who knew Stein/Reis. Taking his notes carefully, Dickinson sifted and sorted findings critically and turned them into a narrative that shed light not only on the fate of one Jew during the Holocaust but also on those who knew him, including, as Hilberg observes, "some of [Stein/Reis's] German acquaintances as they distanced themselves from him, and as they coveted during his last hours in Marburg some of his possessions for 'safekeeping.'"[32]

Hilberg wondered why the 1967 appearance of Dickinson's book did not inspire other studies of a similar kind. While there was still time to do so, studies focused on bystanders and neighbors might have revealed much of importance about the context in which the Holocaust unfolded. In a melancholy mood, Hilberg observed that there was a time "when many people, who as grown men and women had watched the fate of their Jewish neighbors at close range, could still have related in abundant detail what they had seen. But hardly anyone wanted to hear much from such observers, and now the ideal moment for questioning them is gone."[33] Telling it to the world entails small deeds, such as writing an introduction to an unusual but scarcely popular book that one hopes may still attract at least a few readers.[34] Telling it to the world is work for a lifetime. That imperative and the principles that flow from it governed Hilberg's ethics.

Virtues

Putting an ethical outlook into practice depends on the cultivation of virtues, which are the habits of thought and action that turn ideas and ideals into realities. The virtues highlighted and required in Hilberg's ethics are primarily those of scholarship, but such qualities have transferability that reaches well beyond the classroom, library, archive, and writing desk.

Students who studied with Hilberg during his thirty-five years of teaching at the University of Vermont report his saying that one must "know what you're looking at. Study it. Never take anything at face value." Telling it to the world depends on finding out what is true, right, and good. That work cannot be done without study, questioning, and inquiry, all of which refuse to take things as they appear at first glance.

---

32. See Hilberg's introduction in Dickinson, *German & Jew*, xvii.
33. See Hilberg's introduction in Dickinson, *German & Jew*, xvii–xviii.
34. I was unaware of this book until an essay by Hilberg called it to my attention. In 2004, I bought a copy "on sale" from a table of remaindered books at the United States Holocaust Memorial Museum.

As the epigraph for his autobiographical work *The Politics of Memory*, Hilberg selected a sentence from H. G. Adler, the Holocaust survivor who had observed Hilberg's despair and doubt, even his hopelessness, upon reading the first edition of *The Destruction of the European Jews*. "History without tragedy does not exist," wrote Adler, "and knowledge is better and more wholesome than ignorance." In a world so wracked by devastation, loss, and grief, ignorance might be bliss, but not if the imperative is to "tell it to the world." Knowledge is indispensable for that moral task, no matter how hard it is to acquire or difficult to bear. "Researchers," said Hilberg, "do not wait until all the archives are open to them. They begin with whatever is at hand."[35] It takes decisiveness and determination, curiosity and courage, discipline, and always disciplined attention to detail to seek, acquire, and bear the knowledge on which the chance depends for something better and more wholesome than the ruined world that the Holocaust left in its wake. Clear-sightedness and every effort to avoid delusion, mystification, and forgetfulness loom large. One should never conclude that there is nothing more that can and should be done.

Hilberg's *Perpetrators Victims Bystanders* ends with a paragraph devoted to Bernhard Lichtenberg, the Roman Catholic priest who served as Prior of St. Hedwig's Cathedral in Berlin during the Third Reich. After the Kristallnacht pogrom in November 1938, he prayed publicly each day for non-Aryan Christians and Jews. On August 21, 1941, he was denounced to the Gestapo. His arrest followed on October 23. He offered to join Jews who were being deported to the Lodz ghetto in Poland, but instead he was sent to prison for endangering the public peace. Eventually, he was released but only to be sent to Dachau. Taken ill on the way, he was hospitalized and died, after last rites, in the early morning of November 3, 1943. In his brief account of Lichtenberg, Hilberg highlights two brief reminders that he found in Lichtenberg's writings. Marginalia in those documents sometimes said, "Do not delude yourselves" and "This must be said."[36]

Truth-seeking and truth-telling, courage and curiosity, realistic senses of limitation and fallibility and yet a willingness to break new ground, refusal to give up and a lifelong commitment to telling it to the world in spite of hopelessness, despair, and doubt—these qualities are among the cardinal virtues in Hilberg's ethics.

---

35. Hilberg, *Sources*, 202.
36. Hilberg, *Perpetrators*, 268.

Groundings

Hilberg was a self-identified atheist. If one asks about the foundations or groundings for his ethics, he would not and could not locate them in any divine source. Equally clear is the fact that Hilberg was not an ethical relativist. He did not think that might makes right. Nor did he follow Friedrich Nietzsche in claiming that the human will alone is the source of our values and evaluations. I make these claims because there is an important lecture that Hilberg delivered at "Ethics after the Holocaust," a conference at the University of Oregon in 1996.[37] Explaining, as he did more than once, that he did not consider himself a philosopher or a theologian, Hilberg asserted that ethics is the same today as it was yesterday and even the day before yesterday; it is the same after Auschwitz as it was before and during the lethal operations at that place. Especially regarding needless and wanton killing, he emphasized, ethics is the same for everyone, everywhere. Hilberg left no

---

37. Here my commentary is based on my copy of the videotape of Hilberg's lecture at the University of Oregon. To the best of my knowledge, the lecture has not been published, but it is accessible on YouTube: https://www.youtube.com/watch?v=fgogLvAfBfU/. Some of the lecture's historical content, especially comparisons that Hilberg draws between the situations of Jews in Warsaw, Poland, and in Copenhagen, Denmark, can be found in Hilberg, *Destruction*, 1123–24.

Among the moving moments in Hilberg's lecture at the University of Oregon is a story he told about a young soldier whose name Hilberg did not mention. The story is important for detecting his ethics. In the summer of 1945, as Hilberg recounted the episode, a unit of American soldiers was in Europe after the Germans had surrendered in May of that year. Some of the veterans were headed home. The younger and less combat-tested soldiers awaited orders that would send them to the Pacific theater, where many would be destined to lose their lives in the final campaigns against the Japanese. Then, on August 6, 1945, an officer announced that an atomic bomb had been dropped on Hiroshima. "Are there any reactions?" the major asked. If the troops understood that the bomb had likely saved their lives, dead silence prevailed until a nineteen-year-old GI rose and said, "An atomic bombing that destroys a city is an immoral act." He sat down. No one else said a word.

For some time, I wondered how Hilberg knew this story. Perhaps, it occurred to me, that young soldier was Hilberg himself. On February 16–17, 2005, I spoke with Hilberg at the United States Holocaust Memorial Museum. In those conversations, he confirmed my hunch. He also talked about the killing of SS men at Dachau by American soldiers. He did not witness those events firsthand but saw photos of the killing and talked with people who knew about it. Those Americans, Hilberg believed, did not kill sadistically but out of anger after seeing train cars filled with corpses. The victims had simply been left to die after being transported from Buchenwald to Dachau, which did not want to receive them. Hilberg further stated that he had changed his mind about the death penalty after the trial and execution of Adolf Eichmann in 1961. When I asked why, Hilberg gave two reasons. First, on utilitarian grounds, he would have wanted to interview Eichmann and his ilk. Second, as an atheist, he felt that the line that had to be held to prevent nihilism was the right to life, which he took to be absolute.

unclarity. Such killing is wrong. We know that "in our bones," he said, for such knowledge is the heritage of many years.

Hilberg's denial that he was a philosopher notwithstanding, the position reflected in such statements is philosophically provocative and bold. It is provocative because one has to consider what Hilberg's unelaborated propositions mean. It is bold because of what they imply. How should one understand the tantalizing idea that ethical sensibilities are "in our bones," especially if something such as "the heritage of many years," which implies a social formation of the ethical, has put them there? In addition, how would that outlook square with the idea that ethics is the same today as it was yesterday and even the day before yesterday?

It is not clear how these threads—they include intuition or conscience, tradition, and a kind of timelessness—weave together coherently, if they do, but I think that Hilberg's ethics does locate its grounding in the view that social history or evolution produces a deep-seated ethical consciousness that has universal and, in that sense, timeless qualities. Ethical outlooks do have a history, and they are socially formed. Those elements can fuse to make ethical outlooks, at least some of them, so widely accepted that at least the appearance of universality and timelessness attaches to them. But those relationships, even if they are coherent, scarcely put to rest all the questions about the grounding of ethics.

It can be argued that ethical injunctions against needless and wanton killing, for example, obtain normative status because collective experience shows them to have social utility. Thus, such killing is wrong because it threatens individual and social well-being. Over time this lesson is experienced, taught, and driven home so that the ethical norm becomes embedded "in our bones." But what if individuals or social groups do not understand wanton and needless killing in the same way? Himmler and his followers could agree that wanton and needless killing was wrong, but they did not think that description fitted the destruction of the European Jews. Rightly, they should be held accountable for ethical wrongdoing of the most devastating kind, but their deviation from the norm raises suspicion about ethical groundings of the kind that Hilberg's ethics includes. If the grounding is as Hilberg has it, then why did the Nazis do what they did? Why was the heritage of many years, the timelessness of the ethical, as well as the embedding of moral insight in German bones, so obviously insufficient to prevent Himmler and his followers from staining their unwritten pages of "glory" with so much blood? Such questions troubled Hilberg: "No obstruction stopped the German machine of destruction," he wrote. "No moral problem proved insurmountable ... The old moral order did not break through anywhere along the line. This is a phenomenon of the greatest magnitude."[38]

These vexing questions double in complexity because Hilberg's position committed him, I believe, to the view that the Nazis and their collaborators knew that what they were doing to the European Jews was wrong. This issue is a crucial one for consideration of ethics during and after the Holocaust, and Hilberg's analysis in *The Destruction of the European Jews* dwelled on it at some length. One cannot be sure, of course, that the Nazis and their collaborators knew with certainty that their policies toward the Jews were ethically wrong. To have clinching evidence about that fact, trustworthy confessions would be needed, including some explanation of why the perpetrators violated their own ethical sensibilities. Such confessions and explanations we do not have, at least not for the most part, from the perpetrators who were most responsible for the Holocaust.[39] Hilberg, however, pointed to less direct and more circumstantial evidence to make a case that the perpetrators acted in spite of "knowing better."

Hilberg acknowledged that the destruction process "had meaning to its perpetrators," but he argued that the meaning had to vie with what he thought was a "growing uneasiness that pervaded the bureaucracy from the lowest strata to the highest. That uneasiness was the product of moral scruples that were the lingering effect of two thousand years of Western morality and ethics. A Western bureaucracy had never before faced such a chasm between moral precepts and administrative action; an administrative machine had never been burdened with such a drastic task."[40] Rising to the occasion, the German bureaucrats, according to Hilberg, took into account "that at crucial junctures every individual makes decisions, and that every decision is individual," and thus they developed a two-pronged approach—repression and rationalization—that could override, if not entirely assuage, bad conscience.[41]

Illustrated well in Himmler's previously mentioned speech, repression included hiding the truth about mass murder and limiting the flow of

---

38. Hilberg, *Destruction*, 1085.

39. For an insightful source on this point, see Goldensohn, *Nuremberg Interviews*. Goldensohn monitored the mental health of the Nazi defendants who stood trial before the International Military Tribunal at Nuremberg in 1945–1946. He also interviewed Nazis who were witnesses in those trials, including Rudolf Höss, the former SS commandant of Auschwitz, and Otto Ohlendorf, the SS general who commanded Einsatzgruppe D on the eastern front, a shooting squadron responsible for the murder of some ninety thousand Jews. Goldensohn's interviews show these men to be largely devoid of anything resembling guilt, remorse, or repentance for their actions.

40. Hilberg, *Destruction*, 1059, 1084.

41. See Hilberg, *Destruction*, 1085–1104.

information about it, making sure that those who knew were also directly involved in some aspect of the killing, prohibiting criticism, urging perpetrators not to talk about their work, and using euphemistic language to avoid direct reference to killing in reports. Repression was insufficient to do the job of neutralizing conscience. So, rationalizations were provided as well. Two were especially important. First, the destruction of the European Jews was a defensive measure or a preventative countermeasure. Second, it was acknowledged that the individual's role was difficult but also that the hard and dirty work was both necessary and excusable, all the more so because the anti-Jewish actions were not being taken out of any personal vindictiveness. According to the Nazi ideology, the Jews were conspiratorial, criminal, and inferior. Not only their actions but also their very existence threatened German interests. Thus, orders against the Jews had to be followed, but if there were those who were not up to any particular task, opportunities to step aside were available. Furthermore, the division of labor in the destruction process made it possible for one to say that somebody might be doing unethical deeds—outright killing, for instance—but I was not unethical because I was simply doing my duty at this desk or in that office. A receding moral horizon always provided safety for one's conscience, but for anybody who was in the thick of going "through this," as Himmler put it, then there was what Hilberg called "the jungle theory," a last-ditch defense emphasizing that life is a struggle and that those who refused to do what was necessary to preserve their way of life would lose it.

If Hilberg was right when he said that from the German perspective "the most important problems of the destruction process were not administrative but psychological" (would *ethical* be a term at least as apt as *psychological*?), then it is also crucial to see that those problems, too, were solved, at least long enough for the "Final Solution" to sustain itself—until Nazi Germany was crushed by the Allies' superior military might. If ethics is in our bones, then those bones and ethics itself are precariously fragile. If ethics is the result of the heritage of many years, that heritage guarantees very little. If ethics is the same today as it was yesterday and even the day before yesterday, its status remains as vulnerable and problematic as it is fundamental and important.

A Conclusion without Closure

"Within the ranks of the perpetrators," Hilberg contended, "the one premise that shaped all the orders, letters, and reports from 1933 to 1945 was the maxim that the Jews must be removed from German spheres of life."[42] In that compact, understated, and yet emotionally charged sentence, Hilberg identified the imperative that governed much of the Nazi ethic and the "conscience" of Himmler and his men. Even with the philosophical problems that remained unresolved in Hilberg's ethics, his insight provides much of the post-Holocaust response that is needed to strengthen the ethical impulses against genocide, crimes against humanity, and the many other human rights abuses that plague the twenty-first-century world.

The third edition of *The Destruction of the European Jews* ends with a discussion of the 1994 Rwandan genocide. "The disaster of the Tutsis took place in the full view of the world," concluded Hilberg. "History had repeated itself."[43] As Hilberg knew, history may rhyme, but it does not, could not, repeat itself exactly. Nevertheless, its repetitions put in doubt assumptions about progress and (if they do not paralyze us with the despair that studying genocide is bound to produce) continue to be warnings for us. What Hilberg's ethics shows is that there is a way to respond to despair that could help to prevent or check at least some of the conditions and circumstances that cause it. By no means is that a small answer to big questions. If Hilberg's ethics can get under our skin, it may find its way not only into our bones but also into our hearts and minds. The world would be a better place if it did.

In November 2004, the Lessons and Legacies conference on the Holocaust took place at Brown University. It included a panel, organized by the historian Christopher Browning, that was devoted to Hilberg's distinguished scholarly career. With Browning's encouragement, I presented some of my early reflections on Hilberg's ethics. After the papers were presented, Hilberg responded. Four aspects of his response remain vivid.[44]

First, Hilberg's moral anger and his impassioned emphasis on the importance of truth-telling were evident as he spoke about the Holocaust's perpetrators. Second, those moods were evident because Hilberg remained convinced that, for the most part, the perpetrators knew that their murderous policies and actions had crossed a moral dividing line. Third, Hilberg's attention riveted on key questions. Why did the perpetrators do what they did, especially if they knew that their policies and actions crossed a moral dividing line? Why did they do those things so easily and persistently? Coupled with those questions were others pertaining especially to civilian bystanders who witnessed the Nazi onslaught against the Jews. Realistically,

---

42. Hilberg, *Sources*, 134.

43. Hilberg, *Destruction*, 1296.

44. I am indebted to the historian Gregory Weekes, who video-recorded Hilberg's response at Brown University and kindly shared that document with me.

what could have been expected of them? Finally, there was Hilberg's conclusion, which again put the emphasis on questions. For those who live after the Holocaust, he urged, we have to keep asking self-critically whether our own policies and decisions are right. We have to keep pressing the issue: How can the imperative "Never again!" be credible?

As I listened to Hilberg's response, I recalled the 1996 lecture he gave at the University of Oregon's conference on "Ethics after the Holocaust." Its melancholy moments had referred to an observation made by Sigmund Freud in 1915, while World War I was raging. Hilberg recalled Freud's remarking that one should not be too disappointed about humanity's fallen condition, for civilization's moral progress had never been as great as most people believed or hoped. Like Freud, Hilberg kept wondering if anything more than such melancholy deserves to remain. As his passionate insight bears witness when he insisted that we must keep asking "Is it right?" and "How can 'Never again!' be credible?" the future of civilization is in our post-Holocaust hands.

Almost twenty years earlier, on November 1, 1978, the American president Jimmy Carter established the President's Commission on the Holocaust, tasked with the responsibility to prepare a report about the establishment of "an appropriate memorial to those who perished in the Holocaust."[45] This initiative led to the creation of the United States Holocaust Memorial Museum in Washington, DC, which opened on April 22, 1993. Chaired by Elie Wiesel, the Commission had thirty-four members, including Raul Hilberg, who departed for Europe with his Commission colleagues on July 29, 1979, for a two-week mission to visit sites of Holocaust

---

45. See President's Commission on the Holocaust, "Report to the President," The report underscores two guiding principles that provided "the philosophical rationale" for the Commission's work: "the uniqueness of the Holocaust" and "the moral obligation to remember." The first principle entailed that "the systematic, bureaucratic extermination of six million Jews by the Nazis and their collaborators as a central act of state during the Second World War . . . was a crime unique in the annals of human history." In the cover letter that accompanied the "Report to the President," Elie Wiesel, the Commission's chairman, augmented the first principle by adding a theme that achieved mantra status: "The universality of the Holocaust lies in its uniqueness: the Event is essentially Jewish, yet its interpretation is universal." Although widely believed, these claims, whose meaning and validity hinge on how *unique* and *uniqueness* should be understood, have sparked controversy, not least because they seem to privilege the Holocaust as paradigmatic in ways that diminish genocides before and after the Holocaust. The second principle entailed a quest for "lessons of the Holocaust." That concept has also generated debate, which often swirls around questions about what the "lessons" should be and how much or little they depend on Holocaust studies, memorialization, and education. The existence of such discussions corroborates Hilberg's insight that "there is no finality. Findings are always subject to correction and reformulation" (*Sources*, 204).

destruction, to study memorials and museums, and to consult with leaders, historians, and archivists who had knowledge and expertise relevant to the Commission's work.

Sometime after his return, probably in 1979, Hilberg wrote an essay called "The Holocaust Mission," which reflected on his experiences during that trip. To the best of my knowledge, Hilberg did not publish this essay, but on August 3, 2017, my friend, the historian Jonathan Petropoulos, sent me an email message with a typescript of Hilberg's essay attached. Petropoulos explained that our mutual friend and Claremont McKenna College colleague, Wendy Lower, had discovered the essay while exploring archival records from the US Holocaust Memorial Museum on Hilberg's role on the President's Commission and especially his original vision for scholarship at the museum, work she did in conjunction with the museum's twenty-fifth-anniversary observance in the spring of 2018. Knowing my appreciation for Hilberg, Lower and Petropoulos kindly sent me a copy of his paper. It resounds the Hilberg theme that makes a fitting conclusion for this chapter.

Although he had been researching the Holocaust for thirty years, Hilberg noted that he had never been in Poland or the USSR. Auschwitz and Treblinka were places he had never seen. The President's Commission took him to those places and many more, but Hilberg did not count on those visits to make those sites explicable. One cannot be in Auschwitz anymore, he wrote, because the site is now a museum, not a camp. Nor can one be in Treblinka, where sculpture creates a memorial site. In my own ways, I identify with Hilberg's observation. There was a time when I felt the need to visit such Holocaust sites. I have always been glad that I made those visits, which gave me unexpected insight because I expected to understand the Holocaust more and better by being in those places. But that was not quite the case. Yes, I could better "place" Holocaust history and testimony by being at those places. But overall those experiences left me with more questions than answers. For example, I was at Auschwitz-Birkenau late one summer afternoon in 1996 when a thunderstorm drenched the remains of that Nazi killing center where more than a million Jews were murdered. As the storm passed and the sun came out, a rainbow appeared over Auschwitz. The juxtaposition of Birkenau, the reality and aftereffects of that death camp, and a rainbow, with its awesome beauty and symbolic, even biblical meanings of life, hope, and promise, remains jarring and poignant to me. Memory of that intersection, even collision, between history and nature makes me wonder whether human beings can begin to repair the damage we have inflicted on one another.

Years before and after he first went to Auschwitz and Treblinka, Hilberg said in his essay, he was on the Holocaust mission that took him deeply into

German documents. It was in them, he said, that he had most profoundly seen those places—the terrain, operations, and logistics that distinguished them. It was that singular seeing of the Holocaust that took him to the Rose Garden of the White House during the afternoon of September 27, 1979, when the Commission on the Holocaust presented its report to Jimmy Carter. Walking afterwards in Washington that evening, recalled Hilberg, he felt "slightly depressed" as was his usual reaction "after some concluding ceremony." Fringed by that mood, another became the endnote for Hilberg's meditation: "What I had to do now was to plan my research. There were documents I had to read, particularly the records in the Polish archives, and I would have to travel again soon. Next year, in Auschwitz."

Hilberg's travel brought him to Claremont, California, where, on February 7, 2004, it was my honor to confer upon him the first Lifetime Achievement Award from the Claremont McKenna College Center for the Study of the Holocaust, Genocide, and Human Rights (now the Mgrublian Center for Human Rights). Among the accolades in the citation that I wrote for him was recognition that "your awesome knowledge of the Holocaust intensifies, and inspires in others, your ethical commitment to keep advancing research 'lest,' as you say, 'all be relinquished and forgotten.'" Hilberg's research, ethics, and insight continue to inform and focus mine.

6

Friends and Teachers II

In 1972, when the philosopher Frederick Sontag, my friend and teacher, encouraged me to read the writings of Elie Wiesel, I could not have imagined the places I would go and the persons I would meet by following that suggestion. For more than forty years, Claremont McKenna College was my academic home, but my learning and teaching about the Holocaust often took me abroad—to Switzerland and Austria, Israel and the Soviet Union, Japan and South Korea, Ireland and the United Kingdom, Poland and the Czech Republic, Germany and Norway—as well as to the United States Holocaust Memorial Museum and many American colleges and universities. Time in those places deeply influenced my understanding of the Holocaust and its reverberations. During a sabbatical year in Norway, for example, I spent time in the city of Tromsø, which stands far above the Arctic Circle. Only a very few Jews lived in that remote place, but for the Nazis' "Final Solution" to be final, the seventeen Jews—mostly from three families—now named on a Tromsø memorial stone had to be identified, transported to far-distant Oslo, and then by sea to the German port at Stettin (today, Szczecin, Poland) before rail shipment to Auschwitz, where all of them were killed. More than any other object I know, that modest memorial stone in Tromsø sums up for me what the "Final Solution" was all about.

Places map my Holocaust journey, but their direction is surpassed by the friends I have made and by the teachers who have guided me along the way. In this chapter I pay tribute to people who have advanced Holocaust studies, especially mine, not primarily as archival historians but as witnesses to the Holocaust and interpreters of that catastrophe.[1] Absent their input

---

1. More people than I can name have advanced my Holocaust studies as witnesses and interpreters, but in addition to those discussed in this chapter and elsewhere in this book, I acknowledge Giorgio Agamben, Catherine Filloux, Anna and Benno Fischer,

and influence, my grasp of the Holocaust would be impoverished and weak. Their presence enriches and strengthens my insight.

Witnesses

Witnesses have knowledge of events from personal observation or experience. In addition, they may give testimony about what they have witnessed. As far as learning and teaching about the Holocaust are concerned, no witnesses are more important than those who survived the assault and bear witness to it. As far as Holocaust insight is concerned, survivors who became my friends have been my formidable teachers as well. Nothing had greater impact on my students than the visits they made to our classes.

Joe and Helen Freeman

In the late summer of 1994, I received a telephone call from Joseph Freeman, a resident of Pasadena, California, and a Holocaust survivor from Radom, Poland. He asked me to read and comment on the autobiographical manuscript he had written. Thus began a long friendship, which soon included his wife, Helen, an Auschwitz survivor. Joe is no longer alive—he died in 2010—but I still hear his voice.

Joe Freeman's testimony included three books. Especially significant is the one that resulted from the manuscript he asked me to read. It is a distinctive and significant account of a death march that took place from March 16 to April 26, 1945, with Nazi Germany's surrender only days away and well after its killing centers on Polish soil—Auschwitz-Birkenau among them—had been shut down and evacuated.[2] Joe and Helen often met with students in courses about the Holocaust that I taught at Claremont McKenna College. When Joe spoke, two characteristics stood out. First, in spite of the inhumanity he experienced, he had a firm commitment to mend the world. Second, he often repeated the phrase "It's not so easy." The phrase and

---

Dorota Glowacka, Gershon Greenberg, Irving ("Yitz") Greenberg, Sara Horowitz, Steven Katz, Danilo Kiš, Gerda Weissman Klein, Victor Klemperer, Ruth Kluger, Adam Knowles, Gertrud Kolmar, Robert Krell, Carole Lambert, Berel Lang, Lisa Leff, Miles Lerman, Edward Linenthal, John Pawlikowski, Alvin Rosenfeld, Martin Rumscheidt, Harold Schulweis, Amy Shapiro, Oren Stier, Eric Sundquist, James Waller, and James Young.

2. See Freeman, *Road to Hell*. His other books are *Job* and *Kingdom of Night*. The latter is about his spouse, Helen.

the commitment belong together. That is what makes Freeman a memorable source of Holocaust insight for me.

"It's not so easy"—when Joe voiced those words, he was doing what the Holocaust scholar James Young calls "memory-work."[3] Such work not only recalled catastrophe and suffering but also relived it. "It's not so easy" because those requirements permitted little optimism. Freeman's memory-work was done to communicate what he had experienced. But that task was not easy because my students and I could scarcely imagine what he described. He wanted us to understand and be warned by what he had endured. Even though we could not comprehend him fully, perhaps our learning was deepest, our grasp as great as it could be, just when we saw how much he struggled to make clear and vivid what we could only glimpse from afar. Freeman wanted his testimony to make a good difference in the world. When my students and I heard him say, "It's not so easy," we heard that anguished hope in his voice. His presence conferred responsibilities upon us. How could that not be the case whenever testimony about genocide and other mass atrocities is given and received?

Siegfried Halbreich

Numerous survivors of the Holocaust found their way to the Los Angeles area after World War II. In 1952, fourteen of them established the 1939 Club, now the 1939 Society, to sustain remembrance of the Holocaust and to support education about that genocide. I met Siegfried ("Sig") Halbreich in the early 1980s at a workshop for Holocaust educators in which members of the 1939 Club participated. Halbreich had arrived in Los Angeles in 1960, too late to be a founding member of the club, but he served as its president and enthusiastically supported its activities.

One of Halbreich's closest friends was Fred Diament, another Holocaust survivor. Fifteen years younger than Halbreich, who befriended Diament when they were in the Sachsenhausen concentration camp in 1939, they stuck together throughout the Holocaust. Diament called Halbreich, whose Auschwitz tattoo was 68233, one of the very few. "Very few," he said of Halbreich, "maybe I could count them on two hands, survived so many years in the camps."[4] Diament himself belonged in that company. He and Halbreich spent more than five years in Nazi camps, including Auschwitz,

---

3. See Young, *Texture of Memory*.

4. See Roth, "One of the Very Few," my Introduction to Halbreich's memoir, *Before–During–After*, xvii. Diament died at the age of eighty-one in 2004. See Woo, "Fred Diament."

where Diament's older brother, Leo, and two other resisting prisoners were hanged by the Nazis on October 10, 1944. More than ten thousand inmates were forced to witness the execution as a warning against subversion. One of them was Elie Wiesel, whose famous memoir, *Night*, contains his depiction of that event.[5]

Halbreich survived multiple Nazi camps—Gross-Rosen and Nordhausen-Dora in addition to Sachsenhausen and Auschwitz. He also testified in court against Nazi perpetrators. Before dying at ninety-eight, he was a tireless teacher-witness about the Holocaust. That work often brought him to my Claremont classes. When Elaine Woo interviewed me for Halbreich's obituary, which she wrote for the *Los Angeles Times*, I emphasized that what Halbreich accomplished after leaving the camps was also extraordinary.[6] "He would speak with great truthfulness about the hard things he had seen and endured. But there was always a note of determination to go forward, to help people remember that the world can be a brutal and nasty place, but that it doesn't have to be that way." Sig Halbreich's teaching drove home that insight. The world never had to be what it was for him from 1939 to 1945. Human decisions made it that way. Halbreich is a witness who keeps urging me to learn and teach about the Holocaust in ways that encourage better decisions.

Dario Gabbai

My Claremont colleague Jonathan Petropoulos introduced me to Dario Gabbai, a Los Angeles friend of Petropoulos's father. Gabbai was and is many things: cultured (he speaks perfect Greek, Italian, and English), sensitive, generous. But there are other dimensions to him: small-statured, he is also a tough man but deeply saddened and wracked by burdensome memories.

Gabbai's first visit to the Petropoulos-Roth course "Researching the Holocaust" resulted in the most unforgettable moment in my many years of teaching. As Gabbai told the class about his Holocaust experience, he paused and asked for water. During the several minutes it took Petropoulos to get him some, the classroom became completely silent. As Gabbai seemed to wipe tears from his eyes, the silence was as intense as any I have experienced. Here's why.

A Greek Jew, Gabbai, in his early twenties at the time, was deported to Auschwitz in April 1944.[7] Along with his older brother, Jacob, and his

---

5. Wiesel, *Night*, trans. Marion Wiesel, 63–65.

6. See Woo, "Siegfried Halbreich."

7. For more information about Gabbai, see USC Shoah Foundation, "Impact in Profile: Dario Gabbai."

cousins, Morris and Shlomo Venezia, Gabbai was conscripted to work in the Sonderkommando. Tasked with gruesome work in the gas chambers and crematoria, these units did no killing, but they were forced to serve in the destruction process by escorting doomed Jews to the gas chambers, removing the corpses, harvesting valuables from them, burning the bodies in crematoria, and disposing of the ashes.[8] No one saw the "Final Solution" as the men of the Sonderkommando saw it. They knew too much; periodically, the Germans liquidated them.

At the time of this writing in 2019, Gabbai, to the best of my knowledge, is the last survivor of the Auschwitz Sonderkommando. He combined incredible strength with a vulnerability and fragility that became apparent when he talked about his experience. His strength found expression in Auschwitz, where he endured not only the horrifying work detail, but also a highly dangerous situation that resulted from the Sonderkommando uprising in October 1944. Gabbai's unit in Crematorium II was prepared to participate in the revolt, but another Sonderkommando group acted prematurely—before word had been sent to Gabbai and his fellow-prisoners so that they could act in concert. The rebels who had acted were overpowered, killed, and "processed" by a Sonderkommando unit that included Gabbai. The SS guards then planned to liquidate his unit, but before that could happen, Gabbai and others managed to escape from their special compound and meld in with other inmates. The SS searched for them. They tried to find these witnesses, so that those bearers of secrets could never tell what they knew. But Gabbai eluded capture. As the German war effort faltered and the killing operations at Auschwitz were dismantled, he was evacuated from Auschwitz, force-marched to Mauthausen and Ebensee, where he was liberated in May 1945 as the Germans fled and American troops arrived. In 1951, a Jewish community in Cleveland, Ohio, sponsored his entry to the United States. Shortly thereafter, he moved to California.

One February evening at Claremont McKenna College in 2004, I heard Gabbai, his voice quivering with emotion, tell his audience that "there are two men inside of me." One is the person that people ordinarily see—modest and sometimes humorous—and then there is the part that makes him, akin to Halbreich, one of the very few. He saw what very few have seen and did what very few have done. But no comfort comes from that. Day after day, unfortunate men in the Sonderkommando hooked a belt around an Auschwitz corpse and dragged it to a crematorium oven. Week after week, they searched body cavities for valuables. During a lifetime, who

---

8. For more detail about the Sonderkommando, see Greif, *We Wept*; and Venezia, *Inside the Gas Chambers*. Venezia was Gabbai's cousin.

has faced the choiceless choices and done the devastating things required of Gabbai in Auschwitz if his life was to be prolonged? Who can fathom living with the memories that Gabbai carried with him because he survived? His invaluable insight for me: Whenever I think I understand the Holocaust, whenever someone tells me that catastrophe has been explained, I should think again—and again.

Zev Weiss

On that February evening in 2004 when Dario Gabbai spoke at Claremont McKenna College, another Auschwitz survivor, Theodore ("Zev") Weiss was in the audience. My initial contact with this remarkable man took place about fifteen years earlier when a phone call from Weiss started a lasting friendship. He knew about my commitment to learn and teach about the Holocaust. His dedication to such work was as determined and energetic as it was visionary and expansive. Migrating to Canada and then the United States after surviving the Holocaust, Weiss became a leading educator. In 1976, he and his wife, Alice, founded the Holocaust Educational Foundation (HEF). Part of Northwestern University since 2013, HEF advances Holocaust education, especially through its Lessons and Legacies conferences, by supporting teacher-scholars to develop Holocaust courses at universities and colleges around the world.

Gentle, humane, and characterized by an often-surprising sense of humor, Weiss participated in the discussion that ensued after Gabbai's talk ended. His intense comments rejected ranking Holocaust survivors in terms of the extremity of their experiences. But it was hard to tell whether Weiss directed his remarks to a scholar who had done just that in paying tribute to Gabbai, or whether Weiss was addressing Gabbai himself, although the Sonderkommando survivor had made no claims about his uniqueness, let alone superiority.

When the discussion ended, Gabbai and Weiss left. The room cleared, but later a few people regrouped to assess the exchanges they had witnessed. What *had* been said? What had *not* been said? One scholar ventured an opinion: Weiss had lost family members at Auschwitz, including a brother, in late 1944. Was it possible that Dario Gabbai had "processed" Zev Weiss's brother? Probably neither Gabbai nor Weiss could ever know for sure. But I am as sure as I can be that no individual has done more to advance Holocaust education than Zev Weiss. He is a source of Holocaust insight for me because he turns the cliché—one person can make a difference—into a reminding, realistic imperative that must not be forgotten.

Leopold Page/Poldek Pfefferberg

In late 1980, I met Leopold Page during lunch at a Los Angeles workshop on Holocaust education. As conversation developed, I learned much of interest. First, Page and his wife, Mila, were both Holocaust survivors. They had arrived in the United States and moved to Los Angeles in 1950. His leather goods shop in Beverly Hills specialized in high-end Italian imports. Second, Page's name during the Holocaust was Poldek Pfefferberg. He and Mila survived because their names were numbered 173 and 195, respectively, on what came to be known as "Schindler's list." Third, in a "to be continued" way, Page told me about someone I had heard of but knew little about: Oskar Schindler, the opportunistic German industrialist who saved more than a thousand Jews from deportation to Auschwitz. Fourth, Page told me about his chance meeting with an Australian novelist named Thomas Keneally, who went to Page's store one day in October 1980 in search of a replacement for his worn briefcase. As Page told me the story, when conversation revealed to Page that Keneally was a writer, he said to the Australian, "I have a story for you." By the time, Keneally left Page's store, seeds were planted that would grow into Keneally's best-selling *Schindler's List*, which the author dedicated to Pfefferberg as well as to Schindler.

My "to be continued" lunch conversation with Page did continue. It went on until his death at the age of eighty-seven in 2001.[9] Frequently, he and Mila came to Claremont to teach my students. Page had promised that he would do his best to ensure that Schindler was remembered, and he spoke about Schindler with affection and admiration, just as my students and I spoke about Leopold and Mila. He was especially enthusiastic when he told us that Stephen Spielberg planned to produce a film version of *Schindler's List*, which appeared in 1993 and won seven Academy Awards, including best picture and best director honors for Spielberg.

The Holocaust insight that I take from my friendship with Leopold Page emerges from a characteristic that defined him. He was infectiously tenacious. His survival was inseparable from Oskar Schindler. Making that story known was his passion. May his infectious tenacity, his passion, live on.

Samuel Oliner

On Thursday, April 10, 1980, a few months before I met Leopold Page, I flew to San Francisco, but the meeting awaiting me was very different from

---

9. For further information, see Martin, "Leopold Page."

the one I expected. That afternoon I was to participate in a panel called "Perspectives on the Holocaust" at a gathering of the Pacific Sociological Association. Recollections of those talks have faded, but what preceded I remember vividly.

Arriving at the Sheraton-Palace Hotel shortly before noon, I located the room for the afternoon symposium and then went to lunch. On the way, I met the panel's chairman. Strangers at that point, the two of us decided to share a table. After we exchanged pleasantries, our conversation grew more intense. My companion inquired why I was so interested in Adolf Hitler's attempted annihilation of the Jews. My identity as an American, a philosopher, and a Christian, I explained, was what impelled me to explore how the Holocaust happened. When I returned the question, the response provided my first glimpses of Samuel Oliner's complex past, his interest—as passionate as Leopold Page's—in Holocaust rescuers, and his major, growing contributions to Holocaust studies, including *The Altruistic Personality: Rescuers of Jews in Nazi Europe*, which he published with his wife, Pearl M. Oliner, in 1988. It remains important reading for anyone concerned with the ethical questions and implications raised by the Holocaust.

Narrow escapes and restless memories loom large in Oliner's Holocaust survival.[10] On Saturday, June 25, 1994, for example, he returned to Zyndranowa, a village three miles from the Slovak border in southern Poland, where he was born in 1930. On that June day, Oliner spoke at the dedication of the Zalman Jewish Museum, which he had generously helped to build. Situated in a house that had once belonged to Oliner's relatives and named after his grandfather's brother Zalman Polster, the museum honors Jews whose families lived in Poland for eight hundred years before the Holocaust decimated them.

The talk that Oliner gave that day recalled that the Germans had ghettoized his family in June 1942. Two months later, the Bobowa ghetto was "liquidated," the Nazi euphemism for *murdered*. As the killing began, Oliner heard his stepmother say that he must "run and hide" and save himself "to tell the future generations what had happened."

Run he did. Then, with the help of a Polish Christian woman named Balwina Piecuch, her son Staszek, who has been Samuel's longtime friend, and others akin to the rescuers that the sociologist Samuel Oliner would later study with such commitment, the young Samuel Oliner found places to hide and ways to save himself. Eventually he more than fulfilled his stepmother's plea to tell future generations what had happened. Sadly, that narrative had to include the fact that there were no havens for most of Oliner's

---

10. For his memoirs, see Oliner, *Restless Memories*.

immediate family. The Holocaust destroyed nearly all of them, but nevertheless Oliner's narrow escape made it possible for him to conclude his June 1994 remarks at Zyndranowa by thanking those who were caring people.

Above all else, Samuel Oliner is a caring person. He wants there to be more of them. Hence, he has spent his life trying to discern why some people proved to be much more just and caring than others during the Holocaust. Perhaps such questions cannot be answered finally, not even by study as careful as Oliner's. Yet, his research emphasizes important themes: (1) Rescuers, women and men alike, came from different social classes and diverse occupations. (2) They had deeply internalized values such as helpfulness, responsibility, fairness, justice, compassion, and friendship. (3) They had friends in groups outside of their own family circles or immediate communities. (4) They were tolerant of differences and felt responsible for many kinds of people. (5) They had high levels of self-confidence and self-esteem and were not afraid to take calculated risks. (6) They knew what was happening around them, and, in addition, benefitted from a supportive emotional network; typically, their rescue efforts met with approval from family members or others who could be trusted.[11]

I remember Samuel Oliner's belief that if he needed help and could identify persons with these qualities, his chances of receiving assistance would be excellent. His Holocaust insight for me is that the effectiveness of learning and teaching about the Holocaust hinges on their capacity to encourage such people and to enlarge their number.

Interpreters

Interpreters bridge gaps. They translate languages, clarify meanings, add understanding, and penetrate what seem impenetrable. Interpreters also widen gaps because their translations make one aware of how much eludes comprehension. Their clarifications call meaning into question. The understanding they add includes awareness that more inquiry is required, and their penetration of the impenetrable does not, must not, bring closure. Five interpreters have deepened my Holocaust insight in those ways.

---

11. For further information about Oliner's ethical outlook, see Oliner, *Nature of Good and Evil*.

Emil Fackenheim

My lone personal encounter with Emil Fackenheim took place at a conference in England during the summer of 1998. Long before and well after that brief time, his thinking has had lasting influence upon me. Fackenheim fled his native Germany in 1939 after imprisonment in the Nazi concentration camp at Sachsenhausen, taught for many years at the University of Toronto, and then immigrated to Israel, where he died in 2003. In 1968, he delivered the Charles F. Deems Lectures at New York University, which were published two years later as *God's Presence in History: Jewish Affirmations and Philosophical Reflections*. This brief and often reprinted book contains one of the most powerful of the relatively early religious responses to the Holocaust. According to Fackenheim, the Holocaust was the most radically disorienting "epoch-making" event in all Jewish history.[12] He argued that the Jewish people must respond to this shattering challenge with a reaffirmation of God's presence in history.

Fackenheim acknowledged the impossibility of affirming God's saving presence at Auschwitz, but he insisted that while no "redeeming Voice" was heard at Auschwitz, a "commanding Voice" was heard, and it enunciated a "614th commandment" to supplement the 613 commandments of traditional Judaism. The new commandment was that "the authentic Jew of today is forbidden to hand Hitler yet another, posthumous victory." Fackenheim spelled out the 614th commandment, which he first articulated in 1967, as follows:

> We are, first, commanded to survive as Jews, lest the Jewish people perish. We are commanded, second, to remember in our very guts and bones the martyrs of the Holocaust, lest their memory perish. We are forbidden, thirdly, to deny or despair of God, however much we may have to contend with Him or with belief in Him, lest Judaism perish. We are forbidden, finally, to despair of the world as the place which is to become the kingdom of God, lest we help make it a meaningless place in which God is dead or irrelevant and everything is permitted. To abandon any of these imperatives, in response to Hitler's victory at Auschwitz, would be to hand him yet other, posthumous victories.[13]

---

12. See Fackenheim, *God's Presence*, 8–14; and Fackenheim, *To Mend the World*, 9–22.

13. This passage originally appeared in Fackenheim, "Jewish Values," *Judaism* 16 (1967) 272–73. The text of Fackenheim's contribution to that journal's symposium on "Jewish Values in the Post-Holocaust Future" is reprinted in Fackenheim, *Jewish*

Few, if any, post-Holocaust religious statements by a Jewish thinker have become better known.[14] For some time, Fackenheim's 614th commandment struck a deep chord in Jews of every social level and religious commitment. Much, but by no means all, of Fackenheim's writing was on a philosophic and theological level beyond the competence of the ordinary layperson. Not so this passage, which is largely responsible for the fact that Fackenheim's interpretation of the Holocaust arguably became for a time the most influential within the Jewish community. A people that has endured catastrophic defeat is likely to see the survival of their community and its traditions as a supreme imperative. By referring to a divine command, Fackenheim gave potent expression to this aspiration. Instead of questioning whether the traditional Jewish understanding of God could be maintained after Auschwitz, he implied that those who questioned God's presence to Israel were accomplices of the worst destroyer the Jews have ever known.

The passion and the psychological power of Fackenheim's outlook affected me deeply, especially his insistence that one should think and act in ways that deny Hitler posthumous victories. That insight has informed my learning and teaching about the Holocaust. As it has done so, the insight expanded to include awareness that unfortunate consequences lurked in Fackenheim's position. Not only were those Jews "who denied or despaired" of the scriptural God seemingly cast in the role of Hitler's accomplices, a serious and controversial allegation indeed. In addition, Fackenheim went so far as to suggest that those who did not hear the "commanding Voice" from Auschwitz were *willfully* rejecting God: "In my view," he wrote, "nothing less will do than to say that a commanding Voice speaks from Auschwitz, and that there are Jews who hear it and Jews who *stop their ears*."[15] To stop one's ears is a voluntary act. Apparently Fackenheim excluded or ignored the possibility that some Jews, to say nothing of Christians like me, might honestly be unable to believe that God was present in Auschwitz, no matter how metaphorically the idea was presented. Furthermore, in spite of its power,

---

Return, 19–24. See also Fackenheim, *God's Presence*, 84–98. In the 1997 edition of the latter work, Fackenheim includes a new preface, "No Posthumous Victories for Hitler: After Thirty Years, the '614th Commandment' Reconsidered." Noting that the phrase "'no posthumous victories for Hitler' became a slogan, often poorly understood, and as such liked by some, disliked by others, mocked by a few," Fackenheim added that "what 'no posthumous victories for Hitler' asked of Jews was, of course, not to spite Hitler, but to carry on *in spite of* him" (xii, italics original).

14. One of the most noteworthy competitors for that distinction would be Irving Greenberg's "working principle," namely, that "no statement, theological or otherwise, should be made that would not be credible in the presence of the burning children." See Greenberg, "Cloud of Smoke," 23.

15. Fackenheim, *Jewish Return*, 31 (italics added).

Fackenheim's position was not without difficulty even for the tradition he sought to defend. Given his conviction that revelation was inseparable from interpretation, it was not clear whether the commanding Voice was to be taken as real or metaphorical. Subsequently, there was reason to believe that Fackenheim would reject both alternatives and hold that the commandment would have been unreal without an affirmative Jewish response. Taken literally, there does not appear to be any credible evidence that anybody heard the 614th commandment, as indeed Fackenheim's later description of how he came to write the passage indicates. In his 1982 book *To Mend the World*, Fackenheim told his readers that after he had concluded that the Holocaust was a radical challenge to Jewish faith, "my first response was to formulate a '614th commandment.'"[16] Clearly, as understood in traditional Judaism, one does not formulate a commandment. It derives from a divine source. In any event, whatever the psychological power of the 614th commandment, its status as commandment remains ambiguous.

As Fackenheim came to realize that the real difficulty lay in formulating a view of God that took the Holocaust into account, he understood that one could no longer speak of a *saving* presence at Auschwitz. Yet, utter defeat and annihilation could not be the last word. A way out of the ashes had to be found. The 614th commandment expressed what most religious Jews regard as their sacred obligation in response to the Holocaust. In the language of Jewish faith, that response could most appropriately be communicated in the imagery of the commandments.

Fackenheim's 614th commandment is religiously and existentially problematic. That outcome, however, may remain beside the point. It is perhaps best to see Fackenheim's 614th commandment as a cry of the heart, transmuted into the language of the sacred. That would at least help to explain why it has touched so many Jews—and Christians like me—so deeply.[17]

Emmanuel Levinas

The Jewish philosopher Emmanuel Levinas became my teacher not because I knew him personally, which I did not, but because trusted friends insisted that I must read and study him. Levinas argued that ethical theory had failed to concentrate on something as obvious and profound as the human face. By paying close and careful attention to the face of the other person,

---

16. Fackenheim, *To Mend the World*, 10.

17. For further commentary on Fackenheim's thought, see Patterson, *Emil L. Fackenheim*.

he affirmed, there could be a reorientation not only of ethics but also of human life itself, for our seeing of the other person's face would drive home how closely human beings are connected and how much the existence of the other person confers responsibility upon us. When I taught Levinas to my students, those ideas spoke to them.

Levinas did not write explicitly about the Holocaust very often, but traces of that catastrophe appear, and the overt emphases of his thought make plain that the Holocaust was a powerful point of reference between the lines, in the silence—the void even—that shadows his philosophy. On some occasions, however, the Holocaust came to the fore. One example is found in his brief but highly significant 1982 essay called "Useless Suffering." In that article, Levinas explicitly stated a conviction that permeated his thought early and late. "The Holocaust of the Jewish people under the reign of Hitler," said Levinas, "seems to me the paradigm of gratuitous human suffering, in which evil appears in its diabolical horror."[18]

As a French prisoner of war, Levinas did forced labor under the Nazis, and almost all his Lithuanian family perished in the Holocaust. Calling the twentieth century one of "unutterable suffering," he emphasized that suffering of the kind that the Nazis and their collaborators inflicted on Europe's Jews was and is "for nothing." To try to justify such suffering religiously, ethically, or politically was what Levinas called "the source of all immorality."[19]

When Levinas said that the useless suffering inflicted during the Holocaust was "for nothing," he did not overlook Nazi "logic" and what it meant. To the contrary, he took National Socialism to be about arrogant destruction, its grandiose rhetoric about a thousand-year Reich notwithstanding. The chief element in National Socialism's arrogance was that regime's remorseless determination to deface the human face. The Nazis committed that atrocity not in some abstract way, but through useless suffering visited upon Jewish women, children, and men that made Nazism's antisemitic prerogatives dominant until overwhelming force stopped them.

Levinas believed that "all evil relates back to suffering," which is not confined to "persistent or obstinate" bodily pain but includes "helplessness, abandonment and solitude," an abjection intensified when "a moan, a cry, a groan or a sigh" bring no relief but are swallowed up by silence. He distinguished between "*suffering in the other*" and what he called "suffering *in me*." The latter's uselessness could have meaning insofar as it was "a suffering for the suffering (inexorable though it may be) of someone else." As for the

---

18. Levinas, "Useless Suffering," 91–101. The quoted passage is on page 97.

19. The quotations in this paragraph are from Levinas, "Useless Suffering," 93, 94, and 99.

uselessness of the suffering of the other, Levinas thought that striving to relieve it and to resist the forces that created it should be "raised to the level of supreme ethical principle—the only one it is impossible to question—shaping the hopes and commanding the practical discipline of vast human groups."[20]

No sooner did Levinas write those words than he issued a caution about them. In no way should they be construed as a justification for suffering, as a mitigation of suffering's uselessness because such suffering could become the means to the good and the virtue of relieving it. Observing that its temptations should not be underestimated, Levinas rejected all forms of *theodicy*, the attempt to make suffering "comprehensible," to find "in a suffering that is essentially gratuitous and absurd, and apparently arbitrary, a meaning and an order." Noting that "Nietzsche's saying about the death of God" had taken on "the meaning of a quasi-empirical fact" in the Holocaust, and that Fackenheim's allusion to the commanding voice at Auschwitz, which entailed "a revelation from the very God who nevertheless was silent at Auschwitz," was inescapably paradoxical, Levinas nevertheless affirmed that Fackenheim saw something of seminal importance not only for Jews but for humanity itself. Levinas put his point in the form of an extended question: "Must not humanity now, in a faith more difficult than before, in a faith without theodicy, continue to live out Sacred History; a history that now demands even more from the resources of the *I* in each one of us, and from its suffering inspired by the suffering of the other, from its compassion which is a non-useless suffering (or love), which is no longer suffering 'for nothing,' and immediately has meaning?"[21] Levinas's insight—it became mine—was that he could not answer this question, at least not simply, because the response to it depends on how humanity breaks the silence that follows his asking.

Lawrence Langer

Few people have listened more persistently or carefully to the oral testimony of Holocaust survivors than Lawrence Langer, who has been my friend and teacher for more than thirty years.[22] With some of that testimony in mind, he once said that "there is nothing to be learned from a baby torn in two

---

20. The quotations in this paragraph are from Levinas, "Useless Suffering," 92–94.

21. The quotations in this paragraph are from Levinas, "Useless Suffering," 96–97 and 99–100.

22. Especially relevant in this regard is Langer, *Holocaust Testimonies*.

or a woman buried alive."[23] That trenchant comment is emblematic of his rejection of the idea that moral lessons about "the triumph of the human spirit" or about "the transcendence of good over evil" can be learned from the testimony of "former victims," Langer's preferred way of referring to Holocaust survivors, and one that also could identify those who escaped death in other genocides and mass atrocities.

Langer's listening convinced him that the testimony of former victims is laden with what the Auschwitz survivor Charlotte Delbo called "useless knowledge." Such knowledge does not unify, edify, or dignify the lives of former victims. It divides, besieges, and diminishes them instead. If we really let testimony in and do not preempt it for inappropriately optimistic goals, the effects on those of us who receive testimony may be similar. Langer's unflinching analysis of survivor testimonies insists that the truth they tell resists interpretations that console. Instead, the disruption, absence, and irreversible loss recalled by them are a reminder and a warning. The reminder is that the testimonies of former victims need not have existed if the power of those who perpetrate genocide and other mass atrocities had been checked in time, and if those targeted for destruction had not been so defenseless. The warning is related: Although safety and security are never guaranteed, they do depend on the strength and commitment of the communities in which one dwells.

Speaking from his own experience, Langer has rightly insisted that listening to Holocaust testimonies requires extraordinary effort. They can easily be distorted and falsified by the imposition of interpretations—moral, philosophical, psychological, or religious—that rely on what he calls "the grammar of heroism and martyrdom" and thus fall far short because they belong to a universe of normal discourse that the Holocaust eclipsed. The human mind would naturally like to reduce the dissonance that Holocaust testimonies introduce, heal the heartbreak left intact in their wake. The yearning runs deep for justice to prevail, wholeness to be restored, moral expectation to be vindicated, and the human spirit to be triumphant. But that yearning collides with Langer's convincing insistence that the anatomy of melancholy does not favor those hopes.

The insight is that Langer's interpretation splits me. In the ruins of memory, expectation diminishes, and yearning intensifies. As those feelings, conflicted and conflicting, resound in the testimony he has heard, Langer moves me to encounter them and to let the resulting tension remain as it must: unreconciled and unreconciling.

---

23. Langer, *Preempting*, 10.

Zygmunt Bauman

In 1939, Zygmunt Bauman, in his early teens at the time, fled with his family to the Soviet Union after Nazi Germany invaded his native Poland on September 1. Eventually enlisting in the Soviet-controlled First Polish Army, he participated in the conquest of Berlin that spelled the end of the Third Reich. After the war, he studied sociology and taught in Poland at the University of Warsaw until 1968, when an antisemitic political purge forced him to renounce Polish citizenship in order to leave the country. He taught in Israel for a time, and then, in 1971, he relocated to the University of Leeds in England, where he was a professor for twenty years and continued to write for two decades more. In 2010, seven years before his death at the age of ninety-one, the university established the Bauman Institute for Sociology and Social Theory in his honor.

An eminent sociologist and philosopher, Bauman had a discerning eye and ethical insight that led to more than sixty significant books, but none proved more important than *Modernity and the Holocaust*, which appeared in 1989. Two years earlier, Richard Rubenstein and I published the first edition of *Approaches to Auschwitz*. We were pleased that Bauman chose a statement from our book to serve as the epigraph for his first chapter: "Civilization now includes death camps and *Muselmänner* among its material and spiritual products."[24] He quoted each of us further, noting my observation that "had Nazi power prevailed, authority to determine what ought to be would have found that no natural laws were broken and no crimes against God and humanity were committed in the Holocaust," and finding "the ultimate lesson of the Holocaust" in Rubenstein's proposition that the Holocaust "bears witness to the *advance of civilization*."[25]

Bauman underscored that the Holocaust was "a *Jewish tragedy*," but the genocide was neither "simply a *Jewish problem*" nor "an event in *Jewish history* alone." In fact, Bauman, argued, the Holocaust, far from being "an irrational outflow of the not-yet-fully eradicated residues of pre-modern barbarity, ... *was born and executed in our modern rational society, at the high stage of our civilization and at the peak of human cultural achievement*."[26] Bauman cited Rubenstein with approval because Rubenstein's claim about

---

24. Bauman, *Modernity*, 1. See also Rubenstein and Roth, *Approaches to Auschwitz* (1987), 324. For a significant reflection on the *Muselmänner*, prisoners so wasted in the camps that they were living dead before their death arrived, see Agamben, *Remnants of Auschwitz*.

25. Bauman, *Modernity*, 7, 9. See also Roth, "Holocaust Business," 70; and Rubenstein, *Cunning of History*, 91.

26. Bauman, *Modernity*, x, 17 (italics original).

the links between the Holocaust and civilization's advance supported Bauman's keen insight: Not only did Nazi Germany depend on the technology and bureaucracy that made Holocaust-scale mass murder possible but also the instrumental rationality—especially its means-ends calculus and cost-benefit analysis—that had given rise to those modern developments carried within it perspectives and values that aided and abetted genocidal population riddance.

Bauman's position was not immune to criticism. Nazism, some criticisms said, was a reaction against the Enlightenment, not a product of that modern development. Antisemitism, said others, was more salient as a cause of the Holocaust than Bauman thought. Barbarism, still others held, was rife in the Holocaust; emphasis on instrumental rationality, technology, and bureaucracy alone could scarcely explain the genocide. Nevertheless, Bauman's outlook stands strong because his analysis contains a warning as stark as it is grounded in harsh experience: *"we live in a type of society that made the Holocaust possible, and that contained nothing which could stop the Holocaust from happening."*[27]

Bauman saw a forlorn possibility. If there had been stronger ethical commitments for justice and against murder, especially but not only in the Third Reich, the Holocaust might have been prevented. But through its dehumanizing racist and antisemitic propaganda, police-state bureaucracy, nationalistic militarism—thoroughly modern in their scope and dominance—Nazi power quashed that option. So much so, thought Bauman, that his quotation from my essay summarized a key implication embedded in a Third Reich triumphant: Had Nazi power prevailed, authority to determine what ought to be would have found that no natural laws were broken and no crimes against God and humanity were committed in the Holocaust.

Over the years, I have spoken and written less about Bauman than about the persons discussed in this book's chapters titled with their names. But I increasingly recognize that he is a principal source of Holocaust insight because his work was decisive in my understanding of the fragility and failure of ethics. For Bauman, even if modernity included emphases on human rights and human equality, the power of its politically-harnessed instrumental rationality and technology could suppress and override ethical restraints. What's more, that power could manipulate, neutralize, and relativize ethics into irrelevance, or subvert it by repurposing key ethical concepts—duty and responsibility, conscience and loyalty—into "ideals" that legitimate discrimination, patriotism, and violence in ways that become genocidal.

27. Bauman, *Modernity*, 88 (italics original).

Bauman, however, rejected the crippling idea that evil is all-powerful. "It can be resisted," he insisted. Joining other post-Holocaust thinkers, Bauman took that possibility to be forlorn unless a resilient, new ethics can be found and enacted. Taking inspiration from Emmanuel Levinas, whom he called "the greatest moral philosopher of the twentieth century," Bauman envisioned an ethics that had to reach over "socially erected obstacles" and the "reduction of the human self."[28] Advancing such an outlook motivates my learning and teaching about the Holocaust.

Tadeusz Borowksi

On July 3, 1951, before I was much aware of the Holocaust, the Polish writer and journalist Tadeusz Borowski died at the age of twenty-eight. He was not Jewish, but he was among thousands of Poles who were sent to Auschwitz, arriving there in late April 1943. His tattooed camp number was 119198. Honesty about what he saw and took away from Auschwitz makes him a distinctive source of Holocaust insight.

Borowski finished his university degree "underground," because the Germans prohibited such training for Poles. Completing his last examinations just as major roundups began in Warsaw during the spring of 1940, he found work that kept him from being conscripted for labor in Germany. He wrote, too, his poetry and prose appearing in Warsaw's clandestine press. Eventually arrested and jailed for his resistance activities, he spent two months in Pawiak, the notorious prison that stood adjacent to the Warsaw ghetto. From his cell, he saw the Jewish uprising that broke out on April 19, 1943, and the German retaliation. At Auschwitz, he nearly died from pneumonia, but luck was with him, and he found himself assigned to relatively light work, ultimately serving as a medic. Evacuated from Auschwitz in the late summer of 1944, Borowski was liberated at Dachau the next May. In time, he returned to Poland. He seemed destined to be an important voice in the Communist press. That future, however, was cut short when he opened a gas valve in his kitchen on July 1, 1951. Two days later he was dead from likely suicidal gas poisoning.

Published posthumously, a collection called *This Way for the Gas, Ladies and Gentlemen* contains some of the remarkable short stories that Borowski left behind. They are about Auschwitz and Borowski as well. They were written shortly after his release and authored in the first person. The narrator in several of the stories is Vorarbeiter Tadeusz, a deputy kapo in Auschwitz. This perspective gives Borowski's stories uncompromising

---

28. Bauman, *Modernity*, 207, 214, 221.

realism, bitter irony, and humane feeling all at once, each of these qualities complicated by Borowski's experience—involving what Primo Levi would call the "gray zone"—that some boundaries between victim and executioner are blurred.

Less than a thousand words long, a brief post-Auschwitz meditation called "The Visit" appears toward the end of *This Way for the Gas, Ladies and Gentlemen*. Looking out a window, the narrator sits at a writing desk. He recollects: men working, weeping, gathering fortunes, killing; women doing the same. He also recalls those on their way to the gas who "begged the orderlies loading them into the crematorium trucks to remember what they saw. And to tell the truth about mankind to those who do not know it."[29] The narrator ponders the many men and women he saw in Auschwitz. He will write about them, but he wonders "which one of them I should visit today." His selection is complicated, he notes, because "I am troubled by one persistent thought—that I have never been able to look also at myself." In his stories, Borowski did look at himself, perhaps so much so that the looking drove him to the gas. "I do not know," he wrote, "whether we shall survive, but I like to think that one day we shall have the courage to tell the world the whole truth and call it by its proper name."[30] Borowski's "whole truth" fosters disillusionment. No less than his stories, the outcome of his life enjoins Borowski's readers to be troubled, persistently, about what to make of the disillusionment that an honest encounter with the Holocaust unavoidably creates.

In *This Way for the Gas, Ladies and Gentlemen*, disillusionment begins with the statement that "all of us walk around naked." While waiting for a new transport to arrive, Vorarbeiter Tadeusz and his fellow inmates are deloused. Their nakedness, however, turns out to be more than physical. In this Auschwitz block dwell prisoners with privileges. They have enough to eat. Though "a bit coarse to the taste," their bread is "crisp, crunchy." There is bacon, milk, even French wine, because after these laborers unload the trains of people destined for death, they can take some of the food left behind. Other items required to enhance life in Auschwitz can be "organized" later from the huge storage area known as "Canada." Concern mounts when transports do not arrive. Work is hard when the cars roll in, but as Henri says, "They can't run out of people, or we'll starve to death in this blasted camp. All of us live on what they bring."[31]

---

29. Borowski, *This Way*, 175.
30. Borowski, *This Way*, 176, 122.
31. Borowski, *This Way*, 29–31.

Henri's friend, the narrator of this story, does other work. He has not been on the ramp before, that place where the new arrivals undergo selection. Having cleared things with the kapo, Henri invites him along. Off they go to meet Polish Jews from Sosnowiec-Będzin. On this bright, hot day, the first cars reach Auschwitz shortly after noon. The unloading begins. Ironically, "a Red Cross van drives back and forth, back and forth, incessantly: it transports the gas that will kill these people." Darkness brings no relief—until the last of the thousands have been dispatched. Even Henri, who can claim that "since Christmas, at least a million people have passed through my hands," is exhausted. He and his comrades, however, have their reward. For several days the entire camp will be sustained by the Sosnowiec-Będzin Jews, who are already burning. Everyone will agree that "Sosnowiec-Będzin was a good, rich transport."[32]

The Auschwitz described in Borowski's stories is filled with reports of filth, disease, starvation, sadistic violence, and mass murder. His point is that in this world of human domination and destruction such happenings have become so commonplace that it is possible to add, "Work is not unpleasant when one has eaten a breakfast of smoked bacon with bread and garlic and washed it down with a tin of evaporated milk." He suggests that Auschwitz is a new form of human society where living depends on dying; living well depends on access to power that condemns others. Not that the appalling quality of such relationships goes unnoticed—the brutality is not disguised or rationalized—but Borowski's narrator matter-of-factly frames events that seem poles apart and yet are part of the same time and space at Auschwitz. In the spring of 1943, for example, the medical orderlies get to build a soccer field near the hospital barracks. One Sunday, as the narrator reports in "The People Who Walked On," "I was goalkeeper." Although the selection ramp could be viewed from the playing field, the goalkeeper's back was to it when a train arrived. Retrieving a ball that had gone out of bounds, he noticed the arrivals. A short while later, the ball again went astray. A second time the goalkeeper's attention was drawn to the ramp. It stood empty; the train was gone too. Virtually unnoticed—perhaps because the process was so routine, or because the goalkeeper's attention was so much on the game, or both—"between two throw-ins in a soccer game, right behind my back, three thousand people had been put to death."[33]

Borowski's narrator is no unfeeling brute. If he smiles "condescendingly when people speak to me of morality, of law, of tradition, of obligation," he also feels revulsion and outrage over the cruel juxtaposition of events and

---

32. Borowski, *This Way*, 38, 46, 49.
33. Borowski, *This Way*, 58, 83, 84.

believes that evil "ought to be punished. No question about it." Witnessing the incongruity of an infant in Auschwitz, he feels that he would also "like to have a child with rose-colored cheeks and light blond hair."[34] And though he would dismiss that vision as a "ridiculous notion," he has written love letters to his fiancée, who is also an Auschwitz prisoner.

No "philosophic formula" can grasp all that happens at Auschwitz, partly because what seems inexplicable and abnormal has become totally familiar. Without "hocus pocus" or "hypnosis," mass murder happens, and "we have now become a part of it." This, too, is reported matter-of-factly, without self-loathing or righteous indignation. Yet the letter-writer quietly urges an outlook less resigned: "Look carefully at everything around you, and conserve your strength. For a day may come when it will be up to us to give an account of the fraud and mockery to the living—to speak up for the dead."[35]

When it comes to revealing how the Holocaust mocked human life, nothing is more important than to testify that human domination can become so oppressive that it turns hope, that most natural and irrepressible emotion, into a trap. "We were never taught how to give up hope," Borowski says, "and this is why today we perish in gas chambers." He means that, apart from our own power, there is nothing to guarantee that human domination will not reduce a person's life to "a body that has been exploited to the utmost: with a number tattooed on it to save on dog tags, with just enough sleep at night to work during the day, and just enough time to eat. And just enough food so it will not die wastefully . . . If you die—your gold teeth, already recorded in the camp inventory are extracted. Your body is burned and your ashes are used to fertilize the fields or fill in the ponds." Borowski's disillusionment does not stop with the realization that victims fitting those descriptions are real. It also announces honestly how widespread the complicity can be. Disillusionments about safety and immunity must be accompanied by those that unmask pretense about virtue and innocence. Borowski said of the camp, indeed of the whole world, "this is a monstrous lie, a grotesque lie."[36] Hope, too, is deceptively false unless it can be forged out of disillusionment's truth.

Where disillusionment's truth will lead, especially when hope is involved, is uncertain, as a few final glimpses of Borowski's work make clear. In "Silence," a group of released prisoners are about to lynch an SS guard. Unwittingly, a young American officer intervenes when he enters the newly

---

34. Borowski, *This Way*, 110, 90, 89.
35. Borowski, *This Way*, 112–13, 115–16.
36. Borowski, *This Way*, 122, 131, 142.

liberated barracks to urge respect for law and to assure the men that the guilty will be brought to justice. Feigning approval, waiting until the officer had stopped at all the blocks and returned to his headquarters, the ex-prisoners drag the SS man to the floor, "where the entire block, grunting and growling with hatred, trampled him to death."[37]

In "The January Offensive," Borowski recounts a postwar discussion in which some former inmates of concentration camps insist that "morality, national solidarity, patriotism and the ideals of freedom, justice and human dignity had all slid off man like a rotten rag." Listening to them was a Polish poet who responded with an incident that reputedly occurred in January 1945. After fierce fighting, Russian troops had freed a Polish city from German control and were advancing west. Among the Russian soldiers, needing attention at the hospital in that place, was a young woman. Though unwounded, she was pregnant and in labor. Her healthy child born, they stayed at the hospital only a single day. Baby tied to her back, automatic rifle in hand, she resumed her way to Berlin. The former inmates were skeptical. If the poet's story was not made up, it certainly suggested that the Russian woman had not been humane, for she had needlessly endangered the life of her own child. The discussion ended, but in a postscript Borowski adds that one of the Auschwitz comrades eventually received a letter from a woman "whom he had left pregnant in the gypsy camp when in October '44 he was taken in a transport from Birkenau to Gross-Rosen, Flossenburg and Dachau."[38] Along with hundreds of other sick and pregnant women, that mother and her child had been saved by the Russians' January offensive.

Back in Warsaw, Borowski's narrating writer notes that the world has for some time seemed to be "inflating at incredible speed, like some ridiculous soap bubble" which "will dissolve forever into emptiness, as though it were made not of solid matter but only of fleeting sound." He describes his feelings in his new-old postwar city, noting the crumb-dry dust of the ruins, the newly installed windows and freshly painted walls of restored buildings, whose rooms are occupied by people of importance. He goes there to ask, "perhaps a trifle too politely, for things that are perhaps too trivial, but to which nevertheless I am entitled—but which, of course, cannot keep the world from swelling and bursting like an over-ripe pomegranate, leaving behind but a handful of grey, dry ashes." The crowds of people he sees on the streets during the day seem to him to make a weird snarl, a gigantic stew,

---

37. Borowski, *This Way*, 163.
38. Borowski, *This Way*, 166–68.

flowing "along the street, down the gutter," and seeping "into space with a loud gurgle, like water into a sewer."[39]

As darkness falls, he looks out a window, then pushes himself away and heads for his writing desk, engulfed by a feeling that he has lost valuable time. The world still exists. He will try to muster "a tender feeling" for those who remain in it, and "attempt to grasp the true significance of the events, things and people I have seen. For I intend to write a great, immortal epic, worthy of this unchanging, difficult world chiselled out of stone."[40]

Is this ending ironic, perhaps made even more so by Borowski's suicide, or did he accomplish what he intended to do? The answer depends on what can—and cannot—be said. It also depends on how one answers this question: where does the Holocaust's disillusionment lead? In Borowski's case, the answer remains ambiguous and ambivalent, because the truth he could discern did not point in a single, clear-cut direction, least of all to optimism. Unmistakably, though, Borowski placed a premium on exposing illusion. In that respect, the words of his living and the silence of his dying are of one piece. Both resound with his insightful insistence: "It will be up to us to give an account of the fraud and mockery to the living—to speak up for the dead."[41]

Postscript

Without well-educated people to launch, drive, and sustain it, the destruction of the European Jews could not have happened. The resisting German theologian Dietrich Bonhoeffer saw the paradox and irony in those relationships. The Nazis arrested and imprisoned him on April 5, 1943, and, at the age of thirty-nine, he was executed by hanging two years later, on April 9, 1945. Bonhoeffer's insightful writings include a brief but powerful essay called "After Ten Years." Written in December 1942, it assessed what had happened in Germany after the Nazis took control in late January 1933. His thoughts crafted in seventeen short reflections, Bonhoeffer shared them only with a small circle of close friends. In the penultimate section, he wondered whether he and his friends were still of any use.

Then and now, the importance of Bonhoeffer and his friends has been huge. The example of their resistance remains, and Bonhoeffer's writings continue to be studied because they are timely, perceptive, and prophetic. "After Ten Years" fits that description and nowhere more so than in four

---

39. Borowski, *This Way*, 177, 179.
40. Borowski, *This Way*, 180.
41. Borowski, *This Way*, 115–16.

paragraphs that he called "On Stupidity" (Von der Dummheit). They epitomize the paradox that education does not preclude stupidity, at least not completely; they disclose the irony that mass murder not only depends on advanced learning but, stupidly, can thrive within it.

"Stupidity," wrote Bonhoeffer, "is a more dangerous enemy of the good than malice."[42] Here's why Bonhoeffer thought so. "There are human beings," he observed, "who are of remarkably agile intellect yet stupid." Sound reasons do not reach their deaf ears, facts that contradict their prejudgment "simply need not be believed . . . and when facts are irrefutable they are just pushed aside as inconsequential, as incidental." Such stupidity leads to self-satisfaction, and thus to irritation that produces danger when attacks against opposition follow. Bonhoeffer's implication, I believe, is that Nazi ideology was rife with educated stupidity, exemplified by the falsehood that Jews are a pestilential race that must be eliminated root and branch.

Stupidity made Nazism lethal, because, as Bonhoeffer understood, stupidity is "not an intellectual defect but a human one" that has sociological as well as psychological qualities. "People," contended Bonhoeffer, can be "*made stupid* or . . . they allow this to happen to them" because "the overwhelming impact of rising power" can deprive people of "inner independence" so that "one virtually feels that one is dealing not at all with . . . a person, but with slogans, catchwords, and the like." Such stupidity could make people "capable of any evil and at the same time incapable of seeing that it is evil."

An unrelenting effect of Nazi power, stupidity was essential to sustain the policies and practices that constituted the "Final Solution." In Bonhoeffer's view, such stupidity, once entrenched, would not yield to instruction or persuasion, at least not completely. Nevertheless, he was not hopeless. Stupidity, Bonhoeffer emphasized, is not "a congenital defect," nor are most people stupid "in every circumstance." Everything depends, he concluded "on whether those in power expect more from people's stupidity than from their inner independence and wisdom."

Nazi stupidity cost Dietrich Bonhoeffer his life long before I knew anything about him, but my friendship with a Holocaust survivor named Joseph Rebhun, a highly esteemed doctor who lived in Claremont, California, drove home insights related to Bonhoeffer's.[43] Rebhun was born and raised in the Polish city of Przemysl. During World War II, it was under Soviet control

---

42. The quotations from "On Stupidity" are from Bonhoeffer, "After Ten Years," 22–23. Some translations use *folly* to translate the German *Dummheit*. But Bonhoeffer's meaning is better captured by *stupidity*.

43. In addition to his medical expertise as an allergist and immunologist, Rebhun has been a writer who thoughtfully explored his Holocaust experiences. His books include *Leap to Life*, *God and Man*, and *Crisis of Morality*.

for a time, but the Germans took the city in late June 1941. Soon, the Jews were ghettoized, and then deportations to Auschwitz began. Rebhun, twenty-two, and his sixty-eight-year-old mother (the Germans had already killed his father) jumped from their train. He never saw his mother again, but escaping an Auschwitz death, he miraculously—at least to him—managed to get an identity card labeling him a Polish Catholic, survived the Holocaust, met Marie, his wife (a survivor of twelve concentration camps), in postwar Austria, and settled in Claremont after arriving in the United States via Ellis Island.

On one occasion, we participated in a panel on ethics at the Loma Linda University School of Medicine. Rebhun spoke about his medical education, which had partly taken place in Austria after World War II ended. His teachers included former Nazi doctors. Rebhun emphasized their technical competence and their reliable teaching. But he probably agreed with Bonhoeffer that such educated men could also be stupid. I remember asking Rebhun if those erstwhile Nazi doctors knew that he, one of their students, was Jewish. "Yes," he said, adding with an ironic smile I have not forgotten, "they treated me with courtesy and respect."

Most often I saw Rebhun when he visited my courses on the Holocaust. He was patient and gentle with the students and their questions, but intensity grew when he explained what he hoped to accomplish by teaching them about the Holocaust and his personal experience in it. He hoped that his testimony might *inoculate* them—his word, I remember it—against antisemitism and racism. By implication, he was also hoping to provide, even to be, a vaccine against stupidity. Rebhun knew that such inoculations and vaccines do not exist, but his point was neither naïve nor lost. He prescribed what is needed, while realizing, like Bonhoeffer, that what had to be sought instead was inner independence and wisdom.

Education is not enough to secure those virtues, but it is still essential if the stupidity that inflames antisemitism, racism, and mass-atrocity crimes is to be reduced and curbed. So, while "retirement" means that I no longer have the privilege of daily meetings with college students, I have found it worthwhile to return to seventh grade.

For several years, I have met annually with girls and boys at Liberty Bell Middle School, which is near my home in Winthrop, Washington. The students are part of a twenty-year tradition, inspired and sustained by dedicated teachers such as Jane Orme, Jana Mohr Lone, Dani Golden, Laura Schrager, and Cam Alford. Year in and year out, Liberty Bell teachers spend six weeks guiding the students' study of *The Diary of Anne Frank*. I supplement their teaching with background about the Holocaust, the history of antisemitism and Nazism, the power of propaganda and hatred, the importance of resistance and rescue.

Like Bonhoeffer, I sometimes wonder if I am of any use, because what the seventh-graders are studying is full of more complexity, destruction, and loss than their early teen awareness can fathom. But deep down, I know that I must try to impart some Holocaust insight to them. Occasionally, they show me that learning is taking place. They grasp, for example, that Anne's diary contains a sad narrative because it bears witness, partly through her grit, determination, and hope against hope, that something badly wrong happened when Nazi power forced the Frank family to hide, unsuccessfully, for their lives. They are troubled deeply by the betrayal of the Frank family. They wonder, as they put it, "who ratted them out." What's more, the students experience a worthwhile frustration when they learn that we don't know for sure.

One day, while we were talking about antisemitism, discussion led to the swastika, its symbolism and meaning. When we focused on the fact that antisemitism by no means stopped when the Holocaust ended, and I asked the students if they knew that swastikas sometimes deface synagogues and schools in the United States today, we ended up talking about a place or two at Liberty Bell where the students had seen one. Together, we had a teachable moment as powerful as any I have experienced in fifty years.

Learning and teaching about the Holocaust are not a vaccine against stupidity and its allies, but in the seventh grade I have found young friends and savvy teachers who help to convince me that Bonhoeffer had a point, one that echoes themes that Anne Frank explored almost concurrently, when he wrote in December 1942 that while there can certainly be "a stupid, cowardly optimism . . . in its essence optimism is not a way of looking at the present situation but a power of life, a power of hope when others resign, a power to hold our heads high when all seems to have come to naught, a power to tolerate setbacks, a power that never abandons the future to the opponent but lays claim to it."[44] My sources of Holocaust insight are many and varied. They include Bonhoeffer's discernment about stupidity and his realism about optimism, Rebhun's ironic smile and vision of never-to-be-found vaccines, Anne Frank's youthful yearning ("cycling, dancing, whistling, looking out into the world, feeling young, to know that I'm free—that's what I long for") and the learning that can happen in seventh grade.[45]

44. For Bonhoeffer's reflections on optimism, see Bonhoeffer, "After Ten Years," 29.

45. The Anne Frank quotation comes from her diary entry on December 24, 1943. See Frank, *Diary*, 123–24. On that same Christmas Eve, Dietrich Bonhoeffer wrote from his Tegel prison cell to his friends Renate and Eberhard Bethge. "Nothing," he said, "can make up for the absence of someone who we love, and it would be wrong to try to find a substitute; we must simply hold out and see it through" (Bonhoeffer, *Letters and Papers*, 176). Frank and Bonhoeffer both held out. Neither of them, however, saw it through, at least not completely.

7

Sarah Kofman and Charlotte Delbo

One day in 1992, the year before Carol Rittner and I published *Different Voices: Women and the* Holocaust, I was in my college's library looking for words that could help to introduce our book. I found what I needed when I opened *Dark Soliloquy: The Selected Poems of Gertrud Kolmar* and read a poem called "The Woman Poet."[1] The poem's voice urges the reader to take heed, to be aware that "a person lives within the page you thumb." Revealing that line's meaning, the poem ended with a question: "You hear me speak. But do you hear me feel?" As I read what "The Woman Poet" had to say, especially as I felt the powerful question at the end, I knew I had found the right words for *Different Voices*'s governing epigraph.

Gertrud Kolmar was one of the most promising writers of her generation. Like the talent and the lives of so many in her time and place, however, her talent and her life were taken away from her by antisemitism, racism, and genocide. A German Jewish woman, she managed to survive in Berlin until the winter of 1943. In February of that year, the Germans intensified their deportation of the last Jews from that city, even those who worked in war-essential industries. The last writings we have from Kolmar are letters dated February 20–21, 1943. She was most likely caught in the roundup of Jewish workers that took place a few days later. The exact date of Kolmar's death in Auschwitz, the camp to which she was almost certainly deported from Berlin, remains unknown. "You hear me speak. But do you hear me feel?" Kolmar wrote those words sometime before she entered Auschwitz,

---

1. See Kolmar, *Dark Soliloquy*, 55–57. The poem is also accessible online. See the end of the bibliography for the URL that links to the poem. See also Kolmar, *My Gaze*; Kühn, *Gertrud Kolmar*; and Langer, *Versions*.

but especially after Auschwitz her words speak even more poignantly, tragically, and urgently than before.

The same must be said of Sarah Kofman and Charlotte Delbo. Although I never knew them, they also speak to me through their writings. Listening to their words—attempting to see what they want their readers to discern and trying to sense what they want them to feel—makes those women, like Kolmar, sources of Holocaust insight significantly different from all the others I have known.

My listening to Delbo began well before *Different Voices* appeared in 1993, but she played an important part in that book and in my Holocaust insight because she loathed abstraction, rejected sentimentality, and despised dishonesty even more. Kofman affected me later but not less importantly. In the summer of 2001, it was my privilege to lead a two-week seminar at the United States Holocaust Memorial Museum. Focused on "Ethics after the Holocaust," it explored testimonies and texts by important writers such as Emmanuel Levinas and Emil Fackenheim, Hannah Arendt and Charlotte Delbo. Each seminar participant took responsibility for leading discussion on the contributions of one of the writers. My interest in philosophers who wrote about the Holocaust had made me aware of Sarah Kofman, but until I assigned myself responsibility for leading discussion about her contributions to ethics after the Holocaust, I had not read her writings. Listening to her voice in the pages of two small but immensely important books—*Rue Ordener, Rue Labat* and *Smothered Words*—decisively moved me. The lines that follow from *Smothered Words* provide only one telling example.

> How is it possible to speak, when you feel . . . a strange *double bind*: an infinite claim to speak, *a duty to speak infinitely*, imposing itself with irrepressible force, and at the same time, an almost physical impossibility to speak, a *choking* feeling.[2]

Paying close attention to the Holocaust's implications for ethics, a philosopher like me is bound to feel a version of the double bind that Kofman identified. One feels a duty to speak, an obligation to make ethics stronger and less subject to overriding or subversion, an insistence not only to drive home the difference between right and wrong but also to influence action accordingly. Yet such work can produce a choking feeling, a sense that too much harm has been done for a good recovery to be made, a suspicion that ethics may be overwhelmed by the challenges it faces. The bind is double, for the sense of ethical responsibility, real though it is, remains hopelessly

---

2. Kofman, *Smothered Words*, 38–39 (italics original). Parts of this chapter are adapted from Roth, *Holocaust Politics*; Roth and Rubenstein, *Approaches to Auschwitz*; Roth, *Ethics*; Roth, *Failures of Ethics*; and Roth, "Double Binds."

optimistic and naïve unless it grapples with the despair that encounters with the Holocaust are bound to produce. To be touched by that despair, however, scarcely encourages one to believe that ethical responsibilities will be sufficiently accepted. Caught between the post-Holocaust need to speak for ethics and above all to speak ethically and boldly, on the one hand, and the feeling that the key elements of ethics—words, arguments, appeals to reason, persuasion through the example of moral action—may be inadequate, on the other, the question persists: What can and should be made of ethics after Auschwitz? It is doubtful that such a question can be answered, at least if one expects answers to bring finality and closure. But there can be responses, and that is what Holocaust insight attempts to provide, even if in fragmented form such as the glimpses Kofman offers about what she called "the possibility of a new ethics."[3]

Knotted Words

What can words say? What can they do? Words can be put to many uses. They can make statements and ask questions. They can mystify and deconstruct; they can be used against themselves. Speeches, propaganda, orders, laws—these are only a few of the ways language can advance mass murder. Testimonies, memoirs, poems, stories—these are only a few of the ways in which language can bear witness to atrocity. Words can kill. Without them, the Holocaust could not happen. Words are also memory's voice. They can protest and heal, but they cannot do everything. One reason is that words can be smothered or, as Sarah Kofman sometimes said, words can be knotted. The Holocaust produced knotted words, especially for the survivors, for such words, suggested Kofman, are "demanded and yet forbidden, because for too long they have been internalized and withheld." Knotted words, she went on to say, "stick in your throat and cause you to suffocate, to lose your breath"; they "asphyxiate you, taking away the possibility of even beginning."[4]

Kofman understood all too well what she was saying, for this French philosopher was a Holocaust survivor. Like some other important writers who also endured that catastrophe—Jean Améry, Tadeusz Borowski, Paul Celan, and probably Primo Levi—she took her own life. Kofman left behind a rich collection of philosophical works, among them significant writings on Sigmund Freud and Friedrich Nietzsche as well as major contributions to feminist theory. Her voice, which was often heard on French radio and

3. Kofman, *Smothered Words*, 73.
4. Kofman, *Smothered Words*, 39.

in political debate, earned its prominence in an influential generation of French philosophers that included Jacques Derrida, Emmanuel Levinas, and Jean-Luc Nancy, who said of Kofman that "fidelity was for her the very course of life. Not 'truth' but fidelity, the truth of fidelity, which has no final sense but the sense of its very course. Truth that returns to life and not the converse."[5]

Kofman is better known in many philosophical and literary circles than the other survivor-suicides mentioned above, but in the field of Holocaust studies it has thus far been her fate to be too little appreciated and too much overlooked. True, she wrote less—or at least less directly—about the Holocaust than some survivors, including Charlotte Delbo, arguably the woman who has written the most impressively in French about the Holocaust. Kofman's explicit works about the Holocaust consist primarily of two small books, *Paroles suffoquées*, a reflection focused on her father, Berek Kofman, a Parisian rabbi who was deported to Auschwitz in 1942, and *Rue Ordener, Rue Labat*, her memoir about antisemitism, family separation, and hiding during Nazi Germany's occupation of her native France.[6]

Ann Smock, one of her translators, notes that Kofman began writing *Rue Ordener, Rue Labat* during the winter of 1992–1993. She was almost sixty at the time. The memoir takes its title from two Parisian streets, which, Kofman observes, were separated by "one Métro stop."[7] The family home had been on the Rue Ordener, but everything changed when Kofman's father was caught in the roundup of some thirteen thousand Parisian Jews

---

5. Nancy, "Foreword," ix. Deutscher and Oliver provide helpful background—biographical and philosophical—about Kofman in "Sarah Kofman's Skirts," which also contains a detailed bibliography of Kofman's publications. See Deutscher and Oliver 1–22 and 264–75.

6. For the English translations of these books, see Kofman, *Smothered Words*; and Kofman, *Rue Ordener*. Kofman's memory of her father plays an important part in both. *Smothered Words* is dedicated to him and to the philosophers Maurice Blanchot and Robert Antelme. Blanchot's controversial career included the prewar articles that he wrote for right-wing, antisemitic publications, but also assistance to French Jews during the German occupation and postwar reflections on the Holocaust, especially *L'Écriture du désastre*, which influenced Kofman considerably. Antelme, a member of the French Resistance, was arrested by the Germans in June 1944, sent to Buchenwald, and eventually liberated at Dachau. "To have to speak without being able to speak or be understood, to have to choke," wrote Kofman in *Smothered Words* (39), "such is the ethical exigency that Robert Antelme obeys in *The Human Race*." His book *L'Espèce humaine* made an especially strong impression on Kofman. Its inspiration is evident particularly in Kofman's *Smothered Words*. For the English translations of the books by Blanchot and Antelme, see Blanchot, *Writing*; and Antelme, *Human Race*. All citations from Antelme and Blanchot as well as from Kofman, *Rue Ordener*; and Kofman, *Smothered Words* are from the English editions I have noted.

7. Kofman, *Rue Ordener*, 31.

that took place on July 16–17, 1942.⁸ Subsequently Sarah's mother, who survived the Holocaust, had to find hiding places for the children. Kofman's turned out to be on the Rue Labat with a Christian widow named Mémé.⁹

Kofman never saw her father again. In *Smothered Words*, she sums up the bare facts of her father's fate as follows:

> My father: Berek Kofman, born on October 10, 1900, in Sobin (Poland), taken to Drancy on July 16, 1942. Was in convoy no. 12, dated July 29, 1942, a convoy comprising 1,000 deportees, 270 men and 730 women (aged 36–54); 270 men registered 54,153 to 54,422; 514 women selected for work, registered 13,320 to 13,833; 216 other women gassed immediately.¹⁰

The ending of the five-page chapter that contains these words mentions the memorial created by Serge Klarsfeld, a French historian of the Holocaust

---

8. Kofman adds the following information about her father:

> On 16 July 1942, my father knew he was going to be picked up. It had been rumored that a big roundup was planned for that day. He was rabbi of a small synagogue on the Rue Duc in the 18th arrondissement. He had left home very early that day to warn as many Jews as he could to go into hiding immediately.
>
> Then he came home and waited; he was afraid that if he too were to hide his wife and six young children would be taken in his place. He had three girls and three boys between two and twelve years old.
>
> He waited and prayed to God that they would come for him, as long as his wife and children could be saved. (*Rue Ordener*, 5)

About eighty thousand Jews from France were killed in Nazi Germany's extermination camps, mostly at Auschwitz. Approximately one-third of them were French citizens; the majority were immigrants and refugees. Foreign Jews were first deported from France to Auschwitz on March 27, 1942. Facilitated by French police, the roundups and deportations intensified during the summer of 1942. For more background and detail, see Weinberg, "France," 213–22.

9. Among the multiple double binds that the Holocaust created were the complex dilemmas of identity encountered by hidden children. Kofman illustrates an aspect of that bind when she briefly describes the journey that took her from Rue Ordener, her home street, to a place of hiding and relative safety on Rue Labat. Her reaction seems to run as deep as it was physical. Short in distance and time though it was, that journey "seemed endless to me, and I vomited the whole way" (*Rue Ordener*, 31). Kofman indicates that Mémé, her rescuer, was "not without anti-Semitic prejudices." She also detached Kofman from her mother and Judaism. (Mémé, recalls Kofman, "christened me Suzanne because that was the saint's name closest to hers (Claire) on the calendar.") Yet, Kofman says that she came to love Mémé "more than my own mother." Ending *Rue Ordener, Rue Labat* with Mémé on her mind, Kofman writes, "I was unable to attend her funeral. But I know that at her grave the priest recalled how she had saved a little Jewish girl during the war" (*Rue Ordener*, 47, 39, 58, 85).

10. Kofman, *Smothered Words*, 10.

and a hunter of Nazi war criminals. Kofman reproduces a portion of its double-columned, alphabetized list of the French deportees. There, in the left-hand column between the names of Simone Klempen and Grange Kohn, one finds Berek Kofman. Klarsfeld's memorial list, with "its endless columns of names . . . takes your breath away," says Kofman.

> Its "neutral" voice summons you obliquely; in its extreme restraint, it is the very voice of affliction, of this event in which all possibility vanished, and which inflicted on the whole of humanity "the decisive blow which left nothing intact." This voice leaves you without a voice, makes you doubt your common sense and all sense, makes you suffocate in silence: "silence like a cry without words; mute, although crying endlessly."[11]

Her father's death suffocated Kofman, stifled her words. It did so, however, not simply because it was her father's death, grievous enough though a father's death can be for anyone. "Because he was a Jew," as her stifled voice expresses it, "my father died in Auschwitz."[12] And then she adds her double-binding questions: "How can it not be said? And how can it be said?"[13] Not just a father's death but a particular Jewish father's death in Auschwitz—the event, which Kofman calls "my absolute"—made the suffocating difference. She elaborates what she means by suggesting that integral to that difference is the awareness that an Auschwitz death "was worse than death."[14]

---

11. Kofman, *Smothered Words*, 10–11. In this passage Kofman includes two quotations from Blanchot, whose words, along with Antelme's, are frequently quoted in *Smothered Words*. The first quotation is from "After the Fact," Blanchot's afterword to his *Vicious Circles*, 68. The second passage is from *Step Not Beyond*, 61. Elsewhere Blanchot amplifies and complicates the point made in the first passage quoted by Kofman. "The disaster ruins everything," he wrote, "all the while leaving everything intact." That relationship epitomizes another of the Holocaust's double binds, which are so vividly illustrated in Kofman's life and authorship. See Blanchot, *Writing*, 1.

In "A Note on Translation," which helps to introduce *Smothered Words*, Madeleine Dobie observes that Kofman's frequent use of quotations, a style often found in her later writings, "may be seen to attenuate the mastery of the narrative voice through the interposition of the voices of others, and thereby of the Other, the style that Kofman, following Blanchot, calls 'writing without power.' . . . *Paroles suffoquées*," continues Dobie, "is at once a scholarly piece that develops arguments supported by quotations and footnotes, and a meditation in the style of Blanchot, in which the conventional privileging of the signified—arguments or ideas—over the signifier—form or the very process of writing itself—is called into question" (xxiv). This chapter's discussion of Kofman—replete with quotation of her words—modestly tries to emulate her style in this regard.

12. Kofman, *Smothered Words*, 9.

13. Kofman, *Smothered Words*, 9.

14. Kofman, *Smothered Words*, 9. Kofman cites Theodor Adorno's *Negative Dialectics* as an influence on her thinking about this point.

Kofman's point is not restricted to the brutality of that place or even to the systematic, assembly-line character of the mass murder that took place in Birkenau's gas chambers and crematoriums. When she says that an Auschwitz death was worse than death, she is not mystifying that death, let alone denying that death is death. She points instead to the smothering, even the death, of words such as *human* and *humanity*. After Auschwitz, Kofman claimed, people "do not really die" because death itself—in the sense that the death of every man, woman, and child is the death of a human being—reached its nadir as it was degraded and mocked by Nazi Germany's "Final Solution." Auschwitz meant that people died *differently* in the sense that the Nazi extermination camps, whose mass killing went on for months and years, was a devastating assault on the very idea of a shared humanity that puts us all on a common ground of rights and responsibilities, of dignity and respect.

This tragic insight is not solely a lament about the loss of humanity conceived generically, universally, or in terms of some fixed philosophical essence, for, in the words of the philosopher Richard Rorty, "most people—especially people relatively untouched by the European Enlightenment—simply do not think of themselves as, first and foremost, a human being."[15] The loss of humanity involves a destruction of particularity, difference, and the potential for personal development—ingredients without which humanity is an abstraction. Not simply wanton but calculated and intended again and again by Nazi Germany and its collaborators, the destruction of Jews such as Berek Kofman—a particular Jewish rabbi with a distinctive social identity, a specific name, and a singular face whose difference was definitive of his humanity—constitutes the assault on humanity that is also the death of human death. There was, and could be, only one Berek Kofman. The Nazi assault on humanity was systematic, extensive, and devastating. It could only be what it was by destruction that murdered particularity and difference—social and personal—as it destroyed children, women, and men en masse but also one by one by one. Post-Holocaust people, Kofman indicates ironically and tragically, have survived death only to discover, if they will, that reviving suffocated *humanity* is a task that indeed puts us, and perhaps philosophers and ethicists in particular, in "a strange *double bind*: an infinite claim to speak, *a duty to speak infinitely*, imposing itself with irrepressible force, and at the same time, an almost physical impossibility to speak, a *choking* feeling."[16]

---

15. See Rorty, "Human Rights," 251.
16. Kofman, *Smothered Words*, 39. Kofman's italics.

All she has left of her father, Kofman observes at the beginning of *Rue Ordener, Rue Labat*, is his fountain pen. "Patched up with Scotch tape," it can produce words no more, but "right in front of me on my desk," she says, that mute pen "makes me write, write."[17] As she penned those words, Kofman was trying to do what she had not done overtly very much before. "Maybe all my books," she observed, "have been the detours required to bring me to write about 'that.'"[18] *That* included her father's death, the Holocaust, the loss of humanity, the death of death. Kofman had written about some of these matters already and in ways many and diverse, but a direct encounter with the Holocaust, unavoidably including the particularity of her father's death and her own identity in relation to that disaster, created in her something akin to Robert Antelme's predicament after his "liberation" from Dachau:

> It was impossible to bridge the gap we discovered opening up between the words at our disposal and that experience which, in the case of most of us, was still going forward within our bodies. How were we to resign ourselves to not trying to explain how we had got to the state we were in? For we were yet in that state. And even so, it was impossible. No sooner would we begin to tell our story than we would be choking over it.[19]

Confronting this double bind, but not paralyzed by it, at least not completely, Antelme told his story, and Kofman examined the message that she took from it. Antelme believed that the more Hitler and his followers tried to destroy an inclusive sense of *humanity* through their genocidal antisemitism and racism, the more undeniable the "indestructible unity" of humanity became, or, as Antelme put it, "there is only one human race." The SS, claimed Antelme, "can kill a man, but he can't change him into something else."[20]

Kofman seemed to share what she calls Antelme's "pleasure in tearing the Nazis' power to shreds and overturning their mastery," but as much as she admired his resistance, his determination not to permit the Nazis or even his own devastating experience to choke his words completely, Kofman appeared to find Antelme's affirmative understanding of the persistence of a single humanity less than sufficient and therefore not entirely convincing.[21] It was not that she denied the unity, but that Antelme had not emphasized enough how Nazism wreaked havoc on *community*.

17. Kofman, *Rue Ordener*, 3.
18. Kofman, *Rue Ordener*, 3.
19. Antelme, *Human Race*, 3.
20. See Kofman, *Smothered Words*, 58; and Antelme, *Human Race*, 220.
21. Kofman, *Smothered Words*, 66.

Her father's death never far from her consciousness, Kofman starts to draw out what remained only implicit in Antelme's *The Human Race*. The value of a shared sense of humanity, of our belonging to a human species, depends on whether that belonging binds us together in mutual respect and caring, whether it draws people together in community. As Kofman sized up the situation, however, the connections between the unity implied by the word *humanity* and the senses of community that may or may not follow are tenuous and even problematic. First, she pointed out, "no community is possible with the SS."[22] *In my judgment, no Holocaust insight is more important.* With a vengeance, Nazi ideology rejected the idea of an inclusively shared humanity. Regarding difference—especially alleged racial difference—as profoundly threatening, its genocidal impulses took the world to Treblinka and Auschwitz. Nazi Germany, of course, took pride in its own sense of community, which underscores the fact that community is not necessarily humanity's ally, especially if *humanity* is understood to be pluralistic and diverse. So Kofman made a second point: it is crucial to support "the community (of those) without community."[23]

Those without community are outsiders, but Kofman's thinking did not stop with a call to defend and protect those who are threatened and harmed because they are left out. More radically and fundamentally, she rejected all senses of community that are based on "any specific difference or on a shared essence."[24] The right forms of community, she seems to be saying, are those that consciously accept a double bind. This bind acknowledges that every community is particular, different, finite, even exclusive in one way or another, but no community should rest on assumptions about immutable superiority or inferiority. On the contrary, the particularity of one community ought to affirm, protect, and encourage the particularity of others.

Community at its best, she contended, depends on "a shared power to choose, to make incompatible though correlative choices, the power to kill *and* the power to respect and safeguard the incommensurable distance, the relation without relation."[25] Here Kofman's words are not smothered or knotted, but their insights remain less than fully expressed. She provides hints, allusions, signposts pointing to an ethical outlook that would not be the same as old humanisms that appealed to human nature, to the essence of humanity, or to reason as humankind's most decisive characteristic. Instead,

22. Kofman, *Smothered Words*, 70.
23. Kofman, *Smothered Words*, 70.
24. Kofman, *Smothered Words*, 70.
25. Kofman, *Smothered Words*, 70.

she suggests that everyday realities and actions—things such as choices and keeping or betraying one's word—reveal our humanity or the lack of it and make all the difference. The Holocaust reaffirmed that all of those caught in it—perpetrators, victims, bystanders, and more—were human. In some sense, humanity survived the Holocaust, if only to testify, as the French philosopher Maurice Blanchot put it, how human indestructibility reveals "that there is no limit to the destruction of man."[26] But if humanity is to mean more than that, if humanity is to be what Kofman thought it ought to become, then the destruction of old humanisms may make possible the willful reconstitution of a "new kind of 'we,'" even "a new 'humanism' one might say, if it were still acceptable to use this trite and idyllic word."[27]

Unknotted Words?

What about Kofman's guarded hope, her hint of "community (of those) without community" that could be based on "a shared power to choose"? Kofman glimpsed the possibility of a new humanism and a new ethics, a position seemingly at odds with Raul Hilberg. As noted in chapter 5, he asserted that ethics is the same today as it was yesterday and even the day before yesterday; it is the same after Auschwitz as it was before and during the lethal operations at that place. Especially with regard to needless and wanton killing, he emphasized, ethics is the same for everyone, everywhere. Hilberg left no unclarity. Such killing is wrong. We know that "in our bones," he said, for such knowledge is the heritage of many years.

Kofman, I think, would accept Hilberg's claims, but only up to a point, and she would be right before conceding that Hilberg's bold pronouncement unknots the words that ethics after Auschwitz needs to express. True, senses of right and wrong are real. The Holocaust helps to focus them. Even the SS leader Heinrich Himmler knew as much. He and the other perpetrators of the Holocaust were aware of the psychological turmoil created by their orders to kill. They did their best to make those tasks easier, more "humane," by distancing the killers from their victims. Thus, they substituted

---

26. Kofman ends *Smothered Words* (on page 73) with this quotation from Blanchot. The quoted passage comes from Blanchot, *Infinite Conversation*, 135.

27 Kofman, *Smothered Words*, 73. Kofman adds an intriguing note to her allusion about a new "humanism." She writes as follows: "In spite of everything that makes this word unacceptable for us today—after 'the death of God' and the end of man that is its correlate—I nonetheless want to conserve it, while giving it a completely different meaning, displacing and transforming it. I keep it because what other, new 'word' could have as much hold on the old humanism?" (89–90). Here one thinks of the Nietzschean theme of the revaluation of values.

mass gassings for the shootings of the Einsatzgruppen. But did Himmler and the other perpetrators know "in their bones" that what they were doing was wrong? In some cases, there is evidence that says so. The perpetrators covered their tracks as best they could. Many of the killers numbed themselves with alcohol. Some Germans refused orders to kill Jews, especially when children were the target.

On the other hand, such evidence is mostly circumstantial. It was not very often enhanced by admissions of guilt or expressions of remorse. Far more common were excuses that referred to orders that had to be obeyed or to fears of punishment if obedience was not forthcoming. For the most part, Nazi leaders and Holocaust perpetrators remained unrepentant. At the end of the day, their behavior does not show that they knew that their killing of the Jews was wanton, needless, and wrong. On the contrary, their behavior suggests that they believed their killing to be right and good, albeit extremely difficult, even loathsome to do. Kofman was right: no community was possible with the SS because it did not know better than it thought it did. That knowing, as Kofman also understood, depended on an entirely different approach to choosing and fidelity than Nazism required. But absent the force of will, what Kofman called the "shared power to choose" that makes "incompatible though correlative choices, the power to kill *and* the power to respect and safeguard the incommensurable distance, the relation without relation," nothing guarantees that ethics will not be smothered after the Holocaust as it was with such devastating results during that disaster.

"The owl of Minerva," wrote the philosopher Hegel, "spreads its wings only with the falling of the dusk." He meant that human reason and philosophy in particular achieve understanding only in retrospect; they are hard pressed to give "instruction as to what the world ought to be."[28] If Hegel is correct, the tools of moral philosophy and religious ethics are meager. Still, they have a role to play that nothing else can duplicate. Moral reflection, for example, can clarify and intensify feelings of wrong prompted by the Holocaust. Such thinking can show the importance of those feelings by revealing what happens when they fail to work their way into practice. Yet that understanding alone does little to change the world as long as societies concretely reward activities that kill and take punitive action toward those who refuse to cooperate.

If one wants to affirm the United Nations' declaration that "everyone has the right to life, liberty and security of person," one must realize that such claims are as frail as they are abstract.[29] The same is true of the United

---

28. Hegel, *Philosophy of Right*, 12–13.
29. United Nations General Assembly. Resolution 217 A, article 3.

Nations Convention on the Prevention and Punishment of the Crime of Genocide, which the UN's General Assembly approved on December 9, 1948. Forty years later, in November 1988, the United States became a full party to this convention, the ninety-eighth nation to ratify it, but only with significant reservations. Both the long delay and the reservations resulted from fears that if the United States unequivocally agreed to the treaty that makes genocide a crime, Americans and even the state itself might be unjustly indicted by the nation's adversaries. Meanwhile, history continues to testify that power, not pacts, brakes or makes mass killing. Rights, liberty, and security of person are real only in specific times and places, only in actual political circumstances. Apart from such concrete settings those ideals are only that. Granted, they are ideals that attract. They can bring out the best in people. They can even rally powerful forces behind them. They may even have a transcendent status ordained by God. To assume, however, that they are more than ideals until men and women take responsibility to make them a concrete reality may well be an illusion.

Meanwhile, in our pluralistic world, where cultural, religious, and philosophical perspectives vary considerably, a widely held belief is that values are so relative to one's time and place that the "truth" of moral claims is much more a result of subjective preference and political power than a function of objective reality and universal reason. This relativistic outlook meets resistance in the Holocaust, for a widely shared conviction holds that the Holocaust was *wrong*. It was something that should not have happened, and nothing akin to it should ever happen again. Even if people remain skeptical that rational agreement can be obtained about what is right, just, and good, the Holocaust seems to reestablish conviction that what happened at Auschwitz and Treblinka was wrong, unjust, and evil—period. More than that, the scale of the wrongdoing, the magnitude of the injustice, and the devastation of the Holocaust's evil are so radical that we can ill afford not to have our ethical sensibilities informed by them. As Franklin Littell insightfully stressed, "study of the Holocaust is like study of pathology in medicine."[30] Pathology seeks to understand the origins and characteristics of disease and the conditions in which it thrives. If such understanding can be obtained, the prospects for resistance against disease, and perhaps even a cure, may be increased. But so much, perhaps too much, depends on "if" and "may be." The fact remains that the status of ethics after the Holocaust is far from settled.

30. The quotation is from Littell's concluding plenary speech at "Remembering for the Future 2000," a major international conference on the Holocaust held in Oxford, England, July 16–23, 2000. See Roth and Maxwell, eds., *Remembering for the Future*, 3:8.

One might argue that Nazi Germany's defeat shows that right defeated wrong and that goodness subdued evil, thus showing that reality has a fundamentally moral underpinning. The Holocaust, however, is far too awesome for such facile triumphalism. The Nazis did not win, but they came too close for comfort. Even though the Third Reich was destroyed, it is not so easy to say that its defeat was a clear and decisive triumph for goodness, truth, and justice over evil, falsehood, and corruption. Add to those realizations the fact that the Nazis themselves were idealists. They had positive beliefs about right and wrong, good and evil, duty and irresponsibility. We can even identify something that can be called "the Nazi ethic" and "the Nazi conscience." The "Final Solution" was a key part—perhaps the essence—of such outlooks, which were put into practice with a zealous, even apocalyptic, vengeance.[31] It would be too convenient to assume that the Nazi ethic's characteristic blending of loyalty, faith, heroism, and even love for country and cause was simply a passive, mindless obedience. True though the judgment would be, it remains too soothing to say only that the Nazi ethic was really no ethic at all but a deadly perversion of what is truly moral. Most people are unlikely to serve a cause unless that cause makes convincing moral appeals about what is good and worthy of loyalty. Those appeals, of course, can be blind, false, even sinful, and the Nazis' were. Nevertheless, the perceived and persuasive "goodness" of the beliefs that constituted the Nazi ethic—the dedicated SS man embodied them most thoroughly—is crucial to acknowledge if we are to understand why so many Germans willfully followed Hitler into genocidal warfare and stuck with him until the bitter end.

Paradoxically, the "Final Solution" threatens the status, practical and theoretical, of moral norms contrary to those that characterized the Nazi ethic, whose deadly way failed but still prevailed long enough to call into question many of Western civilization's moral assumptions and religious hopes.[32] Hitler and his Nazi followers did not succeed completely in implementing their antisemitism and racism, but they went far enough in establishing what another philosopher-survivor, Jean Améry, aptly called "the

---

31. For important discussions of these themes, see Bialas and Fritze, eds., *Nazi Ideology*; Haas, *Morality after Auschwitz*; Koonz, *Nazi Conscience*; Kühne, "Nazi Morality"; and Roth, "Ethics." Related topics are discussed in Roth, ed., *Ethics after the Holocaust*; and in Roth, *Ethics*.

32. In ethics, the human will is decisive in determining how good and evil, right and wrong are understood. Reason and intuition inform our willing and choosing, but without the latter, our senses of good and evil, right and wrong, lack the force that gives them full reality and makes them effective. Willing and choosing do not alone determine what is ethical, but in the fullest sense no determination of right and wrong takes place without them.

rule of the antiman" that none of our fondest hopes about humanity can be taken for granted.[33]

As Sarah Kofman helped to show, our senses of moral and religious authority have been fragmented and weakened by the accumulated ruins of history and the depersonalized advances of "civilization" that have taken us from a bloody twentieth century into an even more problematic twenty-first. A moral spirit and religious commitment that have the courage to persist *in spite of* humankind's self-inflicted destructiveness are essential, but the question remains how effective these dispositions can be in salvaging moral fragments within a world where power stands at the heart of that destructiveness. To find ways to salvage the fragments, to affect "the powers that be" so that their tendencies to lay waste to human life are checked, ethics after Auschwitz will need to draw on every resource it can find: appeals to human rights, calls for renewed religious sensitivity, respect and honor for people who save lives and resist tyranny, and attention to the Holocaust's warnings, to name only a few. Those efforts will need to be accompanied by efforts that build these concerns into our educational, religious, business, and political institutions.

If one considers human rights after the Holocaust, it is unlikely that humankind will ever reach full agreement on a single worldview that will ground belief in such rights. But it does not follow that appeals to human rights are dashed as well. If people feel the need to ground appeals to human rights, a variety of options—philosophical and religious—may remain credible, even if they will not be universally accepted. More importantly, there may be considerable agreement—especially after the Holocaust—about what the functional interpretation of human rights ought to be. Here, too, there will not be universal agreement, but the Holocaust itself has had an important impact on helping to clarify what ought not to happen to human beings. If we think about what ought not to happen to human beings, moreover, we may find considerable agreement about what should happen.

Sarah Kofman never forgot what the Nazi assault meant, namely, that after July 16, 1942, she never saw her father, Berek, again. Nazism and its Holocaust were an assault on the values that we human beings hold most dear when we are at our best. Resistance to protect them came too late then; hence resistance continues to be urgent now. Kofman warns that nothing human, natural, or divine guarantees respect for those values, but nothing is more important than our commitment to defend them, for they remain as fundamental as they are fragile, as precious as they are endangered. These indispensable insights are among those made clearer by her guarded

---

33. Améry, *Mind's Limits*, 31.

hopes, her hints about "community (of those) without community," and her glimpses of the possibility of a new humanism and a new ethics that might emerge from the Holocaust's double binds.

Useless Knowledge

Sarah Kofman's father was deported from Paris to Auschwitz and did not return. Charlotte Delbo was deported from Paris to Auschwitz and did return. She thought, however, that no one really returned from that place, at least not as one usually thinks of "returning," because, as she put it, "Auschwitz is so deeply etched in my memory that I cannot forget one moment of it."[34]

Delbo was not Jewish. Nevertheless, she was sent to Auschwitz in 1943. Of the 230 French women in her convoy, she was one of forty-nine who survived. Delbo saw what happened to the Jews, her French comrades, and herself. An Auschwitz fate, however, did not have to be hers. When the Germans occupied her native France in June 1940, she was on tour in South America with a theater company. Against the advice of friends, she returned to France in 1941, rejoining her husband, Georges Dudach, and working with him in the Resistance. Arrested by collaborating French police on March 2, 1942, the couple was handed over to the Germans, who imprisoned the two separately. Delbo got a brief visit with her husband just before a firing squad executed him on May 23. A prisoner in France until her deportation, Delbo described her January 1943 arrival at Auschwitz as follows: "The doors of the cattle cars were pushed open, revealing the edge of an icy plain. It was a place from before geography. Where were we? We were to find out—later, at least two months hence; we, that is, those of us who were still alive two months later—that this place was called Auschwitz. We couldn't have given it a name."[35]

Those words come from Delbo's superb trilogy, *Auschwitz and After*, whose anguished visual descriptions and profound reflections on memory make it a powerfully insightful Holocaust testimony. Its three parts begin with *None of Us Will Return*, which she wrote in 1946 after she had been released to the Red Cross from Ravensbrück, a Nazi concentration camp for women. She recuperated in Sweden and then returned to France. Delbo waited nearly twenty years, however, before she allowed *None of Us Will Return* to be published in 1965. Parts of *Useless Knowledge* were also written shortly after Delbo's return to France, but this second volume in the

---

34. Delbo, *Days and Memory*, 2.
35. Delbo, *Auschwitz and After*, 167.

trilogy did not appear until 1970. Its sequel, *The Measure of Our Days*, soon followed.

Delbo stressed that she knew all too well "the difference between before and after."[36] Ordinarily such dimensions of experience cause few problems. Life's continuity makes it possible to feel its connections and relationships without much difficulty. But what if disjunction is more real than continuity? What if devastating gaps break apart *now* and *then*, *here* and *there*, *before* and *after*? What if Auschwitz is the gap? What if memory, far from closing that gap, keeps it open, deep, and terrifying? Delbo tried to move beyond Auschwitz and her memory of it, to leave that horror behind the way a snake sheds its skin when molting. Such escape proved impossible. Auschwitz was no skin to be shed. It remained with her always, imprinted in her very being. True, in the months and years *after*, she relearned what she had forgotten from *before*. *Here* she could do what was never possible *there*—things like using a toothbrush. *Now* she could do what was unthinkable *then*—things like eating calmly with a knife and fork. And yet, as she apparently became once more the person she had been before Auschwitz intervened—charming, cultivated, civilized—she could hardly experience the smell of rain, for example, without recalling that "in Birkenau, rain heightened the odor of diarrhea."[37]

Along with the Auschwitz number—31661—tattooed on her left arm and visible to her every day, such experiences illustrate what Delbo meant by *useless knowledge*. Normally we think of knowledge as useful, but Delbo showed how the Holocaust produced inescapable knowledge about hunger and disease, brutality and suffering, degradation and death that did nothing to respect, enhance, or dignify life. "The sound of fifty blows on a man's back is interminable," she recounted. "Fifty strokes of a club on a man's back is an endless number. They reverberate."[38] Such useless knowledge, which Auschwitz made vast in scope and detail, drove home her point: for the most part, what happened in the Holocaust divided, besieged, and diminished life forever.

None of us will return, Delbo had thought, and after she did, it seemed incredible. So, at times she felt that "the one who was in the camp is not me, is not the person who is here, facing you."[39] Confronting the question, "So you are living with Auschwitz?" Delbo's answer had to be, "No, I live next

---

36. Delbo, *Auschwitz and After*, 258.
37. Delbo, *Days and Memory*, 1.
38. Delbo, *Auschwitz and After*, 58–59.
39. Delbo, *Days and Memory*, 3.

to it."⁴⁰ But that answer did not work completely, because she not only lived "next to it." Rather it also lived in her, a fact that dreams kept showing: "And in those dreams I see myself, yes, my own self such as I know I was . . . and I feel death fasten on me, I feel that I am dying."⁴¹

Delbo could speak and write about her life's disjointed experience but doing so gave her scant consolation. What she could put into words was not the same as what she felt. "Deep memory," she wrote, "preserves sensations, physical imprints," but words do not come from that source. They do not suffice for "explaining the inexplicable."⁴² As she used those words, they did not mystify. Nor were they a philosopher's abstract rendering of some cosmic puzzle. Her dilemma was personal and existential: How does one meaningfully integrate Auschwitz into one's life? One never can, and, Charlotte Delbo might add, that is no answer.

A Box of Memories

Charlotte Delbo lost her life to cancer in 1985, the same year that I began to study her writings. Since that time, she has been a profound source of Holocaust insight for me. In striking ways, she taught me that no matter how long and well I studied the Holocaust, I could never close knowledge gaps that reflected differences between *before* and *after, then* and *now, there* and *here*. Delbo instructed me in a pointed way when she warned, "Today people know / have known for several years/ that this dot on the map / is Auschwitz / This much they know / as for the rest / they think they know."⁴³ But Delbo did more than deepen my awareness of the limitations of Holocaust studies. The insistence that her readers should "try to look. Just try and see"—a theme she states three times at one point in *Auschwitz and After*—made it imperative to envision what I never saw and could not see so that my insight about Auschwitz-and-after would be tempered accordingly.⁴⁴

Steps in those directions included introducing students to Delbo every year that I taught about the Holocaust. They studied *Auschwitz and After* and wrote papers about that experience. One year, an art major named Sarah Yates handed me one of the most unusual and insightful reflections I ever received. Inspired by Delbo's reflection that she has "several faces," including one "weary, worn down, frozen . . . ruined" and another "full of

40. Delbo, *Days and Memory*, 2.
41. Delbo, *Days and Memory*, 3.
42. Delbo, *Days and Memory*, 1, 3.
43. Delbo, *Auschwitz and After*, 138.
44. Delbo, *Auschwitz and After*, 84–86.

light, mobile, the one in our memories,"[45] Sarah's "paper" consisted of a handsome oak box, dark-stained and lacquered. The accompanying written text noted that the box could be "something one might set on a coffee table next to a plate of cookies or a vase of tulips." Like the appearance of Delbo's post-Holocaust life, it could seem to be normal and even decorative. However, Sarah went on to say, "when opened, the box reveals its other 'face,'" an interior of memory fragments, which are not "normal," let alone decorative.

Inside Sarah's "Box of Memories," as she called her project, there were carefully crafted, skillfully decorated, wooden puzzle pieces, each one measuring about 2 x 3 inches. Some fitted together; others did not. Each piece was delicately inscribed on both sides. The inscriptions were words not only from Charlotte Delbo but also from Elie Wiesel, Primo Levi, Raul Hilberg, and other Holocaust-related writers we had read. Their words did not fit together easily, any more than the puzzle pieces themselves, but Sarah's advice was to "dump the pieces out onto your floor or your desk, and then try making and 'reading' different arrangements." Each time, the configuration, the narratives, meanings, and comparisons between them would change, and yet they would not be entirely different. The fragments were real. Many things could be done with them, but not anything or everything, at least not if one respected the memories that the box contained.

Doing as Sarah instructed, I observed—but not closely enough—that the "Box of Memories" was layered. Deep down, covering what turned out to be a face painted at the bottom of the box, there were levels where the puzzle pieces did fit together in a recognizable way that just matched the box's interior. Before I knew it, the fragments were out of the box, and I was arranging them to see what the combinations could be. But when the time came to put the pieces back in the box, I discovered that I could not make them fit.

Without replacing the bottom layers as Sarah had originally arranged them, the pieces would not go back into the box in a way that permitted its lid to be closed. Sarah had color-coded the edges of the bottom layers so she could remember how they went together, but even then, she confessed, closing the "Box of Memories" was hard to do. Later, when Sarah shared the project with her classmates during a period at the end of the semester when the students reported about work they had been doing, a few of the carefully carved memory fragments disappeared. Regretting their loss, Sarah made others—not to replace the irreplaceable but to fill the "Box of Memories" again so that it could not easily be closed.

---

45. Delbo, *Auschwitz and After*, 338.

I keep in contact with Sarah, who has become Sarah Waller, mother of Andrew and Sophia, an educator who continues to be an accomplished artist. As my words bring her to mind, I look again at one of the pieces from her "Box of Memories." It was enclosed in a note she sent me some time ago. "The best compliment that an artist can receive," it said, "is having his/her work mean something to others." The puzzle piece that Sarah included with her note is especially meaningful to me because it recalls two moments evoked by Charlotte Delbo in *Auschwitz and After*.

On an early spring day not yet free of wintery rain and hail, Delbo and her Auschwitz work detail headed for a long day of ditch digging. Their way took them by a house. In one of its windows, she says, "there is a tulip . . . pink between two pale leaves." The women in the labor column slowed down to see it. The SS shouted, "hurry up," but, Delbo recalled, "all day we dream of the tulip." The women saw it again on their way back to camp, and at the roll call that evening, they told other prisoners, "We saw a tulip." Delbo says that the tulip gave the women "a moment of hope," but their work detail never went that way again, and "when we found out that this house belonged to the SS in charge of the fishery, we despised this memory and the tender feeling which had not yet dried up within us."[46]

Against the white background on one side of Sarah's puzzle piece, a delicately painted tulip appears, pink between two pale leaves, and the words, simply ascribed to CD, "All day we dream of the tulip." As seeing and treasuring that Auschwitz tulip collide in the reader's mind with Delbo's despising memory of it, the inexplicable, far from being explained, is made tellingly lucid and poignantly vivid. I again experience emotion that informs insight when Sarah's small puzzle piece is turned over and another moment from *Auschwitz and After* looms large. On the left this time, Sarah finely sketched some greenery. To the right, she drew fencing, and in the middle, something explained by the piece's inscription, again ascribed to CD: "Between the hedge of rosebushes and the barbed wire lies the path leading to the crematorium." The rosebushes, says Delbo, belong to the camp commandant, who "lives close by, just outside the barbed-wire enclosure." His sons play in the garden; sometimes they play "commandant and prisoner." Meanwhile, the path leads to the crematorium: "It is the path taken by stretchers transporting the dead. They go on all day, the whole day. The smokestack spouts its fumes the whole day long. The passing hours shift the smokestack's shadow upon the sandy garden walks and the bright green lawn."[47] Roses growing, kids playing, genocide happening—all in the same

---

46. Delbo, *Auschwitz and After*, 60–61.
47. Delbo, *Auschwitz and After*, 100.

place at the same time, the collision driven home to me not only by Charlotte Delbo's words but also by Sarah Waller's miniature depiction. Once more, the inexplicable eludes explanation but compels attention and makes one ask, what must be done, what can I do, to resist the despair inlayed in the wrenching fragments of Sarah's "Box of Memories" and to make good the hope that the useless knowledge embedded in them does not prevail?

Try to Look

Repeatedly, Delbo challenged her readers to "try to look. Just try and see." Often, this challenge aimed to make them pay attention to the dying and the dead. The challenge within her challenge, indeed her task in focusing her readers' attention so the challenge could be felt, was immense because Delbo knew that her readers had not viewed what her eyes had seen and really never could behold what she remembered. Determined to make her readers try to see the unthinkable, Delbo wanted her words to do their best to inform her readers' vision and to deepen their insight. Her accomplishment is not only that her readers may *begin* to envision what Delbo saw and recollected but also that her word depictions make one aware that the beginning cannot be sustained. In and through that disruption, however, insight about the meaning(s) of death as atrocity may intensify where even the mind's eye unavoidably dims.

One spring evening in Auschwitz, Delbo and her worn-out prisoner companions returned to the camp after another long day of punishing slave labor. This time, her work detail carried the bodies of Berthe and Anne-Marie, two comrades beaten to death—helplessly, hopelessly—when they collapsed from exhaustion that afternoon. Every evening, the Germans required that the prisoners—the dead and the living—had to be counted, and so it was with Berthe and Anne-Marie, who were lined up for "roll call" with those who had carried their lifeless bodies back for the tally. When the count ended, darkness had fallen, but while the roll call lasted, Delbo writes, "we never looked at them." And then her depiction continues, but less with continuity than with disruption: "A corpse. The left eye devoured by a rat. The other open with its fringe of lashes. Try to look. Just try and see."[48]

Whose corpse does Delbo's description identify? During the roll call, Delbo says, "we never looked at them," and yet she urges her readers—and perhaps even herself?—to look. But whose body does she want her readers—and perhaps even herself?—to see? Berthe's? Anne-Marie's? Delbo leaves the corpse unnamed. It's just the one with the rat-devoured left eye,

48. Delbo, *Auschwitz and After*, 84.

the one whose right eye is fringed with lashes and still as open as it is sightless. Delbo leaves her readers—and perhaps even herself?—to bridge the disruption, if that can be done.

This much can be said: The corpse Delbo had in mind was once a living person, a woman or a man with a name, one who had parents and friends, one who was loved and who deserved neither to be robbed of life by genocidal perpetrators nor to be left in degradation after being senselessly beaten to death and reduced to a mark in the death column of an Auschwitz roll call.

This much more must be said: what happened to that person was wrong. But what happened to that person has been repeated, continues to be repeated, again and again. No credible justice has been meted out for such crimes. It may not be possible that any credible justice for such crimes exists, even in principle let alone in practice. The corpse/person Delbo remembers should be remembered forever, but in spite of monumental human efforts—including museums and their walls of names, collections of survivor testimonies, libraries of research, and mandates for education—the chances in favor of that outcome are remote.

The main reason for that grim judgment is not that people are forgetful or indifferent, although those characteristics are prevalent even where the worst atrocities are concerned. Nor is the main reason to be found in the fact that with relatively few exceptions, when events recede into the past, concern about them diminishes as well. The main reason remembrance is likely to fail and meaning is likely to go missing is that if we human beings look, if we "just try and see," the empirical evidence overwhelmingly leads to the conclusion that human consciousness and history, indeed human life itself, are neither everlasting nor eternal but instead are finite and temporary, long-lived though they may be. Birth and death: human life came into existence; it will pass away as well. This process has been and will be in play for ages exceeding recorded history. It is not restricted to particular persons, communities, nations, and traditions but engulfs them all without exception or remainder.

When Delbo urged her readers—and perhaps even herself?—to look and to see that corpse with its "left eye devoured by a rat," the world changed, and nature was not the same as it was before. In spite of that death, the world also went on and so did history. The meanings of both, however, have been affected in ways that can make us see more clearly what fully facing death entails: absent human experience, absent its/our looking and feeling, understanding and incomprehension, outrage and resentment about what happened to that person in Auschwitz and to every victim of genocide and atrocity, there may be nothing to see, let alone any justice that will be done.

In *Auschwitz and After*, poetry mixes and mingles with the death that Delbo wants the living to face. Reminiscent of the tulip and rosebushes she saw in Auschwitz, a portion of her verse recalls the post-Holocaust act of kindness she experienced one day in Sicily when a boy gave her a flower. That day, Delbo says, she told herself "there is no wound that will not heal." From time to time, she adds, she repeats that thought "but not enough to believe it."[49] Delbo's yearning and disbelief have much to do with her saying, "I know the difference between before and after," an outlook that encompassed the fact that death, especially death in and through atrocity, leaves the world so bereft of justice.[50]

Among other things, Delbo's Auschwitz experience left her acutely aware that the Holocaust and its aftermath had fragmented the meaning of words. "There are people," she observed, "who say, 'I'm thirsty.' They step into a café and order a beer."[51] Those words are her ironic conclusion to a chapter in *Auschwitz and After* called "Thirst." It attempts to describe what the "free word" *thirst* can never capture, an experience ungrasped even when Delbo writes that it took her to "the point of losing my mind." The parching that she found no words to describe was so all-consuming that it was only relieved by drinking and drinking some more from a pail, as she was finally able to do in Auschwitz, "like a horse, no, like a dog."[52]

After the Holocaust and other genocides, even apparently simple words such as *after* cannot mean what they did before. What happens, then, to *justice*, a word whose meanings were already fragile, problematic, and contested before genocidal atrocity struck and the Holocaust raged? The word remains and persists after genocide. The fact that it has not been smothered but is still spoken and heard indicates that *justice* is a needed word. But *justice* also is a wounded word because it is primarily and unavoidably an *after*-word.[53]

Cries for and appeals to justice are usually pronounced when something has gone badly wrong. If life were fair, unscarred by greed, terror, war, or genocide, there would be little need to dwell on justice. The Holocaust and other atrocities intensify the need for justice but also make justice impossible, at least as far as the traditional idea of justice as a balancing of scales is concerned. Attempts to restore order, to provide restitution and recompense, even to mete out punishment of perpetrators, can be made.

49. Delbo, *Auschwitz and After*, 241.
50. Delbo, *Auschwitz and After*, 258.
51. Delbo, *Auschwitz and After*, 145.
52. Delbo, *Auschwitz and After*, 142, 144.
53. For elaboration on this theme, see Patterson and Roth, eds., *After-Words*.

Tribunals try to handle matters of this kind. Noble and partially successful though these efforts are, their shortcomings are more striking, because within history no compensation for atrocity is adequate. For the dead, nothing can be done except to remember them. Far from bringing comfort, that remembering—to the extent that it is not swallowed by forgetting and by the death of those left behind—underscores the absence of justice. Memory can encourage efforts to rectify the absence of justice, but when driven by injustice, memory can produce more of the same. It can intensify hostility; it can fuel hate and inflame revenge.

No human quality is more virtuous than the protest and resistance that take the realities of injustice—defined in key ways by the corpses of the Holocaust and genocide—as spurs to try yet again to curb their destructiveness. Absent such determination and defiance, history likely would be much bloodier. But within history, justice is always destined to be an *after*-word. Not only will it be voiced primarily in the wake of useless destruction, harm, and suffering, but justice also will remain elusive. It will be what humanity does not have, what it lacks and, what it is *after* in the sense of seeking.

At best, justice can obtain only in part and incompletely. For it to be complete or even to prevail, more than history and more than human lives that utterly end with death are minimal requirements. Arguably, God would be required as well. The philosopher Immanuel Kant saw those relationships when he held that if ethics and the ideal of justice are fully reasonable—he thought they must be—at least three postulates, as he called them, were fundamental: freedom, human life beyond history and death, and God. The validity of these prerequisites could not be proved, but Kant's insight was a version of the principles that justice makes no sense apart from the freedom to choose, and that justice delayed is justice denied. To the extent that justice is incomplete, injustice prevails, and what is reasonable is thwarted.

So, for the sake of inquiry and perhaps for the sake of justice itself, ponder what the good news might be if human life does not end with death, if history is not all there is, and if a God exists to ensure that justice does prevail completely, a restoration whose full goodness would vanquish all past evils. Next, try to see once more Berthe and Anne-Marie, the two women Delbo saw beaten to death because they could no longer do the slave labor that the Germans demanded of them in Auschwitz. Furthermore, try to look again at the corpse that Delbo wanted her readers to see. Envision them—Berthe, Anne-Marie, the unnamed corpse—alive beyond death. Try to envision a reality in which justice prevails completely over the injustice of genocide's death camps and killing fields. Perhaps God can do so. Perhaps human beings can be transformed beyond death so that they can too. Anything, people sometimes say, is possible. But this scenario of healing and restoration is scarcely thinkable. In fact, if it came into play, ethics and justice would require suspicion about its integrity.

What happened, happened, and unless memory is erased, the injustice will not be forgotten, nor should it be. Even beyond death and with a God who would try to make justice whole, reality is too flawed for that result's credibility to hold. No doubt healing and restoration are badly needed—within history and beyond. They can be obtained in part, but not to an extent that will set everything right. Existence is permanently scarred. Facing death, especially its atrocity in the Holocaust and other genocides, forever diminishes good news about justice.

Carrying the Word

Haunted by the useless knowledge—like seeing corpses with rat-devoured eyes—Delbo ended *Auschwitz and After* by telling her readers that she did not know "if you can still /make something of me / If you have the courage to try..."[54] Part of Delbo's courage was that she kept encouraging her readers to try to look and see. She knew the banality of advice to start life over again. "What an expression," she called it, "if there is a thing you can't do over again, a thing you can't start over again, it is your life."[55] But keeping memory alive was one of the things she could do.

Writing was Delbo's way to keep memory alive. She brought to her writing a sensitive ear for dialogue, which had been tuned by her work in the theater. After the Holocaust, her authorship included numerous plays, including one called *Who Will Carry the Word?*[56] With an entirely female cast, the play is set in the desolate landscape of a death camp. As the third act begins, Denise says: "Seventy days and 'we' no longer means the same thing. Now 'we' is Gina, Francoise and myself. My sister is dead. The others are dead. All of them, all the others." The three women who remain try to keep their resistance going. "All our sentences," says Denise, "start with 'if we come back.'" To which Gina replies: "We must say: 'when we come back.'"

The reason why they must come back is to carry the word. But part of the power of Delbo's play, and the same could be said for Gertrud Kolmar's poetry and Sarah Kofman's testimony, is that it makes us ask: What is "the word" that must be carried? Who will carry it? And to whom will the word be carried? Clearly, the word cannot be any message that simply says "put the past behind" or "good triumphs over evil" or "there's a reason for

---

54. Delbo, *Auschwitz and After*, 352.
55. Delbo, *Auschwitz and After*, 348.
56. The script is available in Skloot, *Theatre of the Holocaust*, 1:267–325.

everything." Not only would such facile chatter trivialize, falsify, and deny the Holocaust, but forgetting is out of the question.

Perhaps the best one can do is just to tell what happened. But even that approach has problems because "what happened" is so destructive, so useless. Carrying the word, Delbo knew, might be spirit-breaking, but she also understood that it must not be. Her response to this dilemma was to use her post-Holocaust life to teach and warn, to help people understand profoundly the importance of taking nothing good for granted.

"Try to look," wrote Delbo. "Just try and see." The more genocidal death is faced, the more likely that heartbreak, melancholy, futility, and despair will invade our minds and occupy our hearts. Anticipation that such moods stalk us, awareness that they can be paralyzing, may make one reluctant to do the looking and seeing that Delbo emphasized. But in spite of those moods, the very looking and seeing that evoke them can have other and better outcomes without preempting those gloomy dispositions and their validity, persistence, and insight.

Carrying the word—Gertrud Kolmar, Charlotte Delbo, and Sarah Kofman did so with penetrating insight that culminates in the challenge with which they leave us. "I beg you," as Delbo put it, "do something . . . / something to justify your existence . . . / because it would be too senseless / after all / for so many to have died / while you live / doing nothing with your life."[57]

---

57. Delbo, *Auschwitz and After*, 230.

8

Philip Hallie and Albert Camus

When the philosopher Philip Hallie said, "Lucidity and passion. That's my motto," he spoke for me and, I believe, for Albert Camus, the other source of Holocaust insight I credit in this chapter.[1] To explain how and why I pair them requires appreciation for the village of Le Chambon-sur-Lignon and its surroundings in the Plateau Vivarais-Lignon, part of the Haute Loire area of south-central France. I first learned about this place when I read Hallie's 1979 book *Lest Innocent Blood Be Shed: The Story of the Village of Le Chambon and How Goodness Happened There*. The book could not have included the updates, corrections, and expansions that later research necessitated, but much that I found in its pages withstands scrutiny and still resonates deeply for me.[2]

Harm and Help

Off the beaten path, Le Chambon and its neighboring villages and farms had long been of little note, but their legacy helped to make them a haven from the Holocaust. Since the sixteenth century, for example, the population of Le Chambon and its surroundings was predominantly Protestant, an anomaly in Catholic France. Even now, many of the villagers are descendants of dissenting Huguenots who fled to that high plateau, seeking to practice their Christianity without fear of persecution, a hope often dashed as hostility

---

1. Hallie, "Cruelty," 120. *Facing Evil*, which contains Hallie's essay, resulted from an important 1987 "Symposium on Understanding Evil," which took place at the Institute for the Humanities at Salado, Texas. The participants included the Holocaust scholar Raul Hilberg.

2. My account of Le Chambon relies on Hallie, *Lest Innocent Blood*; and Hallie, *Eye of the Hurricane*.

against them persisted. Some Le Chambon pastors and their parishioners were hanged or burned at the stake for fidelity to the biblical principles that gave meaning to their lives. Far from weakening their faith, such persecution—and the memory of it—strengthened the solidarity of the Chambonnais. That solidarity, which came to include Catholics and nonbelievers as well as a variety of Protestants, showed itself distinctively soon after Nazi Germany invaded France on May 12, 1940. During the Holocaust many of the region's people made their homes and farms arks of hope in a sea of flames and ashes.

In 1934, André and Magda Trocmé arrived in Le Chambon. Earlier, during World War I, André Trocmé lived in a part of France occupied by Germany. As he saw the war's devastation, he became friends with a German medic who believed that Christians should not kill. Influenced by the medic's example, Trocmé gradually forged a religious outlook that stressed nonviolent resistance to evil. In his view, evil was defined as doing harm to human life. Thus, the injunction not to kill was not enough. It had to be supplemented by positive action to relieve suffering and block harm's way.

Those views informed Trocmé's calling as a Protestant pastor. But they were not widely popular, and so he had been shunted to the backwater community of Le Chambon, where he was serving as the minister of the main church in the area when the Nazi invasion felled France in a few weeks. Geography placed Le Chambon in Vichy, the unoccupied region south of the Loire River where the Germans permitted a puppet government under France's World War I hero, Henri Philippe Pétain. Within a few months of France's defeat, the Vichy regime enacted its own harsh anti-Jewish legislation and authorized the internment of foreign Jews. Measures in the occupied zone were even more punitive and swiftly applied. Deportations of Jews from France to Auschwitz began in March 1942. By late 1942, as the Allies rolled back German gains in North Africa, the Germans occupied the Vichy zone of France, leaving few havens of any kind for Jews on French soil. Le Chambon, however, remained one of them.

Earlier, during the winter of 1940–41, Magda Trocmé had answered an evening knock at her door. A frightened woman identified herself as a German Jew. She had heard that help might be found in Le Chambon. Could she come in? Magda Trocmé's affirmative answer was emblematic of the village and its surroundings. Jewish refugees arrived in the area almost daily. They were fed, hidden, and whenever possible spirited across the Swiss border by helpers, some devout Christians and some not, who were convinced that it was simply wrong to leave anyone in harm's way.[3]

---

3. Criticisms of Hallie's account include that it overemphasized Le Chambon and

Why these acts did not bring German retribution to Le Chambon has not been fully explained, for the activities were never completely secret. One crucial reason, however, has been identified: namely, Major Julius Schmähling, the officer who served as the German military governor for two years when the Germans occupied that region of France. He knew what the people in and around Le Chambon were doing and let it happen. Likewise, André and Magda Trocmé and their followers knew that they had some protection. They did not let their opportunity slip away.

Some seventy-five thousand Jews in France lost their lives in the Holocaust. In the Holocaust's immense destruction, the few thousand rescued in Le Chambon and its surroundings may seem small. Nevertheless, the number stands large because it shows not only what did happen when those people were determined to save lives that were in harm's way but also what might have happened if others had followed their example.

Two other parts of the Le Chambon story are highly significant. First, the people of Le Chambon did what they could. They saved lives and limited the Germans' harmdoing, but the people of Le Chambon did not and could not stop World War II and the Holocaust. Nevertheless, they did what they could. Indeed, without expecting recognition or reward, they arguably did *all* that they could to help the neediest among them.

When asked why they did those things, the rescuers in Le Chambon were modest. Needy people such as those who knocked on Magda Trocmé's door should be helped, they said. It was the natural and right thing to do. Wouldn't anyone do the same? At least to me, however, such reasoning creates huge challenges. The people of Le Chambon were moral heroes or no

---

underplayed rescue efforts that took place in other parts of the Plateau Vivarais-Lignon and beyond. The rescue work done in Le Chambon was part of an extended and extensive network, which importantly reflects the social nature of effective ethical action. Numerous and varied groups in the region were involved, along with Swiss helpers who assisted the Jews who got across the French border. Critics also find that Hallie overemphasized the Trocmés and underplayed the work done by other ministers and people from diverse traditions and walks of life. In addition, debate swirls about the number of Jews saved in the area. Hallie said that Le Chambon "saved the lives of about five thousand refugees (most of them children)" (Hallie, *Lest Innocent Blood*, xiii). Exact statistics are not available, but the number of people rescued in the area may be less than Hallie's estimate. For more detail on these matters see Henry, *We Only Know Men*; Moorehead, *Village of Secrets*; and Sauvage, "French Rescue," a critical review of Moorehead's account. Note also that on January 5, 1971, Yad Vashem, Israel's official memorial to the victims of the Holocaust, recognized André Trocmé and his wife, Magda, as Righteous among the Nations, the special recognition given to non-Jews who rescued Jews during the Holocaust. Thirty-two other residents of Le Chambon sur Lignon have also been awarded that title, and in 1998, Yad Vashem gave the village a special diploma of honor in tribute to their rescue efforts during World War II. For further information on these matters, see Yad Vashem, "André and Magda Trocmé, Daniel Trocmé."

persons could be, but the reason that they were heroic was not because they did "everything" or "saved the world." It was because they did what they could in the times and places where they lived and worked. That challenge is the one that the example of Le Chambon puts before me and anyone who is concerned about ethics and the common good after the Holocaust. It should make us see and remember that limited though our power may be, we still have time and energy that can be used to prevent harm, save lives, and improve the chances for people to care for one another. Such work is not ours to complete, but it is ours to do, lest it goes undone and too little blocks and reverses harm's way.

Second, Hallie was not the only person who played an early part in making Le Chambon well known. In the early 1980s, before I met Philip Hallie for the first time, I became friends with a Los Angeles film maker who took an evening course that I was teaching about the Holocaust and the writings of Elie Wiesel. As I got to know Pierre Sauvage, I learned not only that he was creating a film about Le Chambon but also that he had been born there in 1944 because his parents were among the Jewish refugees who had found refuge in that area. Sauvage established a foundation that helped to build a memorial and museum at Le Chambon, but his film about the village and its surroundings—widely used in teaching about the Holocaust—has done more than anything else to call attention to that place and its moral example.

Sauvage called his film *Weapons of the Spirit*. The title comes from a sermon that André Trocmé preached soon after France fell to Nazi Germany. Trocmé underscored the importance of what Saint Paul called the weapons of the spirit or the weapons of righteousness, which are to be used to resist evil. Those weapons, as Trocmé and Sauvage understood them, are acts that seek to remove people from harm's way, which entails trying to remove the conditions in which harmdoing flourishes.

Meanwhile, both Hallie and Sauvage turned up other fascinating details. One of them was that the novelist and philosopher Albert Camus lived in the vicinity of Le Chambon for a time. Hoping that the mountain air would bring relief from the tuberculosis that besieged him, Camus arrived in the area in August 1942 and stayed until he left for Paris in late 1943. He probably knew about the rescue activities while he was writing *The Plague*, his important metaphorical novel. Sauvage stood in solidarity with Camus and the Chambonnais when he chose to begin *Weapons of the Spirit* with one of *The Plague*'s fundamental insights: "There always comes a time in history when the person who dares to say that two plus two equals four is punished with death. And the issue is not what reward or what punishment will be the outcome of that reasoning. The issue is simply whether or not two plus two equals four."[4]

Set in the Algerian city of Oran in the 1940s, Camus's novel chronicled the battle that Dr. Bernard Rieux fought against a lethal outbreak of bubonic plague. In the story, the disease takes an immense toll before eventually leaving Oran. The toll included the death of Jean Tarrou, a special friend who lived his conviction that "on this earth there are pestilences and there are victims, and it's up to us, so far as possible, not to join forces with the pestilences." Like his friend, Dr. Rieux did all he could to fight the plague. Its siege lifted but not forever. "The plague bacillus never dies or disappears for good," he remembers at the novel's end. The fight against it, he concludes, must be "never ending."[5] The part that the rescuers of Le Chambon and its surroundings played in their struggle against the Nazis' genocidal plague was summed up by Magda Trocmé's observation, "None of us thought that we were heroes. We were just people trying to do our best."[6] Those people may well have been on Camus's mind when he had Dr. Rieux conclude that "there are more things to admire in [people] than to despise."[7]

Hallie's Motto

Returning to Hallie's motto—lucidity and passion—among the perspectives it gave me was something that his Holocaust studies taught him: namely, that "you cannot go down into hell with impunity. You must pay an entrance fee, and an exit fee too."[8] In three major ways, that assessment deepened my Holocaust insight.

First, learning and teaching about the Holocaust require demanding study. Almost without relief, that study plunges one into abysmal darkness. Disorientation, melancholy, despair, even shame—those are among the somber moods that result. Hallie reports that when Elie Wiesel read *Lest Innocent Blood Be Shed* prior to its publication, he told Hallie that the book was about horror as well as love. "Imagine," Wiesel said to Hallie, "what kind of a world this was that made the hospitality of the people of Le Chambon

---

4. Sauvage's translation of Camus's French is slightly different, but see Camus, *Plague*, 132.

5. Camus, *Plague*, 253–54, 308.

6. This account of Le Chambon draws on Rittner and Roth, eds., *Different Voices*, 309–16.

7. Camus, *Plague*, 308.

8. Hallie, *Eye of the Hurricane*, 22. I have often used Hallie's book in my teaching.

so necessary and so extraordinary."[9] Once deeply moved by learning and teaching about the Holocaust, moreover, a person does not easily walk away. One reason is that a serious encounter with Holocaust history raises questions as persistent and disturbing as they are challenging: How must I live differently? What must we do better? Second, as I thought about Hallie's impact on me, I recognized that his statement—you cannot go down into hell with impunity—expresses what I have often felt in writing this book. Third, Hallie's assessment epitomized his larger outlook, which is close to mine.

To enlarge explanation of those three points, I first met Philip Hallie on February 15, 1986, at a University of San Diego conference on ethics. At that time, Hallie was studying Major Julius Schmähling, the aforementioned officer who for some time led the German occupation force around Le Chambon while the rescue activities were underway. Hallie's research after *Lest Innocent Blood Be Shed* reinforced that Schmähling knew what was going on and let it happen, but he was also a loyal soldier in the army of Nazi Germany. Schmähling fascinated Hallie as an example of "maculate," not immaculate, goodness, the term Hallie used in the title of the paper—"Maculate Goodness and Major Julius Schmähling"—on which I was asked to comment during the conference session devoted to "Virtue in Strained Circumstances."

Hallie's paper expressed profound admiration for the Chambonnais rescuers of Jews. His essay identified them as "morally pure."[10] As a former combat artilleryman in Europe during World War II, he said that he felt small and impure in comparison. But Hallie also admitted that his admiration for the Chambonnais harbored some resentment. They had not battled Hitler's armies as he had done. While they saved life without harming it, "decent killers" like him were necessary to stop Hitler.

Highlighting Schmähling's crucial part in Le Chambon's rescue effort, Hallie saw a man who seemed more like him than he took the Chambonnais to be. Both he and Schmähling had done some good, but their harmdoing compromised them both. His interest piqued, Hallie decided to find out more about Schmähling, sensing that important insight could be found in the German officer's "tainted goodness."

Hallie's research revealed that Schmähling was neither religious nor ideological. No clear-cut ethical theory guided him. But Schmähling's long

---

9. Hallie, *Eye of the Hurricane*, 108.

10. I draw from the text in my possession, which, to the best of my knowledge, has not been published in that form, although the paper's depiction of Major Julius Schmähling informed the expanded attention that Hallie gave to him elsewhere. See, for example, Hallie, *Eye of the Hurricane*, 60–90. Hallie, I believe, hoped to write a book about Schmähling, but that project was not finished.

experience as a teacher of history and literature impressed upon him the importance of "making room" for people. In his classrooms and even as the military governor of the Haute Loire in 1943 and 1944, Schmähling's nonreligious, nonideological way opened opportunities for him to do just that. Hallie did not call Schmähling heroic, but the conference paper ended by underscoring that Schmähling's example supported the insight that ethics is not simply a matter of good and evil but a matter of mixtures. Our calling is not to be perfect, but it is to do what we can to make room for caring help and compassionate respect in a world that all too often is cruelly cold and indifferent.

Did Hallie overestimate the moral purity of the Chambonnais and the "maculate goodness" of Schmähling as well? As it should, that question lingers. Meanwhile, the notes I used in my conference commentary on Hallie's 1986 paper still exist. Embedded in them, another question lingers, an important one, I believe, which I asked him to address: Where "maculate goodness" is concerned, how should we assess the harm versus the good that is done? If Schmähling can be called a good man, some who are not too many shades of gray removed from him have been called the same but probably do not deserve that honor. I can no longer document what Hallie said in reply, but my question remains important because the human condition entails that our goodness is far more likely to be maculate than immaculate. The search for Holocaust insight entails trying to think and act in ways that make maculate goodness as good as possible. So, as I look again at my commentary notes, I am glad to be reminded that I began my remarks by thanking Hallie and telling him then what remains even more true now: his work nudges me to keep going.

No Ideas but in Facts

Hallie helped me to understand better how philosophers and philosophy play vital parts in learning and teaching about the Holocaust. Shared elements in our life histories informed that understanding. We were both philosophers influenced by Albert Camus. Our professional lives had been changed by encounters with the Holocaust that made us impatient with the ahistorical tendencies of most academic philosophy. In addition, Hallie's roots, like mine, included the American Midwest. Our educational and career paths were similar too. He had gone to a liberal arts college (Grinnell) and then to a major research university (Harvard) for his graduate work before spending his teaching career as a philosophy professor at a small university (Wesleyan) in Middletown, Connecticut. A similar pattern had taken me from Pomona College to Yale University and then to Claremont McKenna College, in Claremont, California, where I taught for more than forty years.

Our histories had differences too. Hallie was my senior by eighteen years. He grew up in Chicago; my early homes were in small-town Michigan and Indiana. Born in 1922—he died in 1994—Hallie was a veteran of World War II, while I have scarcely any firsthand memories of that cataclysm. Religion was important to us both, but he was Jewish, and I am Christian—a difference that put us more in agreement, I believe, than at odds. Our outlooks, then, could not be the same, and yet again and again Hallie's resonated with mine.

"No ideas but in facts," Hallie liked to say, "no ideas but in things."[11] He called himself a skeptic. I agree with his skepticism, which had two parts: a suspicion of abstraction, closure, and finality and a conviction that details, particularities, and facts contain moral insights and have lessons to teach if we pay attention. Hallie knew much about ancient Greek philosophy. He reminded people that the early skeptics were doctors. Lucidity meant getting as clear as possible about what was happening, especially if disease was the focal point. Knowing what was going on was not enough, however, especially if disease was the focal point. Passion sharpened the focus. Hallie's skepticism entailed that one must be moved to act, to get people out of harm's way, and to help them. The bedrock of his ethics was that "it is better to help than to hurt," that the "vital center" of ethics is deep-down recognition of "the connection between the preciousness of my life and the preciousness of other lives," and that ethics, at its heartfelt best, is about "spreading the joys of living."[12]

One hand washes the other—fondness for that insight from Seneca, a Stoic philosopher, resonated with the resistance in Hallie's skepticism regarding moral indifference and ethical relativism. He liked to quote the British philosopher Geoffrey J. Warnock, who was right when he said: "That it is a bad thing to be tortured or starved, humiliated or hurt, is not an opinion; it is a fact. That it is better for people to be loved and attended to, rather than hated or neglected, is again a plain fact, not a matter of opinion."[13] No one, Warnock added, should be permitted to bully that truth away. In our lethal world, however, such bullying and worse abound. Hallie's blend of lucidity and passion, forged in the continuing collision between his wartime

11. Hallie, "Cruelty," 120.
12. Hallie, *Lest Innocent Blood*, xviii, 277; and Hallie, *Eye of the Hurricane*, 175.
13. Warnock, *Contemporary Moral Philosophy*, 60. See Hallie, *Eye of the Hurricane*, 54.

killing and his moral philosophy's emphasis on the preciousness of individual human life, amplified Warnock's conviction that right and wrong are matters of fact, not opinion. To say that it is wrong to be tortured or starved, or to say that the people of Le Chambon did the right thing when they welcomed Jewish refugees, should not succumb to the relativist's subverting question "who's to say?" When challenged to prove that more than opinion is involved in those judgments, Hallie understood that "I cannot prove this belief the way I can prove that I am alive," but, he argued, there is an expert, qualified judgment in such cases, and it belongs especially to "the drowned ones and the saved ones . . . They know."[14]

For Hallie, knowledge could never be purely "objective," for there is no such thing as pure objectivity. Knowledge roots itself in experience; human experience, in turn, depends upon our embodied selves and the times and places of the communities in which we live and on which we depend. The fact that knowledge exists in a historical context, however, does not mean that it is reduced to opinion on the grounds that human judgments are merely "subjective." Instead, Hallie's skepticism understood that the quality of experience determines the qualifications of the knowledge claims that are made. It is not, for instance, the judgment of the perpetrators or the bystanders that counts the most, if at all, when the claim in question is that the Holocaust was wrong. As Hallie put the point, "cruelty has authority and that authority is its *victims*. The victim of cruelty has an empirical authority like the authority of a doctor who's observing a patient, or better yet, like the authority of a patient about his or her own feelings."[15]

Hallie informed and nourished my Holocaust insight in one more way that requires recognition. His attention to detail and particularity made him an eloquent philosophical storyteller. One of his favorite stories centered on a hurricane.[16] This storm reached his Connecticut home, where he observed its havoc. But havoc was not all that Hallie saw. Even while the storm raged all around, he thought that space for calm and quiet existed within the hurricane's eye. "The eye of the hurricane," he observed, "is in the very middle of destructive power, and that power is always near." Yet, within the eye, he added, "the sky is blue."

Drawn to the blue sky overhead, Hallie had noticed birds that appeared to be "gliding happily high up in the eye of the hurricane," but later a knowledgeable friend told him that the birds "were actually in trouble, fighting to stay aloft in powerful downdrafts. Trapped in the eye, they were

---

14. Hallie, *Eye of the Hurricane*, 54.
15. Hallie, "Cruelty," 120 (italics original).
16. See Hallie, *Eye of the Hurricane*, vi, 51–56; and Hallie, "Cruelty," 128–30.

reeling from having slammed into the wall of wind surrounding it." Despite the plight of the struggling birds, Hallie's hurricane experience contained vision that provided him with moral insight.

> In a world of moral hurricanes some people can and do carve out rather large ethical spaces. In a natural world and a social world swirling in cruelty and love we can make room. We who are not pure ethical beings can push away the choking circle of brute force that is around and within us. We may not be able to push it far . . . , but when we have made as much room as we can, we may know a blue peace that the storm does not know.[17]

Hallie embraced much of Albert Camus's thought, and thus in ways akin to Dr. Rieux's struggle with the plague, Hallie liked to say that "it's the hurricane we're in. Don't forget it." But again like Camus, he did not see that condition as one that should harbor resignation, indifference, and hopelessness. Within the ever-menacing storm, there can be, must be space like the haven provided by Le Chambon. More than that, Hallie's passion was to use his lucidity to do what he could to "expand the blue."[18] Ethically speaking, blue was his favorite color. Some people, Hallie believed, "make a larger space for blue, for peace, for love." He showed me that those who seek Holocaust insight should try to be in that company—no easy task because making a larger space for blue, he added, "takes power as well as love. It takes force of will. It takes assertion and commitment."[19]

A Means to Joy

With World War II and the Holocaust in mind, Albert Camus, who received the Nobel Prize for Literature in 1957, made a statement as stark as it is bold. "Every action today," he wrote, "leads to murder, direct or indirect . . . Murder is the problem today."[20] His outlook implied that human beings live in a murderous web of responsibility that implicates us all. Camus thought that even by its greatest effort, humanity "can only propose to diminish arithmetically the sufferings of the world." But, he insisted, "the injustice and the suffering of the world . . . will not cease to be an outrage," and, he added, "perhaps we cannot prevent this world from being a world in which

---

17. Hallie, *Eye of the Hurricane*, vi.
18. Hallie, "Cruelty," 128.
19. Hallie, "Cruelty," 129.
20. Camus, *Rebel*, 4–5.

children are tortured. But we can reduce the number of tortured children."²¹ That outlook led him to contemplate the fate of Sisyphus, the mythical Greek king who passionately loved life and defied fate by thwarting death itself. The gods condemned Sisyphus to a ceaseless repetition that required him to push a weighty rock up a mountain only to have it roll back to the bottom as he neared the top.

In *The Myth of Sisyphus*, Camus depicted Sisyphus in ways that hone a needed edge for Holocaust insight. "At the very end of his long effort," wrote Camus, "Sisyphus watches the stone rush down . . . whence he will have to push it up again toward the summit. He goes back down to the plain. It is during that return, that pause," said Camus, "that Sisyphus interests me . . . If the descent is . . . sometimes performed in sorrow, it can also take place in joy. This word is not too much . . . The struggle itself toward the heights is enough to fill a man's heart. One must imagine Sisyphus happy."²²

As I age in the troubled and troubling twenty-first century, no insights about the importance of ethical resistance, no matter how great the odds or forlorn the prospects for lasting success, mean more to me than those embedded in Camus's depiction of Sisyphus. Meanwhile, during the late spring of 1959, Philip Hallie was in Paris. Less than a year before Camus lost his life in a car crash at the age of forty-six, Hallie had his only personal meeting with him. One of Hallie's most touching essays, published posthumously, describes the visit and the meaning that Hallie took from it.²³ Camus, wrote Hallie,

> wanted to put himself at the service, not of the makers of history, but rather of the victims of that history. And he would have to do this again and again and again, knowing that his revolt against death would never defeat death. He would just try to limit the harm done. The world is not benign; there will always be victims, but we can feel solidarity with the victims we can embrace; we can feel the joy of helping a few people a few times. The rock will roll down the hill again; but when we are pushing it up the hill with our cheeks against it and our arms spread out on it, we can be close to that hardness and make a little difference, though only temporarily. We can have the joy of friendship, of love, even while we forget nothing, not even murder.²⁴

---

21. Camus, *Rebel*, 303; and Camus, *Resistance*, 55.
22. Camus, *Myth of Sisyphus*, 89–91.
23. Hallie, "Camus's Hug," 428–35.
24. Hallie, "Camus's Hug," 434–35.

In that passage, one increasingly meaningful to me, Hallie emphasizes *joy*—the joy of helping, the joy of friendship and love—while never forgetting murder and always trying to see the murdered dead. Such joy, I believe, is related to the scorn that Camus attributed to Sisyphus. Refusing to be driven to despair by the worst crimes against humanity, such joy defies atrocity, even if not victoriously. With that sense of joy in mind, Camus called Sisyphus happy.

Hallie went a step further, and, again, his insight informs mine: Ethics, he said, including responses to ethical failure, should be "a means of joy."[25] The joy that Camus and Hallie had in mind was not sentimental, occasional, or fleeting. It was scarcely synonymous with fun. Resistant and resilient, the joy they had in mind was what I like to call an *in-spite-of* joy. Kindled and sustained by friendship, by the help that we give as well as receive, by doing what is right and good, by love, such joy sustains solidarity with those who oppose and limit harm, relieve suffering, and save lives. Declining to give in or give up, *in-spite-of* joy keeps people going even though the work of studying, supporting, and defending human rights has no end and, at times, may seem to be a forlorn cause.

Hallie and Camus—my conclusion follows theirs: We neither should nor can eliminate the darkness into which facing death and, in particular, the death unleashed by the Holocaust, genocide, and other mass atrocities plunges us, but working together with others, and standing in solidarity with those who resisted and rescued during the Holocaust, I can try my best to be sure that memory of the Holocaust and other atrocities continues, that education about those catastrophes advances, and that the purposes of those activities include equipping us to resist injustice, to protest when life is disrespected, to live in ways that, in spite of mass-atrocity crimes, still seek to mend the world, and to find and encourage joy when those steps are taken.

We cannot avoid despair over the fact that memory of the Holocaust, genocide, and other mass atrocities, including education about them, have not dislodged the likelihood that death by atrocity will be faced again and again. But working together with others and standing in solidarity with those who resist and rescue, we can try our best to make human existence better than it otherwise will be. Facing death inflicted by the Holocaust and other atrocities reveals human failure as nothing else can. Facing death with that understanding still leaves us to ask what we will do next—today, tomorrow, and the day after tomorrow. Within resistance against moral failure,

---

25. Hallie, "Cruelty," 129. See also Hallie's contributions to *Facing Evil*, a DVD.

contentment should not be found. But in that resistance, meaning and joy must be ours.

Lasting Moral Marks

Through their particularity, stories arguably communicate ethics more accessibly and persuasively than any other form of human communication. That insight was focused by my first encounter with Camus, which took place in the spring of 1960 during my sophomore year at Pomona College. While taking a course on great novels, I studied *The Plague*. It left a lasting moral mark upon me and led to a lifelong engagement with Camus's philosophy, which I later taught to students in my courses on Existentialism, despite the disclaimer that this outlook, which he associated with Jean-Paul Sartre, was not his.

Camus is not remembered primarily as a Holocaust-related writer, but as my commitment to Holocaust studies developed, my appreciation for him grew and deepened. Not only can one scarcely read *The Plague* without thinking of the Holocaust, but also Camus's contributions to Holocaust insight are enormous in other ways. In addition to his lasting moral marks on Philip Hallie and me, Camus explicitly and significantly influenced Richard Rubenstein and Elie Wiesel, two of the foremost sources of my Holocaust insight. Jean Améry, whom I discuss in a later chapter, was more overtly influenced by Sartre, but I am not alone in sensing Camus's presence in his reflections too.[26]

Commenting specifically on *The Plague*, Rubenstein said that no twentieth-century writer had dealt better with the problem, in its universal form, of divine providence and murderous, genocidal destruction. In particular, Camus's novel explored and rejected logic that sees such destruction as punishment for sin—a rejection that resonated with Rubenstein's Holocaust-driven rejection of Judaism's traditional views about the God of history. Camus, said Rubenstein, "accepts the tragedy, the inevitability, and the gratuitous absurdity of suffering, but he refuses to consent to its justice. He would rather live in an absurd, indifferent cosmos in which people suffer and die meaninglessly but still retain a measure of tragic integrity than see every last human event encased in a pitiless framework of meaning which deprives people of even the consolation that suffering, though inevitable, is not entirely merited or earned."[27]

26. See, for example, Anderson, "Absurd Dignity," 74–94.
27. Rubenstein, *After Auschwitz*, 18.

Rubenstein also found Camus on target in an essay called "Summer in Algiers," which Camus wrote in 1936 and included in *The Myth of Sisyphus*. Camus contrasted his native Algiers, its openness to sea and sky, with Europe's old, walled cities, "closed in on themselves."[28] Celebrating an Algerian zest for living in which "no deceptive divinity has traced the signs of hope or of redemption," Camus underscored his discerning that "there is no superhuman happiness, no eternity outside the sweep of days . . . If there is a sin against life, it consists perhaps not so much in despairing of life as in hoping for another life and in eluding the implacable grandeur of this life."[29]

Camus wrote those words before the Holocaust made it harder to avoid despair about life's "implacable grandeur," but Rubenstein stood with Camus, finding him correct "when he suggested that, of all the evils in Pandora's box, none was so great as hope." Rubenstein went on to say that he rejected "ultimate hope completely. I don't mean that I cannot hope that tomorrow I will have a good day or that in the years ahead I may enjoy a measure of fulfillment in life. I reject hope in the sense that I believe that out of Nothingness we have come and to Nothingness we will return. This is our ultimate situation."[30] By no means did Rubenstein's outlook originate from or even depend on Camus's, but as Rubenstein acknowledged, Camus left lasting moral marks upon him.

Sometimes the lasting moral marks that Camus left on me are found in my disagreement with him. I think, for example, that Camus went too far when he said that "hope equals resignation."[31] Hope would be that way if it did not encourage protest and resistance against mass atrocities, but at its realistic best, that is what hope does. True, Sisyphus had no hope that the next time up the hill, his rock would stay put and not have to be pushed uphill again and forever. But his defiant joy can provide and inspire hope that destruction and death may not have the last word, which they do not deserve. And to the extent that such a possibility exists, then Rubenstein's judgment about "our ultimate situation" is not necessarily true either. At the least, questions remain more fundamental than the problematic certitude that Camus and Rubenstein sometimes give their boldest assertions.

Elie Wiesel also indicated that Albert Camus left lasting moral marks on him. In postwar France, Wiesel worked as a journalist and became acquainted with Camus, who was fifteen years older and already a well-established writer. Camus's essays and novels influenced Wiesel early on—"I

---

28. Camus, "Summer in Algiers," in *Myth of Sisyphus*, 104.
29. Camus, "Summer in Algiers," in *Myth of Sisyphus*, 111–13.
30. Rubenstein, "Thomas Altizer's Apocalypse," 129.
31. Camus, "Summer in Algiers," in *Myth of Sisyphus*, 113.

read everything by Camus," said Wiesel—and, throughout his life, Wiesel acknowledged the significance of Camus's thought.[32] In his memoirs, for example, Wiesel suggested that his insistent criticism of indifference had roots in Camus's thought: "One of the main tenets of my life," wrote Wiesel, "has been: '*Lo ta'amod al dam reakha* . . .' Do not be indifferent to the bloodshed inflicted on your fellow man (Leviticus 19:16). Not to take a stand is in itself to take a stand, said Camus."[33] And again: "Surely, when human lives are involved, indifference is not an answer. Not to choose is also a choice, said the French philosopher Albert Camus. Neutrality helps the aggressor, not his victims."[34]

Other moments when Wiesel credited Camus, vital to me because of their connection to the themes of protest and *in-spite-of* joy, can be found in Wiesel's early novel *The Town beyond the Wall*, when Michael, a young Holocaust survivor, returns to his hometown in Hungary, once a place where Nazis deported Jews but now under postwar Communist tyranny. Betrayed, imprisoned, and tortured, Michael finds that memory of his friend Pedro helps him to resist by doing what he can to save his despondent cellmate. Michael's remembering includes Pedro's telling him how "Camus wrote somewhere that to protest against a universe of unhappiness you had to create happiness. That's an arrow pointing the way: it leads to another human being."[35] And again: In a 1967 symposium on "Jewish Values in the Post-Holocaust Future," Wiesel observed that "as Camus would say: one must create happiness to protest against a universe of unhappiness. But—one must *create* it."[36] "As Camus would say"—the acknowledgment in that phrase is emblematic of the lasting moral mark Camus left on Wiesel and on me as well.

Meaning and the Absurd

In his 1968 book *Legends of Our Time*, Elie Wiesel included an essay called "The Guilt We Share." Its point of departure was the 1961 trial of Adolf Eichmann, a key architect and perpetrator of the "Final Solution." Early in that essay, Wiesel recalled asking the literary critic Alfred Kazin "if he

---

32. Wiesel, *All Rivers*, 189. For an account of Camus's impact on the young Wiesel in France, see Lamont, "Elie Wiesel," 80–98.
33. Wiesel, *Sea Is Never Full*, 88.
34. Wiesel, *Sea Is Never Full*, 398.
35. Wiesel, *Town*, 118.
36. See Wiesel's contribution to "Jewish Values in the Post-Holocaust Future," 291.

thought the death of six million Jews could have any meaning." The reply, said Wiesel, was that Kazin "hoped not."[37]

Wiesel's question and Kazin's reply are worth pondering. The reply "I hope not" might seem utterly disrespectful, but Wiesel did not take it that way. Instead, I believe, Wiesel took Kazin's rejection of meaning to be a cautionary injunction, for if we say quickly and easily, "Oh, yes, the Holocaust has meaning," then not only would one have to say what the meaning is, but also in doing that, one might run the risk of justifying or legitimizing the Holocaust by turning that disaster into the means that support or tend toward some great end, or by proclaiming an answer to what Wiesel called "the metaphysical *why*," which would give the Holocaust its "proper" place in the "meaning" of life or in the "meaning" of history or in "God's plan."

More than *having* meaning, the Holocaust *destroyed* meaning. That perspective may *give* the Holocaust meaning, but, if it does, the meaning is primarily and catastrophically negative. Put another way, as Wiesel did in his essay on "The Guilt We Share," the Holocaust and its aftereffects reveal massive human failure, which is ruinous presently and may portend even greater ruin to come. Versions of that perspective haunted and governed the outlook of Albert Camus, who felt that traditional values and ways of life had collapsed during World War II and its aftermath—so much so that the first essay in *The Myth of Sisyphus* began with a judgment as stark as it was bold: "There is but one truly serious philosophical problem, and that is suicide. Judging whether life is or is not worth living amounts to answering the fundamental question of philosophy."[38] For Camus, that inquiry required encountering what he called "the absurd." Reverberations of the Holocaust resound within it, even if Camus did not detail them explicitly.

Camus thought that absurdity comes to us in a feeling that can strike a person "at any streetcorner." One "feels an alien, a stranger"—even to oneself.[39] This feeling results from an encounter between the world and the demands we make as rational beings. Specifically, said Camus, "the real is not entirely rational, nor is the rational entirely real," and absurdity arises from the confrontation between "human need and the unreasonable silence of the world."[40] The Holocaust, genocide, and other mass atrocities lead to a thousand "whys" that lack answers, and countless needs that go unmet. We want solutions, but we stir up absurdity because our efforts to find them seem doomed to come up short.

37. Wiesel, *Legends*, 162.
38. Camus, *Myth of Sisyphus*, 3.
39. Camus, *Myth of Sisyphus*, 5, 9.
40. Camus, *Rebel*, 295; and Camus, *Myth of Sisyphus*, 21.

"The absurd," wrote Camus, "depends as much on [us] as on the world."[41] Thus, when we ask the question of life's meaning, or the meaning of the Holocaust, we realize that our yearning for answers gives rise to the feeling of absurdity as much as any characteristic of the world itself. The problem is that the meaning we seek, and especially the meaning we take for granted, can crumble—almost before we know it—because the "why" gnaws and persists without resolution. The absurd, said Camus, "is essentially a divorce."[42] Intensified by the Holocaust, the absurd is what results when human consciousness and the world collide and split.

Nevertheless, the Holocaust and the absurd do not eliminate meaning, at least not completely, and Camus believed that the quest for answers that satisfy us neither can nor should go away. That quest makes us human. "If, after all, men cannot always make history have a meaning," said Camus, "they can always act so that their own lives have one."[43] Indeed, he thought that human greatness is found in a person's "decision to be stronger than his condition. And if his condition is unjust, he has only one way of overcoming it, which is to be just himself."[44]

Convinced that he could not escape the absurd no matter how long he lived, Camus sometimes spoke of "hopeless hope" but still insisted that existence implies "a total absence of hope."[45] He could see nothing that could make it possible for him to transcend the absurd. Death, however, would put an end to it. Hence, suicide was an option. Indeed, because absurdity infects existence so painfully, would it not make sense to say that the absurd invites us to die, even dictates that we should?

Camus's answer was an emphatic *no*. Of course, the option of suicide remains, and several of my sources of Holocaust insight—Sarah Kofman, for example, Tadeusz Borowski, Jean Améry, and probably Primo Levi—made that choice. But Camus's decision went in a different direction. Absurdity will not go away if we say that we refuse to die. On the contrary, it will remain and even deepen. But Camus thought we should let absurdity remain in order to defy it. Indeed, he even advised that we should make a point of contemplating the absurd, because life can be lived better if it lacks ultimate meaning. Defiance of the absurd maximizes life's passion in a way that would not be possible if, for instance, some transcendent God guaranteed life's significance.

41. Camus, *Myth of Sisyphus*, 16.
42. Camus, *Myth of Sisyphus*, 22–23.
43. Camus, *Resistance*, 79.
44. Camus, *Resistance*, 30.
45. Camus, *Resistance*, 14; and Camus, *Myth of Sisyphus*, 23.

Sisyphus was Camus's absurd hero. He loved life and hated death. His passions condemned him, but Camus thought he never gave up and was never dishonest. Sisyphus accepted his fate so that he could defy it. Thereby he gave meaning to existence, meaning that cannot negate absurdity but refused to succumb to its impact. In no way, then, did the absurd dictate death, but Camus saw that the absurd made another question loom large. If absurdity reigns, then that would seem to imply a demise of ethics that opens the door to nihilism, including the propositions that might makes right and that anything and everything are permitted. Specifically, Camus wondered, does the absurd legitimate murder?

Again, Camus's answer was an emphatic *no*. If the absurd implies that everything is permitted, it does not follow that nothing is forbidden. Building on the insight that the most authentically human response to absurdity is to protest against it, Camus emphasized that such defiance does and should have a social and political component. Absurdity enters existence not so much because my own private needs go unmet, but because disasters such as the Holocaust, genocide, and other mass atrocities waste lives and rob relationships of significance. Hence, far from dictating suicide or legitimizing murder, the absurd should lead to rebellion in the name of justice and human solidarity. As Camus said, "I rebel—therefore we exist."[46]

Another uphill climb no different from that of Sisyphus awaits because Camus's sense of rebellion was governed by moderation. He did not mean that action should be hesitant, dispassionate, or weak, but he did not want the rebel to become the revolutionary who so often destroys life under the pretense of saving it. "The logic of the rebel," said Camus, "is to want to serve justice so as not to add to the injustice of the human condition, to insist on plain language so as not to increase the universal falsehood, and to wage, in spite of human misery, for happiness." Camus was no pacifist. He knew that the rebel, akin to Hallie's "decent killers" and Schmähling's "tainted goodness," might have to resort to violence in defense of justice and freedom. But just as two plus two equals four, lucidity required seeing that violent action ought not be cloaked in unwarranted moral legitimation. Instead, the authentic rebel would honestly accept the dilemma that such action, necessary though it might be, remains unacceptable and "inexcusable."[47] Thus, a true rebel, Camus affirmed and Hallie agreed, will insist that "no cause justifies the death of the innocent," and never say or do anything "to legitimize murder because rebellion, in principle, is a protest against death."[48]

46. Camus, *Rebel*, 22.
47. Camus, *Rebel*, 169.
48. Camus, *Resistance*, 100; and Camus, *Rebel*, 285.

As if the task of rebellion were not difficult enough, Camus again underscored that the true rebel can never expect to escape the fate of Sisyphus. Perhaps things would have been different if the world had been ours to create. But at least, said Camus, "Man is not entirely to blame; it was not he who started history." On the other hand, neither "is he entirely innocent, since he continues it." As one wrestles with meaning and the absurd in this atrocity world of ours, the human task, as Camus said, is "to learn to live and to die, and, in order to be a [human being], to refuse to be a god." And for a Christian like me, Camus, an atheist who dialogued with Christians, got it right when he said insightfully, persistently, "What the world expects of Christians is that Christians should speak out loud and clear, and that they should voice their condemnation in such a way that never a doubt, never the slightest doubt, could rise in the heart of the simplest man. That they should get away from abstraction and confront the blood-stained face history has taken on today."[49]

Camus acknowledged that "there is so much stubborn hope in the human heart," and I continue to have my share, especially about the possibility that Martin Luther King Jr. may have been right when he envisioned what he called "the arc of the moral universe," which is long but bending, he insisted, toward justice.[50] Philip Hallie's Holocaust contemplation, its lucidity and passion, taught him that "you cannot go down into hell with impunity. You must pay an entrance fee, and an exit fee too."[51] Camus joins Hallie to help me see what those fees charge: recognition that more than *having* meaning, the Holocaust *destroyed* meaning; resolve to keep confronting unresolved Holocaust encounters with the absurd; rebellion against the conditions, forces, and persons that will doom the world to wrack and ruin unless their antisemitism and racism are curbed and their tyranny checked; reaffirmation that in such work profound meaning, including an *in-spite-of* joy, can and must be found.

---

49. Camus, *Rebel*, 297, 306; and Camus, *Resistance*, 53.

50. Camus, *Myth of Sisyphus*, 76. See also King, "Where Do We Go from Here?" This address to the Southern Christian Leadership Conference on August 16, 1967, is accessible on the Martin Luther King, Jr. Research and Education Institute website. For the URL that links to the speech, see the bibliography.

51. Hallie, *Eye of the Hurricane*, 22.

9

Friends and Teachers III

Absent perceptive writing—the research and narration, the inspiration and passion, the testimony and search for truth that inform it—Holocaust insight would be diminished. Absent discerning art—the perspective and vision, the tones and moods, the senses of time and place that bring it to life—Holocaust insight would be impoverished. Absent people, the preceding propositions would make no sense because writing requires writers and art depends on artists. For me, it follows that people are my major and fundamental sources of Holocaust insight.[1] This chapter recognizes writers who have been my partners. It pays respect to artists—poets and painters—who keep enriching my inquiry.

Partners

Partners work together. My sources of Holocaust insight include that relationship. Some of my partners are writing companions, and in that way,

---

1. More people than I can name have advanced my Holocaust studies as partners and artists, but in addition to those discussed in this chapter and elsewhere in this book, I acknowledge Mehnaz Afridi, Avril Alba, Sandra and Cornelius Alfers, Alex Alvarez, Gordon Anderson, Martha Andresen, Rachel Baum, Beth Hawkins Benedict, Alan Berger, Sara Bloomfield, Adam Brown, Suzanne Brown-Fleming, Harry James Cargas, Jolene Chu, Leigh Crawford, Lee Ann De Reus, Michael Dobkowski, Robert Ehrenreich, Ivan Fehrenbach, Eva Fleischner, Richard Freedman, Jennifer Geddes, Myrna Goldenberg, Alfred Gottschalk, P. Edward Haley, Marilyn Harran, Stephen Haynes, Alexis Herr, Jaye Houston, Colin Hunter, Björn Krondorfer, Hubert Locke, George R. Lucas Jr., Elisabeth Maxwell, Rochelle Millen, Sarah Pinnock, Elena Procario-Foley, Ravenel Richardson, Alan Rosen, Tharcisse Seminega, Paul Shapiro, Julius Simon, Robert Skloot, James and Stephen Smith, Bonnie and John Snortum, Joel Susel, Samuel Totten, Ellen Trachtenberg, Robert Ventresca, Bret Werb, Carl Wilkins, and Kirsti Zitar.

they are my good friends and trusted teachers. Sometimes partners dance together. I am not a good dancer, and I have never literally danced with any of the people to whom I pay tribute here. But writing together can be a form of dance, and in the metaphorical dancing I have done with the partners identified next, I have received encouragement, meaning, and joy.

Michael Berenbaum

One of the most talented and distinguished Holocaust scholars of his generation, Michael Berenbaum—professor of Jewish studies and director of the Sigi Ziering Institute at the American Jewish University, author or editor of more than twenty books—was the project director tasked with overseeing the creation of the United States Holocaust Memorial Museum and the first director of its research institute. He later served at president and CEO of the Survivors of the Shoah Visual History Foundation. He is the founder and head of the Berenbaum Group, whose film productions and museum designs focus on the Holocaust and other genocides.

In the autumn of 1976, Richard Rubenstein, our friend and mentor in common, introduced me to Berenbaum. Friendship grew, deepened through shared commitment to teaching and writing about the Holocaust. An auspicious moment in our partnership took place on Thursday evening, December 10, 1987, when we outlined a book called *Holocaust: Religious and Philosophical Implications* during dinner at the Old Ebbitt Grill in Washington, DC. Our outline emphasized writings frequently studied at the time, most of them authored by Holocaust survivors or pioneering scholars. Even then, those writings were scattered widely, some in books and journals no longer in print. We decided to make the reflections conveniently accessible, a project that seemed especially important to help students study the Holocaust. Our book appeared in 1989 and has been in print ever since. Its contents remain significant.

In 1994, Berenbaum's advocacy led to President Bill Clinton's appointing me to the United States Holocaust Memorial Council, the governing body for the United States Holocaust Memorial Museum. About the same time, Berenbaum opened the way for me to do some of the most demanding and challenging writing I ever attempted: namely, the text—concise but comprehensive—for the permanent exhibition at Holocaust Museum Houston, which opened in that Texas city on March 3, 1996. My friend's counsel helped me through difficult times in 1998, when I aborted a short-lived appointment to direct the Center for Advanced Holocaust Studies at the United States Holocaust Memorial Museum.[2] "Friendship," said Philip Hallie, a colleague of Berenbaum's at Wesleyan University in the 1970s, "involves wishing good things . . . for one another, but it also involves being there for one another, in misery and in joy."[3] For decades, Berenbaum's friendship has been that way for me.

Berenbaum has long been my partner in recognizing that the power of no event exceeds the power of the Holocaust to raise the right and real questions and to beckon us to reckon with them. Among his many Holocaust insights, none is more important and challenging than his proposition that the Holocaust has become and must remain a "negative absolute."[4] Even if people remain skeptical that rational agreement can be obtained about what is right, just, and good, the Holocaust seems to reestablish conviction that what happened at Auschwitz and Treblinka was wrong, unjust, and evil—period, full stop.

Unfortunately, to identify the Holocaust as a negative absolute that reinstates confidence in moral absolutes is a step that cannot be taken easily. The fact is that the Holocaust signified an immense human failure. It did harm to ethics by showing how ethical teachings could be overridden or even subverted to serve the interests of genocide.[5] When Berenbaum calls the Holocaust a negative absolute, the absoluteness involved means that not even ethics itself was immune from failure and, at times, complicity in the pathological conditions and characteristics that nearly destroyed Jewish life and left the world morally scarred forever. Berenbaum's insight includes a key question: What follows, what should follow if he is right—or wrong—about the Holocaust's status as a negative absolute?

Carol Rittner

"Where," she asked, "are the women?" The voice I heard on the telephone was Carol Rittner's. She had just received a copy of Roth and Berenbaum's *Holocaust: Religious and Philosophical Implications*. It included classic Holocaust reflections by influential writers such Elie Wiesel, Raul Hilberg, Primo Levi, and Jean Améry. Rittner liked the book, but its contents were male-dominated. Her question was justified.

Rittner's question did not come out of the blue. It was raised in friendship that began in 1984, when she invited me to participate in a conference

2. For further information on this episode, see Roth, *Holocaust Politics*, 10–27.
3. Hallie, *Eye of the Hurricane*, 206.
4. Berenbaum, "Who Owns the Holocaust?" 60.
5. On these points see Bauman, *Modernity*; and Glover, *Humanity*.

on "Faith in Humankind, Rescuers of Jews during the Holocaust," which took place that September at the US Department of State with support from Elie Wiesel and sponsorship from the United States Holocaust Memorial Council. When Rittner became the first executive director of the Elie Wiesel Foundation in 1987, I was privileged to work with her on international conferences about "The Anatomy of Hate" and on the establishment of the foundation's annual Ethics Essay Contest, which began in 1989. In addition, Rittner's focus on "The Troubles," the conflict in Northern Ireland, took me there to work with her on reconciliation efforts in the 1990s.

Rittner's inspiration and encouragement have been as long and strong for me as our friendship. Her good question—Where are the women?—nudged us both into action. Published in 1993, *Different Voices: Women and the Holocaust* was our joint response to questions such as "Where were the women during the Holocaust?" and "How do the particularities of women's experiences in that event compare and contrast with those of men?" The Nazi genocide targeted and destroyed women—Jews especially but also non-Jews. The active or passive complicity of other women—Germans but also non-Germans—facilitated and legitimated the process of destruction that annihilated millions. During the Holocaust, women lived in ghettos and in hiding. They struggled to survive in resistance units as well as in concentration camps and killing centers. Other women served in German offices, military operations, killing fields, and camps or made homes for the men who did most of the dirty, killing work that their Nazi oaths of loyalty required. Just as the Nazis tried to persuade German women that no duty was more important than bearing sons for the Third Reich, they also insisted with a vengeance that Jewish motherhood must be eradicated forever.

In the early 1990s, relatively little attention was paid to women's Holocaust-related experiences. In retrospect, it is amazing to recall that when attention turned in that direction, those steps were often contested and criticized. Fortunately, *Different Voices* helped to change perspectives—including mine—for the better. Carol Rittner repeatedly does that important work. No friend has been more important as a source of insight about the Holocaust, its implications and reverberations. A Sister of Mercy, Rittner is one of the most entrepreneurial women I know. She envisions, organizes, and finds the resources to advance one good cause after another. Early on, I learned to follow her suggestions, which often led me to places that otherwise would not have been mine.

Rittner's outcome-oriented outlook usually brings people together to write and publish work that could be used in teaching. As the second decade of the twenty-first century draws to a close, Rittner and I have collaborated on more than a dozen book projects, including sequels to *Different Voices* that focus on rape and other forms of sexualized violence during and after the Holocaust, and on how teachers and students can cope best with that fraught topic.[6]

Next up, a Rittner-Roth book called *Advancing Holocaust Studies* is underway. It brings leading scholar-teachers together to grapple with a challenging fact: Growing and maturing for more than forty years, the field of Holocaust studies faces a world still wracked by antisemitism, racism (including white nationalism), intractable and often violent conflicts, immigration and refugee crises, human rights abuses, mass-atrocity crimes, threats of nuclear war, and environmental degradation. What does the advancement of Holocaust studies signify and mean in that context? Vast resources support study and memorialization of the Holocaust. What assumptions govern that investment? What hopes drive it? Where are the major successes and failures to be found? How should the field of Holocaust studies build upon the successes, and what does it need to do and become to address the shortcomings? Carol Rittner is a source of fundamental insight because she emboldens the courage to care about such issues.

Lenny Grob, Hank Knight, and David Patterson

In 1996, while I was on a Fulbright fellowship in Norway, I applied to participate in a project organized by two friends of mine: the philosopher Leonard (Lenny) Grob and the theologian Henry (Hank) Knight. Their plan called for a symposium on the Holocaust, which would create a group—international, interdisciplinary, interfaith, and intergenerational—that would convene biennially at Fairleigh Dickinson University's Wroxton College campus in Oxfordshire, England.

The application information indicated that the symposium would have a practical orientation. Anchored in Holocaust studies, it would encourage participants to address questions such as these: How are we to respond in word and deed to a radically transformed world, the post-Holocaust world in which "business as usual" must no longer apply? How are we to use our learning from the Holocaust to face, responsibly, the genocidal potentials inherent in our own times and places? The symposium, moreover, would have a limited number of participants—about thirty-five—and it would be designed to stimulate ongoing and sustained collegial work, which would be based in small working groups where shared concerns could be found. An additional expectation was that the work initiated in the small groups would develop and have some concrete results. When I submitted my application

---

6. See Rittner and Roth, eds., *Rape*; and Rittner and Roth, eds., *Teaching about Rape*.

to participate in this project, I scarcely could have imagined what a rich source of insight the Wroxton symposium would be.

My application underscored concern about what had happened to ethics during and after the Holocaust. Other applicants shared that interest, and soon after our arrival at Wroxton College in June 1996, six of us had become the "ethics group." Its members included: Peter Haas, who had done groundbreaking work on what he called the "Nazi ethic"; Didier Pollefeyt, a scholar from the Katholieke Universitet Leuven, Belgium; David Hirsch, now deceased, who did pathbreaking work in Holocaust literature; David Patterson, a prolific and prodigious writer, now at the University of Texas, Dallas, whose thought is destined to have lasting impact on Jewish philosophy and religious reflection; and Lenny Grob, a man of gentle spirit and robust organizational efficiency, who had been led to Holocaust studies through uncovering the history of the destruction of his father's family during the Holocaust. Our work together at Wroxton extended beyond the summer of 1996 as we committed to producing a book. *Ethics After the Holocaust: Perspectives, Critiques, and Responses* appeared three years later.[7] It featured a dialogical format in which essayists responded to one another within the volume.

My work in the Wroxton "ethics group" influenced me in at least two lasting ways. First, Grob, Patterson, and Pollefeyt were deeply engaged with the thought of Emmanuel Levinas. At the time, I knew of him but did not know much about his thinking. My Holocaust insight grew as those three friends took me more thoroughly and deeply into Levinas's ethics. Second, the work of the "ethics group," including the dialogical writing it did, attracted interest from other small groups in the Wroxton circle. Grob, Patterson, and I began to envision a post-Holocaust book series, and when Patterson contacted his editor at the University of Washington Press, we soon had a commitment to develop what became the Stephen S. Weinstein Series in Post-Holocaust Studies, which Patterson and I edited.

As Patterson and I wrote the introductory essays for books in the Weinstein Series, and as I was led to thoroughly study his own work, I discerned that he was giving me a crucial insight about the Holocaust. The Nazis' "Final Solution" sought more than the destruction of Jewish persons. Its violence intended to destroy Jewish traditions and teachings, desecrating God and humankind by wiping out the idea that every child, woman, and man is created in the image of God, which entails an imperative against murder. It is not enough to say that the Nazis targeted Jews for elimination because they were convenient scapegoats for social problems. More fundamental,

---

7. See Roth, ed., *Ethics after the Holocaust*.

Patterson has rightly argued, the Jews' presence in the world contained "a testimony to the sanctity of every human being, and that testimony cannot exist in the same universe with Nazi ideology." Jewish tradition holds that all of humanity stems from common parents, Adam and Eve, and from God, the Holy One. "Undertaking the extermination not only of the Jews but of every idea that arises from them," Patterson aptly underscores, "the Nazis set out to destroy this very idea of a trace of something holy, of something beyond the accidents of nature, that abides at the core of humanity."[8] A key meaning of that "trace of something holy," insists Patterson, is that no individual or people can be inherently, essentially, racially better than others. Utterly at odds with Nazism, Judaism and Jewish ethics had to be destroyed root and branch. The genocide had to do more than eliminate Jewish life, it had to eradicate Jewish thought as well. Hence, although some Jewish artifacts were "saved" to show what the Nazis destroyed, Torah scrolls and synagogues, as well as murdered Jews, were burned and reduced to smoke and ashes.

Sadly, the perpetrators of the Holocaust and other genocides have had advantages. Those who intervene or prosecute or philosophize usually arrive too late. The repetition of genocide since the Holocaust makes it hard to glimpse how prevention can happen so that genocide and other mass-atrocity crimes will ever end. Developed from his Christian perspective, Hank Knight's adroit development of a theology of hospitality moves in that direction by underscoring the importance of welcoming the stranger, but the insight he gives me is that post-Holocaust life teeters in tension between empathic hospitality and the temptation, even likelihood, to succumb to indifference or hostility instead. Knight, a guitar-playing songwriter, rhymes the tension in "Hardly Ever Again," which resounds concerns and echoes moods that should make people think long and hard:

> In '45, remember when
> The world said, "Never, never again!
> Never again: six million lost;
> Never again: The Holocaust."
> "Never," we said, "Never again,"
> But this is now and that was then.
>
> "Hardly ever again."
> Is that what we meant to say?
> "Hardly ever again."

---

8. The quotations are from Patterson, "Assault on the Holy," 481.

Will we turn and walk away?
This is now; that was then.
And we meant "hardly ever again."[9]

Repeatedly, Lenny Grob has been the catalyst that turned Wroxton concerns—such as those in Patterson's outlook regarding the Nazi desecration of God and humankind and in Knight's tension between hospitality and "hardly ever again"—into writing circles and book publication. The insight Grob keeps giving me is that those who learn and teach about the Holocaust should be bold and oriented not only toward what happened then but on what is happening now and what needs to take place in the future. Grob believes that Holocaust scholars and teachers have a responsibility to bring their expertise and insight to bear on contemporary issues: the Palestinian-Israeli conflict, for example; or torture; or relations among Jews, Christians, and Muslims; or global refugee and immigration calamities. His persistent persuasion does not always prevail, but he usually convinced members of the Wroxton group to put reluctance aside and state what their Holocaust insight could helpfully bring to deliberations about predicaments and policies in contemporary life. His influence and inventiveness, his commitment to *tikkun olam* (mending the world), continue to inform what learning and teaching about the Holocaust must mean for me.

Hank Greenspan

Early in my Wroxton experience, I met another remarkable Holocaust scholar, the psychologist and playwright Henry (Hank) Greenspan, who shares my appreciation for the philosopher William James. A close friend of mine for more than twenty-five years, Greenspan is a Holocaust scholar whose in-depth probings of survivor testimony—as mind-changing as they are unusual—have been groundbreaking and penetrating in ways unsurpassed.

One evening at Wroxton College, I witnessed Greenspan's performance of *Remnants*, his one-man play about ongoing conversations he has had with Holocaust survivors over many years. As Greenspan's web site explains, *Remnants* was produced for radio in 1992 and distributed to National Public Radio stations across the United States.[10] Greenspan has performed the forty-minute, award-winning drama hundreds of times, not

---

9. Reprinted by permission of Hank Knight. Initiated by Tom Paxton, the song was published in 1994. A copy of the original version appears in Sachs and Weissman, ed., *Liturgies on the Holocaust*, 194–98.

10. See Greenspan, "Remnants."

only on campuses and in conferences but also in venues such as the United States Holocaust Memorial Museum, the British Library, and the Magdeburg attic theatre in the former Theresienstadt concentration camp—a space used for performances during the Holocaust itself. When Greenspan kindly asked me for a comment that could help to publicize the play, I gladly responded as follows: "*Remnants* combines history and scholarship, art and drama, to inform our understanding of the Holocaust in ways that are as moving and poignant as they are challenging and surprising. Penetrating, gripping, masterful—those are only a few of the words that this distinctive work deserves." Those accolades are as heartfelt now as they were when I wrote them years ago.

Especially regarding the Holocaust, but other genocides and mass atrocities reveal something similar, the gathering of survivor testimony has usually concentrated on obtaining as many testimonies as possible, a methodology that frequently makes the gathering of an individual's testimony a one-time occurrence that also entails formulaic interviewing techniques. Cataloging and organizing these testimonies so they are accessible has posed taxing logistical problems—for example, how to cope with multiple languages, how to index and catalog the testimonies, how to store them, and how to make them accessible to scholars, teachers, and students. While those problems continue to be solved, a "what if" question remains: namely, what if follow-up took place? If testimony were less closed and more ongoing, what would be found?

Owing to aging and death, opportunities for follow-up interviews are rapidly dwindling among Holocaust survivors, but this matter is not hypothetical, at least not entirely, because in-depth gathering of Holocaust testimony has taken place in some cases, and it might happen more thoroughly with the survivors of recent mass atrocities. Greenspan has long been a leader—sometimes a lonely one—in such work, for scarcely anyone has matched his painstaking, crucial attention to repeated and in-depth conversations with Holocaust survivors. Rather than speaking about *testimony*, Greenspan insightfully emphasizes the survivors' *recounting* of their experiences, construing that word as a verb and concentrating on what he calls "the process of retelling."[11] This process discloses that testimony lacks closure and involves layers that include the untellable and the silences that enclose it. Seeing *Remnants* and learning from Greenspan as our friendship grew, I found that my listening to survivor testimony became keener and

---

11. Greenspan has published extensively on his intensive relationships with Holocaust survivors. See, for example, Greenspan, *On Listening*. For an overview of Greenspan's perspectives, see Greenspan, "Survivor Accounts," 414–27. The quoted phrase is from page 414 of that article.

more sensitive, my learning more perceptive and intense than it had been before.

Greenspan rightly points out that "we do a lot more living than speaking... Silence, in the sense of experience never discussed, is the rule. Talk is the exception."[12] Particularly regarding the survivors of the Holocaust and other mass atrocities, silence involves a range and complexity that disaggregate the untellable into the unsaid and the incommunicable, the unbearable and the irretrievable. Greenspan shows that listening to or reading the recounting of survivors is far more complicated and unsettling than we are accustomed to thinking. It is that way because testimony both reveals and hides the worst. As my survivor-friend Joe Freeman once said to me, "There are things we will never talk about."

In 2006, Greenspan wrote a book with a Holocaust survivor named Agi Rubin.[13] Greenspan describes *Reflections: Auschwitz, Memory, and a Life Recreated* as the result of "a twenty-five-year co-authorship between a survivor-diarist and a psychologist-playwright." Reading the results of that partnership after Greenspan invited me to contribute a foreword to the book, I found that *Reflections*, a one-of-a-kind interaction, belongs among the most notable writings to emerge from the Holocaust.

Historical knowledge and ethical insight about the Holocaust depend on access to archives, those repositories of information and evidence that document what happened. Rubin and Greenspan show that no archive is more fundamental than human memory itself. That judgment does not mean that human memory is infallible; nor is memory a substitute for the records that historians examine when they do their essential archival research. Nevertheless, absent human memory and the critical reflection that emerges from it, archival records would be mute and meaningless. In that sense, archives would be closed even if their vaults and files were open.

Reflections takes its readers into a memory archive that is as deep as it is open, as revealing as it is layered, as complex as it is brief and simple, as disconcerting and challenging as it is intense and poignant. Minimalist in their use of words spare and lean, Rubin and Greenspan together crafted a Holocaust document whose impact includes the absences and silences that their voices evoke. Not only are the pages of *Reflections* open in ways that reveal the vulnerability of their authors but also the episodes and vignettes, the images and scenes, open their readers to honest encounters with persons and places that can be profoundly moving. Rubin and Greenspan found that

---

12. Greenspan, "The Unsaid," 229–43.
13. See Rubin and Greenspan, *Reflections*.

some memories are "born in conversation."[14] Sometimes too painful to be borne alone, they found expression as two friends talked in trust. Holocaust insight can be like that. It comes alive for me in conversation—sometimes taking place from afar and in silence—with friends, teachers, and partners such as Michael Berenbaum, Carol Rittner, Lenny Grob, Hank Knight, David Patterson, and Hank Greenspan.

Artists

This book's prologue discussed the philosopher Josiah Royce's understanding of insight. He saw that one of insight's defining characteristics includes discerning "some connected whole of things." He illustrated what he meant by referring to "a landscape as an artist sees it."[15] Because they help me to see connections within and related to the Holocaust, artists—painters and poets—are among the sources of Holocaust insight that I value most.

Samuel Bak

In a magisterial career, Samuel Bak has drawn on his experience as a victim and survivor of the Holocaust to assess the damage done by that catastrophe and to weigh how best to live in what he calls "a world that cries out for repair."[16] A moving example of his work is a 1991 painting called *The Number*.[17] It depicts two stone tablets tipping and falling into a barren, cemetery-like abyss. The tablets themselves suggest signs of death. In the background, cracked and breaking apart, one of the two is inscribed with Hebrew letters that refer to God. In the foreground, the second tablet bears the number 6. Recalling the sixth imperative of the Decalogue or Ten Commandments—"You shall not murder"—Bak's portrayal makes one wonder: In a post-Holocaust world, what remains of the sixth commandment?[18] Has murder silenced God's voice and destroyed the commandment's credibility?

14. Rubin and Greenspan, *Reflections*, 221.
15. Royce, *Sources*, 6.
16. See Bak, "Facing My Own History," 2–4.
17. To view the Bak painting online and for Lawrence L. Langer's commentary about it, two links from Facing History and Ourselves are helpful. For the URL that links to the painting, see the end of the bibliography. Likewise, the URL that links to Langer's commentary can be found at the end of the bibliography.
18. Different traditions number the Ten Commandments differently. Jews and many Protestant Christians, for example, take "You shall not murder" to be the sixth commandment. For Catholics and Lutherans, that injunction is the fifth commandment.

Bak's persistent exploration of such questions continues in a series of paintings called *Just Is*.[19] In the murderous and monstrous atrocity universe that Bak depicts, violence and suffering have laid waste to life and landscape. No casualty of the onslaught is more forlorn than *justice*. Bak's art limns how the Holocaust and other mass atrocity crimes wreck trust that right can withstand wrong, blast hope that goodness will prevail over evil, and scorn faith that someday justice will, as the biblical prophet Amos implores, "roll down like waters, and righteousness like an everflowing stream" (Amos 5:24).

Bak's tersely tense wordplay titles, intensifying his disorienting images, demonstrate his artistic mastery. *Just Is*, for example, can sound like *justice*, seemingly affirming that what is good and right prevails or someday will. Unfortunately, the atrocity universe shatters that benign conjunction. Its wrack and ruin are compounded by indifference that gazes at our battered world—and perhaps even at Bak's artistic portrayals of a cratered existence bereft of justice—and settles for "just is," as in "that's just the way things are." Bak resists that despairing outcome, but his art also insists that one must discern deep down how desperately fraught things are before it can be even remotely credible to affirm that justice "just is."

Bak's atrocity universe can be unrelieved, overwhelming, and exhausting. Those experiences should be parts of any journey—unavoidably somber and sobering—through desolation. But if despair wins, injustice is needlessly compounded. So, a painting in *Just Is* called *After the Before* makes its viewer see the challenges in that connection.[20] Destruction is the *after* of what stood *before*, but Bak paints three people who are present after the wreckage before them. Who are they? What are they trying to do? Can they do anything significant to restore justice after the before? Are they scouts for a salvage team that will try to pick up the pieces and mend the fragments together again?

Bak paints questions, and his question-painting insists on accountability as we live after the before. Easy to say, but another of his *Just Is* paintings, one called *In Vain*, suggests that such responsibility is too hard.[21] In this painting, a lone traveler appears fated to draw that conclusion: the way forward seems blocked by obstruction that contains a blurred figure of Justice, her balancing scales shattered, all obscured with barely traces remaining. What destination was the traveler after before the obstruction of justice?

---

19. See Phillips, *JUST IS*. My reflections about Bak are adapted from my foreword to this Phillips/Bak book.

20. For the painting, see Phillips, *JUST IS*, 112.

21. For the painting, see Phillips, *JUST IS*, 80.

What will happen next? Was the traveler surprised, dismayed, indifferent, or moved to confront the obstruction with determination to try to set things right? If the latter, was the trip in vain? Will matters always be that way because that is just the way things are? *In Vain* may say "perhaps" or even "probably" but also "maybe not."

Despite its bleakness, *Just Is* insists that we should bet our lives on *maybe not*, failing to do so at humanity's peril. That is what two women seem to be doing as they drag broken scales of justice on their way in a work called *Unrelented*.[22] They may seem dejected and in mourning, but Bak's title hints defiantly instead that the women refuse despair and thereby resist injustice no matter what. At the end of the day, and at every day's beginning too, *Just Is* says: Try to be unrelented. Like those women, relentlessly salvage and restore justice as well and as long as we can. That's an insight worth retrieving from the rubble of Bak's atrocity world.

Paul Hunter

Confronting the Holocaust, genocide, and other mass atrocities for almost fifty years, I gradually discerned that I have been following a thread that weaves its way through failure. Inescapable and pervasive, failure riddles existence. Following that thread particularly compels me to contend with the failures of ethics. Exposing fault lines in nature and flaws in reality itself, those failures abound in the multiple shortfalls and shortcomings of thought, character, decision, and action that tempt us human beings to betray what is good, right, virtuous, and just and incite us to inflict incalculable harm.[23] A contemporary American poet, Paul Hunter, has helped me to follow and grasp the thread.

Hunter lives and works in Seattle, Washington, where he also is a self-described "grassroots art activist" and "shade-tree mechanic."[24] He spent formative years on farms, Kentucky fields among them. "It's the lens through which I see the world," I heard him say on a *PBS News Hour* poetry spot. Hunter's diverse interests and talents include repairing things, often things that have been thrown away because, apparently, they have no value. "For most of my adult life now," he says, "I've been finding broken instruments

---

22. For the painting, see Phillips, *JUST IS*, 109.

23. Helpful reflection on failure, including cracks in reality as well as moral shortcomings and shortfalls in human character and conduct, can be found in Feltham, *Failure*.

24. For biographical information about Hunter, see https://www.pbs.org/newshour/arts/poetry/paul-hunter/.

or people give me broken instruments, and I fix them, and they get another life. There's a part of me that's so cheered by that, and it may be part of the same thing that happens with words, with language, that you take a phrase, you take a phrase, you take a set of phrases that are shopworn, that people have had around them and not recognized, and take them and put them into a context that gives them a sharpened meaning of freshness."[25]

This combination of experiences and the moods attending them find expression in poetry by Hunter that concentrates on failures, on mending of the shopworn that can approach miraculous, and on what he calls *Ripening*, the title of one of his poetry books. Two samples of Hunter's perspectives focus insights that inform my learning and teaching about the Holocaust. First, in a poem called "This Failure," Hunter takes his readers into a farm field that won't yield a crop this year. Too much rain or not enough has fallen. The sun has been too hot, or the temperature has dipped too low. Bugs and blights have wreaked their havoc. Cultivation hasn't worked, and what's to be made of this loss? If loss is not to be the end, concludes Hunter, someone must "mow rake and burn off this failure."[26]

The outlook in Paul Hunter's poem "This Failure" is augmented by "For the Miracle," whose tone voices other insightful moods.[27] This time Hunter envisions not a barren field but a cluttered workshop. The partners of its grease-stained bench and well-worn but ever-ready vise jaws are old coffee cans filled with assorted nails and screws, mixed bolts and nuts, waiting to be of use. On the floor are broken, shopworn things, odd parts of this and that, stuff in the way that got consigned to this place by someone, sometime, for who knows what. Hunter sees these elements—maybe trash, good for nothing, to some—as basic elements waiting for the caring, imaginative, creative, and even joyful touch that could beneficially salvage and reconfigure them.

Hunter shows that what is fragmented, what has been ripped apart, let go, broken, heaved, tossed aside, disrespected, and dumped may sometimes have new life and be of use again. But this repairer-of-brokenness should not be misunderstood. Not everything can be fixed and made whole again. Hunter evokes "the muck of history," the sadness, melancholy, and grief that swirl through it.[28] Nevertheless, he advocates doing the best one can to defy the odds that would wear the world out. What's more, he encourages

25. See Hunter, "Hunter Discusses," his interview with Gwen Ifill.

26. Hunter, *Ripening*, 37.

27. This poem, as well as "This Failure," can be found in Hunter, "Hunter Discusses," his interview with Gwen Ifill.

28. See Hunter's "Author's Note" in *Ripenings*, 83.

my sense of an *in-spite-of* joy, the deep-down sense of significance and meaning—happiness even—found when what we do protects, preserves, and enhances precious human life. Such action requires protest and resistance; it embraces the contradiction of holding together persistent melancholy and tenacious hope—the latter understood as what the Israeli writer David Grossman calls "the hope of nevertheless," which "does not disregard the many dangers and obstacles, but refuses to see only them and nothing else."[29]

Arie Galles

A brilliant artist, Arie Galles, a longtime friend of mine, is the son of Holocaust survivors. His complex personality blends a big-hearted, boisterous, cut-to-the-chase sense of humor and a seriousness that can seethe with insightful anger. Friendship with him makes me see connections differently and better. I think of Galles often because an adaptation of his *First Station: Auschwitz-Birkenau* became the cover art for books in the Stephen S. Weinstein Series in Post-Holocaust Studies that David Patterson and I have edited for the University of Washington Press. *First Station* is one of a suite of large-format charcoal drawings called *Fourteen Stations/Hey Yud Dalet*. The Hebrew title is the acronym for *Hashem yinkom daman*, which means "May God avenge their blood." The title of the suite refers both to the Stations of the Cross and to the fact that the Nazi concentration camps and killing centers had to be near railroad stations.

Based on Luftwaffe and Allied aerial photographs of those sites, *Fourteen Stations* is Galles's "Kaddish for all Shoah victims." He makes that tribute concrete and specific by taking parts of that famous Jewish prayer for the dead and embedding them in his drawings. Only a fragment of the prayer is found in any single part of *Fourteen Stations*, but the whole prayer finds intense expression—grief-stricken and life-affirming all at once—in the work as a whole. No part of *Fourteen Stations* has been more painful for Galles than drawing the death camp at Belzec.

In 1942, the most lethal year in Jewish history, Nazi Germany's "Final Solution" destroyed 2.7 million Jews. Scarcely any site in that destruction process was more devastating than Belzec, a Nazi killing center situated in southeastern Poland near the railroad station at a village on the main line between the cities of Lublin and Lvov (L'viv). A specially constructed railroad spur, less than a mile long, led directly to the camp. During Belzec's

---

29. See Grossman, "On Hope and Despair." For instructive reflections on hope, see Martin, *How We Hope*.

brief but deadly operations in a nine-month period from March 17 until mid-December 1942, the relentless gassings and shootings mercilessly carried out by the German SS and their Ukrainian collaborators accounted for about five hundred thousand Jewish deaths. Most of the Jews who were murdered at Belzec came from Poland. Arie Galles's uncle, aunt, and cousins were among them.

Belzec was a place so full of death that Galles portrays it not once but twice—hence fourteen stations but fifteen artworks. It appears first in the *Khurbn Prologue*, where he draws upon an aerial view taken by the Luftwaffe on May 26, 1940. Two years later, virgin woodland near railroad tracks in the Belzec area had been transformed into a fully operational killing center. After the death camp at Belzec had done its worst, the Germans eradicated it as well. Subsequently another Luftwaffe reconnaissance flight captured the remains, which, in Galles's apt words, showed "the camp as a nearly empty lot amid patterned fields along a railway line in eastern Poland."

"Speedily and soon"—those words are included in the Kaddish fragment that Galles embedded in *Belzec*, his fourth station. They come from the part of the prayer that expresses a profound yearning, which is given voice in spite of desolation and despair: "May God establish his kingdom in your lifetime and during your days, and within the life of the entire house of Israel, speedily and soon; and say, Amen." The Holocaust's perpetrators intended to silence that prayer forever. Galles helps me to see how speedily and soon they did so at Belzec, and his before-and-after perspectives about that place become even more awesome when their aerial outlook is combined with a report from ground level.

According to Margaret M. Rubel, a scholar whose work has focused on Belzec, a man named Rudolf Reder was one of only two known survivors from that death camp.[30] With thousands of other Jews from Lvov, Reder, sixty-one, a former soap manufacturer, was deported to Belzec in mid-August 1942. All the Jews who entered Belzec were doomed, but Reder was one of the very few who were temporarily selected for work in the camp's Sonderkommando. The tasks of this Jewish death brigade—it numbered about five hundred brutalized and malnourished prisoners whose ranks were frequently thinned and replenished—involved digging mass burial pits, disposing of corpses, sorting loot (including baskets of gold teeth and vast amounts of women's shorn hair), and maintaining the camp's gas

---

30. Rubel has translated and annotated Reder's eyewitness account of his time in Belzec, which was originally written with the help of a woman named Nella Rost. This unusually important Holocaust document was published by the Jewish Regional Historical Commission in Krakow, Poland, in 1946, but it did not appear in English until 2000. See Reder, "Belzec," 268–89.

chambers, which used the carbon monoxide produced by a large engine that was said to have come from a captured Russian tank. Reder spent about three months in Belzec. Toward the end of November 1942, he managed to escape his guards during a trip to Lvov to obtain building materials for the camp. Remembering the address of his Polish housekeeper, Reder went to her flat, and she gave him refuge until the Red Army liberated the city in late July 1944.

Reder's compressed testimony about Belzec is among the most disturbing survivor narratives to emerge from the Holocaust. Assigned to a variety of jobs, he came to know the camp all too well. It was a place, he said, that "served no other purpose but that of murdering Jews."[31] Every transport—typically there were three a day—got the same treatment. The arriving Jews were ordered to undress and to set their belongings aside. They were told that a bath awaited them before they would be sent to work. Each time people heard that deceptive speech, Reder underscored, he could see "the spark of hope in their eyes." His account continues:

> But a minute later, and with extreme brutality, babies were torn from their mothers, old and sick were thrown on stretchers, while men and little girls were driven with rifle-butts further on to a fenced path leading directly to the gas chambers. At the same time, and with the same brutality, the already naked women were ordered to the barracks, where they had their hair shaved. I knew exactly the moment when they all suddenly realized what was in store. Cries of fear and anguish, terrible moans, mingled with the music played by the orchestra ... Before all six chambers were filled to capacity, those in the first had already been suffering for nearly two hours. It was only when all six chambers were packed with people, when the doors were locked into position, that the engine was set in motion.[32]

At Belzec, systematic murder combined with sadistic torture to produce circumstances in which the most one could really hope for was that death's arrival would come speedily and soon.

After his liberation, Reder returned to Belzec to see what remained. He ended his narrative by observing that the Germans had "covered this graveyard for millions of murdered Jews with fresh greenery ... The railway line was gone. Through a field I reached a young and sweet-smelling pine forest. It was very still. In the middle of it was a large sunny clearing."[33] No

---

31. Reder, "Belzec," 276.
32. Reder, "Belzec," 276–77.
33. Reder, "Belzec," 289.

place, not even Auschwitz-Birkenau, revealed the Holocaust's essence more than Belzec, a camp, Reder said, that "heaved with mass murder."[34]

It is not surprising that Arie Galles found drawing Belzec excruciating. Few, if any, sites on earth have been more explicitly devoted to mass murder. For the Jewish people, and for all who stand in solidarity with them, Belzec signifies a catastrophe that beggars description, let alone comprehension. Belzec would seem to cancel the Kaddish, at least the part about God's kingdom being established "speedily and soon." Yet, Galles insightfully picked the right Kaddish fragment to embed in *Belzec*, for if that prayer does not remain—including its yearning for the world to be mended speedily and soon—the empty hopelessness of Belzec's silence achieves a victory it must never have.

Kay Ryan

One of North America's breathtaking sights is the Niagara River as it becomes Niagara Falls. One can scarcely watch that transformation without feeling terror as well as awe. For the beauty of the place can be chilling as it makes one consider the fate to be met by whatever is swept over the escarpment, plunged into the mist, and dashed on the rocks below.

As I learn and teach about the Holocaust, I think about the Niagara River not because I have recently been to Niagara Falls but because of the California poet Kay Ryan. Former poet laureate of the United States and a Pulitzer Prize winner, she was a stranger to me until I heard her interviewed and listened to her read from *The Niagara River*, a collection of her poems published in 2005. When I got the book, I found it full of poetic provocations. In "Salvage," for instance, Ryan's urban imagery contrasts with Paul Hunter's pastoral themes, but her mood is much the same. Unthinkable disaster has struck, but the salvage begins, the resolute crew determined to keep the wreckage at bay. As if invoking a spirit of *in-spite-of* joy, Ryan's poem seems to ask its reader to hear the salvage squad "whistling as / they work."[35] Can that mood—resistant and resilient—expand so that the salvage crews needed to respond to the Holocaust and its aftermath, including the failures of ethics that led to so much of the worst that happened, become larger, stronger, and better equipped to deal with current humanitarian disasters and to anticipate and forestall catastrophes that may be headed our way?

Ryan's title poem in *The Niagara River* makes affirmative responses imperative. It envisions people floating on the Niagara River, calmly

---

34. Reder, "Belzec," 283.
35. Ryan, *Niagara River*, 35.

conversing, picnicking, and observing the shoreline as they go with the river's flow. They know, the poem says, that they are on the Niagara River. But do they understand, Ryan warns in closing, "what that means."[36]

As with Paul Hunter's poems, I study Kay Ryan's through Holocaust lenses. During and after the genocide, her angles of vision help me to see, so many people, in so many ways, were metaphorically on the Niagara River. We know much about where that journey led between 1933 and 1945. Where might it be leading now?

One of Ryan's *Niagara River* poems ends by saying, "Things shouldn't / be so hard."[37] Why is lucidity—remembering inseparable from it—so tough? Ryan's deft poems are sources of Holocaust insight loaded not only with senses of peril and loss but also with questions that challenge her readers to discern and defend what deserves to matter most.

Carolyn Manosevitz

Another friend for more than twenty years, the petite Carolyn Manosevitz, is a person with a heart more generous and energy more bountiful than most people I know. Born into a family of Jewish immigrants in Winnipeg, Canada, trained in universities in Minnesota and Texas, presently living in the mountains of Colorado, she is also an artist-activist whose work is distinctive because it combines memory of the Holocaust and interreligious engagement. Her Holocaust studies expertise has combined with interfaith interests and concerns in ways that have led to significant visiting faculty appointments, notably at Christian places such as Austin Presbyterian Theological Seminary, the Iliff School of Theology, Wesley Theological Seminary, and Wake Forest University Divinity School. For years, she has organized major interfaith symposia that especially bring together the Abrahamic traditions: Judaism, Christianity, and Islam. This work is supported by the Fund for Interfaith Understanding, which Manosevitz founded in 2010.

Working in what she calls "mixed media on handmade paper," she creates artworks that are delicate and fragile and yet immensely strong and powerful in the feelings they evoke, the encounters they foster, and the insights they contain. "The message that I strive to convey through my art is simple," she says. "We must walk hand in hand into the future—together."[38] So, her creations bear titles such as *Reconstructing the Story*, *Mending the*

---

36. Ryan, *Niagara River*, 1.
37. Ryan, *Niagara River*, 41.
38. Manosevitz's website (http://www.carolynmanosevitz.com) includes numerous examples of her art as well as biographical information and reflection about her work.

Fracture, and *Healing*. But these themes harbor no shallow optimism or banal hope. Hard-earned, they emerge from loss and grief. The insight in Manosevitz's art about reconstructing, mending, and healing would be impossible absent the crafting of art such as *Danger Is Near*, *Leaving Home*, *Mass Grave*, and *The Eternal Presence of Absence*.

While Samuel Bak paints questions and Arie Galles draws the sites of destruction that leave abysmal quandaries without closure, Manosevitz puts her art in the service of rebuilding and restoration. Her deeply centered Jewish identity and its profound spirituality brim with hospitality, inviting and encouraging everyone she meets to explore profound questions, to nurture healing relationships, and to treasure, defend, and serve all that is right and just, beautiful and good. She is a valued source of Holocaust insight for me because her ways show how to make the world the way it ought to be.

Adrienne Rich

Learning and teaching about the Holocaust, its vast scope and its places of destruction, require maps. So, I often consult the United States Holocaust Museum's *Historical Atlas of the Holocaust*. When doing that, I usually think of one of my favorite American writers, the poet Adrienne Rich. Some of her best work appears in *An Atlas of the Difficult World*, which won her the 1992 *Los Angeles Times* Book Award for poetry. I met Rich just once—at the book award celebration—and I treasure the copy of her *Atlas* that she signed for me that evening. The book's title and contents have deep roots in American life. Partly for that reason, they include Holocaust reverberations and insights.

To see how and why, observe that in ancient Greek religion, Atlas was a Titan. He challenged Zeus and paid a price. His punishment was to hold up the sky, although he is sometimes pictured as the one who must shoulder the earth. The mythical Atlas embodies strength. Most often, however, the word *atlas* denotes a book of maps. In that sense, no atlas supports the earth, much less the sky, and yet an atlas does connote strength of another kind. A good atlas helps us to know where in the world we are, where the earth has been, and what has been happening in it.

A sound atlas of the Holocaust is always timely, but most atlases eventually go out of date. The map-drawing and map-revising businesses thrive with the many political, economic, geographical, and religious upheavals that the world has witnessed before, during, and after the Holocaust. In addition to showing where the world has been, good maps, carefully drawn, are needed to help us see where we are going and where we need to be headed.

As the title for a book of poetry, *An Atlas of the Difficult World* suggests a variety of themes: poems as maps, for example, or the poet as Atlas. Rich's poems are about a difficult world, one that she tries to map and perhaps to hold in ways that keep the sky from falling or the earth from going out of orbit.

Rich, who died in 2012, did not view the earth from the sky, at least not primarily. Whether she wrote "From an Old House in America" in Vermont or from out West along California's Pacific shore, she stood firmly on American ground. On one page of her *Atlas*, this poetic cartographer maps that terrain with lines about haunted rivers and seas of indifference, battlefields and shrines, capitals of money and acquiescent suburbs, blind alleys, crumbing bridges, polluted air, and cemeteries of the poor. A voice in the poem protests: this verse is not a map but a mural. No matter, the poem concludes. Map or mural—"where do we see it from is the question."[39] The themes that Rich explores in her *Atlas of the Difficult World*, the dilemmas she probes, the memories and hopes she echoes—all of these elements make contact with deep human yearnings. Their connections to the Holocaust are not far to find.

To see what I mean, focus on some additional examples from Rich's *Atlas*. One of them is a poem about suicides. Drawing on her Jewish tradition and akin to Arie Galles, Rich offers a "Tattered Kaddish," a raveled prayer for the dead. This poem savors the gift and goodness of life, but Rich's praise is inseparable from grief and even rage. "How they loved it, when they could," Rich says in honoring those who lived but could not stand to do so anymore.[40] Yet her "Tattered Kaddish" also questions the gift and, implicitly, the giver of lives that can be so good and yet so broken, so wonderful and yet so full of despair, so filled with love and yet so lonely and bereft.

On May 16, 1942, Rich turned thirteen. About a month later, on June 12, 1942, Anne Frank celebrated her thirteenth birthday too. One of her gifts that day was the diary that she would treasure as she and her family hid for their lives in German-occupied Amsterdam. Rich and Frank never met, but looking back in a 1989–1990 series of poems called "Eastern War Time," Rich wonders what should be made of an American Jewish girl—herself perhaps—who was "trying to grasp the world" but could scarcely anticipate how much a poem could jar by quoting a telegram.[41]

39. Rich, *Atlas*, 6.
40. Rich, *Atlas*, 6.
41. Rich, *Atlas*, 36.

Containing information conveyed by German industrialist Eduard Schulte to Dr. Gerhart Riegner, the World Jewish Congress representative in Geneva, the telegram is dated August 11, 1942. Its message, sent through the American legation in Bern, Switzerland, to the US Department of State in Washington, DC, reported the existence of a plan for the systematic annihilation of Europe's Jews. Those who received the telegram dismissed its message as unbelievable.

I do not know what Adrienne Rich knew about the Holocaust while it was happening. But that catastrophe marked her identity. For instance, in a 1990 poem called "1948: Jews," she apparently ponders her Radcliffe College experience when she observes how complicated it was to be ordinary, let alone fascinating or brilliant, "after the six million."[42] Intent on remembering, on taking the responsibility to be moved by memory, Rich and her *Atlas*, its poetic maps and murals, point ways toward what she called "never-to-be-finished, still unbegun work of repair."[43] She helps me grasp why I want the Holocaust to be at the heart of my answer when "where do we see it from?" is the question.

Postscript

About as far from Auschwitz and Belzec as one can get, the town of Winthrop is where I now make my home. It sits small in the Methow Valley, a place of spectacular beauty on the eastern slope of the majestic Cascade Mountains in the state of Washington. As I consider learning and teaching about the Holocaust, my thoughts often include the poetry of William Stafford, an American national treasure, who loved and wrote about the Methow Valley.

Stafford's poems focus on the natural world, often on humanity's abuse of it. Also drenched in history, his verse laments the carnage we human beings inflict and encourages resistance against it. Although the Holocaust was not Stafford's theme, he knew plenty about war and genocide. In works such as *Traveling through the Dark* and *The Darkness around Us Is Deep* he wondered, as Elie Wiesel did in *Night*, whether, ultimately, only the darkness remains.

About thirty years ago, two Methow Valley forest rangers, Curtis Edwards and Sheela McLean, contacted William Stafford and made an unusual request: Would he help them create "poetry road signs" for the North Cascades Highway and its surroundings? Stafford agreed, and the result was

42. Rich, *Atlas*, 52.
43. Rich, *Atlas*, 11.

a brilliant set that came to be called "The Methow River Poems." Some of those poems appeared on the signs that can still be found here and there.

I am particularly fond of one of Stafford's Methow River poems. Called "Being a Person," it invites a reader/viewer to contemplate the Methow River as its clear, cold water rushes from the Cascades to the Columbia and then to the Pacific. The reflections help me to remember what learning and teaching about the Holocaust implore. "How you stand here is important," Stafford insists.[44] His poem helps me to see that, whatever else they may be, learning and teaching about the Holocaust include what we hear as we listen for what is happening, how we breathe, how we stand. Holocaust insight tells me nothing could be more important.

---

44. Stafford, *Quiet Places*, 89.

10

Primo Levi

In late November 1946, *Minerva Medica*, an Italian medical journal, published a substantial article, whose English title would be "Report on the Hygienic-Sanitary Organization of the Concentration Camp for Jews in Monowitz (Auschwitz—Upper Silesia)." Its authors were survivors of that camp: Leonardo De Benedetti, a forty-six-year-old doctor, and a twenty-five-year-old chemist named Primo Levi. After Auschwitz was liberated by the Red Army in late January 1945, these Italian Jews from Turin found themselves in a Soviet transit camp in the Polish city of Katowice. Soviet authorities wanted information about the conditions in the Nazi camps. One result was the De Benedetti–Levi report, which was drafted in the spring of 1945. This report was not only Levi's first publication but also his earliest writing to assess events that led to his remarkable authorship.[1]

Another significant publication appeared seventy years later when the English-language edition of *The Complete Works of Primo Levi* was published in 2015. The three volumes feature updated translations of Levi's

---

1. For a long time, the report was little noticed, but in the early 1990s, after Levi's death, it was rediscovered and received new life for English-language readers with the appearance of Levi (with De Benedetti), *Auschwitz Report*. The report's coauthorship leaves uncertain where Levi's voice begins and ends, but some sections—for example, the description of the railroad deportation that took De Benedetti and Levi from Italy to Auschwitz in February 1944—anticipate Levi's narrative in *If This Is a Man*, the key book on which he was working when the report appeared in *Minerva Medica*. Levi remained close friends with De Benedetti, whom Levi called "a courageous and gentle man who gave invaluable help to many and never sought help from anyone." See Levi, "Remembrance," 2620–22; and Levi, "Leonardo De Benedetti," 2623–24, especially 2624 for the quotation. My quotations from Levi's writings are taken from the *Complete Works*, as I hereafter shorten the title, but I also cite paperback editions frequently used by Levi's American readers. The original Italian version of the *Complete Works* appeared in two volumes as *Opere* in 1997.

fourteen books, including *Se questo è un uomo* (*If This Is a Man*), his unrivaled memoir about Auschwitz. It is known to most of its American readers as *Survival in Auschwitz*, a much less appropriate title. The chronology of Levi's life that introduces the *Complete Works* notes that in April 1985 he visited the United States for the launch of the translation of *If Not Now, When?*, his successful novel about Jewish partisans in Poland and Russia who fought the Nazis and the genocide against the European Jews. The chronology mentions that during this first and only American visit, Levi gave "talks and readings in New York; Claremont, California; Bloomington, Indiana; and Boston."[2]

One of the books in my library is a yellow-covered, Collier Books paperback copy of *Survival in Auschwitz*, which I bought new for $1.50 in 1976 and often used in my courses about the Holocaust. That book became an especially prized possession when Primo Levi signed it in April 1985 after his talk in Claremont at Harvey Mudd College.[3] His presentation that evening did not focus on *If Not Now, When?* but on a forthcoming book called *The Drowned and the Saved*. Arguably rivaled only by *If This Is a Man* in Levi's distinctive writing about the Holocaust, it was published in 1986. Less than a year later, Levi was dead in Turin, apparently a suicide. Questions linger about the circumstances of Levi's death. But without question, no one has written more profoundly about the Holocaust. Levi remains an unsurpassed source of Holocaust insight.

My personal encounter with Levi in 1985 was fleeting, just long enough to thank him for his Claremont visit and to ask him to sign my well-thumbed, underlined copy of *Survival in Auschwitz*. But his presence in my life endures because even though he was skeptical about philosophers and philosophy—"no, it's not for me"—his exploration of the Holocaust revealed a keen philosophical mind that unflinchingly confronted the Holocaust's most challenging ethical dilemmas.[4] The themes and variations in my appreciation for Levi show that his authorship produced insights that have governed my Holocaust studies. Primary among them is that learning and teaching about the Holocaust entail a challenge as daunting as it is ongoing:

2. Levi, *Complete Works*, liv.

3. For further details about Levi's visit to Claremont, see Viterbi, "Primo Levi." An internationally distinguished scientist whose cousin, Lucia, was married to Levi, Viterbi recalled the Harvey Mudd College presentation in his opening remarks at the Third Annual Symposium on Primo Levi, which he gave on October 25, 2009, in New York at the Centro Primo Levi. For further interpretations of Levi's life and work, see Angier, *Double Bond*; Giuliani, *Centaur in Auschwitz*; Lambert, *Ethics after Auschwitz?*; Lang, *Primo Levi*; and Thomson, *Primo Levi*.

4. Levi, *Voice of Memory*, 175.

Can one keep complexity from overwhelming understanding and make awareness and analysis of complexity yield understanding instead? Levi's responses to that challenge lead to a second insight of disquieting importance: In spite of atrocity and the compromises and ambiguities that accompany it, those who try to learn and teach about the Holocaust should never forsake but to the best of our ability preserve, protect, and defend the affirmation that we are in the world to do good.

A Sunset at Fòssoli

Born in Turin on July 31, 1919, Levi took his degree in chemistry from the university there in 1941. After the Germans occupied northern Italy in the autumn of 1943, he joined a partisan group in the Italian Alps. A few weeks later, on December 13, he was arrested. Fearing that confirmation of his partisan identity would lead to torture and death, he admitted his status as an "Italian citizen of Jewish race," unaware of what that identification held in store for him. Levi was sent to a concentration camp at Fòssoli, near the city of Modena, which had been intended for British and American prisoners of war. By mid-February 1944, more than six hundred Jews were imprisoned there. The arrival of German SS men meant that Levi and the other Jews at Fòssoli would be deported.

On the evening of February 22, 1944, Levi's transport left the train station at Carpi. By then, Levi knew its destination was Auschwitz. That name, he said, was "without significance for us at that time," but soon enough he realized that going there was "a journey toward nothingness, a journey down, toward the bottom."[5] After reaching Auschwitz during the night of Saturday, February 26, Levi was selected for labor, got the number 174517 tattooed on his left arm, and endured Auschwitz for eleven months. For most of that time, he worked at Monowitz, a subcamp in the vast Auschwitz complex. Monowitz—it was also called Auschwitz III or Buna—provided slave labor for the construction of an I. G. Farben plant, the Buna factory, whose name was taken from the synthetic rubber that the Germans wanted to produce there. Liberated by Russian troops on January 27, 1945, Levi eventually returned to Italy, where he resumed his life as an industrial chemist and in due course became a chemical plant manager.

One of Levi's most telling descriptions of Auschwitz involved his camp initiation. On one occasion, he reached out a window to quench his painful thirst with an icicle. When an SS guard snatched it away from him, Levi asked, "*Warum?*" only to be told with a shove, "*Hier ist kein warum*" (There

---

5. Levi, *If This Is a Man*, 13; see also Levi, *Survival in Auschwitz*, 17.

is no why here).[6] Levi's question Why? sought explanation, to say nothing of negotiation, but he got none. No asking was permitted for the likes of Levi. In Auschwitz no why existed—not as a question and certainly not as a satisfying explanation, either.

Plagued by bouts of depression and by what he called survivors' disease, Levi's life ended on April 11, 1987. He left behind a body of work that never stops asking Why? Although largely ignored at first, his Auschwitz memoir *Se questo è un uomo* (1947 and 1958), which was translated into English as *If This Is a Man* (1959) and as *Survival in Auschwitz* (1961), has become a widely read classic. In *Il sistema periodico* (1975), which appeared in English as *The Periodic Table* (1985), Levi used chemistry's basic elements as points of departure for further reflection on his Holocaust experience. His essays in books such as *I sommersi e i salvati* (1986), translated into English as *The Drowned and the Saved* (1988), are required reading, texts to be revisited again and again, for anyone who tries to learn and teach about the Holocaust. In addition, Levi wrote significant fiction, including science fiction, and gave interviews that are among the best examples of survivor testimony.

Unfulfilled, Levi's quest for understanding was unrelenting, an unsettled and unsettling condition reflected in *La chiave a stella* (1978), translated into English as *The Wrench* or, in the United States, as *The Monkey's Wrench* (1986), his semifictional narrative about a skilled, exacting, and loquacious construction rigger named Tino Faussone. This character takes pride in a job well done and swaps stories about his international projects with a chemist-writer who becomes his friend. Their narratives compare the work that fills and complicates their lives. At one point, the chemist-writer says that he feels "a little like Tiresias, and not simply because of my double identity. A long time ago I, too, had stumbled into the middle of a fight between gods; I, too, had come across snakes in my path, and that encounter altered my condition, giving me the strange power of words; and since then, appearing as a chemist before the eyes of the world, yet feeling the blood of a writer in my veins, I felt as if I had two souls in my body, which is one too many."[7]

---

6. Levi, *If This Is a Man*, 25; see also Levi, *Survival in Auschwitz*, 29.

7. Levi, *Wrench*, 997; see also Levi, *Monkey's Wrench*, 52. The Italian title, *La chiave a stella*, literally means "star-shaped key" or "key to the stars," but Levi used it to refer to Faussone's socket wrench, an important tool in his trade. Levi's biographers agree that this book is the happiest and most humorous that he wrote. Nevertheless, there are gray-zoned motifs within it. With specific reference to his remark about two souls, Levi commented in a 1986 interview with the author Philip Roth that "my statement that 'two souls . . . is too many' is half a joke, but half-hints at serious things" (quoted in *Survival in Auschwitz*, 181–82).

Levi described himself as a centaur.[8] That mythological figure—half man, half horse—mirrored his sense of identity. Just as the centaur represents two realities that are improbably, even impossibly, fused into one, Levi's life was a fusion, at times a confusion and collision, of elements—the Italian and the Jew, the chemical plant manager and the writer—that were inseparable from the Holocaust, which left his identity enigmatic. Levi said he was "split in two."[9] Neither his life nor his thought was without fracture and contradiction, but the splitting to which he referred—it resulted from Auschwitz, his survival, and a return-that-was-no-return—was also a blending that contributed to the masterful poetry that added to the variety and brilliance of his writing.

"At certain moments," said Levi, "poetry has seemed to me more appropriate than prose for conveying an idea or an image."[10] His verse epitomized qualities that characterize his other works: a restless questioning, an economy and clarity of mind, a persistent sense of irony and paradox, a keen eye for detail and a love for sensitively crafted language, a patient consideration of historical and psychological complexity, a carefully nuanced moral judgment, an unrelenting honesty, and an unvanquished humanism infused with lucid realism. Poignant yearning also marked Levi's thought, a theme and feeling that appear in one of the poems he wrote not long after World War II ended. In the eight brief lines that make "Sunset at Fòssoli," which is dated February 7, 1946, Levi recalls seeing the sun go down through the barbed wire that imprisoned him in that Auschwitz antechamber. The sun's return may be expected, but he says that he saw the sun die and knows "what it means not to come back."[11] For Levi, the sun both died and lived; he returned and yet did not. Both during and after the Holocaust, Levi realized, his existence was marked by versions of such tension and the inescapable ambiguity and compromise they contained.

8. See Levi, *Voice of Memory*, xvii–xxvi, 84–86; Angier, *Double Bond*, 529–90; Giuliani, *Centaur in Auschwitz*, 27–35.

9. See, for example, Levi's interview with Edoardo Fadini in Levi, *Voice of Memory*, 85.

10. See Levi (trans. Galassi), *Collected Poems*, 1865–2007, esp. 1877; see also Levi (trans. Feldman), *Collected Poems*, which appeared originally as *Ad ora incerta* (*At an Uncertain Hour*) in 1984.

11. Levi, "Sunset at Fòssoli," in Levi (trans. Galassi); and in *Collected Poems*, 1896; Levi (trans. Feldman), *Collected Poems*, 15.

The Gray Zone

Eight months after the Germans sent Levi to Auschwitz in late February 1944, he knew that autumn's receding light and retreating warmth meant that the devastation of another Auschwitz winter was at hand. "From October to April," he understood, "seven out of ten of us will die. Whoever does not die will suffer minute by minute, all day, every day."[12] *Winter*, insisted Levi, was not the right word for that dreadful season. Nor could words like *hunger* and *pain* capture the realities of Auschwitz. "If the Lagers had lasted longer," he observed, "a new, harsh language would have come into being; and we feel the need of this language in order to express what it means to labor all day in the wind, in temperatures below freezing, wearing only a shirt, underpants, a cloth jacket and trousers, and in our body weakness, hunger, and knowledge of the approaching end."[13]

Arguably, the Holocaust did not last long enough to produce fully the new language of which Levi spoke, but as survivors, scholars, and teachers continue their struggle to describe, analyze, and explain what happened during those dark times, new and harsh concepts have emerged. One thinks, for instance, of Lawrence Langer's *choiceless choice*, a term now used to identify the dilemmas created by Nazi Germany and its collaborators, who often put Jews and other victims in circumstances where they had to make decisions among hideous options that could not be described as choosing the "lesser of evils."[14] Or, to cite a second example, Terrence Des Pres wrote about *excremental assault*, the concept he created to refer to the ways in which lack of sanitation in the Holocaust's ghettos and camps—whether intended by the Germans or not—besieged and humiliated every prisoner and killed many of them.[15] Even *genocide*, the word coined by Raphael Lemkin, was added to humanity's vocabulary while the Holocaust raged.[16]

No list of terms belonging to the new vocabulary required by Holocaust studies could begin to be complete if it failed to include Primo Levi's *gray zone*. Especially in *The Drowned and the Saved*, he used that term to

---

12. Levi, *If This Is a Man*, 117; see also Levi, *Survival in Auschwitz*, 123.

13. Levi, *If This Is a Man*, 118; see also Levi, *Survival in Auschwitz*, 123. Victor Klemperer, an important scholar of Jewish descent whose intermarried status spared him from the Holocaust, documented how the Nazis themselves had contributed to a new, harsh language of violence and atrocity. See Klemperer, *Language of the Third Reich*.

14. See, for instance, Langer, *Versions of Survival*, 67–129. Choiceless choices, writes Langer, do not "reflect options between life and death, but between one form of abnormal response and another, both imposed by a situation that was in no way of the victim's own choosing" (72).

15. See Des Pres, *Survivor*, 51–72.

16. See Lemkin, *Axis Rule in Occupied Europe*.

refer to the "incredibly complicated internal structure" of Auschwitz, which created moral ambiguity in ways large and small. He was struck particularly by the ways the German organization of the camp led Jews, however reluctantly, to become complicit in the destruction of their own people. Focusing attention especially on the Sonderkommando, the Jews conscripted to work in the gas chambers and crematoria at Auschwitz-Birkenau, Levi said that "envisioning and organizing [those] squads was National Socialism's most diabolical crime."[17]

Levi's gray zone, however, was not restricted to such radical examples. Emphasizing "the extreme tension of the camp," he noted that the number of "people who are gray, ambiguous, and quick to compromise" was and remains more the rule than the exception in any time or place, but in Auschwitz those ranks swelled, for survival depended on finding or taking some advantage that made nearly all survivors—Levi included himself—"bear their own share of guilt."[18] In *The Drowned and the Saved*, Levi amplified those feelings in a chapter on "Shame," an important sequel to the reflection on "The Gray Zone" that precedes it. "Those who were 'saved' in the camps were not the best of us," said Levi. "What I had seen and experienced," he went on to say, "proved the exact opposite. Generally, those who survived were the worst: the egotists, the violent, the insensitive, the collaborators of the 'gray zone', the informers. It was not a fixed rule (there were no fixed rules, nor are there in human affairs), but it was still a rule. I felt innocent, to be sure, but herded among the saved and thus in permanent search of a justification, in my own eyes and in the eyes of others. Those who survived were the worst, that is to say, the fittest. The best all died."[19]

Levi's understated philosophical view held that "each of us is a mixture of good and not so good," but his interpretation of the gray zone rejected invidious moral equivalencies.[20] "I do not know," he wrote, "nor am I particularly interested in knowing, whether a murderer is lurking deep within me, but I do know that I was an innocent victim and not a murderer."[21] As Levi made clear by his analysis of Muhsfeld, a German perpetrator who

17. Levi (trans. Moore), *Drowned and the Saved*, 2435, 2443; see also Levi (trans. Rosenthal), *Drowned and the Saved*, 42, 53.

18. Levi (trans. Moore), *Drowned and the Saved*, 2440; see also Levi (trans. Rosenthal), *Drowned and the Saved*, 49.

19. Levi (trans. Moore), *Drowned and the Saved*, 2467; see also Levi (trans. Rosenthal), *Drowned and the Saved*, 82.

20. See Levi's 1983 interview with Anna Bravo and Federico Cereja in Levi, *Voice of Memory*, 232.

21. Levi (trans. Moore), *Drowned and the Saved*, 2439; see also Levi (trans. Rosenthal), *Drowned and the Saved*, 48.

momentarily, but only momentarily, showed pity when a Jewish girl somehow remained alive in Auschwitz after gassing, the gray zone could include a wide range of men and women, but immense differences remained among them. Compared to Muhsfeld, Levi could rightly call himself a guiltless victim. Considering himself from other angles, Levi could not exempt himself from guilt, relatively minor though it might be. Mainly, however, Levi did not intend his analysis of the gray zone to result in condemning judgments but instead to show how Auschwitz could "confound our need to judge."[22]

Levi spoke of the gray zone in the singular, but his analysis made clear that this region was multifaceted and multilayered. Nor was it confined to one time or place. Hence, his analysis warned his readers—including me—about the ambiguities and compromises that could be lurking for them. As he experienced and explored the gray zones of Auschwitz, Levi stressed that they contained surprises and shocks that revealed a world that was not only "harrowing, but it was also indecipherable. It did not resemble any model."[23] Levi did not mince words about the fact that the Holocaust epitomized wrongdoing, but clear and distinct moral judgments mixed and mingled with two other dimensions of awareness that made Levi a much more complicated and profound ethical thinker.

Levi saw that gray-zone behavior could not be neatly analyzed in terms of right and wrong, at least not as most traditions of philosophical ethics might try to do. Arguably, those traditions could still be used to judge the National Socialist perpetrators of the Holocaust, but no Aristotelian theory of virtue, Kantian categorical imperative, or utilitarian calculation about consequences had much relevance for judging those who were conscripted into the Sonderkommando, let alone for determining what those hapless men should do, condemned as they were to a fate of choiceless choices before they too were murdered. Next, Levi saw how the gray zone revealed a tragic dysfunctionality for ethics. That dysfunctionality had at least two parts. First, traces of idealism about treating one's neighbor as oneself or of refusing to steal might remain in the gray zone, but within that region of experience such teachings lost their appeal. As Levi put the point: "Since the body's physiological reserves were exhausted after two or three months, death from starvation or from starvation-related illnesses was the normal fate of a prisoner. The only way to avoid it was an extra food ration, and, to obtain that, a privilege, large or small, was needed: in other words, a means—granted or hard won, cunning or violent, licit or illicit—to raise

22. Levi (trans. Moore), *Drowned and the Saved*, 2435; see also Levi (trans. Rosenthal), *Drowned and the Saved*, 42.

23. Levi (trans. Moore), *Drowned and the Saved*, 2431; see also Levi (trans. Rosenthal), *Drowned and the Saved*, 38.

yourself above the norm."²⁴ Second, if the most basic ethical teachings lost their appeal in the gray zone, then that fact scarcely inspired confidence—then or now—that the world has a fundamental, universal moral structure that can be trusted. True, Levi thought that "at least sometimes, and at least in part, historical wrongs are punished," and that the Nazi project had been suicidal.²⁵ But Levi's book *The Drowned and the Saved* was written, overall, in a minor key. Its chapter on the gray zone extends that region beyond the confines of Auschwitz, concluding with reflection on Chaim Rumkowski, whose fate it was to lead the Jewish Council that the Germans forced the Jews to establish in the Lodz ghetto. Rumkowski's story, said Levi, "seems to exemplify the almost physical necessity by which political duress gives rise to the undefined area of ambiguity and compromise" that constitutes the gray zone. "Like Rumkowski," concluded Levi, "we, too, are so blinded by power and prestige that we forget our basic fragility. We make our deals with power, willingly or not, forgetting that we are all in the ghetto, that the ghetto is walled in, that outside the wall are the lords of death, and that not far away the train is waiting."²⁶

Turning into a Writer

No general rule governed survival in Auschwitz, Levi insisted, "except entering the camp in good health and knowing German. Barring this, luck dominated."²⁷ Levi did not take himself to be an exception, but he also emphasized that "for me thinking and observing were survival factors." Although they were not enough to explain his survival, let alone to ensure it, Levi said that he remembered "having lived my Auschwitz year in a condition of exceptional spiritedness. I don't know if this depended on my professional background, or an unsuspected stamina, or on a sound instinct." What did remain clear to Levi was that he "never stopped recording the world and people around me, so much that I still have an unbelievably detailed image of them." Levi insisted that he was "constantly pervaded by a curiosity . . . the curiosity of the naturalist who finds himself transplanted

---

24. Levi (trans. Moore), *Drowned and the Saved*, 2433–34; see also Levi (trans. Rosenthal), 41.

25. Levi (trans. Moore), *Drowned and the Saved*, 2566; see also Levi (trans. Rosenthal), *Drowned and the Saved*, 202.

26. Levi, *Drowned and the Saved*, 2454, 2456; see also Levi (trans. Rosenthal), *Drowned and the Saved*, 67, 69.

27. See Levi, "Conversation with Primo Levi" in *Survival in Auschwitz*, 180.

into an environment that is monstrous but new, monstrously new." He underscored that he had "an intense wish to understand."[28]

Levi's intense wish to understand was less than fulfilled. "I'm leaving much unfinished work," he wrote in a poem called "Unfinished Business," which he completed on April 19, 1981.[29] The Holocaust was too vast to encompass, its gray zones too full of ambiguity and compromise to fathom completely, and then there were the experiences that had been forgotten or repressed—"human memory," said Levi, "is a wonderful but fallible instrument"—as well as the unforgotten horrors that eluded description and muted language.[30]

Levi's account emphasized how the gray zone brought immense and often irresistible pressure to bear on the people within its Auschwitz grip. That structure, however, was complicated and incredible partly because it involved so much contingency and chance. Within his personal gray zone, Levi's fate was and was not his own. Things happened to him arbitrarily; he could control very little. Sometimes he could seize chance opportunities that were unavailable to others; sometimes unexpected advantages just came his way.

Anticipating that production of synthetic rubber might soon begin at Buna/Monowitz, the German "logic" that governed Auschwitz in 1944 resulted in a late spring call for prisoner-chemists. Sensing that some advantage might await him, Levi was among the prisoners who applied and was accepted to work in Kommando 98, the so-called Chemical Kommando. Levi knew, however, not to let his hopes rise too high. Even after passing the examination administered by a German official whom he identifies as Doktor Ingenieur Pannwitz, Levi knew that "in such conditions, those less experienced than us about things in the Lager might even be tempted by the hope of survival and the thought of liberty. Not us, we know how these things go; this is all a gift of fate, to be enjoyed as intensely as possible and at once; there is no certainty about tomorrow."[31]

No synthetic rubber was ever produced at Buna/Monowitz. Nor did the Chemical Kommando's work have much to do with science. It consisted largely of endless moving of backbreaking sacks of caustic chemicals, which often burned the skin and made the prisoners prone to infection.[32] But

28. Levi, "Conversation with Primo Levi," in *Survival in Auschwitz*, 180.

29. Levi, "Unfinished Business," in Levi (trans. Galassi) *Collected Poems*, 1939; see also Levi, (trans. Feldman), *Collected Poems*, 47.

30. Levi (trans. Moore), *Drowned and the Saved*, 2420; see also Levi (trans. Rosenthal), *Drowned and the Saved*, 23.

31. Levi, *If This Is a Man*, 134; see also Levi, *Survival in Auschwitz*, 140.

32. See Angier, *Double Bond*, 324–27.

the Holocaust entailed that one thing could lead to another in strange and unexpectedly beneficial ways. For a time, the Chemical Kommando worked near the British POW camp, where black-market bartering was favorable. In addition, Levi's assignment resulted in work with a bricklaying unit, where he was befriended by Lorenzo Perrone, the Italian civilian who gave him life-saving rations.[33]

"I did not choose to be a writer," said Primo Levi, "I was turned into one."[34] His deportation, his awareness of the gray zone in Auschwitz, his observation of the suffering of others, the help of Lorenzo—those experiences would compel him to write. His encounters with Doktor Pannwitz did so as well. "Pannwitz," wrote Levi, "is tall, thin, blond; he has the eyes, the hair, and the nose that all Germans ought to have." When he gazed at Levi, the prisoner-candidate for a lab job if he passed Pannwitz's chemistry examination, "that look," recalled Levi, "did not pass between two men" but "between two beings who inhabit different worlds." Pannwitz saw Levi only as a member of an inferior species who nevertheless might "contain some useful element." If he could fully explain that look, Levi thought "I would also be able to explain the essence of the great insanity of the Third Reich."[35] But Levi could not do so, which underscored how the Holocaust showed him that "most historical and natural phenomena are not simple, or, rather, not simple in the way we would like."[36]

Levi thought that the human mind tends to equate understanding with simplification. In addition, he thought the desire for simplification was justifiable because there can scarcely be any understanding unless there is some simplification of experience. Both understanding and the communication that make it possible depend on paying attention to *this* instead of *that*. Levi yearned to succeed "in understanding and making other people understand our experience," but he recognized that the Holocaust negated the equation between understanding and simplification.[37] More than that, Levi helped me understand that any declarative sentence one speaks or writes leaves out more than it grasps.

Levi passed the "chemical examination." Some of the work that followed gave him a privileged place in the camp, especially with winter

33. See Thomson, *Primo Levi*, 171–72.

34. See Levi's 1984 interview with Rita Caccamo De Luca and Manuela Olagnero in Levi, *Voice of Memory*, 161.

35. Levi, *If This Is a Man*, 100–101; see also Levi, *Survival in Auschwitz*, 105–6.

36. Levi (trans. Moore), *Drowned and the Saved*, 2431; see also Levi (trans. Rosenthal), *Drowned and the Saved*, 37.

37. Levi (trans. Moore), *Drowned and the Saved*, 2430; see also Levi (trans. Rosenthal), *Drowned and the Saved*, 36.

approaching. "To work," he would later write, "is to push carts, carry ties, break stones, shovel earth, grip with bare hands the repugnant iciness of frozen iron."[38] Levi's verbs—*push, carry, break, shovel, grip*—meant exhaustion and the death that followed. But, said Levi, "I sit all day."[39] He had a notebook, a pencil, and a comrade too. The comrade was not exactly another person, and yet he was, for the comrade was part of Levi himself, an aspect of himself revived by the privileges that were his. In its own way, this self-revival involved gray-zoned ambiguity, compromise, and more because it contained "the pain of remembering, the old fierce anguish of feeling myself a man again, which attacks me like a dog the moment my consciousness comes out of the darkness."[40] With that companion close by, Levi says that he took his pencil and notebook and wrote "what I could never tell anyone."[41]

Later, recalling the notes he had written in the chemical laboratory at Auschwitz in 1944, Levi emphasized that they were real, even though they "never amounted to more than twenty lines." But at the same time, they were not real because "there was no way I could keep them. It was materially impossible. Where could I hide them? In some container, but which? In my pockets? We had nothing, they changed our beds, the mattresses were continually being moved, even our clothes. There was no way of holding on to anything. Except in our memory."[42]

Levi could not keep the words he wrote in Auschwitz. To do so invited death. But even after he was liberated and free to write freely, were there things that he would never dare tell anyone? Levi was an eyewitness to the Holocaust. He wrote about it with the precision and curiosity of the empirical scientist. In that process, Levi revealed much about himself as well. His need to tell the story of his Auschwitz experience was strong. Devoting himself to that work, he tried hard to maintain "a careful balance between the essential and the superfluous," which he regarded as "the decisive element for narrative procedure."[43] Levi found writing to be "a way of creating order," the best one he knew, and he added that he felt "an immense need to put things in order, to put order back into a world of chaos, to explain to myself and to others."[44] But aspects of the chaos, things that he remembered,

---

38. Levi, *If This Is a Man*, 135; see also Levi, *Survival in Auschwitz*, 141.
39. Levi, *If This Is a Man*, 135; see also Levi, *Survival in Auschwitz*, 141.
40. Levi, *If This Is a Man*, 135; see also Levi, *Survival in Auschwitz*, 142.
41. Levi, *If This Is a Man*, 135; see also Levi, *Survival in Auschwitz*, 142.
42. See Levi's 1983 interview with Anna Bravo and Federico Cereja in Levi, *Voice of Memory*, 225.
43. See Levi's 1987 interview with Robert Di Caro in Levi, *Voice of Memory*, 171.
44. See Levi's 1987 interview with Robert Di Caro in Levi, *Voice of Memory*, 174.

could elude telling and thus leave the order incomplete, however much the writing might create or restore it.

Useless Violence

Levi began his memoir *If This Is a Man* with a chapter called "The Journey." His railroad transport to Auschwitz included "twelve freight cars and six hundred and fifty of us; in mine, we were only forty-five, but it was a small car."[45] The journey took four days. Levi describes how the train started and stopped, how slowly it moved. Through a slit in the wagon, he could see "the names of the last Italian cities," and days and nights later there were "known and unknown names of Austrian cities, Salzburg, Vienna; then Czech and, finally, Polish."[46]

Levi recalled the train's stopping for the last time. He remembered that throughout the entire journey a woman had been crushed against him. Although they had known each other for many years, Levi says that they "knew little of one another," but as the train reached Auschwitz, "we said to each other things that are not said among the living. We said farewell and it was short; everybody said farewell to life through his neighbor."[47] Later, Levi would learn that "of our convoy only ninety-six men and twenty-nine women entered the camps, respectively, of Monowitz-Buna and Birkenau, and that of all the others, more than five hundred in number, not one was alive two days later."[48] Of the forty-five persons in his train car, "only four saw their homes again; and ours was by far the most fortunate."[49]

Levi thought again about Holocaust trains in *The Drowned and the Saved* and especially in his powerful chapter about "Useless Violence." Those sealed boxcars, "transformed from a commercial vehicle into a mobile prison or even an instrument of death," were crowded, suffocating, thirst-inflicting, stench-ridden places where German administration of the "Final Solution of the Jewish question" intentionally inflicted what Levi called "a deep wound . . . on human dignity, an obscene and ominous attack, but also the sign of a deliberate, gratuitous malice."[50]

---

45. Levi, *If This Is a Man*, 13; see also Levi, *Survival in Auschwitz*, 16.
46. Levi, *If This Is a Man*, 13–14; see also Levi, *Survival in Auschwitz*, 17–18.
47. Levi, *If This Is a Man*, 15; see also Levi, *Survival in Auschwitz*, 19.
48. Levi, *If This Is a Man*, 16; see also Levi, *Survival in Auschwitz*, 20.
49. Levi, *If This Is a Man*, 14; see also Levi, *Survival in Auschwitz*, 17–18.
50. Levi (trans. Moore), *Drowned and the Saved*, 2488, 2491; see also Levi (trans. Rosenthal), *Drowned and Saved*, 108, 111.

In Levi's apt words, the Holocaust involved many "historical space-times," a variety of geographical and imaginative landscapes, a multiplicity of gray zones. The Holocaust's trains bear witness to that fact, and thus it is not surprising that Levi was not alone—recall Wiesel, for example, and Hilberg—in dwelling on their importance and horror. "The memory's sequence," he wrote, "almost always begins with the train that marked the departure toward the unknown: not only for chronological reasons but also because of the gratuitous cruelty by which those otherwise innocuous convoys of ordinary boxcars were employed for an uncustomary purpose."[51]

The horrors of the trains did not come close to exhausting the Holocaust's useless violence. Levi's probing went deep down because he did not dwell on the obvious—the beatings, hangings, and gassings at Auschwitz. His catalog of useless violence did not overlook the loot collected from the arrivals at Auschwitz, which included tens of thousands of spoons. Lack of a spoon to eat the camps' miserable food brought starvation sooner and closer for Auschwitz prisoners, but no spoons were given to them. Prisoners had to fend as best they could, which might mean spending precious food from the starvation diet to buy a spoon on the black market. Levi also focused on the fact that there were plenty of ways to identify prisoners, but at Auschwitz the Nazis implemented "the violence of the tattoo," which he describes as "gratuitous, an end in itself, a pure insult."[52] The Nazis' useless violence, Levi acknowledges, did have one unredeeming element of utility: "Before dying," Levi observed, "the victim had to be degraded to alleviate the killer's sense of guilt. This explanation is not without logic, but it cries out to the heavens: it is the only use of useless violence."[53] Levi did not go on to say so, but he might have added that the Nazi goal was not simply to lessen guilt's burden but to create practitioners of useless violence who would feel no guilt at all.

With the Holocaust's perpetrators of useless violence in mind, Levi once said that "to forgive is not my verb," but he also articulated conditions that might move him to use it. He would be unwilling to forgive any of the Holocaust's perpetrators "unless they can demonstrate (in deeds: not in words, and not too late) that they are aware of the crimes and errors of fascism, ours and other nations', and are determined to condemn them, to uproot them from their own conscience and that of others. In that case, yes,

---

51. Levi (trans. Moore), *Drowned and Saved*, 2488; see also Levi (trans. Rosenthal), *Drowned and the Saved*, 107–8.

52. Levi (trans. Moore), *Drowned and the Saved*, 2497; see also Levi (trans. Rosenthal), *Drowned and the Saved* 119.

53. Levi (trans. Moore), *Drowned and the Saved*, 2502; see also Levi (trans. Rosenthal), *Drowned and the Saved*, 126.

I, though not a Christian, am willing to follow the Jewish and Christian commandment to forgive my enemy; but an enemy who repents has ceased to be an enemy."[54] Levi found few if any Holocaust perpetrators who met that standard, but that fact did not eliminate the insightful tension between warnings about moral judgment against people caught in the gray zone and insistence that the Holocaust cried out for persistent ethical evaluation.

Levi understood that the human mind's craving for simple understanding includes the need "to separate evil from good, to take sides, to reenact the gesture of Christ on Judgment Day: over here go the righteous, over there the wicked."[55] Although the gray zone defied those neat separations, moral judgments nevertheless resounded in Levi's writing. Recall, for example, that he never hesitated to call the creation of the Sonderkommando a "diabolical crime," the worst committed by National Socialists.[56] Moreover, in his introduction to the German edition of *If This I a Man*, Levi said that he had written that book "to bear witness, to make my voice heard by the German people, to . . . remind them of what they did, and say to them, 'I am alive, and I would like to understand you so that I can judge you.'"[57] Levi added that he did not hate the German people, but then he delivered a comment as devastating as it was understated: "I can't say I understand the Germans."[58]

That statement contained an ethical judgment that went much deeper than conventional moral evaluations, which assume that people are more or

---

54. See Levi's 1986 interview with Giorgio Calcagno regarding *The Drowned and the Saved*, in Levi, *Voice of Memory*, 111. See also the appendix that Levi wrote in 1976 for the school edition of *If This Is a Man*, 167–93, esp. 169. This appendix, which contains Levi's responses to questions he often received, is also published as "A Self-Interview: Afterword to *If This Is a Man* (1976)," in Levi, *Voice of Memory*, 184–207, esp. 186. In the quoted passage, Levi's specification that he is not a Christian is significant. As Levi himself would have understood, his Jewish identity was well known. Ordinarily there would have been no need for him to state that he was not a Christian. He did so, I believe, because he was speaking about forgiveness, even suggesting that there might be Holocaust perpetrators who could once have been worthy of it. Conventional wisdom sometimes holds that forgiveness is more a "Christian" quality than a "Jewish" one. Levi may have wanted to clarify that his outlook was not buying into a Christian ethic of one kind or another.

55. Levi (trans. Moore), *Drowned and the Saved*, 2431; see also Levi (trans. Rosenthal), *Drowned and the Saved*, 37.

56. Levi (trans. Moore), *Drowned and the Saved*, 2443; see also Levi (trans. Rosenthal), *Drowned and the Saved*, 53.

57. Levi (trans. Moore), *Drowned and the Saved*, 2541; see also Levi (trans. Rosenthal), *Drowned and the Saved*, 174.

58. Levi (trans. Moore), *Drowned and Saved*, 2541; see also Levi (trans. Rosenthal), *Drowned and Saved* 174.

less in agreement about shared rights and values, even though they may violate those norms. For Levi, the Germans were not understandable because, as he put it, they had abandoned civilization. Levi clarified these points in comments that he made in 1961 regarding collective guilt:

> The very expression "collective guilt" is a contradiction in terms, and it is a Nazi invention. Every person is singly responsible for their actions. Every German (and non-German) who took part in the murdering is fully guilty; their accomplices are partially guilty...; less guilty but still contemptible are the many who did nothing in the full knowledge of what was happening, and the mass who found ways of not knowing because of their hypocrisy or poverty of spirit.
>
> In this way, we can build up a picture which belies the heroic inventions of Nazi propaganda: not collective guilt, but collective cowardice, a collective failure of intellectual courage, a collective foolishness and abandonment of civilization.[59]

Levi's moral analysis did not stop with Nazi Germany. Acknowledging that he lacked trust in "the moral instinct of humanity, in mankind as 'naturally' good,"[60] Levi warned that the existence of Nazi Germany and the Holocaust meant that realities akin to them could appear again—were even likely to do so—because no community had guaranteed immunity against them.[61] What could humankind do, he wondered, to keep such threats at bay?

One of Levi's responses to that question was to study the gray zone and to grasp why there must be caution as well as boldness about moral judgments. The existence of the Sonderkommando, for example, raised questions for those who want simple understanding: "Why did they accept this job? Why didn't they rebel? Why didn't they prefer death?"[62] Historical inquiry, Levi emphasized, does much to put such questions to rest. "Not everyone did accept," he rightly stated. "Some rebelled, knowing they would die."[63] As for those who did the dismal work, Levi underscored his belief that "no one has the authority to judge them, not those who experienced

---

59. See Levi, *Voice of Memory*, 180–81.

60. Levi, *Voice of Memory*, 180.

61. See Levi (trans. Moore), *Drowned and the Saved*, 2564; see also Levi (trans. Rosenthal), *Drowned and the Saved*, 199.

62. Levi (trans. Moore), *Drowned and the Saved*, 2447; see also Levi (trans. Rosenthal), *Drowned and the Saved*, 58.

63. Levi (trans. Moore), *Drowned and the Saved*, 2447; see also Levi (trans. Rosenthal), *Drowned and the Saved*, 58.

the Lager and, especially, not those who did not."⁶⁴ Levi thought it illogical to think that ordinary men and women would behave like "saints and Stoic philosophers."⁶⁵ Taking the realities of the Lager into account, Levi's insight underscored the importance of remembering that "you are never in someone else's place" and "no one can know how long and what torments his soul can resist before crumpling or breaking."⁶⁶

Levi's position, however, harbored danger. While defending the gray zone's victims against inappropriate moral judgments, would his appeal to human frailty open the door for excuses and thus undermine the moral accountability that Levi so much wanted to support? Would even the Holocaust's perpetrators and bystanders be able to appeal to human frailty to excuse themselves? To disarm the danger, Levi brought attention back to the pressurized structure of the gray zone, where brutality, hunger, choiceless choices, and a persistent desire to live mixed and mingled to produce oppression that diminished civilization, dooming its humanizing ethical categories to be largely inapplicable, if not dysfunctional, as far as the prisoners' struggle to survive was concerned.

By learning to hold moral judgment back appropriately, by not misdirecting it in ways that blame the victims, one can better focus where the ethical critique and its accompanying senses of moral obligation belong. Levi's analysis produces insight that moral judgment should focus on the persons and decisions that created the Holocaust and every other form of genocide. With that judgment there should be an intensification of responsibility to intervene against those powers and circumstances, to honor those who do so, to embrace the survivors with compassion, to restore—as far as possible—what was lost, and to mourn and remember those who were murdered. Levi had his hopes. "There are no problems that cannot be settled around a table," he said, "so long as there is goodwill and mutual trust: or even mutual fear."⁶⁷ Unfortunately, Levi was probably too optimistic. So much hinges on his qualification about goodwill and reciprocal trust. Their scarcity remains one of the Holocaust's most confounding results and one of the most acute challenges in our post-Holocaust world.

---

64. Levi (trans. Moore), *Drowned and the Saved*, 2448; see also Levi (trans. Rosenthal), *Drowned and the Saved*, 59.

65. Levi (trans. Moore), *Drowned and the Saved*, 2440; see also Levi (trans. Rosenthal), *Drowned and the Saved*, 49.

66. Levi (trans. Moore), *Drowned and the Saved*, 2448–49; see also Levi (trans. Rosenthal), *Drowned and the Saved*, 60.

67. Levi (trans. Moore), *Drowned and the Saved*, 2565; see also Levi (trans. Rosenthal), *Drowned and the Saved*, 200.

Kuhn's Prayer

Scarcity of trust and goodwill is at play in the fact that while Levi's writings speak about many things, rarely do they say much directly about God. *If This Is a Man*, however, contains a brief but striking exception to that rule. What led to this exception was an Auschwitz "selection" on a Sunday afternoon in October 1944.

All the prisoners in Levi's part of the camp were ordered to their barracks. In each of them (Levi's was number 48 out of 60), everyone received a card that "bears our number, name, profession, age, and nationality" and obeyed orders to "undress completely, except for shoes."[68] Levi and his comrades then waited for the "selection." It would sentence some to the gas chambers. Others would have to work a while longer.

When the SS inspectors reached Barrack 48 to process Levi's group, the procedure was as random as it was quick and simple. One by one, the prisoners ran a few steps and then surrendered their identity cards to an SS man who, in turn, passed the cards to a man on his right or left. "This," wrote Levi, "is the life or death of each one of us. In three or four minutes a barrack of two hundred men is 'done,' and in the course of the afternoon the entire camp of twelve thousand men."[69] Not quite "done," however, because in Levi's part of the camp it usually took two or three days before those "selected" went to the gas. Meanwhile, the prisoners could figure out whose cards had gone to the left, whose to the right, and what the difference meant.

Levi's description of this October "selection" emphasizes its blending of Nazi logic and capriciousness. October meant that another Auschwitz winter was at hand. In the better weather of spring and summer 1944, the Germans had pitched huge tents to house several thousand prisoners in Levi's part of the camp. As winter approached, the tents came down, and the barracks became increasingly crowded. According to Levi, the Germans disliked such irregularities; they also realized that newly arriving Jewish convoys would make the crowding worse. Thus, the prisoner ranks had to be thinned. Presumably, the October "selection" would cull the weak and useless prisoners, but Levi believed that "the important thing" for the Germans was to ensure that "free places be quickly created, according to a fixed percentage."[70]

Levi drew that conclusion because he witnessed other "irregularities." A prisoner named Sattler, for example, had been in the camp for only twenty

---

68. Levi, *If This Is a Man*, 121; see also Levi, *Survival in Auschwitz*, 127.
69. Levi, *If This Is a Man*, 122; see also Levi, *Survival in Auschwitz*, 128.
70. Levi, *If This Is a Man*, 123; see also Levi, *Survival in Auschwitz*, 129.

days. Even though he was still relatively strong and healthy, the "selection" was his death sentence. In the fast-moving inspection, a young and robust man named René went immediately ahead of Levi. Surely, Levi reflects, it was a mistake that Rene's card went to the left, "the *schlecte Seite*, the bad side."[71] And then it occurred to Levi that, yes, a mistake might well have been made, but it was not simply about René's health. More likely, Levi's card, which went to the right, had been mistaken for René's. "The fact that I was not selected," concluded Levi, "depended almost entirely on chance."[72] Considering the capriciousness that may have spared his life on that Sunday in October, Levi indicates that he felt "no distinct emotion" at the time.[73] Nevertheless, his account does not fully support that judgment, for Levi continues by noting what he observed after the meager portion of soup had been devoured on that postselection evening and how he felt about what he had seen and heard:

> Silence slowly prevails, and then, from my bunk, on the top level, I see and hear old Kuhn praying aloud, with his cap on his head, his torso swaying violently. Kuhn is thanking God that he was not chosen.
>
> Kuhn is out of his mind. Does he not see, in the bunk next to him, Beppo the Greek, who is twenty years old and is going to the gas chamber the day after tomorrow, and knows it, and lies there staring at the light without saying anything and without even thinking anymore? Does Kuhn not know that next time it will be his turn? Does Kuhn not understand that what happened today is an abomination, which no propitiatory prayer, no pardon, no expiation by the guilty—nothing at all in the power of man to do—can ever heal?
>
> If I were God, I would spit Kuhn's prayer out upon the ground.[74]

71. Levi, *If This Is a Man*, 122; see also Levi, *Survival in Auschwitz*, 128.
72. Levi, *If This Is a Man*, 120; see also Levi, *Survival in Auschwitz*, 125.
73. Levi, *If This Is a Man*, 122; see also Levi, *Survival in Auschwitz*, 128.
74. Levi, *If This Is a Man*, 123–24; see also Levi, *Survival in Auschwitz*, 129–30. Levi does not indicate the language Kuhn used in his prayer or how he knew what Kuhn was saying, but clearly Kuhn's prayer left a deep impression on him. In "God and I," Levi's 1983 interview with Giuseppe Grieco, Levi revealed his views about prayer in greater detail. They fit with his understanding of the gray zone and with his responses to Kuhn's prayer. During what he calls "the great selection of 1944," which probably included the episodes surrounding Kuhn's prayer, Levi says that he had a "moment of religious temptation" when "I tried to commend myself to God, and I recall, with shame, having said to myself: 'No, you can't do this, you don't have the right. First, because you don't believe in God; secondly, because asking for favors, without having a special case, is the act of a *mafioso*.' The moral of the story: I gave up the doubtful comfort of prayer

Levi was in his midtwenties when the Germans deported him to Auschwitz in late February 1944. A few months later, in May, Elie Wiesel, fifteen, and his family were deported to Auschwitz from Hungarian territory occupied by the Germans. Levi and Wiesel were both in the Buna subcamp. In Buna, Wiesel said of Levi, "I had spent some time in his barracks. I had seen him without seeing him. He had crossed my path without noticing me."[75] Levi agreed: "Elie Wiesel and I were in the same camp," adding that "probably we did not meet . . . We only got to know each other through our books."[76] From time to time, Wiesel reported, he met "my friend Primo" and spoke with him by telephone, but the divergence in their thought was as significant as the bonds between them.[77] Wiesel focused the crux of the matter when he observed succinctly that during and after Auschwitz, "I needed God, Primo did not."[78]

Levi concurred: "Mine is the life of a man who has lived and who lives without God, indifferent to God."[79] But on another occasion, less than a year before his death, Levi's indifference to God may have been less than complete as he checked the typescript of a series of interviews he had granted to Ferdinando Camon. At the end of one of the interviews, Levi had said, "No, I never have been [a believer]. I'd like to be, but I don't succeed . . . I must say that for me the experience of Auschwitz has been such as to sweep away any remnant of religious education I may have had." Camon sought clarification about those reflections: "Auschwitz," he asked Levi, "is proof of the nonexistence of God?" Levi replied: "There is Auschwitz, and so there cannot be God."

In those few words, Levi's response seemed done. Not quite done, however, because when Camon received the corrected typescript for the

---

and I left it to chance, and whoever else it might be, to decide my fate." In Auschwitz, Levi stated, "I had seen suffering and dying all around me thousands of men more worthy than me, even innocent babies, and conversely, I had seen deplorable, most certainly malicious men survive. Thus salvation and death did not depend on God but on chance." Even if in some sense God does exist, which Levi admitted was a possibility, he thought that God "is indifferent to the matters of mankind. In short, he isn't someone to pray to," and it would be wrong, Levi added, "to invent a God to talk to" (Levi, *Voice of Memory*, 275–76).

75. Wiesel, *Sea Is Never Full*, 345.

76. See Levi's 1986 interview with Anthony Rudolf in Levi, *Voice of Memory*, 27.

77. Wiesel, *Sea Is Never Full*, 345–46.

78. Wiesel, *All Rivers*, 83. Important commentary on this difference between Wiesel and Levi is found in Rubenstein, "Elie Wiesel and Primo Levi," 145–65. This essay also sheds light on Rubenstein's important contributions to post-Holocaust religious thought and ethics.

79. See Levi's 1983 interview with Giuseppi Grieco in Levi, *Voice of Memory*, 272.

interview, he saw that Levi had penciled a margin note beside his not-quite-final comment: "I don't find a solution to this dilemma," Levi had added, "I keep looking, but I don't find it."[80] More than Levi, Wiesel kept looking for God too, and while Levi did not share what he called Wiesel's "endless quarrel with God in whom he keeps believing but whom he keeps on not understanding," Levi was not surprised by Wiesel's impassioned quest, explaining that "I do not find any artifice in his keeping faith with the same theme, because it is an inexhaustible theme."[81]

Looking . . . not finding . . . looking some more: When the question is whether Auschwitz is proof of the nonexistence of God, when the dilemma is whether it could be credible to pray in or after Auschwitz, does that rhythm make sense? By no means would everyone say yes, but I find that Levi's reaction to Kuhn's prayer can intensify reflection about such questions. Levi loathed Kuhn's prayer. Perhaps because of Levi's awareness of the capriciousness of the October "selection," Kuhn's prayer outraged him. Not only did that prayer affirm divine purpose in a place where Levi found none, it also appeared oblivious to chance, which, as Levi knew from his experience just hours earlier, could decisively affect life prospects in Auschwitz. If God did exist, Levi thought, God would despise Kuhn's prayer too. To thank God for one's own survival when Nazi Germany's masters of death were annihilating weak and defenseless people by the millions—often doing so through "mistakes" akin to the kind that Levi saw during the October "selection"—such a prayer included an unawareness or indifference as abhorrent as it was blind and self-centered. The same judgment could apply if Kuhn had asked God to protect and spare persons who were especially dear to him and had done so without regard either for chance or for others beyond his family and friends. But it would not follow that Kuhn should have been unconcerned about or indifferent to what happened to him or to those he cared about most. If lack of awareness or self-centered indifference diminished Kuhn's integrity, it does not follow that he would have been more fully human if his own fate and that of his loved ones had lost special significance for him.

Levi discredits Kuhn's prayer, but not necessarily all prayer during and after the Holocaust. The atrocities, often compounded by their capriciousness, should always leave the reality and character of divinity in doubt. In that sense, Holocaust-related theodicy, a vindication of God's justice in the face of Auschwitz, seems futile, if not dead. Nevertheless, our lives, the histories and contingencies in which they are embedded, the good we value,

---

80. See Camon, *Conversations*, 67–68.
81. See Levi's interview with Rudolf in Levi, *Voice of Memory*, 27–28.

and the evils that may engulf us do not account entirely for themselves. Problematic though they may be, the words that Elie Wiesel and perhaps Levi heard in Auschwitz on Rosh Hashanah eve in 1944—"All the earth and the Universe are God's!"—still have a meaning as awesome as it is ambiguous. At least for some who rebel against reality's absurdity, prayer may retain a legitimate place, even if many prayers do not.

What Auschwitz indicates is that divinity does not necessarily answer or even hear prayer in the ways people prefer or expect. Reality, largely because of the arbitrary, merciless, and murderous devastation it harbors, does not unfold in ways that conform to our needs and desires, but those needs and desires are part of reality, and prayer can help people to pursue them in their best forms. "Prayers," as Wiesel has written, "do not always coincide with reality, and surely not with truth. But so what? It is up to us to modify reality and make the prayers come true."[82]

At its most profound, prayer involves intense awareness, concentration, and yearning for what deserves to matter most to us as human beings. When prayers are said for justice, peace, and freedom, for relief from hunger, racism, violence, war, and genocide, there can be a quieting and opening of ourselves in recognition that life involves power—at times but not always benign—that transcends our own, and value that extends beyond the boundaries of our finite years. It follows, and this is a kind of answer to our needs and petitions, that we may be encouraged to keep trying and to work toward goals that prayer itself has helped us identify as aims ultimately worthy of the best and the most that we can give. Wiesel's prayer-provoked rebellion and Levi's rejection of Kuhn's prayer at Auschwitz alert one to those possibilities by helping to delineate what post-Holocaust prayer should and should not be. Prayer that is offered well resists ignorance, blindness, and self-centeredness. It is an informed expression of and commitment to human solidarity against the masters of death. Prayer is not the only expression of that kind, but humankind would be poorer without it.

A Place for Compassion

Levi, who thought that "each of us is a mixture of good and not so good," lacked trust in "the moral instinct of humanity, in mankind as 'naturally' good."[83] In an essay called "News from the Sky," for example, he noted that the German philosopher Immanuel Kant emphasized two wonders in creation: the starry sky above and the moral law within. "Let's leave aside moral

---

82. Wiesel, *All Rivers*, 84–85.
83. Levi, *Voice of Memory*, 180, 232.

law," said Levi, "is it to be found within everyone? ... Every year that passes only amplifies our doubts."[84] The starry sky seemed to be another matter, but even those considerations gave Levi pause. The stars remain, but the sky—the territory of bombers, hijacked planes, missiles, and drones that can unleash terror and horror capable of annihilating human existence itself—has become an ominous place because of World War II, the Holocaust, and their reverberations.

Levi was not sure that ethics could be salvaged after Auschwitz, but he knew that the failure to try would exact a price higher than humankind could pay. "The universe is strange to us, and we are strange within the universe," he wrote, and "the future of mankind is uncertain."[85] This outlook helps to explain why Levi especially recalled his friend Lorenzo Perrone, the person Levi credited with saving his life in Auschwitz. Not a Jew but an Italian civilian, Lorenzo, a skilled bricklayer, was "officially" a "voluntary" worker helping to build the industrial plant that the Germans were constructing at Monowitz. Lorenzo was not a prisoner. Levi said that Lorenzo and his fellow workers "although not soldiers, lived like soldiers."[86] They had privileges unknown to Levi and his fellow inmates but also obligations to do the Germans' bidding. Levi saw that Lorenzo "hated Germans, their food, their language, their war," but Lorenzo still took pride in work well done. Levi was struck by the fact that Lorenzo, a quiet, "sensitive man, almost illiterate but really sort of a saint," laid his bricks for the Germans "straight and solid, not out of obedience but out of professional dignity."[87]

Probably Lorenzo never encountered Elie Wiesel, but after meeting Levi in late June 1944, he decided to help his fellow Italian, although it was a crime with grave consequences for Lorenzo even to speak to an Auschwitz prisoner. For months, Lorenzo got Levi extra food, which was the physical difference between life and death. "I believe that I owe it to Lorenzo if I am alive today," Levi would write, underscoring that Lorenzo's help meant much more than food alone. What also sustained him was that Lorenzo "constantly reminded me by his presence, by his natural and plain manner of being good, that a just world still existed outside ours, something and someone still pure and whole, not corrupt, not savage, unconnected to

84. Levi (trans. Shugaar), *Other People's Trades*, 2180; see also Levi (trans. Rosenthal), *Other People's Trades*, 20.

85. Levi (trans. Shugaar), *Other People's Trades*, 2182–83; see also Levi (trans. Rosenthal), *Other People's Trades*, 22–23.

86. See "Return of Lorenzo" in Levi, *Lilith*, 1402; and "Lorenzo's Return" in Levi, *Moments*, 150.

87. See Levi's 1985 interview with Gabriel Matola: Matola, "Primo Levi," 201ff. See also Levi, "Conversation with Primo Levi" in *Survival in Auschwitz*, 179.

hatred and fear: something difficult to define, a remote possibility of good, but for which it was worth surviving."[88]

When liberation came, Levi lost track of Lorenzo, but later he became determined to find out what had happened to his life-saving friend. They reconnected in Italy after the war, but soon Lorenzo died. Levi's recollections of him are memorable. "He was not religious," Levi said. "He didn't know the gospel, but instinctively he tried to rescue people, not for pride, not for glory, but out of a good heart and for human comprehension. He asked me once in very laconic words: 'Why are we in the world if not to help each other?' Stop. Period."[89] At one of their postwar meetings, Levi learned that he was not the only Auschwitz prisoner whom Lorenzo had helped, but Levi's friend had rarely told that story. In Lorenzo's view, wrote Levi, "we are in the world to do good, not to boast of it."[90]

Philip Hallie once said that "moral beauty happens when someone carves out a place for compassion in a largely ruthless universe."[91] Moral beauty scarcely existed in the Holocaust and Primo Levi's gray zone, but that fact may make it all the more important to remember Levi's friend Lorenzo, who, Levi said, "constantly reminded me by his presence, by his natural and plain manner of being good, that a just world still existed outside ours, something and someone still pure and whole, not corrupt, not savage, unconnected to hatred and fear: something difficult to define, a remote possibility of good, but for which it was worth surviving." Levi may have been right in thinking, as he did, that no universal human conscience exists, that there is no innate and shared moral compass to guide us all, if only we would pay attention and follow it. But that sensibility does not negate, at least not completely, the reminding presence of Lorenzo, which testifies that "we are in this world to do good." Remote though it often seems, difficult to define though it may be, that possibility remains. More than that, the possibility becomes an imperative if the world is to be less corrupt and savage and more opposed to hatred and terror.

88. Levi, *If This Is a Man*, 115; see also Levi, *Survival in Auschwitz*, 121.

89. See Matola, "Primo Levi," 201ff.

90. Levi, "Return of Lorenzo" in Levi, *Lilith*, 1408; see also "Lorenzo's Return" in Levi, *Moments*, 160. Despite the medical assistance that Levi arranged for him, Perrone, wracked by tuberculosis and alcohol, died in 1952. Significantly, Levi's daughter, Lisa Lorenza, and his son called Renzo were named after Perrone. On June 7, 1998, Perrone was recognized by Yad Vashem, the State of Israel's memorial to the victims of the Holocaust, as one of the Righteous Among the Nations, a special honor for non-Jews who rescued Jews during the Holocaust. For more detail on Perrone, see the Yad Vashem website for the profile of him in "The Stories of Six Righteous Among the Nations in Auschwitz."

91. Hallie, *Eye of the Hurricane*, 173.

Levi was right to suggest that it is difficult to define precisely how it is that we are in this world to do good, but it was not difficult for Levi to feel Lorenzo's "presence" and to discern his "natural and plain manner of being good." Those characteristics were oppression-resisting, hope-sustaining, death-defying, and life-giving. More often than not, ethics at its best involves reminders of the kind embedded in Lorenzo's actions. Reminders are not always welcome or followed. But good reminders of the kind that Lorenzo gave Levi are testimonies about sometimes difficult-to-define realities—justice, compassion, respect, love—that have been experienced, at least at times, in word and deed. Reminders about those realities may be especially crucial when human flourishing is threatened, and hope is in short supply. Knowing that, Levi testified with insistence that Lorenzo's reminder—we are in this world to do good—should always be vivid and never abandoned. When that vision guides and compels human conduct, chances for joy *in spite of* atrocity are improved, and even possibilities for happiness *in spite of* carnage are enhanced. Such insight remains much needed in our dangerous and endangered world.

11

Jean Améry

Less than three weeks before dying at the age of eighty-two on November 7, 2016, the great Canadian singer-songwriter Leonard Cohen released the last of his fourteen albums. He called it *You Want It Darker*, echoing the album's title track, which, in January 2018, won a Grammy Award for Best Rock Performance. Cohen was steeped in his Jewish identity and quarrelsome in ways reminiscent of Elie Wiesel, and Cohen's song makes God the You who apparently wants things darker in a world where millions of candles burn for help that never comes. I like Cohen's song for its bold and challenging lamentation, which includes honest world-weariness that admits the time comes, as Cohen says, to be "out of the game."

Cohen's gravelly voicing, "You want it darker," reminds me of Jean Améry—Jewish philosopher, victim of Nazi torture, and survivor of Auschwitz. He is a profound source of Holocaust insight because he could also be the You in Cohen's song. No Holocaust survivor-writer—not Wiesel or Levi, not Delbo or Kofman—made the Holocaust darker. Plunging me deep down into darkness, Améry shows how learning and teaching about the Holocaust entail losing trust in the world and deciding what to do after that.

No Illusions, No Delusions

As though countering Cohen, Les Schwab Tires, more than 450-stores strong in the American west, has promoted itself by wordplay: "Our Business Is Earning Your Trust." That goal might well be everyone's business, but in this deceitful world of ours, trust is in short supply. Arguably, a slogan more accurate than Les Schwab's would say: "The world's business, including America's, is destroying our trust."

But hold on. Not so fast. Perhaps the reality is that our times and circumstances are very different and much better than that. Consider, for example, what the January 15, 2018, issue of *Time* magazine had to say. Guest-edited by Bill Gates, the Microsoft founder and philanthropist, a section of that issue featured what the cover called "The Optimists." Gates's introduction acknowledged that recent events such as "Hurricanes in the Americas. Horrific mass shootings. Global tensions over nuclear arms, crisis in Myanmar, bloody civil wars in Syria and Yemen" could make it "feel like the world is falling apart." But not so, Gates argued: "On the whole, the world is getting better."

Eight months earlier, in mid-May 2017, Gates expressed the same trust in the world, producing buzz and booming sales for a book when he sent a tweet aimed at that year's graduating classes. "If I could give each of you a graduation present," said Gates, "it would be this—the most inspiring book I've ever read."[1] Authored by Harvard psychology professor Steven Pinker, the enthusiastically recommended volume was *The Better Angels of Our Nature: Why Violence Has Declined*. A few months after his "graduation present" comments, however, Gates found a book he liked even better. Also authored by Pinker, *Enlightenment Now: The Case for Reason, Science, Humanism, and Progress*, said Gates, is "my new favorite book of all time" because of its compelling argument that, in Pinker's words, "there is no limit to the betterments we can attain if we continue to apply knowledge to enhance human flourishing."[2]

Enlightenment Now became available with wide acclaim when Amazon released it on February 13, 2018.[3] The next afternoon, on Valentine's Day, Nikolas Cruz, nineteen, mocked the purported decline of violence. At Marjory Stoneman Douglas High School in Parkland, Florida, he opened fire with a legally purchased AR-15 semiautomatic rifle and, in six deadly minutes, murdered seventeen students and faculty members, wounded many others, and plunged a community into mourning. The five-hundred-plus pages of *Enlightenment Now* were scant comfort to the bereaved in Parkland or to the grief-stricken from more than 130 shootings at elementary, middle and high schools, and fifty-eight others at colleges and universities

---

1. See Fung, "Bill Gates."
2. See Gates, "My New Favorite Book."
3. When the paperback edition of *Enlightenment Now* appeared in January 2019, Pinker used the occasion to publish a lengthy article about "the controversies that have flared up in the year since the book appeared." See Pinker, "Enlightenment Wars." The article includes a substantial list of reviews and commentaries that the book has received.

in the United States from 2000 through early 2018.⁴ Nevertheless, Pinker claimed that his *Better Angels of Our Nature* identifies "what may be the most important thing that has ever happened in human history . . . violence has declined over long stretches of time, and today we may be living in the most peaceable era in our species' existence."⁵ Thanks to evolution and the trends and historical forces of modernity, plus the data and analytical perspectives provided by "atrocitology," Pinker thinks we can discern progress that makes "the decline of violence . . . an accomplishment we can savor, and an impetus to cherish the forces of civilization and enlightenment that made it possible."⁶

To be fair, while Pinker thinks the decline in violence is unmistakable, he acknowledges that the progress "has not been smooth; it has not brought violence down to zero; and it is not guaranteed to continue."⁷ But his trust that progress will continue is fortified, at least in part, by widespread memory of the Holocaust and testimony about it, which includes, in particular, recognition that Anne Frank's *Diary* and Elie Wiesel's *Night* have helped to increase "public awareness of the suffering of people who might otherwise have been ignored." Such awareness advances "new ideas about moral values and the social order," and reorients "our conception of history" in ways that encourage "humanitarian sensibilities."⁸

Especially in the wake of Parkland and countless other contemporary atrocities, how soon and how fully we should celebrate such claims depends

---

4. On these matters, see Bump, "Eighteen Years of Gun Violence," https://www.washingtonpost.com/news/politics/wp/2018/02/14/eighteen-years-of-gun-violence-in-u-s-schools-mapped/?utm_term=.78a0425dfe95.

5. Pinker, *Better Angels*, preface. The book was initially published in 2011.

6. Pinker, *Better Angels*, 696. Pinker's arguments in favor of these propositions result in claims that will strike most Holocaust and genocide scholars and educators as problematic if not false. Five examples include: (1) "There is no indication that anyone but Hitler and a few fanatical henchmen thought it was a good idea for the Jews to be exterminated." (2) "Could World War II be an isolated peak in a declining sawtooth—the last gasp in a long slide of major war into historical obsolescence? Again, we will see that this possibility is not as dreamy as it sounds." (3) Discussing so-called new wars or "low-intensity conflicts" as well as "the mass killing of ethnic and political groups" and terrorism, Pinker contends that "*all these kinds of killing are in decline*" (his italics). (4) "What changed in the 20th century was not so much the occurrence of genocide as the recognition that genocide was something bad." (5) "Readers of this book (and as we shall see, people in most of the rest of the world) no longer have to worry about . . . the prospect of a nuclear world war that would put an end to civilization or to human life itself." See 331, 192, 297, 643, 29–30.

7. Pinker, *Better Angels*, preface.

8. Pinker, *Better Angels*, 177, 335.

on how much of Pinker's account is accurate, credible, and persuasive.[9] He fills eight hundred pages to convince his readers, but insofar as Pinker may intend to restore trust in the world, his tribute to progress does not work for me. The reasons involve not only American school shootings but also events that took place in Europe years before *The Better Angels of Our Nature* appeared.

A Human Being Needs a Home

According to the foundational 1951 United Nations Convention on the Status of Refugees, which was signed at Geneva, Switzerland, on July 28, 1951, and entered into force on April 22, 1954, "the term 'refugee' shall apply to any person who . . . owing to well-founded fear of being persecuted for reasons of race, religion, nationality, membership of a particular social group or political opinion, is outside the country of his nationality and is unable or, owing to such fear, is unwilling to avail himself of the protection of that country; or who, not having a nationality and being outside the country of his former habitual residence as a result of such events, is unable or, owing to such fear, is unwilling to return to it."[10] Necessary though it is, such definitional language says far too little and leaves far too much in silence. Refugees, for instance, are not only persons outside their country of origin or "habitual residence." At least in the short term, they are homeless. Not only do refugees have "well-founded fear" about "persecution" and indeed about their very lives. They are often besieged and plagued by *homesickness*.

Forced into refugee status before the UN defined the term, Jean Améry reflected on the multiple aspects of that forlorn condition, particularly in an essay called "How Much Home Does a Person Need?" His voice emphasizes an observation so fundamental—"a human being needs a home"—that it stands now, like it did then, as a searing indictment and an inescapable imperative.[11]

To see how such realities affected Améry and made him a pivotal source of Holocaust insight, note that troops from Nazi Germany crossed the Austrian border on March 12, 1938. By the next day, the Anschluss, as

---

9. Critiques of Pinker's outlook are as pointed as they are numerous, often attacking his methodology and statistics as well as his optimistic findings. See, for example, Bartlett, "Why Do People Love to Hate"; Gray, "Steven Pinker Is Wrong"; and Kolbert, "Peace in Our Time."

10. See Article 1, A.2 in the full text—United Nations, Office of the High Commissioner for Refugees, *Commission and Protocol*.

11. Améry, *Mind's Limits*, 60.

the annexation of Austria became known, had made that country part of Adolf Hitler's intensely antisemitic Third Reich. While hundreds of thousands of enthusiastic Austrian supporters greeted his triumphal arrival in Vienna, Hitler soon found that he had to deal with a major demographic problem: one hundred ninety thousand Austrian Jews, a tally larger than the number of Jews who had left Germany in the previous five years.

National Socialist strategies sought to make life so uncomfortable for German Jews that they would get out, but those tactics were not entirely successful. The dimensions of the "Jewish problem" created by the Anschluss called for more effective measures. One of those put in charge was a young SS officer named Adolf Eichmann. He orchestrated a campaign of persecution, expropriation, and forced emigration that overwhelmed Austrian Jews more rapidly and thoroughly than anything that German Jews had hitherto experienced. In six months, Eichmann expelled nearly forty-five thousand Jews from Austria, about twice the number who left Germany in any year since 1933. By May 1939, some one hundred thousand Jews—more than 50 percent of Austria's Jewish population—had left. The Nazi leadership noticed Eichmann's success. Eventually he would be put in charge of deportations that took Jews from every quarter of Europe to the death camps that the Nazis established in Poland.

The Anschluss and Eichmann's system of forced emigration escalated an international refugee problem. Attempts to address that problem took place from July 6 to 15, 1938, when delegates from thirty-two nations, representatives of numerous relief agencies (many of them Jewish), and scores of reporters met at the luxurious Hotel Royal in the French resort of Evian-les-Bains on Lake Geneva, near the Swiss border. Nazi Germany did not attend but permitted representation from the German and Austrian Jewish communities. Initiated by US president Franklin D. Roosevelt, the Evian Conference might have helped the mounting number of Jewish refugees, but the meeting and its aftermath unmasked that illusion. For instance, speaking for Belgium on July 7, 1938, Robert de Foy, head of his country's state security service, offered a perspective widely embraced by other national delegations. Arguing that "immigration has reached the point of saturation," de Foy stated that "in view of the large number of refugees already established on her territory, Belgium, to her great regret, is nevertheless under the urgent necessity of reconsidering the problem of refugees before she accepts fresh international obligations."[12]

---

12. In the bibliography see Evian Committee, "Second Meeting (Public)," for the URL linking to the report from the Evian Committee for July 7, 1938.

De Foy's remarks underscored what he called Belgium's "tradition of generous hospitality" toward refugees. That comment had merit. In 1938, Belgium's population was about 8.3 million, including approximately seventy-five thousand Jews. Residing primarily in Brussels and Antwerp, where many were engaged in the diamond trade, a majority were not Belgian citizens. By the end of the 1930s, Belgian policies reflected De Foy's restrictive outlook, but earlier in that decade, Belgium was relatively generous to refugees. Between 1933 and 1940, an estimated thirty thousand Jewish refugees entered Belgium—approximately half before 1938 and the rest, including numerous Austrian Jews, after the March Anschluss.[13] Other Evian Conference delegates echoed De Foy in expressing sympathy for the Jewish refugees, but they also made excuses that meant the doors of their countries would not be opened much, if at all.

A Dead Man on Leave

One of the persons affected profoundly by European events in 1938 was an Austrian Jew born Hans Maier on October 31, 1912, the only child of a Jewish-Catholic mother and a Jewish father who died as an Austrian solider in 1917. Maier preferred Mayer as the spelling of his surname, which complicated life more than once when he had to document his identity. Whether Maier or Mayer, until his midtwenties he thought of himself as Austrian more than Jewish, not least because his father's family had lived in that land since the seventeenth century.[14] But Mayer—I follow his preference—lived in the twentieth century, and thus it was that in September 1935 he studied a newspaper in a Vienna coffeehouse. The Nuremberg Laws had just been promulgated in Nazi Germany. Mayer's reading led him to see that even if he did not much think of himself as Jewish, and no matter the spelling of his name, the Nazis' definitions meant that the cunning of history had nonetheless—and decisively—made him a Jew, at least as far as Nazi Germany was concerned.

---

13. Clandestine entry means that the figures can scarcely be precise, but see Bauer, *My Brother's Keeper*.

14. Mayer's boyhood included Catholic influences along with awareness that he was a Jew, but he received little training in Judaism or education about Jewish history, tradition, and culture. On these matters, see Améry, *Mind's Limits*, 83. See also Heidelberger-Leonard's biography of Améry, *Philosopher of Auschwitz*, esp. 4-6, 10-11. Quoting from an Améry manuscript dated January 1957 and called "Gasthof zur Stadt Graz," Heidelberger-Leonard supplies Améry's description of his mother as "half-Jewish, and on her marriage [she] had converted from the Catholic Church to become a member of the Jewish Community." See Heidelberger-Leonard, *Philosopher of Auschwitz*, 6, 261n2.

Mayer lacked the authority to define social reality in the mid-1930s. Increasingly, however, the Nazi state did possess such power. If that power engulfed him, its laws would make him Jewish even if his consciousness did not. As he confronted that reality, the fateful unavoidability of his being Jewish took on another dimension. By identifying him as a Jew, Maier later would write, Nazi power made him "a dead man on leave, someone to be murdered, who only by chance was not yet where he properly belonged."[15]

By the time Nazi Germany occupied Austria in March 1938, Mayer was a largely self-taught intellectual with deep interests in literature and philosophy and ambitions as a writer. He remained in Vienna long enough to witness Kristallnacht, the November pogrom whose savagery throughout the Third Reich made clear that no Jew could expect to live a normal life under the swastika. By the end of 1938, Mayer and his wife, Regine (Gina) Berger-Baumgarten, had become refugees, suddenly fleeing "without making any preparations, without money, armed only with invalid Austrian identity cards" and crossing the Belgian border clandestinely.[16]

After World War II began in September 1939 with Nazi Germany's invasion of Poland, most of the Jews in Belgium were foreign and stateless. The limited safety from Nazi terror that those refugees had obtained was interrupted all too soon. On May 10, 1940, Nazi Germany attacked the Netherlands and Belgium. Mayer, who had found work as a writer and teacher in Antwerp, was regarded as a German refugee and, in these circumstances, as an enemy alien. So, he was among the refugees deported from Belgium to internment camps in southern France. On the way to the camp at St. Cyprien, Mayer jumped from the train only to be arrested and eventually sent, on July 28, 1940, to the internment camp at Gurs, which came under the authority of the collaborationist Vichy France regime after the French capitulated to Nazi Germany's invasion in June 1940. Escaping about a year later, Mayer made his way back to occupied Belgium. Reunited with his wife, he also joined what he later described as "a small German-speaking organization within the Belgian resistance movement, [which] was spreading anti-Nazi propaganda among the members of the German occupation forces."[17]

For some time, Mayer had feared that his refugee status meant that "I was not a writer, not an intellectual, I had no name, no origin and . . . most certainly I had no future."[18] If Mayer's straits were not quite that dire

15. Améry, *Mind's Limits*, 86.
16. Heidelberger-Leonard, *Philosopher of Auschwitz*, 49.
17. Améry, *Mind's Limits*, 24.
18. Améry quoted in Heidelberger-Leonard, *Philosopher of Auschwitz*, 49.

as the summer of 1943 arrived, his prospects definitely took a turn for the worse on July 23 when the Gestapo caught him in Brussels carrying resistance flyers, one of which "bore the message, which was just as succinct as it was propagandistically ineffectual, 'Death to the SS bandits and Gestapo hangmen!'"[19] Subsequently tortured at Belgium's Fort Breendonk, Mayer was deported to Auschwitz when his German captors determined that he had no useful information and was Jewish besides. His transport left the Mechelen transit camp on January 15, 1944, reaching Auschwitz on January 17. According to the historian Danuta Czech, the transport included 657 Jews: "309 men and 37 boys and 286 women and 25 girls. After the selection, 140 men and 98 women are admitted to the camp as prisoners and receive Nos. 172296–172435 and 74512–74609. The remaining 419 people are killed in the gas chambers."[20] Mayer's transport was one of twenty-eight that departed Mechelen between August 4, 1942, and July 31, 1944. Those trains deported 25,484 Jews and 352 Roma (Gypsies) from Belgium and northern France, nearly all of them to Auschwitz. Less than thirteen hundred (about 5 percent) of the deportees survived.[21]

Tattooed with number 172364, which is inscribed on his gravestone in the Vienna Central Cemetery, Mayer was sent to the Auschwitz subcamp known variously as Buna, Monowitz, or Auschwitz III, the same place where Primo Levi and Elie Wiesel were sent some weeks later.[22] By the summer of 1944, the camp's sixty barracks housed more than eleven thousand prisoners in miserable conditions. At first assigned to a labor group, Améry got office work in June 1944 because, unlike many of his fellow prisoners, he could accurately read and write German. When Soviet troops neared the Auschwitz complex in January 1945, Mayer was among the prisoners who were force marched to Gleiwitz and then sent off to Dora-Mittelbau before liberation from Bergen-Belsen on April 15, 1945, ended his captivity in German prisons and camps. Mayer returned to Belgium hoping to find his wife, Gina, who was one of some fifteen thousand Jews who went into

19. Améry, *Mind's Limits*, 24.

20. Czech, *Auschwitz Chronicle*, 571. Czech indicates that this transport also included 351 Roma (Gypsies) who were "Belgian, French, Dutch, German, and Norwegian citizens."

21. These statistics are from Belgium's Kazerne Dossin: Memorial, Museum, and Documentation Center on the Holocaust and Human Rights. For the URL that links to the statistics, see the end of the bibliography.

22. A helpful source for further information about this camp is the website for the Wollheim Memorial. Another useful source is the website for the Auschwitz-Birkenau Memorial Museum, especially the webpage on the history of the Monowitz subcamp. The URLs that link to the websites for the Wollheim Memorial and for the Auschwitz-Birkenau Memorial Museum can be found at the end of the bibliography.

hiding there. His hunt for her unsuccessful, Mayer learned several years later that she had died of heart failure in late April 1944.

Once the war ended, Mayer was determined to take up writing again and to advance his ambitions as a novelist. Already in the late spring and early summer of 1945, he wrote about his torture and imprisonment, but these writings remained unpublished as he took the journalistic assignments and freelance commissions that provided much of his livelihood for some time. Looking back on the first two decades of his postwar life, Mayer noted the "somewhat melancholy fact" that he did not achieve major literary success until his early fifties but in no way had he idled away time for writing during those years. To the contrary, he underscored, "if I attempt to estimate the quantity of what I committed to paper during this period, then I arrive at the dismaying figure of some five thousand newspaper articles that together would amount to about 15,000 pages, an almost frighteningly voluminous production."[23] Mayer's characteristic self-deprecation obscured the brilliance of his journalism, but that work did deprive him of time to work on projects of his own choosing.

Mayer's journalism took him to major European cities—Cologne, London, Paris, Zurich—but Brussels became his permanent place of residence, although never fully his home. Despite gratitude to Belgium for receiving him as a refugee, Mayer felt that he was, at most, a visitor there.[24] Meanwhile, although 1955 was not the turning point that would follow about a decade later, that year included two significant changes for him. First, on April 2, Mayer married his longtime friend Maria Leitner, a gentile from Vienna, who had also been close with his wife Gina during the Mayers' early time in Belgium. Maria did much to support Mayer and to encourage his literary hopes. Dying in 2004, she outlived him by more than fifteen years. Biographer Irène Heidelberger-Leonard sums up their relationship: "He did not make things easy for her in the course of his turbulent life. He never set much store by fidelity, but knew how much he owed her, and loved her in his own fashion."[25] Second, Mayer decided to resolve long-standing ambivalence about his name. Correspondence with Maria Leitner indicates that as early as 1949 he had in mind the change he wanted to make, but not until 1955 did he consistently call himself Jean Améry. Hans Maier/Mayer—the dead man on leave—did not cease to exist, but the anagram-name became the one by which he is best known and remembered. How that name became

---

23. Améry, *Radical Humanism*, 1–2.
24. See Heidelberger-Leonard, *Philosopher of Auschwitz*, 98.
25. Heidelberger-Leonard, *Philosopher of Auschwitz*, 87.

important, however, entails not only what happened to Hans Mayer before 1955 but also what affected him decisively after that pivotal year.

In 1947, the Italian Jew Primo Levi published his Holocaust memoir *Se questo è un uomo* (translated into English as *If This Is a Man* in 1959 and subsequently as *Survival in Auschwitz: The Nazi Assault on Humanity*). A German translation, *Ist das ein Mensch?* appeared in 1961. This book and its author provoked Améry. As inmates in Auschwitz III, the two were barely acquainted.[26] But after Auschwitz, although they had scarcely any direct personal contact, these Holocaust survivors loomed large for each other—one could call them rivals. Améry regarded Levi as too conciliatory, even forgiving, toward the Germans, a criticism that Levi rejected and resented. Levi reflected most extensively on Améry in an essay called "The Intellectual in Auschwitz," the sixth chapter of Levi's book *The Drowned and the Saved*, which appeared in 1986, eight years after Améry's death. Levi began by saying that "to enter into an argument with the deceased is embarrassing and unfair, especially when the absent party is a potential friend and a privileged interlocutor; but it can also be forced upon you."[27] This odd tone continued as Levi expressed agreement and disagreement with Améry, whom Levi did not always describe accurately or, arguably, understand well enough.[28] As for Elie Wiesel, a fellow prisoner with Améry and Levi in Auschwitz III, he did not know Améry personally and had little to say about him, but he did know *At the Mind's Limits*, and it affected him.[29]

Meanwhile, in 1963, another Holocaust-related book further piqued Améry's anger. It was Hannah Arendt's *Eichmann in Jerusalem: A Report on the Banality of Evil*, her still controversial reflection on the 1961 Israeli trial of the Holocaust perpetrator Adolf Eichmann and the "banality of evil" that she thought he embodied. Améry felt that Arendt did not know deeply enough what she was trying to confront. "For there is no 'banality of evil,'" said Améry, who had experienced evil and seen the likes of Eichmann up close and personal. In Améry's view, "Hannah Arendt, who wrote about it

---

26. For accounts of their relationship, see Améry, *Mind's Limits*, 3, and Levi, "Intellectual in Auschwitz" in *Drowned and the Saved*, 2503–20, esp. 2505 and (1989), 127–48, esp. 130. An earlier brief essay by Levi, "Jean Améry, the Philosopher-Suicide," anticipates the chapter in *The Drowned and the Saved*. It appeared in the Italian newspaper *La Stampa* on December 7, 1978, a few weeks after Améry's death. In the essay, which is found in *Uncollected Stories*, 1262–64, Levi was scarcely charitable to Améry, calling him "a bad-tempered and solitary philosopher" whose essays in *At the Mind's Limits* are "bitter and chilling."

27. Levi (trans. Moore), *Drowned and the Saved*, 2503; see also Levi (trans. Rosenthal), *Drowned and the Saved*, 127.

28. On these points, see Heidelberger-Leonard, *Philosopher of Auschwitz*, 65–72.

29. Wiesel, *All Rivers*, 85–86 and Wiesel, *Sea Is Never Full*, 102–3.

[the banality of evil] in her Eichmann book, knew the enemy of mankind only from hearsay, saw him only through the glass cage. When an event places the most extreme demands on us, one ought not to speak of banality."[30]

Convinced that Levi and Arendt missed and misunderstood a great deal but received accolades nonetheless, Améry also witnessed the burgeoning popular interest aroused by the lengthy Auschwitz Trial that began, after several years of preparation, in the West German city of Frankfurt on December 20, 1963. The trial began with twenty-two defendants, all of them indicted as Auschwitz perpetrators. By the litigation's end on August 20, 1965, there had been 183 trial sessions, which included testimony by several hundred witnesses, more than two hundred Auschwitz survivors among them, and thousands of pages of documentation. Of the twenty defendants who remained in the dock when verdicts and sentences were handed down—earlier, two defendants had their cases suspended for health reasons—seven were found guilty of murder, ten were convicted as accessories to murder, and three were acquitted. The sentences ranged from life imprisonment to about three years, with the lighter penalties often reduced to time served.[31]

The trials of Eichmann and the Auschwitz perpetrators, the writings of Levi and Arendt—these events brought Auschwitz to the fore, but Améry grew increasingly convinced that the attention lacked the perspective that his insight could provide. For a few years, Améry had contributed to German radio broadcasts as a Brussels correspondent, and on January 18, 1964, as Heidelberger-Leonard explains, he advanced his perspective by writing to Karl Schwedhelm at South German Radio: "I am in the process of writing a reconstructed Auschwitz diary," he told him, "not a documentary account, of which there are many already, but reflections in diary form on fundamental existential problems of the world of the concentration camps, and more particularly the reactions of an *intellectual*."[32] Stating his belief that "no one has yet written on the camps in this particular manner," Améry suggested that his writing would make good radio content. One step led to another, and with the encouragement of Helmut Heissenbüttel, head of the Radio-Essay department of South German Radio, Améry himself broadcast—from Stuttgart on October 19, 1964—his reflection called "At the Mind's Limits: Essay on the Intellectual's Experience of Auschwitz."

30. Améry, *Mind's Limits*, 25.

31. For further information about the trial, see Pendas, *Frankfurt Auschwitz Trial*, esp. 1–2, and Wittmann, "Punishment," 524–39, esp. 536.

32. See Heidelberger-Leonard, *Philosopher of Auschwitz*, 139 (italics Améry's).

It took Améry almost twenty fraught years to reach this point, but when he did, the result was a series of five remarkable essays, each aired on German radio. In 1966, they were published as *Jenseits von Schuld and Sühne* (Beyond guilt and atonement; translated into English as *At the Mind's Limits: Contemplations by a Survivor on Auschwitz and Its Realities*). Subsequently, Améry published important reflections on aging and suicide—voluntary death, as he preferred to call it—as well as some novels, but *At the Mind's Limits* remains his greatest achievement.[33] Nothing written by Primo Levi, Elie Wiesel, or any other Holocaust survivor surpasses it.

At the Mind's Limits

In his preface to the first edition of *At the Mind's Limits*, Améry looked back on his work and noted how he began with the assumption that he "could remain circumspect and distant and face the reader with refined objectivity" only to see that what "demanded telling" but for two decades "had been difficult for me to talk about" required what Améry called "a personal confession refracted through meditation."[34] He further explained that the five essays were not "arranged according to the chronology of events, but in the order of their writing." He believed that the sequence revealed "contradictions in which I myself got caught up" and described "the state of someone who was overcome."[35] Thus, the first essay, "At the Mind's Limits," showed how Auschwitz undermined, contradicted, and eclipsed the assumption that human rationality, especially as embodied in the Enlightenment-inspired humanistic commitments of an intellectual like himself, could withstand, let alone fully comprehend and transcend, the degradation and devastation of humanity that took place there. Immensely useful in everyday as well as in academic experience, "rational-analytic thinking," said Améry, was "no help" in Auschwitz.[36] Nor did anything about that place make its intellectual inmates "wiser ... better, more human, more humane, and more mature

---

33. Only recently has one of Améry's novels been translated into English. See Améry, *Charles Bovary*. Originally published in 1978, just a few months before Améry took his own life, the novel, which at times reads like a philosophical essay, defends Charles Bovary, who in Gustave Flaubert's celebrated *Madame Bovary* is unjustly reduced, at least in Améry's view, to bungling mediocrity and incompetence and thus robbed of his own voice and his right to respect. Echoing Améry's other writings, this novel protests against power, in this case literary power, that denies humanity and life itself to those judged inferiors, a disposition that paved the way to Auschwitz.

34. Améry, *Mind's Limits*, xiii.

35. Améry, *Mind's Limits*, xiv.

36. Améry, *Mind's Limits*, 10.

ethically." Améry held that survivors, at least those like him (intellectual, philosophical, nonreligious), "emerged from the camp stripped, robbed, emptied out, disoriented—and it was a long time before we were able even to learn the ordinary language of freedom. Still today," he added, "we speak it with discomfort and without real trust in its validity."[37]

Pushed to the limits though he was, Améry did not give up on the mind's capability to probe the causes and conditions that ultimately stymied rational comprehension. So, Améry intended his reflections to be deeply personal and intensely subjective, but at the same time he used the particularity of his experience to give his readers as much lucidity and even enlightenment as he could muster about the abysmal realities, reverberations, and repercussions of Nazism, the Holocaust, and especially Auschwitz. Probably the best known of his book's five essays, the second, simply called "Torture," excels in that regard. It is grounded in the fact that before Auschwitz pushed Améry to the mind's limits, torture at Fort Breendonk had done the same in different but related ways. The mind cannot prepare one for torture; nor can the mind do justice to torture by thinking about it afterwards. Nevertheless, Améry concentrated to write about torture with unrivaled insight.

Describing what happened to him, Améry stated not only that "torture was the essence of National Socialism" but also that "torture is the most horrible event a human being can retain within himself."[38] Testifying that torture does not end when it ends because "whoever was tortured, stays tortured . . . and whoever has succumbed to torture can no longer feel at home in the world, " Améry sharpened the lucidity: "The expectation of help, the certainty of help," he wrote, "is indeed one of the fundamental experiences of human beings." But with the torturer's very first blow, the tortured person loses "trust in the world, . . . the certainty that by reason of written or unwritten social contracts the other person will spare me—more precisely stated, that he will respect my physical, and with it also my metaphysical, being."[39] Contradicting such assumptions, negating such expectations, a world in which "somewhere, someone is crying out under torture . . . perhaps in this hour, this second" drives the mind to its limits by blocking "the view into a world in which the principle of hope rules."[40]

Adolf Hitler and his Nazi regime intended the annihilation of Jewish life to signify the destruction of the very idea of a common humanity that all people share. Améry, who noted that the Nazis "hated the word 'humanity,'"

37. Améry, *Mind's Limits*, 19–20.
38. Améry, *Mind's Limits*, 22, 30.
39. Améry, *Mind's Limits*, 28, 34, 40.
40. Améry, *Mind's Limits*, 24, 40.

amplified such points when he stated, "Torture was no invention of National Socialism. But it was its apotheosis."[41] I think he meant that the Third Reich aimed to produce men, women, and children whose hardness would transcend humanity in favor of a racially pure and culturally superior form of life that could be called Aryan or German but not merely "human." Insofar as *humanity* referred to universal equality, suggested a shared and even divine source of life, or implied any of the other trappings of weakness and sentimentality that Hitler and his most dedicated followers ascribed to such concepts, National Socialism intentionally went beyond humanity. That arrogance entailed more than killing so-called inferior forms of life that were thought to threaten German superiority. Moving beyond humanity made it essential to inflict torture—not only to show that "humanity" or "subhumanity" deserved no respect in and of itself but also to ensure that those who had moved beyond humanity, and thus were recognizing the respect deserved only by Germans or Aryans, had really done so.

Before Améry's humanity was disrespected by torture and degraded in Auschwitz, he was a refugee. That experience also took him to the mind's limits because he had been at home in his native Austria only to experience the Nazi domination that wrecked his homeland, forced him to flee, and made it impossible for him ever to go home or to be at home again. Thus, the title of the third chapter of *At the Mind's Limits* raised a question, "How Much Home Does a Person Need?" Like other Jews in the vast number snared by Nazi Germany's genocidal antisemitism, like multitudes before and after the Holocaust, Améry underscored that he "went into exile because he *had* to."[42] Taking that decision entailed not only crossing "so many borders illegally that even now it still seems strange and wondrous to me when I pass a customs post in my car, well provided with all the necessary travel papers" but also suffering continually from "homesickness, a nasty, gnawing sickness, which does not have a folk song–like, homey quality."[43]

Améry called this nasty, gnawing homesickness "alienation from the self." No abstraction, that concept included his loss of a shared language, with its dialect and familiar way of pronouncing his "plain German name." The concept captured many other losses too. He had become "a person who could no longer say 'we.'" That also meant that "I was no longer an I," a condition that left him with "no passport, and no past, and no money, and

---

41. Améry, *Mind's Limits*, 30–31.
42. Améry, *Mind's Limits*, 42 (italics original).
43. Améry, *Mind's Limits*, 41, 43.

no history... I was completely uprooted... Genuine homesickness... was self-destruction."⁴⁴

Torture shattered trust in the world, which drove home to Améry that "trusting belongs in the broader psychological area of feeling secure," a realization showing that "reduced to the positive psychological basic content of the idea, home is *security*."⁴⁵ As Améry plumbed the depths of that insight, he discerned that identifying home with security meant that the mind would again meet its limits, faltering in attempts to answer the question, How much home does a person need? In a sense, argued Améry, that question is not genuine, partly because responses to it elude quantification and, more importantly, because the detailed particularity of the security that creates and sustains home encompasses and requires more than words can say: memories and feelings, familiar landscapes and places, a language and country of one's own, a history and culture with which one can identify, a social and political order that respects and thereby allows one to flourish and to be able to say both "I" and "we" in ways that curb the destructive conditions that produce the nasty, gnawing homesickness that so profoundly afflicted Améry. At the end of the chapter, what remained for Améry was "the most matter-of-fact observation"—a telling understatement—"it is not good to have no home."⁴⁶

In his preface to the 1977 reissue of *At the Mind's Limits*, Améry very simply and passionately said, "What happened, happened. But *that* it happened cannot be so easily accepted."⁴⁷ The surrounding context deserves quotation at length because the passage well amplifies what he meant by that restraint, which sets the stage especially for "Resentments," the fourth chapter of his book.

> I always proceed from the concrete event, but never become lost in it; rather I always take it as an occasion for reflections that extend beyond reasoning and the pleasure in logical argument to areas of thought that lie in an uncertain twilight and will remain therein, no matter how much I strive to attain the clarity necessary in order to lend them contour. However—and in this I must still persist—enlightenment is not the same as clarification. I had no clarity when I was writing this little book, I do not have it today, and I hope that I never will. Clarification also would amount to disposal, settlement of the case, which can

---

44. Améry, *Mind's Limits*, 43–45, 51.
45. Améry, *Mind's Limits*, 46–47 (italics original).
46. Améry, *Mind's Limits*, 61.
47. Améry, *Mind's Limits*, xi.

then be placed in the files of history. My book is meant to aid in preventing precisely this. For nothing is resolved, no conflict is settled, no remembering has become a mere memory . . . I rebel: against my past, against history, and against a present that places the incomprehensible in the cold storage of history and thus falsifies it in a revolting way. Nothing has healed.[48]

Exile, refugee status, torture, Auschwitz—in their particularity each and all took Améry to the mind's limits, which he then interrogated ever more deeply for himself and his readers. Life went on after Auschwitz. That did nothing, however, to restore what Améry had lost. To the contrary, "long personal and historical development" produced resentments not only about what had happened but also about the repression and denial regarding what had taken place. Especially in West Germany, he found a reprehensible lack of remorse about what had happened, which was made all the more obvious to Améry because it was accompanied by prosperous economic recovery, rapid acceptance of the Federal Republic into the community of nations, and even a sense that the Germans were victims of brutal wartime violence and dismemberment of the country that came with Nazism's defeat.

As Améry used the terms *resentments* or *resentment*, he was not encouraging revenge, let alone equating their meaning with it. Connoting deep-down ethical anger and indignation, even grudge-holding outrage, Améry used those words to emphasize that the atrocities of Nazi Germany constituted a "moral chasm" and to hold accountable—without forgiveness—all those responsible for that abyss. Repudiating "hollow, thoughtless, utterly false conciliatoriness," he thought it better to let the Holocaust's moral chasm "remain wide open."[49]

Améry seemed to retain some hope that his expressions of resentment might help to establish a post-Holocaust German "national community that would reject everything, but absolutely everything, that it accomplished in the days of its own deepest degradation." Germany has made progress in that direction, but when Améry published those words in 1966, he was only able "to imagine vaguely" a Germany of that kind.[50] Subsequently, his outlook may have been less hopeful than that. For example, what he and other Holocaust victims went through, he wrote on another occasion,

> must *not happen again, never, nowhere*. Therefore—and I have said and written this over and over—I refuse any reconciliation with the criminals, and with those who only by accident did not

48. Améry, *Mind's Limits*, xi.
49. Améry, *Mind's Limits*, ix.
50. Améry, *Mind's Limits*, 78.

happen to commit atrocities, and finally, all those who helped prepare the unspeakable acts with their words. Only if Nazi crimes like the genocide of European Jewry are not subject to a statute of limitations now or in the future, only if everyone who committed atrocities is hunted down and finally caught, will the potential murderers of tomorrow and the day after tomorrow be prevented from realizing their criminal potential.[51]

Améry harbored no illusions about moral progress, no delusions that remorse and repentance, let alone empathy and altruism, would prevail. His doubts ran deep, so much so, he believed, that the ultimate status of events could not be verified, a dilemma that reinforced the mind's limits. One could not dismiss out of hand the outlook that "atrocity as atrocity has no objective character. Mass murder, torture, injury of every kind are objectively nothing but chains of physical events, describable in the formalized language of the natural sciences. They are facts within a physical system, not deeds within a moral system."[52] Nevertheless, Améry defended "the moral truth of the blows that even today roar in my skull."[53] The blows were not only those inflicted by "the Flemish SS-man Wajs, who—inspired by his German masters—beat me on the head with a shovel handle whenever I didn't work fast enough."[54] They included every crime of National Socialism.

For Améry, the "roar in my skull" resounded in resentment. His defiance went beyond vehement rejection of forgetting and forgiving to an unrelenting protest against the perpetrators and bystanders who advance torture and genocide. Especially with his torturers in mind, Améry intended his resentment to make "the crime become a moral reality for the criminal, in order that he be swept into the truth of his atrocity."[55]

Despite the intensity of his resentment, which stands in stark contrast to Steven Pinker's scientific calm and confidence, Améry understood that his resentment would fail. No "nullification of what happened" was possible.[56] Far from being on Améry's side, time's passage favored a statute of limitations on atrocity. Even if it were remembered that atrocity has been rampant, even if pledges have been made about never forgetting, Améry held—and resented—that "natural time," as he called it, "will reject the moral demands of our resentment and finally extinguish them," because

51. See Améry's contribution to Wiesenthal, *Sunflower*, 105–9, esp. 108.
52. Améry, *Mind's Limits*, 70.
53. Améry, *Mind's Limits*, 70.
54. Améry, *Mind's Limits*, 70.
55. Améry, *Mind's Limits*, 70.
56. Améry, *Mind's Limits*, 68.

prevailing sensibilities ensure that "what will be tomorrow is more valuable than what was yesterday."⁵⁷

In addition, Améry saw no reason to think that his moral perspectives had any privileged position in the cosmic scheme of things. Injury of every kind, including the infliction of death itself, could be described as "nothing but chains of physical events." But even if one called that outlook into question, rightly introducing skepticism about why priority should be given to the natural sciences, Améry thought it "logically senseless" to assume that his experience or, for that matter, anything human could comprehend, let alone determine, what was ultimately real.⁵⁸ In those regards, finitude, fallibility, and failure pervade human life. Death testifies to that.

Nevertheless, in spite of and because of those insights, Améry's resentment intensified, refusing to make peace with events, with existence, so riddled with unmitigated atrocity and unredeemable death as to be nothing less than outrageous. Compounding the outrage, Améry believed, the meaningless oblivion of death—"the negating not," as he named it—awaits everything human.⁵⁹ Mourning that inevitability would change little. Nor would resentment matter much in the long run. Its defiant honesty, however, accompanied by protest and resistance, could make at least some temporary space for moral truth, forlorn though that struggle would be.

Resentment pushed Améry to the mind's limits. It did so because resentment revealed what should not have happened and what ought to be the case instead, but at the same time showed that what did happen meant that what ought to be the case instead was all too much impossible. Related contradictions permeated the final chapter of *At the Mind's Limits*, which Améry called "On the Necessity and Impossibility of Being a Jew."

In one way or another, everything Améry explored in the book's earlier chapters pivoted around a Jewish identity thrust upon him much more than it was rooted in his upbringing. "Everyone," he said, "must be who he was in the first years of his life, even if later these were buried under. No one can become what he cannot find in his memories."⁶⁰ In that sense, it was impossible for Améry to be the Jew that he never was—oriented religiously toward Judaism and engaged with Jewish tradition. And yet he found, again at the mind's limits, that the necessity of being a Jew was more powerful and compelling than the impossibility because Jewish identity was conferred upon him with such a lethal vengeance.

57. Améry, *Mind's Limits*, 76, 79.
58. Améry, *Mind's Limits*, 70.
59. Améry, *Suicide*, 77.
60. Améry, *Mind's Limits*, 84.

After Améry read the Nuremberg Laws in a Vienna coffeehouse in 1935, he was "no more Jewish than a half hour before," but insisting that he was not "inadmissibly projecting Auschwitz and the Final Solution back to 1935," he understood that Nazi power counted him as Jewish and made him "a quarry of Death . . . Our sole right, our sole duty was to disappear from the face of the earth."[61] Améry saw that these circumstances imposed impossibilities upon him. Under the swastika, he could not claim that he was a human being with dignity that deserved respect. On the contrary, he was a Jew, which necessitated his death. Améry's response was to make an imposed necessity *his*: confronting the Nazi judgment "with the decision to overcome it through revolt, . . . I took it upon myself to be a Jew."[62]

Améry sometimes referred to himself as a "Holocaust Jew," and he affirmed that "the Holocaust is truly the existential reference point for all Jews."[63] That insight has done much to deepen my commitment to learning and teaching about the Holocaust. Améry would wonder, and makes me wonder, about rhetoric like Pinker's that confidently trusts "the forces of modernity—reason, science, humanism, individual rights" or hopefully pledges and promises "Never Again."[64] He even would warn against putting too much stock in so-called lessons of the Holocaust.[65] "Every morning when I get up," he said, "I can read the Auschwitz number on my forearm . . . Every day anew I lose my trust in the world . . . Declarations of human rights, democratic constitutions, the free world and the free press, nothing," he went on to say, "can lull me into the slumber of security from which I awoke in 1935."[66]

Far from scorning the human dignity that those institutions emphasize, Améry yearned for the right to live, which he equated with dignity itself, and he defended the Enlightenment's commitment to progress, humanization, and reason, arguing that "*all* of the freedoms we enjoy and are obliged to pass on are [its] fruits."[67] But unlike Pinker, far from finding that tradition vindicated by progress, Améry invoked it as essential to keep disaster at bay, for his experience taught him that "it is certainly true that dignity can be bestowed only by society, whether it be the dignity of some office, a professional or, very generally speaking, civil dignity; and

---

61. Améry, *Mind's Limits*, 85–86.
62. Améry, *Mind's Limits*, 90.
63. Améry, *Mind's Limits*, 93, 99.
64. Pinker, *Better Angels*, 694.
65. For important reflections on this theme, see Marrus, *Lessons*.
66. Améry, *Mind's Limits*, 94–95.
67. Améry, *Radical Humanism*, 136 (italics original).

the merely individual, subjective claim ('I am a human being and as such I have my dignity, no matter what you may do or say!') is an empty academic game, or madness."[68] Lucidity, believed Améry, demanded the recognition of this reality, but lucidity did not end there. He thought it also entailed rebellion against power that would make anyone a "dead man on leave." Unfortunately, it must also be acknowledged that Améry's hopes for such protest were scarcely optimistic. On October 17, 1978, the impossibility and necessity of being a Jew—and much more—reached the mind's limits as he took leave, becoming a dead man by his own hand.

Beyond Homesickness?

Asserting that "reality is reasonable only so long as it is moral," Améry embodied an unrelieved revolt against reality insofar as it shows itself to be indifferent if not hostile to moral truth.[69] So, when he concluded his essay "How Much Home Does a Person Need?" by saying that "it is not good to have no home," his understatement implied an imperative: *Everyone ought to have a home*. Améry did not trust the language of human rights, but it can be instructive to cast the imperative that way: *Every person has the right to a home*. If his implied imperative were obeyed, if the inferred right to a home were honored, then, arguably, that outcome would relieve the "nasty, gnawing" homesickness that afflicts refugees because it would shrink if not eliminate refugee status. As Améry underscored, however, reality is not reasonable because it is scarcely moral.

How far human life falls short of that mark is evident when one notes that while there may be widespread agreement that it is not good to have no home and even considerable conviction that everyone ought to have a home, who seriously believes that every person has the right to a home, let alone that such a right, if it exists, is anywhere close to being honored? And yet, a case can be made that fundamental commitments about such vital matters remain. For example, the Universal Declaration of Human Rights

---

68. Améry, *Mind's Limits*, 89.

69. Améry, *Radical Humanism*, 65. See also Sebald, *Natural History*. In his chapter "Against the Irreversible: On Jean Améry," Sebald aptly says (155–56), "One of the most impressive aspects of Améry's stance as a writer is that although he knew the real limits of the power to resist as few others did, he maintains the validity of resistance even to the point of absurdity. Resistance without any confidence that it will be effective, resistance ... out of a principle of solidarity with victims and as a deliberate affront to those who simply let the stream of history sweep them along, is the essence of Améry's philosophy."

(1948) still stands and defends many of the elements that Améry regarded as essential for the home that every person needs. That declaration affirms:

> Everyone, as a member of society, has the right to social security and is entitled to realization, through national effort and international co-operation and in accordance with the organization and resources of each State, of the economic, social and cultural rights indispensable for his dignity and the free development of his personality. (Article 22)
>
> Everyone has the right to a standard of living adequate for the health and well-being of himself and of his family, including food, clothing, housing and medical care and necessary social services, and the right to security in the event of unemployment, sickness, disability, widowhood, old age or other lack of livelihood in circumstances beyond his control. (Article 25.1)[70]

If Améry knew those words, they would be among the declarations that never again lulled him into "the slumber of security from which I awoke in 1935." No doubt his resentment extended to the fact that such propositions about human rights were much too late and far too little.[71]

Améry insisted that his moral outrage was "no neurosis, but rather precisely reflected reality." He declared that "the neurosis is on the part of the historical occurrence." He, the refugee, "was not deranged"; rather those who create and sustain the conditions that plunge persons into the homesickness of the refugee are the "madmen." Too much power remains in their hands—so much so, Améry felt, that "my own mental lucidity is entirely irrelevant."[72]

No one who goes to the mind's limits with Jean Améry will fail to be profoundly affected by his sense that our world is never likely to move beyond the refugee's homesickness. But that recognition points to a further insight: whether Améry's mental lucidity is entirely irrelevant is neither for him alone to say nor the last word for those who travel with him. The rebellion and revolt embodied in his testimony, even in his voluntary death, still survive. They can reject the impossibility of resisting the powers that inflict refugee status and its homesickness and can embrace the necessity of defending every person's right to have a home.

---

70. See the full text of the Declaration: United Nations General Assembly, Resolution 217 A. The bibliography includes the URL that links to the Declaration and the Resolution.

71. For insightful reflection on related themes, see Moyn, *Not Enough*.

72. Améry, *Mind's Limits*, 96.

Sober, Somber, Modest

Perhaps with refugee status and its gnawing homesickness in mind, Améry, whose Holocaust experience robbed him of the possibility of feeling at home in the world, concluded *At the Mind's Limits* by saying,

> In the end, nothing else differentiates me from the people among whom I pass my days than a vague, sometimes more, sometimes less perceptible restiveness. But it is a *social* unrest, not a metaphysical one. It is not Being that oppresses me, or Nothingness, or God, or the Absence of God, only society ... It and only it robbed me of my trust in the world ... In my incessant effort to explore the basic condition of being a victim, in conflict with the necessity to be a Jew and the impossibility of being one, I believe to have recognized that the most extreme expectations and demands directed at us are of a physical and social nature. That such knowledge has made me unfit for profound and lofty speculation, I know. It is my hope that it has better equipped me to recognize reality.[73]

Améry's recognition of reality stands in stark contrast to Steven Pinker's and also to Donald Trump's, at least as indicated by his presidential comments during the United States Holocaust Memorial Museum's April 2017 Days of Remembrance. Grandiose to the point of banality, Trump's rhetoric at the Capitol Rotunda and elsewhere during that time favored the glib imperative to "stamp out prejudice and antisemitism everywhere it is found," facile pledges "to never be bystanders to evil," cheap encouragement to "celebrate humanity's victory over tyranny and evil," the nebulous admonition that "we must defeat terrorism," the hazy promise that "we will never, ever be silent in the face of evil again," and simplistic instruction that "every generation must learn and apply the lessons of the Holocaust."

Seemingly oblivious to the genocides and other mass-atrocity crimes that have scourged and pervaded the post-Holocaust world, as well as to the genocidal violence that climate change could unleash, to say nothing of threats of nuclear war that exceed any since the Cuban missile crisis of the early 1960s, Trump intoned to no purpose the most hackneyed cliché of all: "Never again. I say it, never again."[74] If that platitude did not strain credulity enough, he far too easily affirmed that "we know that in the end, good will

---

73. Améry, *Mind's Limits*, 100–101.

74. For a prescient analysis of the genocidal implications of climate change, see Alvarez, *Unstable Ground*.

triumph over evil, and that as long as we refuse to close our eyes or to silence our voices, we know that justice will ultimately prevail."[75]

As the life and work of Jean Améry much more credibly bear witness, *we know no such thing*. Trump's pretentious verbiage about Holocaust remembrance might fit with Pinker's account of the better angels of our nature, but it is about as far from Améry's insightful testimony as one can get. Typically, as though undercutting such trivializing in advance, Améry's words were not only passionate but also somber and modest. They had to contend with melancholy and despair as they voiced warning and urged resistance against powers and failures that likely will keep ensuring that prejudice and antisemitism will not go away, at least not completely; that humanity will fall short of victory over tyranny and evil; that injustice will threaten and perhaps even trump justice as long as human life continues—unless courage can be found to keep disaster at bay, which is anything but a foregone conclusion.[76]

On the night of October 16, 1978, Améry committed suicide in a Salzburg hotel. Two years earlier and ten years after *At the Mind's Limits* appeared, he had published *On Suicide*, a reflection on "voluntary death." Regarding the voluntary taking of one's own life as "a privilege of the human," he held that act to be a dignity-affirming and freedom-confirming assertion against "the irreversibility of total ruin" and absurdity.[77] Voluntary death, he contended, did not bring "peace." No entry to eternal "sleep," let alone a step toward God, its flight was "from the absurdity of existence into the absurdity of nothing."[78]

Améry called death "the future of all futures . . . the negative that carries nothing positive within it."[79] Ultimately, he thought, it negates every vestige of human existence and its moral truths. His painstaking struggle to fathom voluntary death was not, however, a recommendation to encourage

---

75. The Trump quotations come from three of his 2017 Days of Remembrance statements: Trump's speech to the delegates of the World Jewish Congress Plenary Assembly in New York on April 23, his April 24 proclamation of the Days of Remembrance of Victims of the Holocaust, and his April 25 remarks in the Capitol Rotunda at the United States Holocaust Memorial Museum National Days of Remembrance. Some of these texts have apparently been removed from the White House press office links, but others can still be found online. See Trump, "Remarks" (Capitol Rotunda speech); Trump, "'We Must Stamp Out Prejudice'" (World Jewish Congress speech); and Webb, "'Never Again'" (Days of Remembrance proclamation). Trump made similar promises and stated similar convictions when he spoke in Jerusalem at Yad Vashem, Israel's Holocaust memorial, on May 23, 2017. See Yad Vashem, "President."

76. For further exploration of these points, see Roth, *Failures of Ethics*.

77. Améry, *On Suicide*, 41, 43.

78. Améry, *On Suicide*, 46.

79. Améry, *On Aging*, 109, 110.

that choice, although he was determined to defend its integrity. While he saw no exit from absurdity, Améry pondered the "message" that, no matter how paradoxically and indeed impossibly, voluntary death seeks to transmit. What Améry meant by the message is not confined to or even expressed by so-called suicide notes, including the ones he wrote before dying. I think he had in mind the idea that voluntary death, at least for the one who chooses it, *stops* the world's lack of dignity, humanity, and freedom, even though the death does not change the world much, if at all.[80] Thus, the message of voluntary death is that the world *should* stop—at least in the sense that moral truth requires, which includes assertion that torture and genocide must be no more.

Wanting It Darker

Améry wanted it darker—not as an end in itself but as a way of resisting the darkness. Thus, he remains one of my most influential sources of Holocaust insight. He makes me think twice about experiences and convictions that I hold dear. Explored earlier in this book, one of them is that what I call an *in-spite-of* joy comes from a deep-down sense of purpose embodied in helping, caring, befriending, and loving that do not ignore or forget atrocity, that do not depend upon, let alone assume, progress but steadfastly respond to atrocity in resisting and healing ways.

Recognizing and yet defying the worst that human beings have done and may still do, an *in-spite-of* joy enlarges and nourishes—it even defines—the aim and meaning of resistance, protest, and healing. Refusing to be driven to despair, such joy rebels against disaster, even if not victoriously. Kindled and sustained by friendship, by the help that we give as well as receive, by doing what is right and good, by love, such joy emerges from and sustains solidarity with those who oppose and limit harm, relieve suffering, and save lives. Declining to give in or give up, an *in-spite-of* joy can keep people going even though the work of defending human rights has no end and may even be a lost cause.

Améry wanted it darker—not to aid indifference and abet atrocity but to enlighten those who learn and teach about the Holocaust how much responsibility is theirs. Thus, he cautions me: Do not put more weight on an *in-spite-of* joy than it can bear. Primo Levi thought that Améry's "severe and intransigent positions" made him "unable to find joy in life, in living."[81] Was

80. Améry, *On Suicide*, 106–11, 152.

81. Levi (trans. Moore), *Drowned and the Saved*, 2510; see also Levi (trans. Rosenthal), *Drowned and the Saved*, 136.

Levi right? Who can say with confidence, one way or the other? To the best of my knowledge, Améry told no myth of Sisyphus, nor did he comment on Camus's interpretation of that story and its emphasis on joy. But of this much I am confident. Defiance, more than severity, characterized Améry. Resistance, more than intransigence, was his hallmark. Even when the cause was forlorn, he defended art and inquiry, justice and truth, especially at the mind's limits. Even when little, if anything, in his experience made him think that the world would ever conform to his demands, Améry insisted that "reality is reasonable only so long as it is moral."[82] His work and even his decision to end his life aimed in that direction.

These commitments affirm that, in his complex and distinctive ways, Jean Améry, like Levi's friend, Lorenzo, was in the world to do good. Perhaps there was no *in-spite-of* joy for him in any of that living, a possibility that warns against making more of such joy than it deserves. So, let that warning stand. Its caution does not deny that an *in-spite-of* joy is real and important. Its caveat does not cancel the possibility that, from time to time, a version of that experience might have been Améry's. The warning—steeped in his wanting it darker—does mean that all experiences of an *in-spite-of* joy need to include awareness that such joy is always hard-won, never enough, and ever likely to confront the mind's limits, if not to succumb to them.

---

82. Améry, *Radical Humanism*, 65.

Epilogue

Take Nothing Good for Granted

A symposium on "The Ethical and Moral Foundations of Holocaust Studies," which I planned with Victoria Barnett, Wendy Lower, and Carol Rittner, convened on May 8, 2018, at the United States Holocaust Memorial Museum as part of its twenty-fifth anniversary celebration. The day before those discussions, which brought leading Holocaust scholars and educators together, I toured the David and Fela Shapell Family Collections, Conservation and Research Center, a forty-million-dollar storage and research facility—more than one hundred thousand square feet in size—that opened in 2017. The center's specialized laboratories, equipment, and climate-controlled environments house the museum's artifacts, large and small, including more than 100 million pages of documents, 110,000 photographs and images, 1,000 hours of film footage, and more than 16,000 oral testimonies of survivors, witnesses, and perpetrators. Travis Roxlau, the center's director, indicated that the museum's collection is likely to double during the next ten to fifteen years as aging Holocaust survivors die. Plans for the future allow for an additional twenty thousand square feet of storage space.

One stop on my tour of the center took me to what seemed like a medical operating room. There, a highly trained technician was doing "surgery" on a toy animal, one of the countless, much-loved possessions of the hundreds of thousands of Jewish children engulfed in the Holocaust. The repairs were not intended to make that teddy bear as good as new but to save it from further decay. Roxlau and the technician muted sentimentality about the once-cuddled companion. Like the other objects in the center's holdings, said Roxlau, the teddy bear must be preserved because it is evidence of a crime, an understated but accurate way to identify the Holocaust, for if the Holocaust was not a crime, there could be no such thing.

An artifact preservation project more impressive than the Shapell Center's can scarcely be imagined. But "inconvenient truths," as Primo Levi said, "have a difficult road," and Roxlau stressed one of them: preservation cannot be for eternity, just for as long as possible.[1] No matter how careful the preservation, the Center's holdings will eventually decay. No matter how hard we try to salvage the material evidence of the Holocaust, Roxlau was saying, it will turn to dust and be no more.

What about Holocaust insight and its sources? Are they doomed to that fate too? As far as *Sources of Holocaust Insight* is concerned, this book will not be an exception to the rule. Only time will tell whether Holocaust insight and its ingredients—facts and theories, questions and inquiries, testimonies and narratives, interpretations and imperatives—have better chances of surviving the unrelenting tests of time. Forlorn though that hope may be, let a metaphorical time capsule contain key elements of the Holocaust insight that writing this book imparts to me.

- The Holocaust targeted a particular people, the Jews, for utter destruction. Reliable insight can emerge from that catastrophe only by carefully studying how and why it happened.
- Much is known about how the Holocaust happened and why. Therefore, build learning and teaching about the Holocaust on this foundation.
- Much remains unknown and arguably unknowable about the Holocaust, its vastness and reverberations. Therefore, inquire and teach diligently, persistently, and with the respectful modesty that the task requires.
- No event has more power than the Holocaust to raise the right questions, the ones that we need to pursue to help make life worth living. Therefore, learning and teaching about the Holocaust remain imperative.
- The Holocaust was wrong—or nothing could be. Affirm that fact, defend that truth. Lives hang in the balance.
- The Holocaust signifies immense failure—ethical, religious, political. Therefore, refuse to let that fact be the last judgment.
- The Holocaust and its reverberations reveal "the fatal interdependence of all human actions."[2] Individuals remain responsible for their action and its consequences, but persons are and must be responsible for each other too.

1. Levi (trans. Moore), *Drowned and Saved*, 2529; see also Levi (trans. Rosenthal), *Drowned and the Saved*, 159.
2. The quoted phrase is Gitta Sereny's. See Sereny, *Into That Darkness*, 15.

- The Holocaust shattered trust in the world. Therefore, insist that we must be in the world to do good.
- The Holocaust did not have to happen. Therefore, resist the forces that made it happen, among them what Bonhoeffer called "the huge masquerade of evil" that throws "all ethical concepts into confusion" by making evil (including genocide) "appear in the form of light, good deeds, historical necessity, social justice."[3] Remember too that there were people who risked everything to help others. Do not allow indifference to forget or abandon them; instead, try to follow their example.
- The Holocaust fractured and fragmented what we hold dear when we are at our best. Therefore, salvage the fragments and mend the fractures.
- The Holocaust is a warning. Therefore, do not overestimate the degree to which the Holocaust gave antisemitism and racism a bad name.
- The Holocaust can be a much-needed compass. Let the Holocaust-as-compass orient attention, guide priorities, and direct discernment about what's right and wrong.
- Seeing differently, seeing better—sound learning and teaching about the Holocaust aim for what may be the most important Holocaust insight of all: Take nothing good for granted.

For many years, another source of Holocaust insight, my friend Jim Quay, who loves and writes poetry, directed the California Council for the Humanities (now Cal Humanities), one of the fifty-six humanities councils located in all US states and jurisdictions. With support from the National Endowment for the Humanities, these vital organizations expand understanding of the histories, contexts, and cultures in which Americans live, work, and serve. Learning and teaching about the Holocaust primarily in academic settings, I became engaged in the work of the state councils in California and Washington and nationally through the Federation of State Humanities Councils because I applauded the public outreach that makes the humanities fields—history, literature, philosophy and its emphasis on ethics—more fertile by cultivating them beyond college and university campuses.

One day in February 1995, almost twenty-five years before I crafted this epilogue at the end of February 2019, I received "For John Roth," the calligraphed poem that Quay had written for me. I keep it near my writing desk. Day by day, I recognize its challenging insight.

---

3. Bonhoeffer, "After Ten Years," 18.

> The scholar bends on his hands and knees over the deep hole of history.
> His light spills into the darkness, as he looks for reflections
> Far beneath the surface.
> It's work he does at night, better to see the faint glint,
> And without gloves, better to grasp the stories waiting to be
> Plucked from oblivion.
> This work can only be done by a hopeful man willing to be sad.
> Sometimes he cuts his finger on a fragment, sometimes his vision blurs,
> Or he loses his balance, falls, and sits all night,
> Rocking in the darkness, until voices of the living lead him home.
> When, during the day, he discusses dreams with his students,
> The ashes on his pants and the scars on his hands make them listen,
> Make them believe.
> Their faith in dreams is the gift of a hopeful man willing to be sad.

In *Souls on Fire*, Elie Wiesel devoted a few pages to the Hasidic master Rebbe Zusia. According to tradition, Zusia, his death approaching, said: "When I shall face the celestial tribunal, I shall not be asked why I was not Abraham, Jacob, or Moses. I shall be asked why I was not Zusia."[4] That story has been on my mind during the writing of this book. My aspiration has not been to mimic, much less to embody, my sources but to let them help me get Holocaust insight of my own. My task is to be that odd person, an American Christian philosopher who has spent a lifetime learning and teaching about the Holocaust, seeking and finding Holocaust insight, always with the indispensable help of others but with the responsibility to make that insight mine. So, this book could have been composed or structured in a different way. That or this source of Holocaust insight. Texts and tales different from those found here. But these insights and their sources, as I discern and understand them, mean much to me. If they work that way for any reader of these thoughts—including Jim Quay's poem, which sums up the aims of my learning and teaching about the genocide—then my quest to get Holocaust insight will have been amply rewarded.

---

4. Wiesel, *Souls on Fire*, 120.

Bibliography

Aderet, Ofer. "Newly Unearthed Version of Elie Wiesel's Seminal Work Is a Scathing Indictment of God, Jewish World." *Haaretz* (May 1, 2016). https://www.haaretz.com/jewish/.premium-harsher-version-of-night-found-in-elie-wiesel-archive-1.5377614.

———. "Why the Opening Chapter of Elie Wiesel's 'Night' Was Scrapped." *Haaretz* (November 29, 2016). https://www.haaretz.com/israel-news/culture/premium-why-the-opening-chapter-of-elie-wiesel-s-night-was-scrapped-1.5466813.

Adorno, Theodor. *Negative Dialectics*. Translated by E. B. Ashton. New York: Seabury, 1973.

Agamben, Giorgio. *Remnants of Auschwitz: The Witness and the Archive*. Translated by Daniel Heller-Roazen. New York: Zone, 1999.

Alvarez, Alex. *Unstable Ground: Climate Change, Conflict, and Genocide*. Studies in Genocide: Religion, History, and Human Rights. Lanham, MD: Rowman & Littlefield, 2017.

Améry, Jean. *At the Mind's Limits: Contemplations by a Survivor on Auschwitz and Its Realities*. Translated by Sidney Rosenfeld and Stella P. Rosenfeld. Bloomington: Indiana University Press, 1980.

———. *Charles Bovary, Country Doctor: Portrait of a Simple Man*. Translated by Adrian Nathan West. New York Review of Books Classics. New York: New York Review, 2018.

———. *On Aging: Revolt and Resignation*. Translated by John D. Barlow. Bloomington: Indiana University Press, 1994.

———. *On Suicide: A Discourse on Voluntary Death*. Translated by John D. Barlow. Bloomington: Indiana University Press, 1999.

———. *Radical Humanism: Selected Essays*. Translated and edited by Sidney Rosenfeld and Stella P. Rosenfeld. Bloomington: Indiana University Press, 1984.

Anderson, Ingrid L. "Absurd Dignity: The Rebel and His Cause in Améry and Camus." *Journal of French and Francophone Philosophy* 24 (2016) 74–94.

———. *Ethics and Suffering since the Holocaust: Making Ethics "First Philosophy" in Levinas, Wiesel and Rubenstein*. New York: Routledge, 2016.

Angier, Carole. *The Double Bond: Primo Levi, a Biography*. New York: Farrar, Straus & Giroux, 2002.

Antelme, Robert. *The Human Race*. Translated by Jeffrey Haight and Annie Mahler. Evanston, IL: Malboro Press/Northwestern University Press, 1998.

Bak, Samuel. "Facing My Own History and My Story with *Facing History and Ourselves*." In *Illuminations: The Art of Samuel Bak*, 2–4. Brookline, MA: Facing History and Ourselves, 2010.

Bartlett, Tom. "Why Do People Love to Hate Steven Pinker?" *Chronicle of Higher Education* (March 8, 2019). https://www.chronicle.com/interactives/hating-pinker.

Bauer, Yehuda. *My Brother's Keeper: A History of the American Joint Distribution Committee, 1929–1939*. Philadelphia: Jewish Publication Society of America, 1974.

———. *Rethinking the Holocaust*. New Haven: Yale University Press, 2001.

Bauman, Zygmunt. *Modernity and the Holocaust*. Ithaca: Cornell University Press, 1989; 1991.

Benz, Wolfgang. *The Holocaust: A German Historian Examines the Genocide*. Translated by Jane Sydenham-Kwiet. New York: Columbia University Press, 1999.

Berenbaum, Michael. "Who Owns the Holocaust?" *Moment* 25 (2000) 60–72.

———. *The World Must Know: The History of the Holocaust as Told in the United States Holocaust Memorial Museum*. 2nd ed. Washington, DC: United States Holocaust Memorial Museum, 2006.

Berger, Alan L., ed. *Elie Wiesel: Teacher, Mentor, and Friend*. Eugene, OR: Cascade Books, 2018.

Bialas, Wolfgang, and Lothar Fritze, eds. *Nazi Ideology and Ethics*. Newcastle, UK: Cambridge Scholars, 2014.

Blanchot, Maurice. *The Infinite Conversation*. Translation and foreword by Susan Hanson. Theory and History of Literature 82. Minneapolis: University of Minnesota Press, 1993.

———. *The Step Not Beyond*. Translated with an introduction by Lycette Nelson. Intersections: Philosophy and Critical Theory. Albany: SUNY Press, 1992.

———. *Vicious Circles: Two Fictions & "After the Fact."* Translated by Paul Auster. Barrytown, NY: Station Hill, 1985.

———. *The Writing of the Disaster*. Translated by Ann Smock. Lincoln: University of Nebraska Press, 1986.

Blau, Reuven. "Family and Friends Bid Farewell to Elie Wiesel . . ." *New York Daily News* (July 3, 2016). http://www.nydailynews.com/news/world/exclusive-family-friends-mourn-loss-elie-wiesel-funeral-article-1.2697799.

Bloom, Harold, ed. *Elie Wiesel's "Night."* New ed. New York: Infobase, 2010.

Bonhoeffer, Dietrich. "After Ten Years: An Account at the Turn of the Year 1942–1943." In *"After Ten Years": Dietrich Bonhoeffer and Our Times*, edited by Victoria J. Barnett and translated by Barbara and Martin Rumscheidt, 17–31. Minneapolis: Fortress, 2017.

———. *Letters and Papers from Prison*. Enlarged ed. Edited by Eberhard Bethge. New York: Macmillan, 1972.

Borowski, Tadeusz. *This Way for the Gas, Ladies and Gentlemen*. Translated by Barbara Vedder. New York: Penguin, 1967.

Browning, Christopher R. *Collected Memories: Holocaust History and Postwar Testimony*. George L. Mosse Series in Modern European Cultural and Intellectual History. Madison: University of Wisconsin Press, 2003.

———. *Nazi Policy, Jewish Workers, German Killers*. Cambridge: Cambridge University Press, 2000.

———. *Ordinary Men: Reserve Police Battalion 101 and the Final Solution in Poland*. With a new afterword. Rev. ed. New York: Harper Perennial, 2017.

Browning, Christopher R., Peter Hayes, and Raul Hilberg. *German Railroads, Jewish Souls: The Reichsbahn, Bureaucracy, and the Final Solution*. New York: Berghahn, 2020.
Bump, Philip. "Eighteen Years of Gun Violence in U.S. Schools, Mapped." *Washington Post* (February 14, 2018). https://www.washingtonpost.com/news/politics/wp/2018/02/14/eighteen-years-of-gun-violence-in-u-s-schools-mapped/?utm_term=.3781f107c3e7.
Burger, Ariel. *Witness: Lessons from Elie Wiesel's Classroom*. New York: Houghton Mifflin Harcourt, 2018.
Camon, Ferdinando. *Conversations with Primo Levi*. Translated by John Shepley. Marlboro, VT: Marlboro, 1989.
Camus, Albert. *The Myth of Sisyphus, and Other Essays*. Translated by Justin O'Brien. New York: Vintage, 1955.
———. *The Plague*. Translated by Gilbert Stuart. Vintage International. New York: Vintage, 1991.
———. *The Rebel: An Essay on Man in Revolt*. With a foreword by (Sir) Herbert Read. Translated by Anthony Bower. New York: Vintage, 1956.
———. *Resistance, Rebellion, and Death*. Translated by Justin O'Brien. New York: Modern Library, 1963.
Cargas, Harry James. "Elie Wiesel: Christian Responses." In *Responses to Elie Wiesel: Critical Essays by Major Jewish and Christian Scholars*, edited by Harry James Cargas, 281–91. New York: Persea, 1978.
———. *Shadows of Auschwitz: A Christian Response to the Holocaust*. Rev. ed. New York: Crossroad, 1990.
Czech, Danuta. *Auschwitz Chronicle 1939–1945*. Translated by Barbara Harshav et al. New York: Holt, 1990.
Delbo, Charlotte. *Auschwitz and After*. Translated by Rosette C. Lamont. New Haven: Yale University Press, 1995.
———. *Days and Memory*. Translated by Rosette C. Lamont. Marlboro, VT: Marlboro, 1990.
Des Pres, Terrence. *The Survivor: An Anatomy of Life in the Death Camps*. Oxford: Oxford University Press, 1976.
Dickinson, John K. *German & Jew: The Life and Death of Sigmund Stein*. Chicago: Dee, 2001.
Evian Committee. "Second Meeting (Public). Held on Thursday, July 7th, 1938, at 3.30 p.m." On *History Central* (website). https://www.historycentral.com/20th/Part2.html.
Fackenheim, Emil L. *God's Presence in History: Jewish Affirmations and Philosophical Reflections*. Northvale, NJ: Aronson, 1997.
———. *The Jewish Return into History: Reflections in the Age of Auschwitz and a New Jerusalem*. New York: Schocken, 1978.
———. "Jewish Values in the Post-Holocaust Future." *Judaism* 16 (1967) 269–73, 289–90, 295–96.
———. *To Mend the World: Foundations of Future Jewish Thought*. New York: Schocken, 1982.
Feltham, Colin. *Failure*. New York: Routledge, 2014.
Filkins, Peter. *H. G. Adler: A Life in Many Worlds*. New York: Oxford University Press, 2019.

Frank, Anne. *The Diary of a Young Girl*. Translated by B. M. Mooyaart-Doubleday. New York: Bantam, 1993.
Freeman, Joseph. *Job: The Story of a Holocaust Survivor*. Westport, CT: Praeger, 1996.
———. *Kingdom of Night: The Saga of a Woman's Struggle for Survival*. Lanham, MD: University Press of America, 2006.
———. *The Road to Hell: Recollections of the Nazi Death March*. St. Paul: Paragon, 1998.
Friedländer, Saul. *Nazi Germany and the Jews*. Vol. 1, *The Years of Persecution, 1933–1939*. New York: HarperCollins, 1997.
———. *Nazi Germany and the Jews*. Vol. 2, *The Years of Extermination: Nazi Germany and the Jews, 1939–1945*. New York: HarperCollins, 2007.
———. "Prologue." In *Memory, History, and Responsibility: Reassessments of the Holocaust, Implications for the Future*, edited by Jonathan Petropoulos, Lynn Rapaport, and John K. Roth, 3–15. Lessons and Legacies 9. Evanston, IL: Northwestern University Press, 2010.
———. *When Memory Comes*. Translated by Helen R. Lane. New York: Farrar, Straus, Giroux, 1979.
———. *Where Memory Leads*. Translated by Helen R. Lane. New York: Other Press, 2016.
Fung, Brian. "Bill Gates Told New Grads to Read This Book. Now It's Surging on Amazon." *Washington Post* (May 15, 2017). https://www.washingtonpost.com/news/the-switch/wp/2017/05/15/bill-gates-told-new-grads-to-read-this-book-now-its-surging-on-amazon/?utm_term=.6f2a40af38d9.
Gates, Bill. "My New Favorite Book of All Time." *GatesNotes: The Blog of Bill Gates* (January 26, 2018). https://www.gatesnotes.com/Books/Enlightenment-Now.
Giuliani, Massimo. *A Centaur in Auschwitz: Reflections on Primo Levi's Thinking*. Lanham, MD: Lexington, 2002.
Glover, Jonathan. *Humanity: A Moral History of the Twentieth Century*. New Haven: Yale University Press, 2000.
Goldensohn, Leon. *The Nuremberg Interviews: An American Psychiatrist's Conversations with Defendants and Witnesses*. Edited and introduced by Robert Gellately. New York: Knopf, 2004.
Gray, John. "Steven Pinker Is Wrong about Violence and War." *Guardian* (March 13, 2015). https://www.theguardian.com/books/2015/mar/13/john-gray-steven-pinker-wrong-violence-war-declining.
Greenberg, Irving. "Cloud of Smoke, Pillar of Fire: Judaism, Christianity, and Modernity after the Holocaust." In *Auschwitz: Beginning of a New Era?*, edited by Eva Fleischner, 7–55. New York: Ktav, 1977.
Greenspan, Henry. "The Humanities of Contingency: Interviewing and Teaching beyond 'Testimony' with Holocaust Survivors." *Oral History Review* 46 (2019) 360–79.
———. *On Listening to Holocaust Survivors: Beyond Testimony*. 2nd ed. St. Paul: Paragon, 2010.
———. "Remnants" (webpage). *Henry (Hank) Greenspan, Ph.D.* (website). http://www.henrygreenspan.com/work2.htm.
———. "Survivors' Accounts." In *The Oxford Handbook of Holocaust Studies*, edited by Peter Hayes and John K. Roth, 414–27. Oxford: Oxford University Press, 2010.
———. "The Unsaid, the Incommunicable, the Unbearable, and the Irretrievable." *Oral History Review* 41 (2014) 229–43.

Greif, Gideon. *We Wept without Tears: Testimonies of the Jewish Sonderkommando from Auschwitz*. New Haven: Yale University Press, 2005.

Grob, Leonard, and John K. Roth, eds. *Encountering the Stranger: A Jewish-Christian-Muslim Trialogue*. The Stephen S. Weinstein Series in Post-Holocaust Studies. Seattle: University of Washington Press, 2012.

———, eds. *Losing Trust in the World: Holocaust Scholars Confront Torture*. The Stephen S. Weinstein Series in Post-Holocaust Studies. Seattle: University of Washington Press, 2017.

Grossman, David. "On Hope and Despair in the Middle East." *Haaretz* (July 8, 2014). http://www.haaretz.com/news/diplomacy-defense/2.1434/1.601993.

Gutman, Israel, and Robert Rozett. "Estimated Jewish Losses in the Holocaust." In *Encyclopedia of the Holocaust*, edited by Israel Gutman, 1797–802. 4 vols. New York: Macmillan, 1990.

Haas, Peter J. *Morality after Auschwitz: The Radical Challenge of the Nazi Ethic*. 1988. Reprint, Eugene, OR: Wipf & Stock, 2014.

Halbreich, Siegfried. *Before–During–After: Surviving the Holocaust*. New York: Vantage, 1991.

Hallie, Philip P. "Camus's Hug." *American Scholar* 64 (1995) 428–35.

———. "Cruelty: The Empirical Evil." In *Facing Evil: Light at the Core of Darkness*, edited by Paul Woodruff and Harry A. Wilmer, 119–37. LaSalle, IL: Open Court, 1994.

———. *In the Eye of the Hurricane: Tales of Good and Evil, Help and Harm*. Middletown, CT: Wesleyan University Press, 2001.

———. *Lest Innocent Blood Be Shed: The Story of the Village of Le Chambon and How Goodness Happened There*. New York: HarperPerennial, 1994.

Hayes, Peter. "Ethics and Corporate History in Nazi Germany." In *Memory, History, and Responsibility: Reassessments of the Holocaust, Implications for the Future*, edited by Jonathan Petropoulos, Lynn Rapaport, and John K. Roth, 300–303. Lessons & Legacies 9. Evanston, IL: Northwestern University Press, 2010.

———, ed. *How Was It Possible? A Holocaust Reader*. Lincoln: University of Nebraska Press, 2015.

———. *Why? Explaining the Holocaust*. New York: Norton, 2017.

Haynes, Stephen R., and John K. Roth, eds. *The Death of God Movement and the Holocaust: Radical Theology Encounters the Shoah*. Contributions to the Study of Religion 55. Christianity and the Holocaust—Core Issues. Westport, CT: Greenwood, 1999.

Hegel, Georg Wilhelm Friedrich. *Philosophy of History*. Translated by Leo Rauch. Indianapolis: Hackett, 1988.

———. *Philosophy of Right*. Translated by T. M. Knox. London: Oxford University Press, 1967.

Heidelberger-Leonard, Irène. *The Philosopher of Auschwitz: Jean Améry and Living with the Holocaust*. Translated by Anthea Bell. London: Taurus, 2010.

Henry, Patrick. *We Only Know Men: The Rescue of Jews in France during the Holocaust*. Washington, DC: Catholic University of America Press, 2007.

Hilberg, Raul. *The Destruction of the European Jews*. 3 vols. 3rd ed. New Haven: Yale University Press, 2003.

———, ed. *Documents of Destruction: Germany and Jewry 1933–1945*. Chicago: Quadrangle, 1971.

———. "German Railroads/Jewish Souls." *Society* 14 (1976) 60–74.
———. "The Holocaust." In *Facing Evil: Light at the Core of Darkness*, edited by Paul Woodruff and Harry A. Wilmer, 99–117. LaSalle, IL: Open Court, 1994.
———. "Incompleteness in Holocaust Historiography." In *Gray Zones: Ambiguity and Compromise in the Holocaust and Its Aftermath*, edited by Jonathan Petropoulos and John K. Roth, 81–92. Studies on War and Genocide 6. New York: Berghahn, 2005.
———. Lecture delivered at Ethics and the Holocaust, a conference at the University of Oregon, Eugene, OR, May 6–8, 1996. https://www.youtube.com/watch?v=fgogLvAfBfU.
———. *Perpetrators, Victims, Bystanders: The Jewish Catastrophe, 1933–1945*. New York: HarperCollins, 1992.
———. *The Politics of Memory: The Journey of a Holocaust Historian*. Chicago: Dee, 1996.
———. *Sources of Holocaust Research: An Analysis*. Chicago: Dee, 2001.
Hunter, Paul. "Hunter Discusses Reshaping 'Shopworn' Language." Interview with Paul Hunter. By Gwen Ifill. *PBS News Hour*, July 9, 2007. https://www.pbs.org/newshour/show/hunter-discusses-reshaping-shopworn-language#transcript.
———. *Ripening: Poems*. Eugene, OR: Silverfish Review Press, 2007.
James, William. "The Teaching of Philosophy in Our Colleges." *Nation* 23 (1876) 178.
Katz, Steven T., and Alan Rosen, eds. *Elie Wiesel: Jewish, Literary, and Moral Perspectives*. Jewish Literature and Culture. Bloomington: Indiana University Press, 2013.
King, Martin Luther, Jr. "Where Do We Go From Here?" Address delivered at the eleventh annual SCLC convention, Atlanta, August 16, 1967. Published by the Martin Luther King, Jr. Research and Education Institute at Stanford University. *The Martin Luther King, Jr. Research and Education Institute* (website). https://kinginstitute.stanford.edu/king-papers/documents/where-do-we-go-here-address-delivered-eleventh-annual-sclc-convention.
Klemperer, Victor. *The Language of the Third Reich: LTI—Lingua Tertii Imperii; A Philologist's Notebook*. Translated by Martin Brady. New York: Continuum, 2002.
Knowles, Adam. *Heidegger's Fascist Affinities: A Politics of Silence*. Stanford: Stanford University Press, 2019.
Kofman, Sarah. *Rue Ordener, Rue Labat*. Translated by Ann Smock. Stages 7. Lincoln: University of Nebraska Press, 1996.
———. *Smothered Words*. Translated by Madeleine Dobie. Evanston, IL: Northwestern University Press, 2001.
Kolbert, Elizabeth. "Peace in Our Time: Steven Pinker's History of Violence." Review of *The Better Angels of Our Nature: Why Violence Has Declined*, by Steven Pinker. Books. *New Yorker*, October 3, 2011. https://www.newyorker.com/magazine/2011/10/03/peace-in-our-time-elizabeth-kolbert.
Kolmar, Gertrud. *Dark Soliloquy: The Selected Poems of Gertrud Kolmar*. Translated by Henry A. Smith. A Continuum Book. New York: Seabury, 1975.
———. *My Gaze Is Turned Inward: Letters, 1934–1943*. Translated with a preface by Brigitte Goldstein. Edited with an afterword by Johanna Woltmann. Jewish Lives. Evanston, IL: Northwestern University Press, 2004.
Koonz, Claudia. *The Nazi Conscience*. Cambridge: Harvard University Press, 2003.

Kühn, Dieter. *Gertrud Kolmar: A Literary Life.* Translated by Linda Marianielo, with poetry translated by Franz Vote. Evanston, IL: Northwestern University Press, 2013.

Kühne, Thomas. "Nazi Morality." In *A Companion to Nazi Germany*, edited by Shelley Baranowsk et al., 215–29. Wiley Blackwell Companions to World History. Hoboken, NJ: Wiley, 2018.

Lambert, Carole J. *Ethics after Auschwitz? Primo Levi's & Elie Wiesel's Response.* American University Studies. VII, Theology and Religion 305. New York: Lang, 2011.

Lamont, Rosette C. "Elie Wiesel: In Search of a Tongue." In *Confronting the Holocaust: The Impact of Elie Wiesel*, edited by Alvin H. Rosenfeld and Irving Greenberg, 80–98. Bloomington: Indiana University Press, 1978.

Lang, Berel. *Primo Levi: The Matter of a Life.* Jewish Lives. New Haven: Yale University Press, 2013.

Langer, Lawrence L. *Holocaust Testimonies: The Ruins of Memory.* New Haven: Yale University Press, 1991.

———. *Preempting the Holocaust.* New Haven: Yale University Press, 1998.

———. *Versions of Survival: The Holocaust and the Human Spirit.* SUNY Series in Modern Jewish Literature and Culture. Albany: SUNY Press, 1982.

Lanzmann, Claude. *Shoah: An Oral History of the Holocaust; the Complete Text of the Film.* New York: Pantheon, 1985.

Lemkin, Raphael. *Axis Rule in Occupied Europe: Laws of Occupation, Analysis of Government, Proposals for Redress.* Publications of the Carnegie Endowment for International Peace, Division of International Law. Washington, DC: Carnegie Endowment for International Peace, 1944.

Levi, Primo. *Collected Poems.* Translated by Jonathan Galassi. In *The Complete Works of Primo Levi*, 3:1865–2007. Edited by Ann Goldstein. 3 vols. New York: Liveright, 2015.

———. *Collected Poems.* Translated by Ruth Feldman and Brian Swan. London: Faber & Faber, 1988.

———. *The Drowned and the Saved.* Translated by Michael F. Moore. In *The Complete Works of Primo Levi*, 3:2405–2567. Edited by Ann Goldstein, 3 vols. New York: Liveright, 2015.

———. *The Drowned and the Saved.* Translated by Raymond Rosenthal. New York: Vintage, 1989.

———. *If This Is a Man.* Translated by Stuart Wolff. New York: Orion, 1959.

———. *If This Is a Man.* Translated by Stuart Wolff. In *The Complete Works of Primo Levi*, 1:1–193. Edited by Ann Goldstein. 3 vols. New York: Liveright, 2015.

———. *Lilith and Other Stories.* Translated by Ann Goldstein. In *The Complete Works of Primo Levi*, 2:1343–545. Edited by Ann Goldstein. 3 vols. New York: Liveright, 2015.

———. *Moments of Reprieve: A Memoir of Auschwitz.* Translated by Ruth Feldman. New York: Penguin, 1987.

———. *The Monkey's Wrench.* Translated by William Weaver. New York: Summit, 1986.

———. *Other People's Trades.* Translated by Antony Shugaar. In *The Complete Works of Primo Levi*, 3:2009–252. Edited by Ann Goldstein. 3 vols. New York: Liveright, 2015.

———. *Other People's Trades*. Translated by Raymond Rosenthal. New York: Summit, 1989.

———. *Survival in Auschwitz: The Nazi Assault on Humanity*. Translated by Stuart Wolff. New York: Simon & Schuster, 1996.

———. *The Voice of Memory: Interviews, 1961–1987*. Edited by Marco Belpoliti and Robert Gordon. Translated by Robert Gordon. New York: New Press, 2001.

———. *Uncollected Stories and Essays: 1981–1987*. Translated by Alessandra Bastagli and Francesco Bastagli. In *The Complete Works of Primo Levi*, 3:2575–2792. Edited by Ann Goldstein. 3 vols. New York: Liveright, 2015.

———. *The Wrench*. Translated by Nathaniel Rich. In *The Complete Works of Primo Levi*, 2:947–1113. Edited by Ann Goldstein. 3 vols. New York: Liveright, 2015.

Levi, Primo, with Leonardo de Benedetti. *Auschwitz Report*. Translated by Judith Wolff. Edited by Robert S. C. Gordon. London: Verso, 2006.

Levinas, Emmanuel. "Useless Suffering." In *Entre Nous: On Thinking-of-the-Other*, 91–101. Translated by Michael B. Smith and Barbara Harshav. European Perspectives. New York: Columbia University Press, 1998.

Lipstadt, Deborah E. *Antisemitism: Here and Now*. New York: Schocken, 2019.

———. *Holocaust: An American Understanding*. Key Words in Jewish Studies 7. New Brunswick, NJ: Rutgers University Press, 2016.

Littell, Franklin H. "Closing Address." In *Remembering for the Future: The Holocaust in an Age of Genocide*, 3:8–9, edited by John K. Roth and Elisabeth Maxwell. 3 vols. New York: Palgrave, 2001.

———. *The Crucifixion of the Jews: The Failure of Christians to Understand the Jewish Experience*. 1975. ROSE 12. Reprint, Macon, GA: Mercer University Press, 1986.

———. "An Interview with Prof. Rev. Franklin H. Littell: Christian Antisemitism and Its Influence on Nazi Ideology." By Yehuda Bauer. Conducted under the auspices of the Department of Religion, Temple University at Yad Vashem, Jerusalem, on July 23, 1998. On *Eclipse of Humanity: The History of the Shoah*, a multimedia CD by the Holocaust Remembrance Authority. Jerusalem: Yad Vashem, 2000. Reprinted by the Shoah Resource Center at Yad Vashem: The International School for Holocaust Studies. https://www.yadvashem.org/odot_pdf/Microsoft%20Word%20-%203725.pdf.

———. "Proclaiming the Silence." In *Telling the Tale: A Tribute to Elie Wiesel*, edited by Harry James Cargas, 62–66. St. Louis: Time Being, 1993.

Littell, Franklin H., and Hubert G. Locke, eds. *The German Church Struggle and the Holocaust*. Detroit: Wayne State University Press, 1974.

Littell, Marcia Sachs, and Sharon Weissman Gutman, eds. *Liturgies on the Holocaust: An Interfaith Anthology*. New and rev. ed. Valley Forge, PA: Trinity, 1996.

Lower, Wendy. "Decentering Berlin—Europeanization of Holocaust History." *Journal of Modern European History* 16 (2018) 32–39.

———. "The History and Future of Holocaust Research." Culture News. *Tablet* (April 26, 2018). https://www.tabletmag.com/jewish-arts-and-culture/culture-news/260677/history-future-holocaust-research.

———. *Hitler's Furies: German Women in the Nazi Killing Fields*. Boston: Houghton Mifflin Harcourt, 2013.

———. "Holocaust Studies: The Spatial Turn." In *A Companion to Nazi Germany*, edited by Shelley Baranowski et al., 565–79. Wiley Blackwell Companions to World History. Hoboken, NJ: Wiley, 2018.

Manseau, Peter. "Revising *Night*: Elie Wiesel and the Hazards of Holocaust Theology." *Crosscurrents* 56 (2006) 387–99.

Marrus, Michael R. *Lessons of the Holocaust*. Toronto: University of Toronto Press, 2016.

Martin, Adrienne M. *How We Hope: A Moral Psychology*. Princeton: Princeton University Press, 2014.

Martin, Douglas. "Leopold Page, Who Promoted Story of Schindler, Dies at 87." *New York Times* (March 15, 2001). https://www.nytimes.com/2001/03/15/us/leopold-page-who-promoted-story-of-schindler-dies-at-87.html.

Moorehead, Caroline. *Village of Secrets: Defying the Nazis in Vichy France*. New York: HarperCollins, 2014.

Motola, Gabriel. "Primo Levi: The Art of Fiction CXL." *Paris Review* 37 (1995) 201–20.

Moyers, Bill, et al. *Facing Evil*. Moyers Collection on DVD. DVD. Princeton: Films for the Humanities & Sciences, 2005.

Moyn, Samuel. *Not Enough: Human Rights in an Unequal World*. Cambridge: Harvard University Press, 2018.

Nancy, Jean-Luc. "Foreword: Run, Sarah!" In *Enigmas: Essays on Sarah Kofman*, edited by Penelope Deutscher and Kelly Oliver, viii–xvi. Ithaca, NY: Cornell University Press, 1999.

Oliner, Samuel P. *The Nature of Good and Evil: Understanding the Many Acts of Moral and Immoral Behavior*. St. Paul: Paragon, 2011.

———. *Restless Memories: Recollections of the Holocaust Years*. 2nd ed. Berkeley: Judah L. Magness Museum, 1986.

Oliner, Samuel P., and Pearl M. Oliner. *The Altruistic Personality: Rescuers of Jews in Nazi Europe*. New York: Free Press, 1988.

Patterson, David. "The Assault on the Holy within the Human: The Account of the Holocaust Diaries." In *Remembering for the Future: The Holocaust in an Age of Genocide*, edited by John K. Roth and Elisabeth Maxwell, 1:481–94. 3 vols. New York: Palgrave, 2001.

———. *Emil L. Fackenheim: A Jewish Philosopher's Response to the Holocaust*. Religion, Theology and the Holocaust. Syracuse: Syracuse University Press, 2008.

Patterson, David, and Marcia Sachs Littell, eds. *Legacy of an Impassioned Plea: Franklin H. Littell's "The Crucifixion of the Jews."* St. Paul: Paragon, 2018.

Patterson, David, and John K. Roth, eds. *After-Words: Post-Holocaust Struggles with Forgiveness, Reconciliation, Justice*. The Pastora Goldner Series in Post-Holocaust Studies. Seattle: University of Washington Press, 2004.

Pendas, Devon O. *The Frankfurt Auschwitz Trial, 1963–1965: Genocide, History, and the Limits of Law*. Cambridge: Cambridge University Press, 2006.

Petropoulos, Jonathan. *The Faustian Bargain: The Art World in Nazi Germany*. Oxford: Oxford University Press, 2000.

Phillips, Gary A. *Just Is in the Art of Samuel Bak*. Boston: Pucker Art Publications, 2018.

Pinker, Steven. *The Better Angels of Our Nature: Why Violence Has Declined*. New York: Penguin, 2012.

———. *Enlightenment Now: The Case for Reason, Science, Humanism, and Progress*. New York: Viking, 2018.

———. "Enlightenment Wars: Some Reflections on 'Enlightenment Now,' One Year Later." *Quillette* (January 14, 2019). https://quillette.com/2019/01/14/enlightenment-wars-some-reflections-on-enlightenment-now-one-year-later.

President's Commission on the Holocaust, Elie Wiesel, Chairman. "Report to the President." September 27, 1979. https://www.ushmm.org/m/pdfs/20050707-pres-commission-79.pdf.

Rebhun, Joseph. *Crisis of Morality and Reaction to the Holocaust*. Cabin John, MD: Wildside, 2010.

——. *God and Man: In Two Worlds*. Claremont, CA: OR Publishing, 1985.

——. *Leap to Life: Triumph over Nazi Evil*. Valley Stream, NY: Ardor Scribendi, 2000.

Reder, Rudolf. "Belzec." Translated by Margaret M. Rubel. In *Focusing on the Holocaust and Its Aftermath*, edited by Antony Polonsky, 268–89. Polin: Studies in Polish Jewry 13. London: Littman Library of Jewish Civilization, 2000.

Rich, Adrienne. *An Atlas of the Difficult World: Poems 1988–1991*. New York: Norton, 1991.

Rittner, Carol, and John K. Roth, eds. *Different Voices: Women and the Holocaust*. St. Paul: Paragon, 1993.

——, eds. *Rape: Weapon of War and Genocide*. St. Paul: Paragon, 2012.

——, eds. *Teaching about Rape in War and Genocide*. Palgrave Pivot. Basingstoke, UK: Palgrave Macmillan, 2016.

Rorty, Richard. "Human Rights, Rationality, and Sentimentality." In *The Philosophy of Human Rights: Readings in Context*, edited by Patrick Hayden, 241–56. Paragon Issues in Philosophy. St. Paul: Paragon, 2001.

Rosen, Alan. *Approaches to Teaching Wiesel's "Night."* Approaches to Teaching World Literature. New York: Modern Language Association of America, 2007.

Rosenbaum, Alan S., ed. *Is the Holocaust Unique? Perspectives on Comparative Genocide*. 3rd ed. Boulder, CO: Westview, 2009.

Roth, John K. "Connections and Exchanges: Elie Wiesel, Richard L. Rubenstein, and Franklin H. H. Littell." In *Legacy of an Impassioned Plea: Franklin H. Littell's "The Crucifixion of the Jews,"* edited by David Patterson and Marcia Sachs Littell, 61–78. St. Paul: Paragon, 2018.

——. *A Consuming Fire: Encounters with Elie Wiesel and the Holocaust*. 1979. Reprint, Eugene, OR: Wipf & Stock, 2016.

——. "The Death of God in American Theology." In *The American Religious Experience: The Roots, Trends, and Future of American Theology*, by Frederick Sontag and John K. Roth, 201–35. New York: Harper & Row, 1972.

——. "Double Binds: Ethics after Auschwitz." In *The Double Binds of Ethics after the Holocaust: Salvaging the Fragments*, edited by Jennifer L. Geddes et al., 5–23. New York: Palgrave Macmillan, 2009.

——, ed. *Ethics after the Holocaust: Perspectives, Critiques, and Responses*. St. Paul: Paragon, 1999.

——. *Ethics during and after the Holocaust: In the Shadow of Birkenau*. New York: Palgrave Macmillan, 2005.

——. *The Failures of Ethics: Confronting the Holocaust, Genocide, and Other Mass Atrocities*. Oxford: Oxford University Press, 2015.

——. "Foreword." In *Just Is in the Art of Samuel Bak*, by Gary A. Phillips, 1–3. Boston: Pucker Art Publications, 2018.

——. *Freedom and the Moral Life: The Ethics of William James*. Philadelphia: Westminster, 1969.

——, ed. *Genocide and Human Rights: A Philosophical Guide*. New York: Palgrave Macmillan, 2005.

———. "Holocaust Business: Some Reflections on *Arbeit Macht Frei*." In *Reflections on the Holocaust: Historical, Philosophical, and Educational Dimensions*, edited by Irene G. Shur et al., 68–82. The Annals of the American Academy of Political and Social Science 450. Philadelphia: American Academy of Political and Social Science, 1980.

———. *Holocaust Politics*. 2001. Reprint, Eugene, OR: Wipf & Stock, 2016.

———. "Is God Dead? Some Aftereffects and Aftershocks of the Holocaust." In *Resurrecting the Death of God: The Origins, Influence, and Return of Radical Theology*, edited by Daniel J. Peterson and G. Michael Zbaraschuk, 43–57. Albany: SUNY Press, 2014.

———. "One of the Very Few." In *Before–During–After: Surviving the Holocaust*, by Siegfried Halbreich, xvii–xxiii. New York: Vantage, 1991.

———, ed. *The Philosophy of Josiah Royce*. 1971. Reprint, Indianapolis: Hackett, 1982.

———. "Tears and Elie Wiesel." *Princeton Seminary Bulletin* 65 (1972) 42–48. http://commons.ptsem.edu/id/princetonseminar6521prin-dmd009.

Roth, John K., and Michael Berenbaum, eds. *Holocaust: Religious and Philosophical Implications*. With a new preface. 30th anniversary printing. St. Paul: Paragon, 2018.

Royce, Josiah. *The Sources of Religious Insight*. Edinburgh: T. & T. Clark, 1912.

Rubenstein, Richard L. *After Auschwitz: History, Theology, and Contemporary Judaism*. 2nd ed. Johns Hopkins Jewish Studies. Baltimore: Johns Hopkins University Press, 1992.

———. *The Age of Triage: Fear and Hope in an Overcrowded World*. Boston: Beacon, 1983.

———. *The Cunning of History: The Holocaust and the American Future*. New York: Harper, 1987.

———. "Elie Wiesel and Primo Levi." In *Perspectives on the Holocaust: Essays in Honor of Raul Hilberg*, edited by James S. Pacy and Alan P. Wertheimer, 145–65. Boulder, CO: Westview, 1995.

———. *Jihad and Genocide*. Studies in Genocide. Lanham, MD: Rowman & Littlefield, 2010.

———. "Naming the Unnamable; Thinking the Unthinkable: A Review Essay of Arthur Cohen's *The Tremendum*." *Journal of Reform Judaism* 31/2 (1984) 43–55.

———. *Power Struggle*. New York: Scribner, 1974.

———. "Some Perspectives on Religious Faith after Auschwitz." In *Holocaust: Religious and Philosophical Implications*, edited by John K. Roth and Michael Berenbaum, 349–61. With a new preface. 30th anniversary printing. St. Paul: Paragon, 2018.

———. "Thomas Altizer's Apocalypse." In *The Theology of Altizer: Critique and Response*, edited by John B. Cobb Jr., 125–37. Philadelphia: Westminster, 1970.

Rubenstein, Richard L., and John K. Roth. *Approaches to Auschwitz: The Holocaust and Its Legacy*. Rev. ed. Louisville: Westminster John Knox, 2003.

———. *Approaches to Auschwitz: The Holocaust and Its Legacy*. Atlanta: John Knox, 1987.

Rubin, Agi, and Henry Greenspan. *Reflections: Auschwitz, Memory, and a Life Recreated*. St. Paul: Paragon, 2006.

Ryan, Kay. *The Niagara River: Poems*. The Grove Press Poetry Series. New York: Grove Press, 2005.

Sauvage, Pierre. "Does 'Village of Secrets' Falsify French Rescue during the Holocaust?" Review of *Village of Secrets*, by Caroline Moorhead. *Tablet* (October 31, 2014). https://www.tabletmag.com/jewish-arts-and-culture/books/186652/moorehead-le-chambon.

Sebald, W. G. *On the Natural History of Destruction*. Translated by Anthea Bell. New York: Random House, 2003.

Seidman, Naomi. "Elie Wiesel and the Scandal of Jewish Rage." *Jewish Social Studies* 3 (1996) 1–19.

———. *Faithful Renderings: Jewish-Christian Difference and the Politics of Translation*. Afterlives of the Bible. Chicago: University of Chicago Press, 2006.

Sereny, Gitta. *Into That Darkness: An Examination of Conscience*. New York: Vintage, 1983.

Skloot, Robert, ed. *The Theatre of the Holocaust*. 2 vols. Madison: University of Wisconsin Press, 1983.

Stafford, William. *The Darkness around Us Is Deep: Selected Poems of William Stafford*. Edited by Robert Bly. New York: HarperCollins, 1993.

———. *Even in Quiet Places: Poems by William Stafford*. Lewiston, ID: Confluence, 1996.

———. *Traveling through the Dark*. New York: Harper & Row, 1962.

Swazo, Norman Kenneth. "Questioning Islamic Belief in Post-Genocide Bangladesh: Mu'tazilites and Ash'arites, Maya and Sohail." *Holocaust and Genocide Studies* 32 (2018) 272–90.

Thomson, Ian. *Primo Levi*. London: Hutchinson, 2002.

Trump, Donald. "Remarks by President Trump at United States Holocaust Memorial Museum National Days of Remembrance." Delivered at the United States Capitol on April 25, 2017. https://www.whitehouse.gov/briefings-statements/remarks-president-trump-united-states-holocaust-memorial-museum-national-days-remembrance.

———."'We Must Stamp out Prejudice and Anti-Semitism Everywhere,' Trump Tells World Jewish Congress." *World Jewish Congress* (website), April 25, 2017. https://www.worldjewishcongress.org/en/news/we-must-stamp-out-prejudice-and-anti-semitism-everywhere-trump-tells-world-jewish-congress-4-0-2017?print=true.

United Nations General Assembly. Office of the High Commissioner for Refugees. *Convention and Protocol relating to the Status of Refugees: Text of the 1951 Convention Relating to the Status of the Refugees; Text of the 1967 Protocol relating to the Status of Refugees; Resolution 2198 (XXI) adopted by the United Nations General Assembly*. Geneva: UNHCR, 2007. See the URL to this resolution at the end of the bibliography.

———. Resolution 217 A, Universal Declaration on Human Rights (December 10, 1948). https://www.ohchr.org/EN/UDHR/Documents/UDHR_Translations/eng.pdf.

———. Resolution 260 A (III), Convention on the Prevention and Punishment of the Crime of Genocide (December 9, 1948). https://www.ohchr.org/en/professionalinterest/pages/crimeofgenocide.aspx.

———. *Statistical Yearbooks* (website). "Figures at a Glance." https://www.unhcr.org/en-us/figures-at-a-glance.html.

United States Holocaust Memorial Museum. "Introduction to the Holocaust." In *United States Holocaust Memorial Museum* (website) *Holocaust Encyclopedia*. https://encyclopedia.ushmm.org/content/en/article/introduction-to-the-holocaust.

The USC Shoah Foundation. "Impact in Profile: Dario Gabbai." https://sfi.usc.edu/profiles/dario-gabbai.

Venezia, Shlomo. *Inside the Gas Chambers: Eight Months in the Sonderkommando of Auschwitz*. Edited by Jean Mouttapa. Translated by Andrew Brown. Cambridge: Polity, 2009.

Veterbi, Andrew J. "Prmo Levi: A Family Memory; Opening Remarks at Third Annual Symposium on Primo Levi." *Centro Primo Levi Online Monthly* (website). September 22, 2019. Primo Levi Center. Printed Matter. https://primolevicenter.org/printed-matter/primo-levi-a-family-memory/

Warnock, G. J. *Contemporary Moral Philosophy*. New Studies in Ethics. London: Macmillan, 1967.

Webb, Kristina. "'Never Again': Trump Marks Holocaust Days of Remembrance in Proclamation." *Palm Beach Post*, April 24, 2017. https://www.palmbeachpost.com/news/national-govt--politics/never-again-trump-marks-holocaust-days-remembrance-proclamation/tbngdSFAlRSnPCgT71NMiN.

Weinberg, David. "France." In *The Holocaust Encyclopedia*, edited by Walter Laqueur, 213–22. New Haven: Yale University Press, 2001.

Wiesel, Elie. *All Rivers Run to the Sea: Memoirs*. New York: Knopf, 1995.

———. *And the Sea Is Never Full: Memoirs, 1969-*. Translated by Marion Wiesel. New York: Knopf, 1999.

———. "Auschwitz—Another Planet." In *Against Silence: The Voice and Vision of Elie Wiesel*, edited by Irving Abrahamson, 2:292–94. 3 vols. New York: Holocaust Library, 1985.

———. *Day*. Translated by Anne Borchardt. New York: Hill & Wang, 2006.

———. "Exile and the Human Condition." In *Against Silence: The Voice and Vision of Elie Wiesel*, edited by Irving Abrahamson, 1:179–83. 3 vols. New York: Holocaust Library, 1985.

———. "Foreword." In *Shadows of Auschwitz: A Christian Response to the Holocaust*, ix–x. Rev. ed. New York: Crossroad, 1990.

———. *Four Hasidic Masters and Their Struggle against Melancholy*. Ward-Phillips Lectures in English Language and Literature 9. Notre Dame, IN: University of Notre Dame Press, 1978.

———. "The Gates of the Holocaust." In *Against Silence: The Voice and Vision of Elie Wiesel*, edited by Irving Abrahamson, 1:211–12. 3 vols. New York: Holocaust Library, 1985.

———. *A Jew Today*. Translated by Marion Wiesel. New York: Random House, 1978.

———. "Jewish Values in the Post-Holocaust Future." *Judaism* 16 (1967) 291–94.

———. *Legends of Our Time*. New York: Holt, Rinehart and Winston, 1968.

———. *Messengers of God: Biblical Portraits and Legends*. Translated by Marion Wiesel. New York: Simon & Schuster, 2005.

———. *Night*. Translated by Stella Rodway. 25th anniversary ed. New York: Bantam, 1982.

———. *Night*. Translated by Marion Wiesel. New York: Hill & Wang, 2006.

———. *The Night Trilogy*. New York: Hill & Wang, 2008.

———. *The Oath*. Translated by Marion Wiesel. New York: Random House, 1973.

———. *One Generation After*. Translated by Lily Edelman and Elie Wiesel. 1970. Reprint, New York: Schocken, 2011.

———. "One Must Not Forget." Interview with Elie Wiesel. By Alvin P. Sanoff. *US News and World Report* (October 27, 1968), 68.

———. *Open Heart*. Translated by Marion Wiesel. New York: Knopf, 2012.

———. "A Prayer for the Days of Awe." Opinion. *New York Times*, October 2, 1997. http://www.nytimes.com/1997/10/02/opinion/a-prayer-for-the-days-of-awe.html.

———. "Preface to the New Translation." In *Night*, viii–xv. Translated by Marion Wiesel. New York: Hill & Wang, 2006.

———. *Sages and Dreamers: Biblical, Talmudic, and Hasidic Portraits and Legends*. Translated by Marion Wiesel. New York: Summit, 1991.

———. *Somewhere a Master: Further Hasidic Portraits and Legends*. Translated by Marion Wiesel. New York: Summit, 1982.

———. *Souls on Fire: Portraits and Legends of Hasidic Masters*. Translated by Marion Wiesel. New York: Random House, 1972.

———. "Talking and Writing and Keeping Silent." In *Holocaust: Religious and Philosophical Implications*, edited by John K. Roth and Michael Berenbaum, 362–69. With a new preface. 30th anniversary printing. St. Paul: Paragon, 2018.

———. "Telling the Tale." In *Against Silence: The Voice and Vision of Elie Wiesel*, edited by Irving Abrahamson, 1:234–38. 3 vols. New York: Holocaust Library, 1985.

———. *The Testament: A Novel*. Translated by Marion Wiesel. New York: Summit, 1981.

———. *The Town beyond the Wall*. Translated by Stephen Becker. New York: Schocken, 1995.

———. "The Trial of Man." In *Against Silence: The Voice and Vision of Elie Wiesel*, edited by Irving Abrahamson, 1:175–78. 3 vols., New York: Holocaust Library, 1985.

———. "Trivializing the Holocaust: Semi-Fact and Semi-Fiction." In *Against Silence: The Voice and Vision of Elie Wiesel*, edited by Irving Abrahamson, 1:155–58. 3 vols. New York: Holocaust Library, 1985.

———. "The Use of Words and the Weight of Silence." In *Against Silence: The Voice and Vision of Elie Wiesel*, edited by Irving Abrahamson, 2:75–84. 3 vols. New York: Holocaust Library, 1985.

———. "What Is a Jew?" In *Against Silence: The Voice and Vision of Elie Wiesel*, edited by Irving Abrahamson, 1:271–75. 3 vols. New York: Holocaust Library, 1985.

———. "Why I Write." Translated by Rosette C. Lamont. In *Confronting the Holocaust: The Impact of Elie Wiesel*, edited by Alvin H. Rosenfeld and Irving Greenberg, 200–206. Bloomington: Indiana University Press, 1978.

———. "Why Should People Care?" In John K. Roth, *A Consuming Fire: Encounters with Elie Wiesel and the Holocaust*, 15–18. 1979. Reprint, Eugene, OR: Wipf & Stock, 2016.

———. *Wise Men and Their Tales: Portraits of Biblical, Talmudic, and Hasidic Masters*. New York: Schocken, 2003.

Wiesel, Elie, et al. "Remarks at Millennium Evening: The Perils of Indifference; Lessons Learned from a Violent Century." East Room of the White House, April 12, 1999. On *History Place* (website). http://www.historyplace.com/speeches/wiesel-transcript.htm/

Wiesenthal, Simon. *The Sunflower: On the Possibilities and Limits of Forgiveness*. With a symposium edited by Harry James Cargas and Bonny V. Fetterman. Rev. and expanded ed. 2nd paperback ed. New York: Schocken, 1998.

Winter, Jay M. "Demography of the War." In *The Oxford Companion to World War II*, edited by Ian C. B. Dear, 289–92. Oxford: Oxford University Press, 1995.

Wittmann, Rebecca. "Punishment." In *The Oxford Handbook of Holocaust Studies*, edited by Peter Hayes and John K. Roth, 524–39. Oxford Handbooks. Oxford: Oxford University Press, 2010.

Woo, Elaine. "Fred Diament, 81: Survivor of the Holocaust Taught Many about It." *Los Angeles Times*, November 28, 2004. http://articles.latimes.com/2004/nov/28/local/me-diament28.

———. "Siegfried Halbreich Dies at 98; Holocaust Survivor Lectured on His Experience." *Los Angeles Times*, September 21, 2008. https://www.latimes.com/local/obituaries/la-me-halbreich21-2008sep21-story.html.

Woodruff, Paul, and Harry A. Wilmer, eds. *Facing Evil: Light at the Core of Darkness*. La Salle, IL: Open Court, 1994.

The World Counts (website). "World Population Clock Live." http://www.theworldcounts.com/counters/shocking_environmental_facts_and_statistics/world_population_clock_live.

Wyatt, Edward. "The Translation of Wiesel's 'Night' Is New, but Old Questions Are Raised." *New York Times* (January 19, 2006). http://www.nytimes.com/2006/01/19/books/19nigh.html.

Yad Vashem. "André and Magda Trocmé, Daniel Trocmé." In *The Righteous among the Nations, Featured Stories*. On *Yad Vashem* (website). https://www.yadvashem.org/righteous/stories/trocme.html.

———. "Lorenzo Perrone." In *The Stories of Six Righteous among the Nations in Auschwitz: Flickers of Light*. On *Yad Vashem* (website). https://www.yadvashem.org/yv/en/exhibitions/righteous-auschwitz/perrone.asp.

———. "President Donald J. Trump's Speech at Yad Vashem" (May 23, 2017). On *Yad Vashem* (website). https://www.yadvashem.org/yv/trump/index.asp.

Young, James E. *The Texture of Memory: Holocaust Memorials and Meaning*. New Haven: Yale University Press, 1993.

Zeidman, Lawrence A., and Jaap Cohen. "Walking a Fine Line: The Extraordinary Deeds of Dutch Neuroscientist C. U. Ariëns Kappers before and during World War II." *Journal of the History of the Neurosciences* 23 (2014) 252–72. https://www.researchgate.net/publication/262339527_Walking_a_Fine_Scientific_Line_The_Extraordinary_Deeds_of_Dutch_Neuroscientist_C_U_Ariens_Kappers_Before_and_During_World_War_II.

Bibliography

~~~

The website for Siddha Yoga, mentioned in chapter 1, can be found here; the URL given links to the page of essential teachings: http://www.siddhayoga.org/teachings/essential.

The David Moffie photograph mentioned in chapter 3 and in n. 34 can be found at: https://www.google.com/search?q=david+moffie&rlz=1C1MKDC_enUS774US774&tbm=isch&source=iu&ictx=1&fir=S6l6a0yk5F-YOM%253A%252CypncEteh_8E_6M%252C_&vet=1&usg=AI4_-kSuBf3rAYUJ9HIpYKdCOMQU2msC0Q&sa=X&ved=2ahUKEwi4oMGu1cPhAhVDqJ4KHQinCygQ9QEwAXoECAkQBA#imgrc=S6l6aoyk5F-YOM:.

"The Woman Poet," by Gertrud Kolmar, mentioned in chapter 7, can be found at: http://apoemaday.tumblr.com/post/167347166129/the-woman-poet.

The Samuel Bak painting mentioned in chapter 9, can be found at: https://www.facinghistory.org/chunk/478?backlink=for-educators/educator-resources/resource-collections/illuminations/samuel-bak-paintings. Likewise, Langer's commentary, mentioned in chapter 9, can also be found at: https://www.facinghistory.org/For-Educators/Educator-Resources/Resource-Collections/Illuminations/Introduction-Professor-Lawrence-L-Langer.

The website for the Wollheim Memorial, mentioned in chapter 11, can be found at: http://www.wollheim-memorial.de/en/home.

The website for the Auschwitz-Birkenau Memorial Museum, mentioned in chapter 11, and especially the webpage on the history of the Monowitz subcamp can be found at: http://www.auschwitz.org/en/history/auschwitz-sub-camps/monowitz.

The URL that links to the United Nations Convention and Protocol relating to the Status of Refugees, mentioned in chapter 11, can be found at: https://www.unhcr.org/cgi-bin/texis/vtx/search?page=search&docid=3b66c2aa10&query=Convention%20relating%20to%20the%20Status%20of%20Refugees.

The statistics mentioned in chapter 11 from Belgium's Kazerne Dossin: Memorial, Museum, and Documentation Center on the Holocaust and Human Rights can be found in English at: https://www.kazernedossin.eu/EN/Museumsite/Museum/Thema-Dood.

Index

Note: n indicates footnotes, and italicized page numbers indicate illustrations.

Abel, 84
Abraham, 39, 84, 260
Academy Award, 120
The Accident (Wiesel), 75n5
acts of recognition, 1–9
Adam, 84, 190
Adler, H. G., 99, 105
Adorno, Theodor, 145n14
Adunka, Evelyn, 99
Advancing Holocaust Studies (Rittner and Roth, eds.), 188
Africa, 166
Afridi, Mehnaz, 184n1
After Auschwitz (Rubenstein), 11, 12n8, 13–14, 30
"After Ten Years" (Bonhoeffer), 136
After the Before (Bak), 195
"After the Fact" (Blanchot), 145n11
"Afterword" (Browning), 48
"Against the Irreversible: On Jean Améry" (Sebald), 251n69
Agamben, Giorgio, 114n1
The Age of Triage: Fear and Hope in an Overcrowded World (Rubenstein), 20–22
Alba, Avril, 184n1
Aleppo, Syria, 80
Alfers, Cornelius, 184n1
Alfers, Sandra, 184n1

Alford, Cam, 138
Algeria, 169, 178
Algiers, Algeria, 178
All Rivers Run to the Sea (Wiesel), 30
Allah, 16n15
Allies, 18, 109, 166, 198
Alps, Italian, 209
al-Qaeda, 24, 80
Altizer, Thomas, 13
The Altruistic Personality: Rescuers of Jews in Nazi Europe (Oliner and Oliner), 121
Alvarez, Alex, 184n1
Aly, Götz, 47n1
Amazon, 233
American Jewish University, 185
Améry, Jean, 142, 152, 177, 181, 186, 232–56
Amos, 195
Amsterdam, Netherlands, 61, 204
Amsterdam Neurological Association, 60n34
"The Anatomy of Hate" [conference], 187
Anderson, Gordon, 184n1
Andresen, Martha, 184n1
Anschluss, 93, 235–37
Antelme, Robert, 143n6, 145n11, 147–48

278 Index

antisemitism
  acts of recognition, 6
  friends and teachers, 138–39
  Holocaust insight
    Améry, 236, 245, 253–54
    Bauer, 55
    Bauman, 129–30
    Friedländer, 58–59
    Hallie and Camus, 183
    Kofman and Delbo, 140, 143, 144n9, 147, 152
    Levinas, 126
    Littell, 69, 71–72, 77, 81–82, 84
    Lower and Petropoulos, 65
    Rittner, 188
    Rubenstein, 16–17, 21, 25
    Wiesel, 31
  taking nothing good for granted, 259
Antwerp, Belgium, 237–38
Approaches to Auschwitz (Rubenstein and Roth), 24, 129
Arbeit macht frei, 18
Arctic Circle, 114
Arendt, Hannah, 141, 241–42
Army, First Polish, 129
Army, Red, 200, 207
Army, US, 93
Ash Wednesday, 69
At the Mind's Limits (Améry), 241, 243, 245–46, 249, 253–54
"At the Mind's Limits: Essay on the Intellectual's Experience of Auschwitz" (Améry), 242–43
atheism, 13, 106, 183
Atlas, 203–4
An Atlas of the Difficult World (Rich), 204–5
Auschwitz
  acts of recognition, 5, 8–9
  friends and teachers, 114, 138, 205
  Holocaust insight
    Améry, 232, 239, 241–45, 247, 250
    Bauer, 57
    Berenbaum, 186
    Borowski, 131–35
    Fackenheim, 123–25
    Freeman and Freeman, 115
    Friedländer, 59–60
    Gabbai, 117–19
    Galles, 201
    Halbreich, 116–17
    Hallie and Camus, 166
    Hilberg, 94, 99, 103, 106, 108n39, 112–13
    Kofman and Delbo, 140–43, 144n8, 145–46, 148–49, 151, 153–56, 158–62
    Langer, 128
    Levi, 207–20, 224, 226–30
    Levinas, 127
    Littell, 70, 75–76
    Page, 120
    Rubenstein, 11, 13, 15, 24
    Weiss, 119
    Wiesel, 28–29, 35–37, 42
Auschwitz and After (Delbo), 154, 156, 158, 161, 163
Auschwitz III. *See* Monowitz
Auschwitz Report (De Benedetti and Levi), 207n1
Auschwitz Trial, 242
Auschwitz-Birkenau Memorial Museum, 239n22
Austin Presbyterian Theological Seminary, 202
Austria
  friends and teachers, 114, 138
  Holocaust insight
    Améry, 236–38, 240, 245, 250, 254
    Hilberg, 93, 99
    Levi, 219

Bak, Samuel, 194–96, 203
Bangladesh, 16n15
Barnes & Noble, 98
Barnett, Victoria, 47n1, 257
Barrack 48, 224
Bartov, Omer, 47n1
Bauer, Yehuda, 54–58, 67, 71
Baum, Rachel, 184n1
Bauman, Zygmunt, 129–31
Bauman Institute for Sociology and Social Theory, 129

BDS movement, 81
Becker, Carl, 54
"Being a Person" (Stafford), 206
Belgium, 189, 236–40, 242
Belzec, 198–201, 205
Belzec (Galles), 199, 201
Benedict, Beth Hawkins, 184n1
Benz, Wolfgang, 1n1
Berenbaum, Michael, 17, 185–86, 194
Berenbaum Group, 185
Bergen, Doris, 47n1
Bergen-Belsen, 239
Berger, Alan, 184n1
Berger-Baumgarten, Regine (Gina), 238–40
Berlin, Germany, 12, 105, 129, 135, 140
Bern, Switzerland, 205
Bethge, Eberhard, 139n45
Bethge, Renate, 139n45
The Better Angels of Our Nature: Why Violence Has Declined (Pinker), 233–35
Beverly Hills, California, 120
Beyle, Marie-Henri. *See* Stendhal
Bible, 77–78
Birkenau
   acts of recognition, 8–9
   Holocaust insight
      Borowski, 135
      Freeman and Freeman, 115
      Friedländer, 60
      Galles, 201
      Hilberg, 112
      Kofman and Delbo, 146, 155
      Levi, 213, 219
      Wiesel, 28–29, 33, 35
Blanchot, Maurice, 143n6, 145n11, 149
Bloomfield, Sara, 184n1
Bloomington, Indiana, 208
Bloxham, Donald, 47n1
Bobowa ghetto, 121
Bohemia, 99n18
Boko Haram, 80
Bonhoeffer, Dietrich, 136–39, 259
Bonn, Germany, 12
Book Award, *Los Angeles Times*, 203

Borowski, Tadeusz, 131–36, 142, 181
Boston, Massachusetts, 30, 98–99, 208
Boston University, 30
Bovary, Charles, 243n33
Braunstein, Paul, 74, 75
British Library, 192
Brown, Adam, 184n1
Brown University, 110
Brown-Fleming, Suzanne, 184n1
Browning, Christopher R., 48–50, 55, 67, 92–93n11, 110
Brussels, Belgium, 237, 239–40, 242
Buchenwald, 106n37, 143n6
Buchner, Ernst, 66
Buddha, 23
Buna. *See* Monowitz
Bundesbahn, 90
Bundespressamt, 12
Bundestag, 57
Burger, Ariel, 30
Burlington, Vermont, 90

Cain, 84
Cal Humanities (California Council for the Humanities), 259
California
   friends and teachers, 137–38
   Holocaust insight
      Browning, 48
      Freeman and Freeman, 115
      Gabbai, 117–18
      Halbreich, 116
      Hallie and Camus, 168, 172
      Hayes, 50
      Hilberg, 113
      Levi, 208
      Oliner, 120
      Page, 120
      Rich, 204
      Ryan, 201
   taking nothing good for granted, 259
California Council for the Humanities (Cal Humanities), 259
Camon, Ferdinando, 226
Camus, Albert, 76, 165–83, 256
Canada, 119, 132, 202
Capitol, US, 253, 254n75

Index

Cargas, Harry James, 74, *74*, 76–77, 184n1
Carpi, Italy, 209
Carter, Jimmy, 111, 113
Cascade Mountains, 205–6
Catholicism, 69, 75–76, 105, 138, 165–66, 194n18, 237
Celan, Paul, 142
Celemenski, Jacob, 102–3
Center for Advanced Holocaust Studies, 185
Center for the Study of the Holocaust, Genocide, and Human Rights. *See* Mgrublian Center for Human Rights
Central Office for Jewish Emigration, 99n18
Centro Primo Levi, 208n3
Cesarani, David, 47n1
Charles Bovary (Améry), 243n33
Charles F. Deems Lectures, 123
Chemical Kommando, 216–17
Chicago, Illinois, 172
Christianity
  acts of recognition, 1
  Holocaust insight
    Bak, 194n18
    Fackenheim, 124–25
    Grob, Knight, and Patterson, 190–91
    Hallie and Camus, 165–66, 172, 183
    Hilberg, 105
    Kofman and Delbo, 144
    Levi, 221
    Littell, 69–74, 76–79, 81–82, 84
    Manosevitz, 202
    Oliner, 121
    Rubenstein, 10–17, 20, 26
    Wiesel, 43–44
  taking nothing good for granted, 260
Chu, Jolene, 184n1
Claremont, California, 48, 113, 137–38, 172, 208
Claremont McKenna College
  friends and teachers, 114
  Holocaust insight
    Browning, 48
    Freeman and Freeman, 115
    Friedländer, 58
    Gabbai, 117–18
    Halbreich, 117
    Hallie and Camus, 172
    Hayes, 50
    Hilberg, 112
    Lower and Petropoulos, 63, 66
    Page, 120
    Rubenstein, 25
    Weiss, 119
    Wiesel, 31
Cleveland, Ohio, 118
Clinton, Bill, 39, 185
Clinton, Hillary, 39
Cohen, Leonard, 232
Cold War, 12, 81
Collier Books, 208
Cologne, Germany, 240
Colorado, 202
Columbia River, 206
Columbia University, 93
The Complete Works of Primo Levi (Levi), 207–8
Confessing Church, 77
Confino, Alon, 47n1
Confucius, 23
Congress, US, 33n24
Connecticut, 171, 173
A Consuming Fire: Encounters with Elie Wiesel and the Holocaust (Roth), 10
Convention on the Prevention and Punishment of the Crime of Genocide, UN, 150–51
Convention on the Status of Refugees, UN, 235
Copenhagen, Denmark, 106n37
Covenant Theology, 76
Crawford, Leigh, 184n1
Crematorium II, Auschwitz, 118
Crisis of Morality (Rebhun), 137n43
The Crucifixion of the Jews (Littell), 72–73, 77, 79–84
Cruz, Nikolas, 233
Cuba, 93
Cuban missile crisis, 253

The Cunning of History: The Holocaust and the American Future (Rubenstein), 10–11, 16, 18, 20
Czech, Danuta, 239
Czech Republic, 114
Czerniakow, Adam, 7, 100

Dachau, 105, 106n37, 131, 135, 143n6, 147
Dahlem, Germany, 12
Danger Is Near (Manosevitz), 203
Darfur, 6, 73
Dark Soliloquy: The Selected Poems of Gertrud Kolmar (Kolmar), 140
The Darkness around Us Is Deep (Stafford), 205
David and Fela Shapell Family Collections, Conservation and Research Center, 257–58
David Moffie Prize, 60n34
Dawn (Wiesel), 75n5
Day (Wiesel), 75n5
Days of Remembrance of Victims of the Holocaust, 253, 254n75
De Benedetti, Leonardo, 207
de Foy, Robert, 236–37
De Reus, Lee Ann, 184n1
Dean, Martin, 47n1
"The Dean and the Chosen People" (Rubenstein), 12n8
Decalogue. See Ten Commandments
Declaration of Independence, US, 18
Delbo, Charlotte, 47, 128, 140–64, 232
Denmark, 106n37
Department of State, US, 187, 205
Derrida, Jacques, 143
Des Pres, Terrence, 212
Desbois, Patrick, 47n1
The Destruction of the European Jews (Hilberg)
  acts of recognition, 2, 7
  Holocaust insight
    Hilberg, 90, 92n9, 94, 98–99, 101, 105, 108, 110
    Littell, 75
Deutsche Reichsbahn, 89–90
Deutscher, Penelope, 143n5
Diament, Fred, 116

Diament, Leo, 117
The Diary of Anne Frank (Frank), 138, 234
Dickinson, John K., 103–4
Different Voices: Women and the Holocaust (Rittner and Roth, eds.), 140–41, 187
Dobie, Madeleine, 145n11
Dobkowski, Michael, 184n1
Documents of Destruction: Germany and Jewry 1933–1945 (Hilberg), 101
Dora-Mittelbau, 239
Drancy, 144
The Drowned and the Saved (Levi), 208, 210, 212–13, 215, 219, 241
Dudach, Georges, 154
Dwork, Debórah, 1, 47n1

East Berlin, Germany, 12
"Eastern War Time" (Rich), 204
Ebensee, 118
Editions de Seuil, 84
Edwards, Curtis, 205
Ehrenreich, Robert, 184n1
Eichmann, Adolf, 12, 106n37, 179, 236, 241–42
Eichmann in Jerusalem: A Report on the Banality of Evil (Arendt), 241
Einsatzgruppe D, 108n39
Einsatzgruppen, 150
Eitinger, Leo, 74, 75–76
Elie Wiesel Foundation, 187
Elie Wiesel Genocide and Atrocities Prevention Act, 33
"Elie Wiesel: The Man and His Work" [symposium], 74, 87
Ellis Island, 138
Emory University, 73
England, 123, 129, 151n30, 188, 240
Enlightenment, 130, 146, 243, 250
Enlightenment Now: The Case for Reason, Science, Humanism, and Progress (Pinker), 233
Ericksen, Robert, 47n1
Ernest, Stefan, 63
The Eternal Presence of Absence (Manosevitz), 203

"The Ethical and Moral Foundations of Holocaust Studies" [symposium], 257
"Ethics after the Holocaust" [lecture by Hilberg], 106, 111
"Ethics after the Holocaust" [seminar], 141
Ethics After the Holocaust: Perspectives, Critiques, and Responses (Roth, ed.), 189
"Ethics during and after the Holocaust" [conference session], 50
Ethics Essay Contest, 187
Europe
  acts of recognition, 1–2, 5
  Holocaust insight
    Améry, 235–36
    Browning, 49
    Friedländer, 58, 62
    Hallie and Camus, 170, 178
    Hilberg, 89, 93, 106n37, 111
    Levinas, 126
    Littell, 80–81
    Rich, 205
    Rubenstein, 19
    Wiesel, 40
Evans, Richard J., 47n1
Eve, 84, 190
Evian Conference, 236–37
Evian-les-Bains, 236
Existentialism, 177

Facing History and Ourselves, 194n17
Fackenheim, Emil, 123–25, 127, 141
Fahrplananordnung 587, 7, 97
The Failures of Ethics (Roth), 45
Fairleigh Dickinson University, 188
"Faith in Humankind, Rescuers of Jews during the Holocaust" [conference], 187
Faussone, Tino, 210
The Faustinian Bargain: The Art World in Nazi Germany (Petropoulos), 66
Federal Republic, 247
Federation of State Humanities Councils, 259
Fehrenbach, Ivan, 184n1

Filloux, Catherine, 114n1
"Final Solution"
  acts of recognition, 2
  friends and teachers, 114, 137
  Holocaust insight
    Améry, 250
    Friedländer, 59–60
    Gabbai, 118
    Galles, 198
    Grob, Knight, and Patterson, 189
    Hallie and Camus, 179
    Hilberg, 89, 100, 109
    Kofman and Delbo, 146, 152
    Levi, 219
    Rubenstein, 16, 18
Finance Ministry, German, 17
First Station: Auschwitz-Birkenau (Galles), 198
Fischer, Anna, 114n1
Fischer, Benno, 114n1
Flannery, Edward, 72
Flaubert, Gustave, 243n33
Fleischner, Eva, 184n1
Florida, 93, 233–34
Flossenburg, 135
"For John Roth" (Quay), 259
"For the Miracle" (Hunter), 197
Fort Breendonk, 239, 244
Fòssoli, Italy, 209
Fourteen Stations/Hey Yud Dalet (Galles), 198
France
  Holocaust insight
    Améry, 238–40
    Hallie and Camus, 165–71, 173–75, 178
    Hilberg, 93
    Kofman and Delbo, 143, 144n8, 154
Frank, Anne, 139, 204, 234
Frankfurt, Germany, 242
Freedman, Richard, 184n1
Freeman, Helen, 115–16
Freeman, Joe, 115–16, 193
French Resistance, 143n6, 154
Freud, Sigmund, 111, 142
Friedländer, Saul, 58–64

Index 283

friends and teachers, 47–68, 114–39, 184–206
Fritzsche, Peter, 47n1
"From an Old House in America" (Rich), 204
Fulbright fellowship, 188
Fund for Interfaith Understanding, 202

Gabbai, Dario, 117–19
Gabbai, Jacob, 117
Galilee [historical], 69
Galles, Arie, 198–201, 203–4
Ganeshpuri, India, 23
Gates, Bill, 233
Geddes, Jennifer, 184n1
General Assembly, UN, 57, 151
Geneva, Switzerland, 205, 235
Gentiles. See non-Jews
German & Jew: The Life and Death of Sigmund Stein (Dickinson), 103
The German Church Struggle and the Holocaust (Littell and Locke, eds.), 73
German Order Police, 49
Germany
  acts of recognition, 1–2
  friends and teachers, 114, 136, 139n45
  Holocaust insight
    Améry, 235–38, 240, 242, 245, 247
    Bauman, 129–30
    Borowski, 131, 135
    Fackenheim, 123
    Freeman and Freeman, 115
    Friedländer, 59
    Galles, 198
    Hallie and Camus, 166, 168, 170
    Hilberg, 90, 94, 100, 103–5, 108n39, 109
    Kofman and Delbo, 140, 143, 144n8, 146, 148, 152
    Levi, 212, 222, 227
    Littell, 70–73
    Lower and Petropoulos, 67
    Rubenstein, 12, 15, 17–18
Gestapo, 105, 239

Gibson, Mel, 69–70
Gleiwitz, 239
Glowacka, Dorota, 115n1
God
  acts of recognition, 5–6, 9
  Holocaust insight
    Améry, 232, 253–54
    Bak, 194
    Bauer, 56
    Bauman, 129–30
    Fackenheim, 123–25
    Galles, 198–99, 201
    Grob, Knight, and Patterson, 189–91
    Hallie and Camus, 177, 180–81
    Hilberg, 88
    Kofman and Delbo, 144n8, 149n27, 151, 162–63
    Levi, 224–28
    Levinas, 127
    Littell, 69–70, 76–80, 82–87
    Rubenstein, 10–17, 19, 23n37, 24
    Wiesel, 29, 31–32, 34, 39–45
"God and I" (Levi), 225n74
God and Man (Rebhun), 137n43
God's Presence in History: Jewish Affirmations and Philosophical Reflections (Fackenheim), 123
Golden, Dani, 138
Goldenberg, Myrna, 184n1
Goldensohn, Leon, 108n39
Goldhagen, Daniel, 48
Golleschau, 103
Gottschalk, Alfred, 184n1
Grammy Awards, 232
"Gray Zones: Ambiguity and Compromise in the Holocaust and Its Aftermath" [conference], 50
Greenberg, Gershon, 115n1
Greenberg, Irving "Yitz," 74, 76, 115n1, 124n14
Greenspan, Henry "Hank," 88n1, 191–94
Grieco, Giuseppe, 225n74
Grinnell College, 171
Grob, Lenny, 188–91, 194
Grossman, David, 198
Gross-Rosen, 117, 135

284 Index

Grüber, Heinrich, 12–13
Gruner, Wolf, 47n1
"The Guilt We Share" (Wiesel), 179–80
Günther, Hans. *See* Adler, H. G.
Gurs, 238
Gutman, Israel, 1n1
Gypsies, 2

Haas, Peter, 189
Haberstock, Karl, 66
Halbreich, Siegfried, 116–18
Haley, P. Edward, 184n1
Hallie, Philip, 165–83, 186, 230
Hamas, 26
Hamilton, William, 13
"Hardly Ever Again," (Knight) 190
Harran, Marilyn, 184n1
Harvard University, 3, 171, 233
Harvey Mudd College, 208
Hasidic Judaism, 32, 40–41, 260
Haute Loire, France, 165, 171
Hayes, Peter, 49–52, 55, 67
Haynes, Stephen, 184n1
Healing (Manosevitz), 203
Heberer, Patricia, 47n1
Hebrew University, 73
Hegel, Georg W. F., 19, 80, 150
Heidegger, Martin, 17
Heidelberger-Leonard, Irène, 237n14, 240, 242
Heissenbüttel, Helmut, 242
Herr, Alexis, 184n1
Heydrich, Reinhard, 49
Heyen, William, 74, 75–76
High Commissioner for Refugees, UN, 20
High Holy Days, 42
Hilberg, Raul
 acts of recognition, 1n1, 2–4, 7–9
 friends and teachers, 47–48
 Holocaust insight, 88–113
  Bauer, 54
  Hallie and Camus, 165n1
  Kofman and Delbo, 149, 157
  Levi, 220
  Littell, 75
  Rittner, 186

 photo, 74
Himmler, Heinrich, 49, 102–3, 107–10, 149–50
Hinduism, 23n37
Hiroshima, Japan, 106n37
Hirsch, David, 189
Historical Atlas of the Holocaust, 203
Hitler, Adolf
 acts of recognition, 2
 Holocaust insight
  Améry, 234n6, 236, 244–45
  Bauer, 55
  Browning, 49
  Fackenheim, 123–24
  Friedländer, 58
  Hallie and Camus, 170
  Hilberg, 93, 101
  Kofman and Delbo, 147, 152
  Levinas, 126
  Littell, 71, 73, 77, 81
  Lower and Petropoulos, 63, 65
  Oliner, 121
  Rubenstein, 13, 15, 17–18
  Wiesel, 35
Hitler's Furies: German Women in the Nazi Killing Fields (Lower), 63–64
Holocaust Educational Foundation, 50, 119
Holocaust Memorial Council, US, 74, 185, 187
Holocaust Memorial Museum, US
 acts of recognition, 2
 friends and teachers, 114
 Holocaust insight
  Améry, 253, 254n75
  Berenbaum, 185–86
  Greenspan, 192
  Hilberg, 104n34, 106n37, 111–12
  Kofman and Delbo, 141
  Littell, 74, 76
  Rich, 203
  Wiesel, 33
 taking nothing good for granted, 257
"The Holocaust Mission" (Hilberg), 112
Holocaust Museum Houston, 185

Holocaust Politics (Roth), 25
Holocaust: Religious and Philosophical Implications (Berenbaum and Roth, eds.), 185–86
Horowitz, Sara, 115n1
Höss, Rudolf, 108n39
Hotel Royal, 236
Houston, Jaye, 184n1
"How Much Home Does a Person Need?" (Améry), 235, 245, 251
How Was It Possible? (Hayes), 51
Huguenots, 165
The Human Race (Antelme), 143n6, 148
Hume, David, 36
Hungary, 5, 27, 179
Hunter, Colin, 184n1
Hunter, Paul, 196–98, 201–2

I. G. Farben, 209
If Not Now, When? (Levi), 208
If This Is a Man (Levi), 207n1, 208, 210, 219, 221, 224, 241
Iliff School of Theology, 202
Illinois, 50, 172
In Vain (Bak), 195
India, 23
Indiana, 172, 208
Institute for the Humanities, 165n1
"The Intellectual in Auschwitz" (Levi), 241
International Governing Board, Yad Vashem, 74
International Holocaust Remembrance Day, 57
International Military Tribunal, 108n39
Iran, 26, 81
Ireland, 114, 187
Isaac, 39, 84
ISIS, 6
Islam, 16n15, 25–26, 80, 82, 202
Israel
  friends and teachers, 114
  Holocaust insight
    Améry, 254n75
    Bauman, 129

    Fackenheim, 123
    Hallie and Camus, 167n3
    Levi, 230n90
    Littell, 71–73, 79, 81, 86
    Rubenstein, 12, 26
Israel, Maggid of Kozhenitz, R., 41
Italy, 161, 207–9, 230

Jacob, 84, 260
James, William, 3, 88, 191
"The January Offensive" (Borowski), 135
Japan, 106n37, 114
"Jean Améry, the Philosopher-Suicide" (Levi), 241n26
Jefferson, Thomas, 18
Jehovah's Witnesses, 2
Jerusalem [historical], 17
Jerusalem, Israel, 12, 71, 73, 81, 254n75
Jesus Christ, 17, 23, 44, 69–70, 76, 221
A Jew Today (Wiesel), 33
Jewish Council, Amsterdam, 61
Jewish Council, Lodz, 215
Jewish Council, Warsaw, 100
Jewish Regional Historical Commission, 199n30
"Jewish Values in the Post-Holocaust Future" [symposium], 179
Jihad and Genocide (Rubenstein), 24–26
Job, 39, 84–86
Job (Freeman), 115n2
Joseph, 84
Judenrat, 7
Judeo-Roman War, 17
Judgment Day, 221
Just Is (Bak), 195–96
Just Man, 40

Kaddish, 198–99, 201
Kant, Immanuel, 6, 36, 162, 228
Kaplan, Marion, 47n1
Kappers, Ariëns, 59n34
Katholieke Universiteit Leuven, 189
Katowice, Poland, 207
Katz, Steven, 115n1

Kazerne Dossin: Memorial, Museum, and Documentation Center on the Holocaust and Human Rights, 239n21
Kazin, Alfred, 179–80
Keneally, Thomas, 120
Kentucky, 196
Kershaw, Ian, 47n1
Khurbn Prologue (Galles), 199
Kierkegaard, Søren, 43
King Jr., Martin Luther, 183
Kingdom of Night (Freeman), 115n2
Kiš, Danilo, 115n1
Klarsfeld, Serge, 144–45
Klein, Gerda Weissman, 115n1
Klempen, Simone, 145
Klemperer, Victor, 115n1, 212n13
Kluger, Ruth, 115n1
Knight, Hank, 188–91, 194
Knowles, Adam, 115n1
Kofman, Berek, 143–46, 153
Kofman, Sarah, 140–64, 181, 232
Kohn, Grange, 145
Kolmar, Gertrud, 115n1, 140–41, 163–64
Kommando 98, 216–17
Koonz, Claudia, 47n1, 50
Korea, 81, 114
Kosovo, 39
Krakow, Poland, 199n30
Krell, Robert, 115n1
Kristallnacht, 105, 238
Krondorfer, Björn, 184n1
Kühne, Thomas, 47n1
Kuhn's prayer, 225, 227–28

La Stampa, 241n26
Lake Geneva, 236
Lambert, Carole, 115n1
Lang, Berel, 50, 115n1
Langer, Lawrence, 127–28, 194n17, 212
Lanzmann, Claude, 7, 90–91, 97, 100
The Last Hurrah, 98
Le Chambon-sur-Lignon, France, 165–70, 173–74
Leap to Life (Rebhun), 137n43

Leaving Home (Manosevitz), 203
Leff, Lisa, 115n1
Legends of Our Time (Wiesel), 179
Leitner, Maria, 240
Lemkin, Raphael, 212
Lent, 69
Lerman, Miles, 115n1
Les Schwab Tires, 232
"Lessons and Legacies" [conference], 50, 58n31, 110, 119
Lessons of the Holocaust (Marrus), 51–54
Lest Innocent Blood Be Shed: The Story of the Village of Le Chambon and How Goodness Happened There (Hallie), 165, 169–70
Levi, Lisa Lorenza, 230n90
Levi, Lucia, 208n3
Levi, Primo
   friends and teachers, 47
   Holocaust insight, 207–31
      Améry, 232, 239, 241–43, 255–56
      Borowski, 132
      Hallie and Camus, 181
      Kofman and Delbo, 142, 157
      Rittner, 186
      Wiesel, 226–28
   taking nothing good for granted, 258
Levi, Renzo, 230n90
Levi Yitzchak of Berditchev, R., 41
Levinas, Emmanuel, 125–27, 131, 141, 143, 189
Liberty Bell Middle School, 138–39
Library of Congress, US, 72–73
Lichtenberg, Bernhard, 105
Lifetime Achievement Award, Mgrublian Center for Human Rights, 113
Linenthal, Edward, 115n1
Lipstadt, Deborah, 47n1
"The Literature of the Holocaust" (Wiesel), 76
Littell, Franklin H., 11, 69–87, 74, 151
Locke, Hubert, 11, 73, 87, 184n1
Lodz ghetto, 105, 215
Loire River, 166

Loma Linda University School of Medicine, 138
London, England, 240
Lone, Jana Mohr, 138
Los Angeles, California, 116–17, 120, 168
Los Angeles Times, 117, 203
Lower, Wendy, 63–67, 112, 257
Lublin, Poland, 198
Lucas Jr., George R., 184n1
Luftwaffe, 198–99
Lutheranism, 194n18
Lvov (L'viv), Poland, 198–200

"Maculate Goodness and Major Julius Schmähling" (Hallie), 170
Madame Bovary (Flaubert), 243n33
Magdeburg, Germany, 192
Maier/Mayer, Hans. *See* Améry, Jean
Manosevitz, Carolyn, 202–3
Marburg, Germany, 103–4
Marjory Stoneman Douglas High School, 233
Marrus, Michael R., 51–54
Mass Grave (Manosevitz), 203
Massachusetts, 30, 98–99, 208
Matthäus, Jürgen, 47n1
Mauthausen, 118
Maxwell, Elisabeth, 184n1
McLean, Sheela, 205
The Measure of Our Days (Delbo), 155
Mechelen, 239
Mémé, 144
Menahem-Mendl of Kotzk, R., 32–34, 41
Mending the Fracture (Manosevitz), 202–3
Messengers of God: Biblical Portraits and Legends (Wiesel), 84, 86
Methodism, 44, 72
Methow River, 206
"The Methow River Poems" (Stafford), 206
Methow Valley, 205
Mgrublian Center for Human Rights, 50, 66, 113
Miami, Florida, 93

Michigan, 172
Microsoft, 233
Middle East, 82
Middletown, Connecticut, 171
Millen, Rochelle, 184n1
Milosevic, Slobodan, 39
Minerva, 150
Minerva Medica, 207
Minnesota, 202
Missouri, 74
Modena, Italy, 209
Modern Orthodox Judaism, 76
Modernity and the Holocaust (Bauman), 129
Moffie, David, 59–62
Mohammed, 23
The Monkey's Wrench (Levi), 210
Monowitz, 209, 216, 219, 226, 239, 241
Moravia, 99n18
Moses, 23, 39, 84–85, 260
Mosse, George, 93n11
"A Mother and Her Daughter" (Wiesel), 33
Mühlmann, Kajetan, 66
Muhsfeld, Erich, 213–14
Muktananda, Swami, 23–24
Muselmänner, 129
Myanmar, 233
The Myth of Sisyphus (Camus), 175, 178, 180

Nahman of Bratzlav, R., 41
Nancy, Jean-Luc, 143
National Endowment for the Humanities, 10, 259
National Humanities Institute, Yale University, 10
National Public Radio, 191
National Socialism
  Holocaust insight
    Améry, 236, 244–45, 248
    Hilberg, 101
    Levi, 213–14, 221
    Levinas, 126
    Rubenstein, 17, 25
NATO, 39

Nazareth, 44
Nazi Policy, Jewish Workers, German Killers (Browning), 49
Nazism
  acts of recognition, 1–2
  friends and teachers, 114, 136–39
  Holocaust insight
    Améry, 232, 235–38, 244–45, 247–48, 250
    Bauer, 55
    Bauman, 129–30
    Fackenheim, 123
    Freeman and Freeman, 115
    Friedländer, 58–60, 62
    Galles, 198
    Grob, Knight, and Patterson, 189–91
    Halbreich, 116–17
    Hallie and Camus, 166, 168–70, 179
    Hilberg, 89–90, 94, 99n18, 101, 103, 107–10, 111n45, 112
    Kofman and Delbo, 143, 144n8, 145–48, 150, 152–54
    Levi, 207–8, 212, 215, 220, 222, 224, 227
    Levinas, 126
    Littell, 70–73, 77, 84
    Lower and Petropoulos, 64–67
    Oliner, 121
    Rittner, 187
    Rubenstein, 11–12, 15–18, 20–21, 25
    Wiesel, 27, 35
Negative Dialectics (Adorno), 145n14
Netherlands, the, 59, 61, 204, 238
Neumann, Franz, 94
New Testament, 16, 44, 70, 72
New York, 25, 30, 40n43, 75–76, 93, 208, 254n75
New York Review of Books, 10
New York Times, 42, 98
New York University, 123
"News from the Sky" (Levi), 228
Niagara Falls, 201
Niagara River, 201–2
The Niagara River (Ryan), 201–2
Nietzsche, Friedrich, 106, 127, 142

Nigeria, 81
Night (Wiesel)
  acts of recognition, 5
  friends and teachers, 205
  Holocaust insight
    Améry, 234
    Halbreich, 117
    Littell, 74, 75n3, 75n5
    Wiesel, 27, 29–30, 35
9/11, 6, 24–25, 80
"1948: Jews" (Rich), 205
1939 Club, 116
1939 Society, 116
92nd Street Y, 40n43
Nobel Peace Prize, 33, 38
Nobel Prize for Literature, 174
None of Us Will Return (Delbo), 154
non-Jews, 27n1, 121, 167n3, 187, 230n90, 240
Nordhausen-Dora, 117
North Africa, 166
North America, 201
North Cascades Highway, 205
North Korea, 81
Northwestern University, 50, 119
Norway, 75, 114, 188
"A Note on Translation" (Dobie), 145n11
The Number (Bak), 194
Nuremberg, Germany, 108n39
Nuremberg Laws, 237, 250

The Oath (Wiesel), 45–46
Occident, 23
Ohio, 118
Ohlendorf, Otto, 108n39
Old Ebbitt Grill, 185
Oliner, Pearl M., 121
Oliner, Samuel, 120–22
Oliver, Kelly, 143n5
"On Stupidity" (Bonhoeffer), 137
On Suicide (Améry), 254
"On the Necessity and Impossibility of Being a Jew" (Améry), 249
Open Heart (Wiesel), 42–43
Opere (Levi), 207n1
Oran, Algeria, 169

Ordinary Men: Reserve Police Battalion 101 and the Final Solution in Poland (Browning), 48–49
Orient, 23
Orme, Jane, 138
Oslo, Norway, 114
Other, the, 145n11
Oxford (Oxfordshire), England, 151n30, 188
The Oxford Handbook of Holocaust Studies (Hayes and Roth, eds.), 49
Oxford University, 54
Oxford University Press, 49

Pacific Ocean, 204, 206
Pacific Sociological Association, 121
Pacific theater, 106n37
Page, Leopold, 120–21
Page, Mila, 120
Pannwitz, Doktor Ingenieur, 216–17
Paris, France, 154, 168, 175, 240
Parkes, James, 72
Parkland, Florida, 233–34
Paroles suffoquées (Kofman), 143, 145n11
Pasadena, California, 115
The Passion of the Christ (Gibson), 69–71
Patterson, David, 188–91, 194, 198
Paul, 168
Paulsson, Steve, 47n1
Pawiak, 131
Pawlikowski, John, 115n1
Paxton, Tom, 191n9
PBS News Hour, 196
Pentagon, 25, 80
"The People Who Walked On" (Borowski), 133
"The Perils of Indifference: Lessons Learned from a Violent Century" (Wiesel), 39
The Periodic Table (Levi), 210
Perpetrators Victims Bystanders (Hilberg), 98, 105
Perrone, Lorenzo, 217, 229–31, 256
"Perspectives on the Holocaust" [panel], 121
Pétain, Henri Philippe, 166

Petropoulos, Jonathan, 63–67, 112, 117
Pfefferberg, Poldek. *See* Page, Leopold
Piecuch, Balwina, 121
Piecuch, Staszek, 121
Pinker, Steven, 233–35, 248, 250, 253–54
Pinnock, Sarah, 184n1
The Plague (Camus), 168, 177
Plateau Vivarais-Lignon, France, 165, 167n3
Plenary Assembly, World Jewish Congress, 254n75
Poland
    friends and teachers, 114, 137
    Holocaust insight
        Améry, 236, 238
        Bauman, 129
        Borowski, 131, 133, 135
        Freeman and Freeman, 115
        Friedländer, 63
        Galles, 198–200
        Hilberg, 93, 100, 105, 106n37, 112
        Kofman and Delbo, 144
        Levi, 207–8
        Oliner, 121–22
        Wiesel, 32
Police Battalion 101, 48–49
The Politics of Memory (Hilberg), 89, 98, 105
Pollefeyt, Didier, 189
Polster, Zalman, 121
Pomona College, 30, 172, 177
Pontius Pilate, 69
Pook, Hermann, 101
"A Prayer for the Days of Awe" (Wiesel), 42
Presidential Advisory Commission on Holocaust Assets in the United States, 66
President's Commission on the Holocaust, 111–13
Procario-Foley, Elena, 184n1
Protestantism, 13–14, 72, 76, 165–66, 194n18
Przemysl, Poland, 137
Pulitzer Prize, 201

Quay, Jim, 259–60
"Questioning Islamic Belief" (Swazo), 16n15
Qureshi, Lucy, 49

Radcliffe College, 205
Radom, Poland, 115
Rappel, Joel, 27n1
Ravensbrück, 154
Rebhun, Joseph, 137–39
Rebhun, Marie, 138
recognition, acts of, 1–9
Reconstructing the Story (Manosevitz), 202
Red Cross, 133, 154
Reder, Rudolf, 199–200
Reflections: Auschwitz, Memory, and a Life Recreated (Greenspan and Rubin), 193
Reichsbahn, 89–90
Reifenstahl, Leni, 18
Reis, Hermann. *See* Stein, Sigmund
"Remembering for the Future" [conference], 54, 151n30
Remnants (Greenspan), 191–92
"Report on the Hygienic-Sanitary Organization of the Concentration Camp for Jews in Monowitz (Auschwitz–Upper Silesia)" (De Benedetti and Levi), 207
"Report to the President" (President's Commission on the Holocaust), 111n45
"Researching the Holocaust" [course], 66, 117
"Resentments" (Améry), 246
Reserve Police Battalion 101, 48–49
Rethinking the Holocaust (Bauer), 54–55, 57
Rich, Adrienne, 203–5
Richard Stockton College of New Jersey. *See* Stockton University
Richardson, Ravenel, 184n1
Riegner, Gerhart, 205
Rieux, Bernard, 169, 174
Righteous Among the Nations, 167n3, 230n90
Ripening (Hunter), 197

Rittner, Carol, 63, 140, 186–88, 194, 257
Roma, 2
Roman Catholicism, 69, 105
Roosevelt, Franklin D., 236
Rorty, Richard, 146
Rose Garden, White House, 113
Rosen, Alan, 184n1
Rosenfeld, Alvin, 115n1
Rosh Hashanah, 228
Rost, Nella, 199n30
Roth, John K., 74
Roth, Josiah, 48
Roth, Philip, 210n7
Roth, Sarah, 31
Rotunda, US Capitol, 253, 254n75
Roxlau, Travis, 257–58
Royce, Josiah, 3–5, 194
Rozett, Robert, 1n1
Rubel, Margaret M., 199
Rubenstein, Richard L.
   Holocaust insight, 10–26
     Bauman, 129
     Berenbaum, 185
     Hallie and Camus, 177–78
     Levi, 226n78
     Littell, 73, 76–78, 83, 86–87
     Wiesel, 30
Rubin, Agi, 193
Rue Duc, 144n8
Rue Labat, 144
Rue Ordener, 143, 144n9
Rue Ordener, Rue Labat (Kofman), 141, 143, 144n9, 147
Rumkowski, Chaim, 215
Rumscheidt, Martin, 115n1
Russia, 32, 81, 208
Rwanda, 6, 73, 80
Ryan, Kay, 201–2

Sachsenhausen, 12, 116–17, 123
Salado, Texas, 165n1
"Salvage" (Ryan), 201
Salzburg, Austria, 219, 254
San Francisco, California, 120
"Sarah Kofman's Skirts" (Deutscher and Oliver), 143n5
Sartre, Jean-Paul, 177

Sauvage, Pierre, 168
Schächter, Mrs., 28–30
Schindler, Oskar, 120
Schindler's list, 120
Schindler's List (Keneally), 120
Schmähling, Julius, 167, 170–71, 182
Scholars' Conference on the Holocaust and the Churches, 11, 73, 76
Schrager, Laura, 138
Schulte, Eduard, 205
Schulweis, Harold, 115n1
Schwab, Les, 232
Schwedhelm, Karl, 242
Seattle, Washington, 196
Sebald, W. G., 251n69
Seidman, Naomi, 27n1
Seminega, Tharcisse, 184n1
Seneca, 172
Serbia, 39
Sereny, Gitta, 47n1
Shapiro, Amy, 115n1
Shapiro, Paul, 184n1
Sheraton-Palace Hotel, 121
Shoah [movie], 7, 90–91, 97, 100
Shoah Foundation, USC, 47
Sicily, Italy, 161
Siddha Yoga, 23n37
Siddha Yoga Dham Associates Foundation, 23n37
Sighet, Romania/Hungary, 5, 27
Sigi Ziering Institute, 185
"Silence" (Borowski), 134
Simon, Julius, 184n1
Sinti, 2
Sisyphus, 175–76, 178, 182–83, 256
Skloot, Robert, 184n1
Slovakia, 121
Smith, James, 184n1
Smith, Stephen, 184n1
Smock, Ann, 143
Smothered Words (Kofman), 141, 143n6, 144, 145n11, 149n26
Snortum, Bonnie, 184n1
Snortum, John, 184n1
Snyder, Timothy, 47n1
Sobin, Poland, 144
Sodom, 40

Soelle, Dorothee, 74, 76
Somalia, 81
"Some Perspectives on Religious Faith After Auschwitz" (Rubenstein), 12
Sonderkommando, 118–19, 199, 213–14, 221–22
Sontag, Frederick, 30, 114
Sophie's Choice (Styron), 10
Sosnowiec-Będzin, Poland, 133
Souls on Fire (Wiesel), 47, 260
Sources of Holocaust Research (Hilberg), 2–3, 54, 98–99
The Sources of Religious Insight (Royce), 3
South America, 154
South German Radio, 242
South Korea, 114
South Sudan, 81
Soviet Union, 112, 114, 129
Spielberg, Steven, 120
SS
  Holocaust insight
    Améry, 236, 239, 248
    Borowski, 134–35
    Gabbai, 118
    Galles, 199
    Hilberg, 90, 101–2, 106n37, 108n39
    Kofman and Delbo, 147–50, 152, 158
    Levi, 209, 224
    Littell, 71
St. Cyprien, 238
St. Hedwig's Cathedral, 105
St. Louis, Missouri, 74
Stafford, William, 205–6
Stations of the Cross, 198
Stein, Sigmund, 103–4
Steinweis, Alan, 47n1
Stendhal, 11
Step Not Beyond (Blanchot), 145n11
Stephen S. Weinstein Series in Post-Holocaust Studies, 189, 198
Stettin, Poland, 114
Stier, Oren, 115n1
Stockton University, 73–74
Stuttgart, Germany, 242

Styron, William, 10
Sudan, 81
"Summer in Algiers" (Camus), 178
Sundquist, Eric, 115n1
"Sunset at Fòssoli" (Levi), 211
Survival in Auschwitz (Levi), 208, 210, 241
Survivors of the Shoah Visual History Foundation, 185
Susel, Joel, 184n1
Swazo, Norman Kenneth, 16n15
Sweden, 154
Switzerland, 114, 205, 235, 240
"Symposium on Primo Levi," 208n3
"Symposium on Understanding Evil," 165n1
Syria, 80, 233
Szczecin, Poland, 114

Tadeusz, Vorarbeiter, 131–32
taking nothing good for granted, 257–60
Tarrou, Jean, 169
"Tattered Kaddish" (Rich), 204
teachers and friends, 47–68, 114–39, 184–206
"Tears and Elie Wiesel" (Roth), 31
Tegel, Germany, 139n45
Tel Aviv, Israel, 81
Temple University, 73
Ten Commandments, 57, 194
Texas, 165n1, 185, 202
Theresienstadt, 99, 192
Third Reich
    acts of recognition, 2
    Holocaust insight
        Améry, 236, 238, 245
        Bauman, 129–30
        Hayes, 50
        Hilberg, 105
        Kofman and Delbo, 152
        Levi, 217
        Littell, 84
        Lower and Petropoulos, 66–67
        Rittner, 187
        Rubenstein, 18, 21
        Wiesel, 31, 36
"This Failure" (Hunter), 197

This Way for the Gas, Ladies and Gentlemen (Borowski), 131–32
Time, 13, 233
Tiresias, 210
"To a Young Jew of Today" (Wiesel), 10
To Mend the World (Fackenheim), 125
Torah, 76, 84, 190
"Torture" (Améry), 244
Totten, Samuel, 184n1
The Town beyond the Wall (Wiesel), 179
Trachtenberg, Ellen, 184n1
Traveling through the Dark (Stafford), 205
Treblinka
    acts of recognition, 7
    Holocaust insight
        Berenbaum, 186
        Friedländer, 59
        Hilberg, 97, 112
        Kofman and Delbo, 148, 151
        Rubenstein, 11
Trocmé, André, 166–68
Trocmé, Magda, 166–67, 169
Tromsø, Norway, 114
The Troubles, 187
Trump, Donald, 80, 253–54
Turin, Italy, 207–9
Tutsi, 110
"Twenty-five Years Later" (Browning), 48

Ukraine, 63
Uncollected Stories (Levi), 241n26
"Unfinished Business" (Levi), 216
Union Theological Seminary, 76
United Kingdom, 114
United Nations, 20, 57, 150–51, 235
Universal Declaration of Human Rights, 251
University of Amsterdam, 59
University of California, Los Angeles, 58
University of Leeds, 129
University of Oregon, 106, 111
University of Oslo, 75n3
University of San Diego, 170

University of Southern California, 47
University of Texas, Dallas, 189
University of Toronto, 123
University of Vermont, 104
University of Warsaw, 129
University of Washington Press, 189, 198
University of Washington, Seattle, 48
Unrelented (Bak), 196
Useless Knowledge (Delbo), 154
"Useless Suffering" (Levinas), 126
USSR. *See* Soviet Union

van Buren, Paul M., 13–14
Van Pelt, Robert Jan, 47n1
Venezia, Morris, 118
Venezia, Shlomo, 118
Ventresca, Robert, 184n1
Vermont, 90, 204
Vichy, France, 166, 238
Vicious Circles (Blanchot), 145n11
Vienna, Austria, 99, 219, 236–38, 240, 250
Vienna Central Cemetery, 239
"Virtue in Strained Circumstances" [conference session], 170
"The Visit" (Borowski), 132
Viterbi, Andrew, 208n3

Wachsmann, Nikolaus, 47n1
Wajs, 248
Wake Forest University Divinity School, 202
Waller, Andrew, 158
Waller, James, 115n1
Waller, Sarah Yates, 156–59
Waller, Sophia, 158
Warnock, Geoffrey J., 172–73
Warsaw, Poland, 63, 100, 106n37, 131, 135
The Warsaw Diary of Adam Czerniakow (Czerniakow), 90
Warsaw ghetto, 7, 100, 131
Washington, DC, 25, 66, 74, 111, 113, 185, 205
Washington, state of, 138, 196, 205, 259
Wayne State University, 11, 73, 87

Weapons of the Spirit (Sauvage), 168
Webster University, 74, 76–77, 87
Weekes, Gregory, 110n44
Wehrmacht, 12
Weinberg, Gerhard, 47n1
Weiss, Alice, 119
Weiss, Zev, 119
Werb, Bret, 184n1
Wesley Theological Seminary, 202
Wesleyan University, 171, 186
West Bank, 81
West Berlin, Germany, 12
West Germany, 12, 247
"Western Society after the Holocaust" [symposium], 48
When Memory Comes (Friedländer), 58n31
Where Memory Leads (Friedländer), 58n31
White House, 39, 113, 254n75
Who Will Carry the Word? (Delbo), 163
Why? Explaining the Holocaust (Hayes), 50–51
Wiesel, Elie
  acts of recognition, 5–8
  friends and teachers, 114, 205
  Holocaust insight, 27–46
    Améry, 232, 234, 239, 241, 243
    Halbreich, 117
    Hallie and Camus, 168–69, 177–80
    Hilberg, 111
    Kofman and Delbo, 157
    Levi, 220, 226–29
    Littell, 73–79, 82–87
    Rittner, 186–87
    Rubenstein, 11–12
  photo, 74
  taking nothing good for granted, 260
Wiesel, Elisha, 31, 42
Wiesel, Marion, 27n1
Wiesel, Sarah, 29
Wiesel, Shlomo, 29
Wiesel, Tzipora, 29
Wilkins, Carl, 184n1
Winnipeg, Canada, 202

Winthrop, Washington, 138, 205
Wirtschafts-Verwaltungshauptamt, SS, 101
Wittmann, Rebecca, 50
Wollheim Memorial, 239n22
"The Woman Poet" (Kolmar), 140
Woo, Elaine, 117
The World Counts, 20n26
World Jewish Congress, 205, 254n75
World Population Clock Live, 20n26
World Trade Center, 24–25, 80
World War I, 111, 166
World War II
   acts of recognition, 1–2
   friends and teachers, 137–38
   Holocaust insight
      Améry, 234n6, 238
      Halbreich, 116
      Hallie and Camus, 167, 170, 172, 174, 180
      Hilberg, 89, 93, 111n45
      Levi, 211, 229
      Rubenstein, 12, 25
The Wrench (Levi), 210

The Writing of the Disaster (Blanchot), 143n6
Wroxton College, 188–89, 191

Yad Vashem, 71, 74, 167n3, 230n90, 254n75
Yale University, 10–11, 88, 172
Yates (Waller), Sarah, 156–59
The Years of Extermination (Friedländer), 59, 62–63
Yemen, 81, 233
Yom Kippur War, 79
You Want It Darker (Cohen), 232
Young, James, 115n1, 116
Yugoslavia, 6, 73, 80

Zalman Jewish Museum, 121
Zeus, 203
Zitar, Kirsti, 184n1
Zurich, Switzerland, 240
Zusia, R., 260
Zyklon B, 18
Zyndranowa, Poland, 121–22

www.ingramcontent.com/pod-product-compliance
Lightning Source LLC
Chambersburg PA
CBHW021652230426
43668CB00008B/600